TRANSFORMING
THE
CURRICULUM

TRANSFORMING THE CURRICULUM

Ethnic Studies and Women's Studies

edited by
Johnnella E. Butler
and
John C. Walter

State University of New York Press

Published by
State University of New York Press, Albany

For information, address State University of New York
Press, State University Plaza, Albany, N.Y., 12246

Production by Diane Ganeles
Marketing by Fran Keneston

Library of Congress Cataloging-in-Publication Data

Transforming the curriculum : ethnic studies and women's studies
    edited by Johnnella E. Butler and John C. Walter.
        p.   cm.
    Includes index.
    ISBN 0-7914-0586-9 (alk. paper). — ISBN 0-7914-0587-7 (pbk.
alk. paper)
        1. Women's studies—United States.   2. Ethnology—Study and
    teaching (Graduate)—United States.   I. Butler, Johnnella E.
    II. Walter, John C., 1933–
    HQ1181.U5T73   1991
    305.4'071'173—dc20   90-37670
                                                                      CIP

10   9   8   7   6   5   4   3

To Emma and Sidney Kaplan,
Transformation Pioneers

Contents

Part IV: Ethnic Studies, Women's Studies, and the Liberal Arts Curriculum: Retrospect and Prospect

Acknowledgments

We owe a special debt of thanks to Katharine Bolland, a former Smith student and currently our Research Coordinator at the University of Washington. Not only did she assist in details of getting what we thought was the final draft off, but she also entered the entire manuscript on disks accurately and in an unimaginably short amount of time as became necessary when SUNY Press changed its procedure. Eileen Hayes, our research assistant, worked unselfishly to correct the copy-edited manuscript. Smith undergraduates Nima Eshghi, Leisa Jenkins, and Karen Perkins spent weeks doing research for us during the early conceptualization stages of this book. We also appreciate the stimulating and challenging classes at Smith College from 1982 through 1987: The Literature of Black Women, taught by Professor Butler; Women and Philosophy, taught by Professors Elizabeth Spelman and Butler; and The Afro-American Woman and the Feminist Movement, taught by Professor Walter.

Professors James Banks, Gail Nomura, Betty Schmitz, Stephen Sumida and Ines Talamantez gave supportive and useful critical advice during the preparation of the manuscript. It is impossible to acknowledge all the conversations that helped shape this work, but thank you to all the curriculum transformation projects, participants and colleagues for the opportunities to work together. And to Professor Margo Culley of the University of Massachusetts, thank you for your vision and calm perseverance.

Foreword

Laurel Wilkening

Studying Western Civilization was a wonderful experience for me. From the study of texts of a great sweep of time and places came an understanding of the human common quest: the search for the meaning of human existence. Whether the search was pursued through the travels of Odysseus, the introspection of Aquinas, or the loves and lusts of Shakespeare's characters, it was a compelling, intellectual story with a lesson. We peculiar animals, gifted with the ability to contemplate our existence and converse about our contemplations, have shared this search across time and place. Inspiring as I find this lesson, is it unique to Western civilization? Could I not have gained a similar understanding of humanity through the study of the complex tapestry of intellectual and religious writings and from the art of those who, for millennia, have occupied Africa, the Indian subcontinent, or the vast expanse of China? Or, was there something uniquely "Western" about Western civilization that was to be learned?

Some strong advocates of Western Civilization stress its role in identifying and emphasizing the common ground among all cultures, races, and gender. However, the sad truth is that for too long the common ground has been identified by white protestant males as the attributes common only to this group. The assumption seems to be that these attributes are the reason for our patently superior modern Western society. There is much to question in this assumption. If one learns anything at all about history from the study of the Western Civilization curriculum, it is that today's superior society is tomorrow's declining and falling empire. But my greater concern is that the definition of these common attributes disconnects those of us who are not white protestant males from the curriculum and, therefore, from the common moral, which is the lesson to be learned. Women have been disadvantaged for centuries by the fact that the norm in health and behavior was defined "male" by the scientists and philosophers studying the human body and behavior. Women were described and defined by their difference from that norm. This custom has not totally disappeared.

My skepticism about the traditional canon began early. I had the good fortune to grow up in the cradle of European-American civilization of the western United States, namely, the Rio Grande valley of New Mexico. I well remember the incredulity of my Hispanic, middle school classmates, whose families traced their heritage on the American continent back to the early 1600s, over the effusive textbook accounts of the Pilgrims and the "settling" of New England in 1620. Through the study of their own history they knew that before the Pilgrims had experienced their first crop failure, their Spanish forebears had sufficient successful harvests to have constructed villages still in use today. Because we had to, we labored through the textbooks, which assumed for us the aura of irrelevant novels. The history of our part of the country, with its rich diversity of players, was ignored except for "cowboys and Indians." I cannot begin to imagine the feeling of the American Indian students, whose families had resided in communities in that part of our country for thousands of years, long before the Spanish. They were not in our classes. What were they taught about the Pilgrims, about the Spanish, in the Indian boarding schools?

So the textbook writers had feet of clay. What about the "real" scholars? As in any other enterprise, quality varies. I will always remember being shown a computerized database on Spanish colonial history. With justifiable pride, my host asked me to pick a person or place for a demonstration search. I suggested he select one of the Spanish women who was with Francisco Vasquez de Coronado on his 1542 expedition into what is now the Southwest and Plains States of the United States. He replied that there were no women with Coronado. I wish I could say that an uncomfortable silence followed but, in fact, it was necessary to challenge the scholar on this point. At least two Spanish women and numerous native women participated in Coronado's expedition. This is not a particularly obscure historical fact, but it was invisible to that scholar.

Those who are invisible to the traditional scholars were not necessarily invisible in their time. Absence of evidence is not evidence of absence. Coronado's expedition went forward because of the role of a remarkable African, Estevanico. He was with Alvar Nuñez Cabeza de Vaca on the perilous journey to Mexico City, made by the four survivors of an ill-fated Spanish colony in Florida. The small group survived because of the personality and linguistic skills of Estevanico. It was this group that in 1636 in Mexico City told the tales of the Seven Cities of Cibola, thereby motivating Coronado's expedition. That journey was not the final role in history for Estevanico. The Viceroy of New Spain, Antonio de Mendoza, sent Estevanico in the company of a hapless friar, Marcos de Niza, ahead of Coronado on a reconnaissance mission to affirm or deny the existence of the "cities of gold." Estevanico was murdered as he reached the first of the pueblos. As the putative first non-native to enter what is now the state of Arizona, Fray Marcos de Niza has a few streets, schools, and hotels in Arizona and Sonora named after him. To my knowledge, Estevanico the Moor, probably the real first non-native to enter Arizona, is invisible, both to the public and on paper.

It is this disconnection, the disenfranchisement of the invisible people— invisible because of gender, race, or religion—and their hidden philosophies, literature, and arts that leads me to advocate the supplementation, expansion, and, yes, even replacement of portions of the Western Civilization curriculum. The basic truths of human behavior and experience and the human quest for the meaning of life can also be found in modern and ancient "non-Western," nontraditional history, art, and literature. The inclusion of this material in our curriculum could only serve to reinforce our common experience and aspirations as human beings. Possibly, it is a fear of this shared nature all humans experience that leads advocates of the Western Civilization curriculum to cling to the "westernness" of civilization. This book helps to provide visibility to some of those long-hidden connections and explores their meaning for our diverse, yet shared, experiences.

Introduction

Johnnella E. Butler

In 1979 I went off to Tuscaloosa, Alabama to spend six weeks studying at a National Endowment of the Humanities (NEH) seminar on Women's Nontraditional Literature. Although I deliberately chose to apply for admission to this seminar because I wanted to become involved academically in Women's Studies, I had no idea that those hot, humid days of determining, among other salient things, just what constituted nontraditional literature, would result in significant scholarly commitment on my part to bringing together the scholarship of Women's Studies and Black Studies. Those Alabama days marked the beginning of my trying to articulate clearly and usefully just why I and other Black women insisted that race and culture had to be taken seriously when discussing Black women. Many of us in Alabama that summer, and at fledgling Women's Studies and women's issues conferences, meetings, and organizing efforts, tried to make clear that gender was not a sufficient commonality, in and of itself, for bonding. Women of color came to this understanding early and from different vantage points.

From one perspective, this book is a product of my initial decision to become involved in Women's Studies because I wanted to assist in making sure that the experiences of Black women and other, what we called then Third World/U.S.A. women, were accurately presented and discussed. Many of us chose various routes to the same goal, and thus we have many complementary approaches to the representation of women of color on their own terms. My particular concern began with the inclusion of Black women into Black Studies and the inclusion of Black women into Women's Studies. At that fateful Alabama seminar, I met Professor Margo Culley of the University of Massachusetts, a white woman and dedicated scholar of American literature, women's literature, and Women's Studies, who shared that concern. Margo and I became true and trusted friends and colleagues as we worked through our ideas and feelings, resulting in the 1981–1983 Fund for the Improvement of Postsecondary Education (FIPSE) faculty development grant, *Black Studies/Women's Studies: An Overdue Partnership*.

From the perspective of that grant and its implications, this book is the realization of our earlier intentions to coauthor a volume based on that particular experience. However, somehow it never seemed complete and "right" enough to simply base a book on the grant experience, for upon the completion of that project we were poignantly aware of the overwhelming amount of work that still had to be done. We had begun an aspect of the very difficult dialogue around full incorporation of women and men of color and white women into the liberal arts curriculum, but our work was only a minute part of the tip of the iceberg. Our work seemed to be centered around the relationship among Black Studies, other ethnic-specific studies, and Women's Studies. The fact that these relationships must be worked out in the context of utilizing the best of the existing liberal arts curriculum, as well as in the context of struggling with its biases, shortsightedness, and sometimes outright bigotry, suggested the imagery of a quadruple-edged sword at the least.

Could the book address and demonstrate to some extent not simply what the dialogue entails, but also what theory and scholarship might emerge from the dialogues? Could it maintain an awareness of the debates around diversity, the hostility towards the recognition of the political and cultural hegemony inherent in curricula and pedagogy without addressing such attacks at the expense of the dialogue between Ethnic Studies and Women's Studies?

It took awhile for ideas to meld and for Ethnic Studies to begin to be recognized by a significant number of scholars and students as a bona fide field of study. Frequently when mentioning the necessity of bringing together Ethnic Studies and Women's Studies, people would assume I meant Immigrant Studies. Others assumed that ethnic groups of Europe were the topic of concern. Still others insisted on addressing Euro-American immigrant ethnic groups, while others queried whether Anglo-Americans were ethnic. These questions indicate the difficulty of naming the body of scholarship on American people of color within the academy. This book intends at least to bring clarification to the debate of nomenclature, if not settle it.

Then, thinking further, I wondered, shouldn't the book tackle the question of just where Jewish Studies falls? Anti-semitism is not the same as racism, but there are strong similarities as well as strong differences. While American Jews face(d) assimilation, Americanization, and the attendant anti-semitism, racism is an embedded characteristic of our institutions. For the most part in this country, Jewish Americans are Euro-American ethnic. They suffered, and still do to some extent, religious discrimination. They do not form a distinct race, and they generally can opt to enjoy the privileges of white skin. Is Jewish Studies European-based or American-based? What are the cultural and social realities of American Jews? Are they and anti-semitism analogous to the racial colonial discourses and experiences of people of color here and abroad? This book intends to address this issue, raising salient aspects of the question within the context of Ethnic Studies and Women's Studies, hoping to begin and encourage reasoned, informed dialogue. The dialogues around the issues of incorporation of women and men of color and white women into the curriculum are complex and numerous. The goal has grown from balancing, mainstreaming, and integration (essentially addition) to *transformation* (radical paradigm shifts). There are interracial and intercultural dialogues, intraracial and intracultural dialogues, inter- and intraclass and inter- and intragender dialogues around all sorts of issues and concerns salient to each field. This book intends to clarify that *transformation* of the curriculum cannot be done by Women's Studies alone—especially by a Women's Studies that naively assumes a sameness among women in the United States, minimizing, if not disregarding class, race, and ethnicity. To transform the contents of the liberal arts curriculum, Ethnic Studies and Women's Studies must first be transformed and then incorporated into the curriculum to do a properly transformative work.

Over the years, Margo became committed to other related efforts of scholarship and pedagogy, and I became involved—perhaps overly so—in sustaining efforts and accomplishments in building African American Studies on a campus that did not want the significant changes that was bringing about. The book went to a back burner for quite awhile.

Finally, after eight intensive years travelling nationally developing syllabi, consulting and conducting workshops for and with Women's Studies programs and departments, Black Studies programs and departments, and English departments, often helping entire faculties begin projects around issues of greater participation of "minorities and women" in the university and college curricula, I felt I had learned enough to try my hand at bringing it all together somehow. My friend and colleague, John Walter, had been prodding me to begin, and we agreed that it would be significant for him to coedit the volume, as an African American male professor (originally from the West Indies) who had participated in that early FIPSE grant and who had made a conscientious effort to transform his courses.

There are quite a few people across the country involved in transformation efforts. I will not try to list them for fear of inadvertently omitting someone. However, the scholarship produced over the past twenty years owes a particular debt to pioneering works like *Sturdy Black Bridges, This Bridge Called My Back: Writings by Radical Women of Color, Home Girls*, the works of Bell Hooks, and new anthologies like *The Forbidden Stitch: An Asian American Women's Anthology*. These works and others began and continue the dialogue upon which can be based full incorporation of white women and men and women of color into the liberal arts curriculum. The experience of the woman of color is the bridge that joins us all—white male, men of color, white women, and women of color. She is the link between Ethnic Studies and Women's Studies content, and as such occupies a pivotal place in curricular change.

We have collected examples of scholarship and provided theory, in some instances focusing primarily on Ethnic Studies, in other instances focusing primarily on Women's Studies, and still in other instances bringing the two together. We believe the chapters in this book reflect the current state of the transformation effort. Women's Studies has characteristically focused its attention on dismantling the patriarchy, yet, to paraphrase Audre Lorde, it has used the master's tools. Thus its scholarship has, only with outstanding exceptions, reflected the racial and cultural biases of Western scholarship. Black Studies and other Ethnic Studies characteristically focused their attention on dismantling racism and colonialism, and in most instances has used the master's tools, reflecting the patriarchal biases of Western scholarship. In our assessment, neither field has done justice to class and classism. This text reflects some of the problems inherent in our flawed traditions in Women's Studies and Ethnic Studies, while it simultaneously attempts to correct those same flaws. We see this text as *generative*. As such it should be read as a collection of interactive works. All works put forth need improvement and invite debate, clarification, even correction. We hope the problems and issues the book raises overtly, and the hidden problems and issues implicit in some of the works, will be identified and addressed by reviewers and colleagues in Ethnic Studies and Women's Studies in the Freirean spirit of praxis.

By no means do we think we have said all that can and should be said, contoured all that can be contoured, or completed anything. It is John's hope and my hope that this book will *lend direction to and contribute to* all our efforts to better the liberal arts, to make our classrooms places where the closest approximation of the truth can be reached for the bettering of the conditions of all.

PART I

Ethnic Studies and Women's Studies: Interrelationships

This section explores some of the not so obvious ways in which Ethnic Studies (African American Studies, Asian American Studies, American Indian Studies, and Latino Studies) and Women's Studies are interrelated—as they affect curricular change, as they evolve pedagogically, and as they compete for funding outside the college and university structure. Johnnella Butler, besides projecting a vision of a transformed curriculum, identifies what has become the scope of Ethnic Studies, insisting that Ethnic Studies and Women's Studies must be transformed to reflect the matrix interaction among race, class, gender, and ethnicity or culture. Suggesting a conceptual framework for these tasks, she clarifies the contours of the dialogues that must take place within the academy between Ethnic Studies and Women's Studies while maintaining no illusions regarding the characteristic resistant posture of the arts and sciences. This chapter is closely related to her "Transforming the Curriculum: Teaching About Women of Color," in part II.

Caryn Musil and Ruby Sales, and Katharine Bolland and John Walter present much needed information on kinds and sources of funding for Women's Studies and Ethnic Studies respectively. Musil and Sales detail the various funding sources for Women's Studies since 1969 and track the pattern of granting among private, semi-private, and public agencies. They end with an assessment of the present state of funding and suggest strategies for future funding.

Katharine Bolland and John Walter trace private funding for Ethnic Studies since 1972, analyze the patterns of private funding, and suggest areas considered most viable for future grant application. They concentrate on private funding due to the lack of information available on grants to Ethnic Studies departments and programs from public funding agencies. This is an area that demands further attention.

The final chapter in this section, by Johnnella Butler and Betty Schmitz, first appeared in the autumn 1989 issue (no. 37) of *Radical Teacher*. A description of the 1988 Ford-funded Different Voices Institute at the University of Washington, the chapter provides a successful model in which Ethnic

Studies and Women's Studies faculty bring their content to bear on core courses. From the perspective of this book, one of the most valuable revelations of the Different Voices Institute resulted from the sharing among Ethnic Studies faculty. As they commented on one another's presentations, similar and complementary paradigms and approaches on content emerged. Such comparative analyses and discussion is essential to both ethnic-specific fields and to the transformation of Women's Studies and traditional disciplines.

CHAPTER 1

The Difficult Dialogue of Curriculum Transformation: Ethnic Studies and Women's Studies

Johnnella E. Butler

During the past twenty years in the United States, we have established Women's Studies, Black Studies, Latino Studies, Asian American Studies, and Native American Studies as legitimate scholarly areas of inquiry and as academic majors and minors. The Black Studies movement served as a catalyst for other Ethnic Studies programs and provided a catalyst for Women's Studies to challenge gender bias in the academy. Struggles in Women's Studies to mainstream, balance, and integrate the curriculum have taken place alongside struggles to maintain departments and programs of Afro-American and the more inclusive Black or Africana Studies, and to develop Puerto Rican Studies, Chicano Studies, Asian American Studies, and Native American Studies. The dialogue between Women's Studies and Ethnic Studies is limited, often indirect, and hampered by mutual distrust stemming from racism, sexism, heterosexism, ethnocentrism, and classism. The centrality of each field to women of color, however, can provide a foundation for the two fields to produce complete scholarship and pedagogy, challenging the Eurocentric, male-biased, heterosexist, sexist, racist, and classist orientation of college and university curricula.

The extent of and depth of that challenge is succinctly characterized by an advertisement,"Is the Curriculum Biased? A Statement by the National Association of Scholars" in the November 8, 1989 *Chronicle of Higher Education*.[1] Attention to texts by and about white women and men and women of color is reduced to the argument of standards, supported by the assumption that these texts are inferior and their inclusion decided upon simply on the "principle of proportional representation of authors, classified ethnically, biologically, or geographically. The inclusion of works by white women, and men and women of color is perceived to be for the purpose of simply avoiding " [the discouraging of students for not having encountered] more works by members of their own race, sex, or ethnic group, [and even if] substantiated,

1

would not justify adding inferior works." The study of white women, and men and women of color is reduced to simply studying "social problems," and it is argued that "other cultures, minority subcultures, and social problems have long been studied in the liberal arts curriculum in such established disciplines as history, literature, comparative religion, economics, political science, anthropology, and sociology." No attention or validity is given to the reality of most of our curricula either not representing, for example African or American Indian religions as world religions, or at best insulting them by viewing them from a Eurocentric perspective.

Discussion of the demands for inclusion is reduced to assertions implying the Eurocentric, Anglocentric, colonialist assumptions and perspectives that make it possible to state that "the idea that the traditional curriculum 'excludes' is patently false" and "that the liberal arts oppress minorities and women is yet more ludicrous." Diversity is simplistically reduced to "the idea that people of different sexes, races or ethnic backgrounds necessarily see things differently." Intellectual honesty is seen to exist only where political realities are ignored or reduced to "polemics," where cultural differences are transcended rather than acknowledged and utilized, and where studies of the West seem curiously separate from the study of the traditions and experiences that make up the United States. Most curiously, in the face of the reality of the near extirpation of American Indians, in the face of the reality of the enslavement of people of African ancestry, in the face of the reality of the sexist and heterosexist behavior to all women, in the face of these and other like realities and their legacies, the National Association of Scholars publicly advertises its racism, sexism, ethnocentrism, and classism in the patronizing closing of its advertisement:

The National Association of Scholars is in favor of ethnic studies, the study of non-Western cultures, and the study of the special problems of women and minorities in our society, but it opposes subordinating the entire humanities and social science curricula to such studies and it views with alarm their growing politicization. Efforts purportedly made to introduce "other points of view" and "pluralism" often seem in fact designed to restrict attention to a narrow set of issues, tendentiously defined. An examination of many women's studies and minority studies courses and programs discloses little study of other cultures and much excoriation of our society for its alleged oppression of women, blacks, and others. The banner of "cultural diversity" is apparently being raised by some whose paramount interest actually lies in attacking the West and its institutions. . . . We must also reject the allegations of "racism" and "sexism" that are frequently leveled against honest critics of the new proposals, and which only have the effect of stifling much-needed debate.[2]

The "much needed debate" called upon in the closing statement can hardly take place as long as racism, sexism, heterosexism, ethnocentrism, classism, and colonialism are either ignored or reduced to "a narrow set of issues." Furthermore, until the validity and usefulness of the best of the traditions of both the so-called West and those of its myriad peoples are recognized, studied in their own right, and utilized in scholarship, we will perpetuate a seriously flawed and damaged scholarship and society. As long as the political dimensions of the existing curriculum are obscured and passed off as objective subject content and as long as the past and present realities of white women, women of color, and men of color are deemed a "narrow set of issues," to be studied, at best, from the perspective of their inferiority and deviance, the "much-needed" debate will be a rather lopsided, intellectual game of "defending" the West. Curriculum transformation is not about such games at all.

In my experience, the statement by the National Association of Scholars represents the parameters of the current debate within the academy around Ethnic Studies and Women's Studies. And within this myopic, hostile, ethnocentric context, with its paternalistic overtones, many of us urge a scholarly conversation and sharing between the faculty and content of Ethnic Studies and Women's Studies. I wish to suggest a broader conceptualization of transformative work in the academy, to lend a coherence, a productive perspective, and clear directions for the difficult dialogues that have begun and must continue in order to provide an education worthy of and essential to the well-being of our citizens.

Henry Adams, in his late-nineteenth-century search for unity in thought and action and between the two, oddly enough may be seen as very similar to his contemporary, W. E. B. DuBois, and to more recent scholars and advocates of Black Studies, Asian American, American Indian, and Latino Studies; and Women's Studies. Adams realized, as they, that his education was useless to cope with rapid social, cultural, and technological change. More distressingly, he realized that his education did not provide him with the attitudes and skills necessary for progress toward a positive end for humanity. Through his efforts to understand human thought and history as energetic forces comparable to the forces of physical, scientific energy, he prophetically predicted that the huge electric dynamos of the Chicago and Paris expos of 1893 and 1900 respectively were symbolic of the coming age in which "the human race may commit suicide by blowing up the world." Furthermore, he explicated the power of the spiritual unity of philosophy, art, and vision. He deplored his own age, of which ours is a direct extension, as having no unity except in "the unsolved mystery of the atom."

The kind of unity that Adams sought was limited and doomed in its inherent ethnocentrism and sexism; nonetheless, it provided a significant step,

I think, towards our taking seriously the need for a humaneness in thought and action that might prevent humankind's self-destruction through group, cultural, and societal genocide, and encourage the potential for full human development. Furthermore, as DuBois predicted in 1903, the problem of the twentieth century is the problem of the color line, with all its social, political, economic, and cultural ramifications.[3] The current challenges to academia that white women and women and men of color present to the curriculum are articulations of the problem in academia, just as the Civil Rights and Black Power movements articulated the problem of the color line in the body politic. The greater presence of minorities of color and white women on college and university campuses clearly raises the question of essential change within the academic community structure. Their mere presence, however, does not mandate that the curriculum be changed to reflect the strengths and weaknesses, the beautiful and ugly of our essentially pluralistic collective history. The goal of good, honest scholarship, reflective of the closest approximation of the truth, mandates essential change. Their presence suggests the need to prepare all students to live and work in a rapidly changing and increasingly diverse world. Those of us who have become involved in curriculum transformation efforts are attempting to assist universities, colleges, and their faculty in doing just that.

Most will agree that we are a nation founded essentially on the concept of individualism with a national culture defined by Anglo-American ethnicity with European roots, essentially British and neoclassical Greek and Roman. Serious, unbiased attention to the American historical, social, political, economic, and cultural experiences and present reality of men of color, white women, and women of color in the United States reveals that the democratic ideals of the United States have failed many of its myriad peoples because of the inherent contradiction between the structure and the essence of our projected national culture and the essentially pluralist composition of our people. What Harold Cruse has defined as the "integrationist ethic" conveys not simply "freedom and justice for all," but moreover the myth of the melting pot—the coercion of the American Dream at the expense of one another, a vicious rugged individualism, an ethnocentrism, sexism, classism, and racism maintaining an inherent contradiction between the structure and essence of our national culture and the essentially pluralist composition of our people at a significant, defining, "credo" level.[4]

The implicit, inherent message for all Euro-Americans as well as for Americans of other racial and cultural heritages has been and remains that integration/assimilation means negation of one's own cultural values and a melting or blending of the self into the dominant ideal. That dominant ideal, then, defines the greater part of one's cultural and personal identity. In most possibilities for a sharing of cultural values, the values and ways of people of color are appropriated to uses and definitions that result, at best, in a distorting compromise. American ethnic, cultural, social, and economic realities are then defined by an individual, bootstrap, competitive, evolving, puritanical ethic. What results, perhaps unwittingly, is the distortion and constantly threatened destruction of a sustaining ethnic potential other than the "American," read "Anglo-American," or subscribers to that norm. Only in short-lived instances where the ethnic group has power and status for a given period of time do we see an apparent flourishing of the democratic ideal in its intended pluralistic concept of "We, the people . . ."

The ramifications of the integrationist ethic on scholarship are quite visible and incur a figurative as well as concrete violence on the social, cultural, political, and economic realities of most men and women of color in the United States and most white women. It incurs another violence on white men, beginning with an exaggerated sense of self-worth. As a historical tendency stimulated by the Anglo-American ideology (reminder: my use of Anglo-American indicates a cultural, social, political, and economic national heritage), the integrationist ethic subverts and blocks the underlying American propensity toward a democratic pluralism, a pluralism inclusive of the Anglo-American ethic but not defined by that or any one ethic subscribed to by a power structure. It is further supported by racism, which upholds rampant individualism and an Americanism with the implied goal of nullification of all competing subcultures indigenous to what is now the United States. Briefly stated, knowing and acting out of the full, true story of our shared American pasts and presents, and learning that story through a constructive generative process, is the only hope for our becoming a literate nation.

As Paulo Friere has shown, literacy implies more than the ability to read and count. As the history of American slavery reminds us, learning to read and count was closely connected to the slaves perceiving fully their human condition and to the Christian misuse of the Bible to justify slavery, and led, if not directly to revolt, to an intense desire for freedom. Literacy is inextricably joined with a freedom that is dependent on our knowing one another, becoming conversant with one another, and building on the best of our traditions in the approximation, if not the achievement, of wholeness.

In the curricular context, the attempt at wholeness includes a comprehensive sense of unity, somewhat reminiscent of Henry Adams and others, but much more transformative. That unity is expressed by:

• The identification of the connections between and interaction among the disciplines (interdisciplinary study would not simply mean bringing several scholars together to investigate a subject. Rather, it would mean an approach to scholarship evolving from the confluence and convergence of disciplinary approaches)

• The study and definition of the experience and the aesthetics of those large groups of people who are neglected, studied not in comparison to the dominant group, not as problems to a dominant group, but in and of themselves and in relation to one another

• The correction of the distortions of the majority and the minority that have occurred due to the insistence of exclusion

• The defining and structuring of a curriculum that through its content and process affirms the interconnectedness of human life, experience, and creativity and its constant evolutionary nature

In such a curriculum, the stories of Euro-American assimilation would find their place in the disciplines and in interdisciplinary study as well as in the transformation of the concept of what and who is American. The Anglo-American experience would take its rightful place as a heritage that has defined much of the national character, to which most Euro-Americans have subscribed, and that has wielded an inordinate amount of power in determining various norms and privileges. The scholarship of Black Studies and other Ethnic Studies, and the scholarship of Women's Studies, as both separate entities and as interdisciplinary fields of study interacting with the traditional disciplines, would then move us to a content and pedagogy that begins to define and characterize a curriculum more reflective of our American cultural reality (and here I use "cultural" in its most comprehensive sense), and more reflective of the need that human beings constantly exhibit to understand who they are in order to act responsibly toward one another in the world.

Given the American social and cultural reality, the greater participation of men and women of color and white women in higher education has far-reaching implications for not only who the students and professors are in our colleges and universities, but also for *what* and *how* we teach. The Afro-American, the Latino American, the Asian American, and the American Indian bring with them a cultural and historical reality integral to the understanding of the United States' past and present. Women—Anglo-American and other Euro-American women, and women of color—foreground the diversity implicit in our many misleading collective nouns, such as "women." These realities are vital to laying the groundwork for a productive, vibrant future. Their incorporation into the curriculum began and directs the discussion of curricular change, as well as the more ambitious transformation.

In his 1985 *Report to the Ford Foundation*, the late Nathan Huggins reviews the transition of the American University during the mid twentieth century from "Cardinal Newman's idealism and from the shaping influence of the German university" to an "unprecedented expansion and transformation."

That transformation occurred in regards to curriculum as well as in regards to the composition of the student body. He reminds us that:

> When in the late sixties, black students challenged the curriculum, their main target was the parochial character of the humanities as taught. They saw the humanities as exclusive rather than universal. They saw humanists as arrogant white men in self-congratulatory identification with a grand European culture. To those students, such arrogance justified the charge of "racism."[5]

Consistent with this transformation, humanities scholars, Huggins points out, had become more and more specialized and were even more incompetent, he implies, to meet this challenge than those imbued with Matthew Arnold's conceptualization of the proper liberal arts content that at least went somewhat beyond the confines of Western civilization. Huggins succinctly further reminds us that Black students and scholars also began to "challenge the 'objectivity' of mainstream social science," and demanded a "discussion of what they saw to be the inherent racism in these normative assumptions and for a shift in perspective that would destigmatize blacks and reexamine the 'normalcy' of the white middle class."

Catherine Stimpson in her 1986 *Report to the Ford Foundation: Women's Studies in the United States*, argues that it is appropriate to view Women's Studies within the framework of curricular reform beginning in the 1820s, of which the mid-twentieth-century shifts of foci may be seen as a part. She points out that

> Black studies and the larger black power movement that helped create black studies made several significant contributions to the theory and practice of women's studies, providing an intellectual agenda for women's studies in its initial stages. The black power movement believed that a revolution by the oppressed must be preceded by a transformation of consciousness in order to succeed. The battle for self-esteem proceeded on two fronts—on the popular level through slogans like "black is beautiful" and in institutions of higher learning through the black studies movement. Black studies, like women's studies after it, sought, first, to reclaim the past and, second, to analyze the causes of oppression.[6]

What Huggins and Stimpson refer to is more correctly labelled reform, for early Black Studies and Women's Studies did not demand any fundamental shifts in foci of the entire liberal arts curriculum. The emphasis was on adding the "other" to the curriculum. Indeed, reflecting on the program and departmental status of Women's Studies and Black Studies, we quickly realize that they were most frequently on the periphery of the curriculum, struggling with one another over limited funds. Course approvals, tenure, and reappointments did not come easily. There are many casualties, for example in Black Studies, of scholars who were denied tenure by white (usually male) professors who have built their careers on studying Black people and their lives.[7] The fact that now we have two burgeoning fields of study that by their very nature challenge the accepted subject matter and foci of the liberal arts suggests movement beyond reform to transformation.

In "Transforming the Curriculum: Teaching About Women of Color," I define and describe transformation in the context of scholarship on the United States, emphasizing that it involves taking race, class, gender, and ethnicity seriously as categories of analysis functioning simultaneously separately and together in a matrix-like fashion. During the early eighties, many of us in Women's Studies in particular began to understand the difference between reform and transform as we observed that balancing, mainstreaming, and integrating were essentially simply adding women of color to Women's Studies syllabi as an afterthought or as an aberration. The books *Sturdy Black Bridges* and *But Some of Us are Brave: Black Women's Studies* publicly demonstrated the need for transformation, and two early faculty development projects articulated in the academic community ways of transforming courses: the FIPSE-funded Black Studies/Women's Studies, an Overdue Partnership faculty development grant in Massachusetts, and the state-funded Cross Cultural Perspectives in the Curriculum in California.[8]

More recently, focusing on the incorporation of content on women of color into core and introductory courses, Ford has funded eleven Women's Research Centers to work with the Ethnic Studies components on their campuses. Virginia, through a competitive effort, has funded faculty development projects on incorporating race, class, gender, and ethnicity into the curriculum.[9] Similar efforts are occurring on campuses across the nation, not in insignificant numbers, but not nearly as much as needed. Ethnic Studies and Women's Studies have the content and are developing the methodologies and pedagogies needed to incorporate race, class, gender, and ethnicity into the curriculum. The task calls for approaches to scholarship and teaching beyond those of the traditional disciplines. It also demands dropping courses repetitive of the Euro-American and Western experience from the liberal arts curriculum.

However, transformation of the academy will not occur unless Women's Studies and Ethnic Studies themselves are transformed. *That is, significant curricular change regarding the experiences of women depends on the radical transformation of Women's Studies to reflect all women's experience. Significant curricular change regarding the experience of people of color depends on the radical transformation of Ethnic Studies to reflect the experience of women of color.* Simply put, Women's Studies must divest itself of white-skin privilege, racism, and the feminist insistence on the primacy of gender; Ethnic Studies must divest itself of male-centered scholarship, sexism, and hetero-sexism, and must lend credibility to gender as a valid, viable, and necessary category of analysis. The emerging dialogue is most productive when viewed as part of the ongoing development of the American university and the re—structuring of knowledge as our nation and its needs grow and change. Its rough, jagged edges begin to smooth as we find ways to recognize and incorporate difference, correct omissions and distortions. Clarifying the use of the term "Ethnic Studies" and envisioning a curriculum help to reveal the possible.

The fact that the term Ethnic Studies has come to signify the body of knowledge of people of color in the United States as well as academic pro-grams and departments organized to study in an interdisciplinary fashion these experiences, is transformative. Ethnic Studies serves as a collective noun for Black Studies, Asian American Studies, American Indian Studies, and Latino Studies. Programmatically, Ethnic Studies can exist as Black Studies, Asian American Studies, American Indian Studies, and Latino Studies, independently and/or in a comparative context. Arguments in the academy over the use of the term generally question its use to the exclusion of Euro-American ethnics. In Werner Sollers's *Beyond Ethnicity*, the discussion of the origin of the term "ethnic" clarifies that it is a time-bound and group-situation-bound term. His work tends to reinforce the historical use of the term that simultane-ously affirms assimilation (the melting pot worked) while affirming plural coexistence (cultural pluralism reigns), as if one can have it both ways. Race, gender, and class, while not ignored, do not seem to be taken seriously as categories of definition that also have institutional and cultural manifestations in and of themselves and in the form of their "-isms."[10]

It has become fairly obvious that while most Euro-American ethnic groups maintain an identity around the heritage of their country of origin, most have assimilated in the most significant ways to the Anglo-American norm. Racism has not been a constant factor preventing that assimilation. Scandinavian Studies, for example, may mean studying European Scandina-vian countries and populations or it may mean studying assimilated Ameri-cans of Scandinavian experience. In the American context, it does not provide us with extensive legal studies, a history that is pervasive throughout and in many ways central to American history, or a distinct cultural experience within the United States that provides distinct and significant paradigms for the study of literature, psychology, sociology, politics, and economics. While the Irish American, for example, may have more ethnic visibility in some aspects of American life, that experience, because of assimilation, does not provide a centrality, as do the experiences of people of color in the United States.

Furthermore, it is testimony to the peculiar and complex racial and ethnic definitions in the United States that there is confusion as to where the American Jewish experience "fits." Are they Jewish and therefore ethnic? Are they white and therefore assimilated, despite anti-semitism? Is anti-semitism the same as racism? Does it have the institutional ramifications of racism? Howard Adelman argues in this volume that Jewish Studies is ethnic. Within a European context, indeed, the study of Semitics and of the European Jew may be viewed as Ethnic Studies. In the American context, however, it may be argued that because of white-skin privilege, Jewish Americans have been able to assimilate. Their distinguishing feature is their religion.[11] The Armenian American women whom Arlene Avakian describes in this text may be viewed as in the process of classic assimilation.

What has emerged, I think, is a transformation in the American reality and consciousness that sees ethnicity and race as overlapping, making ethnicity applicable as a category to American people of color. Whites, it seems, have for the most part assimilated. Euro-American ethnic differences have evolved for the most part in this century to be variations on a theme that is primarily American (read Anglo-American).[12] People of color have not been allowed, for the most part, to assimilate. Ethnic/racial differences signal "other." The move then within the academy to study the content of Ethnic Studies and Women's Studies may be seen as an effort to examine the beautiful and the ugly of this important aspect of the American experience, in order to reveal and develop the paradigms and methodologies necessary to understand these experiences in and of themselves, in comparison to one another, in the context of the larger American society, and indeed to understand fully American society in its entirety. This describes transformation. It does not stop at adding and celebrating diversity. It demands that we do something with these experiences, this diversity, in order ultimately to understand the whole. It demands that we add, delete, decenter, re-vision and reorganize in order to transform our curricula to reflect a kind of unity, a wholeness that is all-inclusive in its content, methodology, and pedagogy.

A curriculum, methodology, and pedagogy that examines the unity among disciplines, experiences, events, and humans, that explores subject matter comparatively as well as singly, will begin to correct some of the basic ills of the academy:

1. *A lack of a sense of human commonality and communality.*
    Because the curriculum content does not assert or imply a commonality or a communality among humans and human experience, course material

seems distant, irrelevant, or perhaps ideal and abstract. And because it is ethnocentric, it is frequently repetitive. Few connections, if any, are apparent between the past, present, and the future; science and math appear formulaic and abstract, distant from humans. The lack of an understood commonality and communality makes it difficult for professors to identify the needs of students who come from backgrounds unlike their own. This lack makes it impossible for professors to draw analogies to experiences with which they are unfamiliar, both when teaching and when deciding on process, or to recognize similar behavior patterns or learning processes. Rarely do students embrace the learning process because they feel connected with the content and the professors in relation to content and process. Rarely do professors feel connected with content and process and with students.

2. *A distorted sense of the value of the aesthetics, ideals, history, and heritage of the Anglo, upper-middle to upper class white American.*

Scholars, professors, and students weigh all experience against the stated and implied norm of a white, idealized sense of Western culture. Thus, other aesthetics, ideals, histories, and heritages are ignored. They are seen as subordinate to and only within the context of the implied norm, or seen as deviant. In such a way is the literary canon established; historical periods defined; sociological, economic, and political formulae devised, and so on. Failure to achieve the American Dream is ascribed to cultural deprivation and perhaps "lacking the necessaries," that is inherent racial and/or ethnic difference.

3. *A distortion of American history and culture through the distortion of the meaning of race and ethnicity in American social and scholarly contexts.*

The history and heritage of groups of color are presented as additional to, instead of integral to, American history and heritage, that is, if included at all. Thus, there is the accepted version of American history and heritage that is only minimally affected by Afro-American history and heritage, Asian American history and heritage, Latino American history and heritage, American Indian history and heritage, and white women's history and heritage. Similarly, Euro-American history and heritage is modulated by Anglo-American norm imposition and privilege.

4. *A distorted and limited treatment of gender difference and similarities.*

The curriculum is characterized by a valuing of the masculine over the feminine and a simplistic tendency to equate the two to suggest equity and fairness. Failure of women to achieve is often seen as part and parcel of the female reality. Likewise, cultural, academic, social, and political achievements of women are valued less than those of men. This valuing and devaluing is modulated by ethnocentrism, racism, and classism.

5. *A distortion of American class realities.*

In pursuit of the "norm" as coerced by the integrationist ethic, class differences are weighed against the upper-middle to upper class norm that is part of the Anglo-American ideal. Together with the myth of rugged individualism, the American Dream, the melting pot, racism, sexism, and ethnocentrism, the upper-middle class to upper class norm allows scholarship and teaching to act as if class differences do not exist or have negligible significance, or to ascribe failure to achieve the American Dream to inherent class characteristics.

6. *A limitation and restriction of education to a static state.*

The entire educational process becomes one that must remain primarily static in order to maintain the imbalance of power sustained by racism, classism, sexism, and ethnocentrism. Only changes defined and limited by the dominant cultural norm are tolerated. Professors generally control and fill "the empty receptacles of students' minds." The "leading out" of the mind inherent in the definition of the verb "to educate" is ignored. Specialization and marketable skills ensure quick returns. Therefore, critical thinking, comprehension of the dynamics of culture and human life, and the relationship of the sciences, humanities, and social sciences to humankind and to one another are devalued and viewed as unnecessary to individual, material well-being. The lack of perceived unity among the different kinds of people, lifestyles, classes, cultures, and among disciplines, content, professors, and students, and so on, supports the cultural and personal expression that either imitates or is of the norm. Education maintains that norm instead of catalyzing growth.

7. *A gross limitation of the human potential.*

By the narrow adherence to an idealized norm, we fail to identify and utilize the best of our collective traditions. Hence, a large segment of the American population, both "minority" and "majority," fail to develop as part of the larger culture that which is in them. For example, our national enthusiasm and commitment to foreign language teaching is dampened. Only languages deemed acceptable within the context of the idealized norm are supported. Our tolerance of non-English-speaking peoples is limited. Teaching reading and writing using foreign language or the regional or cultural dialect of English as building blocks is largely disdained, and in some quarters viewed as un-American.

The serious, radical deconstruction and subsequent reconstruction through transformation can ensure the education our students need to strive toward an informed, intelligent, creative, plural, multidimensional, and humane life. Rarely do expediency and moral justice converge. However, if we desire a literate citizenry, then we must encourage an academic atmosphere that corrects distortions and exclusions, and allows for syncretism and an interaction among differences and samenesses so that we see all of our selves as vibrant parts of the past, present, and future of the many dimensions of this nation.[13]

Academic institutions, by their very nature and reason for existence, define and perpetuate the national culture. It might be convincingly argued that this purpose has become more and more obscure as the population grows more and more out of touch with the static curriculum. By now demographic statistics are well known. Numbers of the elite white are dwindling. In addition, the population pool for the majority of colleges and universities is rapidly becoming Latino, Asian American, Afro-American, American Indian, and middle- and lower-economic-class white American. The complexion of the elite class reflects flecks of brown and yellow. A curriculum that does not propose and explicate the values of our total population—its past and present, its encounter with technological and social change—will be useless in the working, cultural, and social world of the twenty-first century. Worst of all, it will continue to stifle the human imagination and potential so that fear of one another and protection and isolation from one another will maintain enlarged possibilities for mutual destruction.

It is impossible to describe in detail the curriculum implied by the chapters in this book; however, I can provide a working overview. The changes needed must occur over a period of time. Change in the nature of the disciplines, the relationships among disciplines, between departments and programs, and in interdisciplinary approaches and disciplinary approaches, only begin to outline the nature of this change. Furthermore, the most fundamental characteristic of the projected curriculum is generative change. Generative change is inherent in and emanates from pedagogy, methodology, and content itself (for all academic content is, in one way or another, a reflection of human lives and conditions). The ideas and actions resulting from study that reflects the conditions and needs of the humans they serve constitute this change.

The foundation of the overall liberal arts curriculum would be core or distribution general education courses providing knowledge of African, Asian, Native American, and Western civilizations. Content of such courses would include essential philosophies, cultures, and aesthetics of these civilizations. Methodology and pedagogy would focus on examination of the interactions among these civilizations, the balances and imbalances of power within and among these civilizations, value systems, comparative value systems, and identification of what has been and what can be possible when these civilizations have and do come together. Such core or general education courses would form a sequence over a period of at least four semesters. This institution of required courses—whether distribution or core general education courses concentrating on other cultures, on "minority" experience and on women's experience—by some colleges and universities during the past few years is often viewed negatively as a band-aid approach or stopgap measure for addressing the ills of higher education. However, more positively, these efforts provide initial foundations for recognition of the relevance of such content to the liberal arts education. And more importantly, they point to more sophisticated, inclusive foundation courses.

Ethnic Studies (either comparative, including ethnic-specific programs for example, or simply ethnic-specific programs or departments) and Women's Studies departments or programs are essential to the proposed curriculum. Whether the program or department structure serves best depends on the particular university or college structure. In some institutions it is only possible for interdisciplinary departments to cross-list courses, share joint appointments, and have significant academic exchange with the traditionally discipline-based departments. In others the program format works well, allowing for the necessary interaction with related disciplines and fields while simultaneously maintaining the integrity of the fields of Ethnic Studies and Women's Studies. (In deciding upon structure, we should recognize that the department is the structural entity for recognition of scholarship, for tenure, budget lines, etc.) The academic entities of Women's Studies and Ethnic Studies provide the basic structure within which scholarship from those fields is generated as well as the structure within which undergraduates may major, minor, or select electives. Faculty from these departments, and faculty in disciplines who share content and the interdisciplinary approach most likely would have the interest and scholarly background to begin the shaping of the required courses.

The treatment of literature in English in this projected curriculum provides a useful example for imagining humanities and suggests implications for the social sciences and the sciences. What passes for our nation's literary history and heritage espouses the aesthetics and tenets of Western, specifically British and Anglo-American traditions. Definition and description of those traditions' beautiful and ugly, of their significances, are relevant to them; however, the definitions are imposed on what should be recognized as other American traditions and other world literary traditions (such as African literature and Indian literature being designated "Commonwealth Literature"). Consequently, the literary aesthetic is limited to the idealization of the Anglo and Anglo-American norm. The origins, and indeed the existence of other traditions in English, are traced to the Anglo and Anglo-American aesthetics, and so limited and defined. The American literary tradition excludes, usurps, and obliterates the lives, works, and thoughts of people who either are not of that tradition or who do not subscribe to it. Reclaiming those lives, works, and thoughts provides for a more truthful consideration of the apparently dominant tradition; demands a non-hierarchal analysis of other existing and burgeoning traditions both in and of themselves and in relation to one another; and demands a demystification of the Anglo and Anglo-American traditions as dominant and, rather, a positing of them as one among many.

To those who question "What of the 'classics'?" the response is at least twofold. First, the sequence and content of the curriculum would be informed by a pluralistic concept of the art of the written word. The student would be encouraged to read as widely as possible while studying the nature and development of literary traditions, their evolution, and their comparisons. Comprehension of the multidimensional American literary tradition, for example, demands comparative, interdisciplinary, and disciplinary approaches. The point is not to read everything of great significance in each American literary tradition. Rather, the point is to develop an understanding of works from each tradition and a comprehension of the essentials and aesthetics of the traditions. This builds on the two-semester distribution or core general education courses that examine the various cultural contexts of world civilizations and of American ethnic groups of which Anglo-American is one.

Second, the proposed curriculum necessitates the redefinition of the classics in terms of the vernacular of each aesthetic and within the context of a non-hierarchal, pluralistic sense of aesthetics. Hawthorne and Twain would stand next to Kate Chopin and Charles Chesnutt; Wheatley Bradstreet would find places in the same tradition with Thoreau and David Walker; Yezierska, Larsen, Silko, Momaday, and Carlos Bulosan, among other writers usually excluded from the American literary tradition, would be designated as twentieth-century "classics." Writers whose works are repetitive of the Anglo-American tradition would be dropped. Transformation does not necessitate six years in college.

Standards for assessing literature would be determined by its cultural and aesthetic context. For example, the use of the oral tradition, of African-based Afro-American folk ritual, of elements of the Blues, and of signifying, serve as signposts in Afro-American writing; the combination of Anglo-based devices to explore Afro-American contexts or the use of Anglo-based devices to explore Afro-American topics serve in other instances. What is "romantic Primitivism" in Anglo terms becomes metaphysical realism in American Indian terms, or simply realism. Implied in that literature is a definition of realism that encompasses the rational and intuitive worlds, the material and physical worlds in a way essentially alien to Western thought. Perhaps even new literary terms must be devised to accommodate this world view which we find in American Indian, Afro-American, Asian American, and Latino American literatures.

Briefly, the literature in English curriculum would require a course explicating the roots and literary manifestations of the Afro-American, Anglo-American, Asian American, Latino American, and American Indian traditions. Familiarization with these literary traditions and their evolution, and their interactions with the Anglo-American tradition are the objective that determines what texts would be employed. It seems reasonable to require knowledge of at least two traditions with an upper-level, required, two-semester seminar in comparative American aesthetics. The required general education course would prepare students to encounter the comparative and interdisciplinary approaches and the interactions of race, class, gender, and their negative "-isms."

I have attempted to give a projection, and there are many variations in literature, sociology, history, economics, and the natural and physical sciences. The importance of foreign language departments and religion departments should not be underestimated either. Once we accept the fact that language does not *determine* culture, the breadth of literary expression expands tremendously. Caribbean literatures, as well as African and Indian literatures become visible on their own terms, terms influenced by, but by no means defined by, the colonialism of the French, British, Portuguese, and Spanish. Once we accept the fact that religion has many manifestations as logical and as sacred to the corresponding cultures as Christianity is to much of the United States or as Judaism is to Israel, then we develop an informed curiosity about American Indian rituals, African traditional religions, Islam, and their contacts with one another and with Christianity. No longer do we then designate Buddhism as exotic or African religion and philosophy as savage. Studying "the other" in and of themselves and in relation to colonial realities and discourse, both here and abroad, begins to clarify the connections between, the boundaries of, and the content of traditions. The American tradition is expanded and transformed, for example, in regard to content and aesthetics.

Most significantly, to achieve the transformed curriculum demands fundamental change within the professor, the scholar. When we sit alone in our studies creating scholarship and devising syllabi, we have to confront those deterrents of white skin-privilege, racism, sexism, homophobia, classism, and ethnocentrism. Women's Studies' relationship to the academy is bound up with the power inherent in white-skin privilege. I think this is why Women's Studies has insisted on the lens of gender as being primary, why many Women's Studies professors find it easy to say it is too difficult and too much of a bother to find a woman of color scholar to teach, to consult. It is this same privilege that gives many whites the "permission" to respond to discussions regarding the relationship between American literature by people of color and Anglo-American literature by demanding "What's wrong with the West?" The resistance to removing white Anglo-American literature from the center urges many of us to support such derailments and question the validity of literature by people of color.

The tenacity of feeling that whites ought by nature to be at the center and by nature to define is tremendous. A non-hierarchal methodology would refuse primacy to either race, class, gender, or ethnicity, demanding instead the recognition of their matrix-like interaction. As Lillian Smith points out in *Killers of the Dream*, racism in the segregated South was sustained by the position of white women that is defined by sexism.[14] Speaking generally, the sexism the Black woman experiences, whether instigated by white or Black males, is reinforced and defined in its nature by the racism and ethnocentrism of the oppressors. Class, of course, creates additional variations. Embracing a non-hierarchal methodology increases in whites the fear of displacement from the center, the locus of control. For people of color who are fighting for validation within the traditional norms, such a methodology increases the fear of being relegated to the periphery because no one enjoys the center exclusively. All of us trained traditionally, even as we challenge, experience an uneasiness with interdisciplinary approaches as they defy the (false) boundaries of knowledge.

Although Ethnic Studies are generally male-centered and frequently homophobic, they are not as closely tied to the academy as is Women's Studies. The Afro-centric methodology of Black Studies and the emphasis on the significance of the mother cultures to Asian American, Latino, and American Indian Studies distance and even alienate their approaches from Anglo- and Western-centered disciplines. Although Women's Studies is new, until very recently white women in the academy have shared the academy's cultural framework and methodology. Black scholars, if not denied admittance into the academy, have been alienated if only for their race—not to mention their subject matter, their cultural reality, and the perception of them as distinctly inferior, inhuman beings incapable of competing in any fashion on human terms. Other people of color generally figure as a variation on this theme.

Thus, while political questions as to the wisdom of maintaining a dialogue with Women's Studies weigh heavily and sometimes unkindly, the sexism and homophobia of Ethnic Studies is frequently mediated by cultural and historical realities. Racial stereotyping that may surface in the efforts of comparative Ethnic Studies is most frequently mediated by shared oppressions; it seldom parallels the dimensions of white racism, which is endemic to society in the United States.

The academic and personal efforts that are needed in Women's Studies and Ethnic Studies and other disciplines and fields is enormous. The way is clear; we have begun the dialogue. We know that insisting on the primacy of gender obliterates the reality of the matrix-like interactions among racism, classism, sexism, and ethnocentrism. We know that insisting on the primacy of race and culture likewise obliterates the same reality (see especially Spelman, this volume, and Butler, ". . . Teaching About Women of Color," this volume). Whether or not we take up the challenge is yet to be seen.

Notes

1. "Is the Curriculum Biased? A Statement by the National Association of Scholars. *Chronicle of Higher Education,* November 8, 1989, p. A23.

2. Ibid.

3. W. E. B. Dubois, *The Souls of Black Folk* in John Hope Franklin, ed. *Three Negro Classics* (Signet, 1903) (New York: Avon, 1971).

4. Harold Cruse, "The Creative and Performing Arts and the Struggle for Identity and Credibility" in Harry A. Johnson, ed., *Negotiating the Mainstream: A Survey of the Afro-American Experience* (Chicago: American Library Association, 1972), pp. 47–102.

5. Nathan Huggins, *Afro-American Studies* (New York: Ford Foundation, 1985), p. 13.

6. Catherine Stimpson with Nina Kressner Cobb, *Women's Studies in the United States* (New York: Ford Foundation, 1986), p. 11.

7. This has long been a known, undocumented fact within the Black Studies community. See Michael A. Olivas, "An Elite Priesthood of White Males Dominates the Central Areas of Civil Rights Scholarship," *The Chronicle of Higher Education,* May 24, 1989, pp. B1–B2.

8. Roseann P. Bell, Bettye J. Parker, Beverly Guy-Sheftall, eds., *Sturdy Black Bridges: Visions of Black Women in Literature* (New York: Anchor, 1979); Gloria T. Hull, Patricia Bell Scott, Barbara Smith, eds., *But Some of Us Are Brave, Black Women's Studies* (Old Westbury, N.Y.: 1982; Margo Culley and I were the project investigators and co-directors of the F.I.P.S.E. project. See Johnnella E. Butler, "Complicating the Question: Black Studies and Women's Studies in Marilyn Schuster and Susan Van Dyne, eds., *Women's Place in the Academy: Transforming the Liberal Arts Curriculum* (New Jersey: Rowman and Allanheld, 1985). Deborah Rosenfelt and Carol Lee Sanchez co-directed the California project at San Francisco State University.

9. The two Virginia projects are at Mary Washington College, Fredericksburg and Virginia Polytechnic Institute and State University, Blacksburg.

10. See Chapter I in Werner Sollers, *Beyond Ethnicity: Consent and Descent in American Culture* (New York: Oxford, 1986).

11. Anti-semitism in this country cannot be equated with that in Nazi Germany and which is extant in the Soviet Union. Here it refers to a religious and ethnic prejudice, existing in an entirely different context, altered largely by Jewish white skin privilege, class and, at times, ethnic privilege.

12. For a model transformation of American literature based on American cultural pluralism, see Paul Lauter, ed., *Reconstructing American Literature: Courses, Syllabi, Issues* (Old Westbury, New York: The Feminist Press, 1983).

13. Taking seriously information that is found in our efforts to correct racist, sexist, classist, and bigoted scholarship in many instances calls for a complete change in the ways we conceptualize our cultural selves. John Pappademos, Professor of Physics at the University of Illinois at Chicago, as part of a panel presentation at a conference on the core curriculum, sponsored by the Texas Higher Education Coordinating Board (July 21, 1990) presented an unpublished paper on "The Role of Africa in the History of Science."

He noted that a survey of introductory physics and physical science texts revealed that of "African and African American achievements in science there was not a word." While this survey was done in 1980, he said that one or two recent texts "try to remedy the omissions of past and present achievements of women scientists;" but that "Africa and Black people have been stricken from the record as far as science's history is concerned (p. 1)". Demonstrating that ancient Egypt's racial makeup was predominantly Black African, he detailed Black African achievements in science, most of which have been obliterated as such by blatantly racist 19th century scholars (see Martin Bernal, *Black Athena* (New Brunswick, NJ: Rutgers University Press, 1989). From the world's first scientific method of measuring time, to identifying the retrograde motion of the planet Mars, to quadratic equations, to establishing a thousand years before Galileo (and known to Galileo) that bodies of different mass fall with the same acceleration, he provided sufficient information to prove his point that the Greeks had learned from the Black Egyptians most of what we credit them and other Europeans for. We need to contemplate just what such information means for transforming our curricula; what it means for the reconceptualization of the origins of Western Civilization and for the excluded and dispossessed cultures of our curricula. Might we not only correct distortions but also learn of different ways of being that might be useful in rescuing ourselves from our oppressive excesses? See Bernal, cited above; John Pappademos, "An outline of Africa in the History of Physics," *Journal of African Civilization*, Vol. II, no. 1,2 (September 1980, pp. 40–59; Pappademos, "The Newtonian Synthesis in Physical Science, Roots in the Nile Valley," *Journal of African Civilizations*, vol. VI, no. 2 (November 1984), pp. 84–101. Various works by Ivan Van Sertima and Frank Snowden also address the Black African origins of science and mathematics.

14. Lillian Smith, *Killers of the Dream* (New York: Norton, 1978).

CHAPTER 2

Funding Women's Studies

Caryn McTighe Musil and Ruby Sales

Despite a technologically sophisticated world with its developing consciousness about race, class, and gender as fundamental categories in our culture, tracking financial support awarded for research on women and women's issues continues to be masked by inadequate subject headings and insufficient tracking of data. This invisibility haunts statistics on funders and funding. Such poverty of information is compounded by the fact that there is no single source or group that monitors funding levels for women. Nor is there a group pressing agencies to provide descriptions of funded projects detailed enough that they would permit more concrete and broader analyses of gender, race, and class. Lacking such a central, sustained monitoring body erases any hope of continuity, which is essential to raising the level of discourse on funding Women's Studies from rudimentary questions to complex issues such as funding patterns, needs assessments, and strategies for future survival. Establishing such a monitoring agency, which simultaneously acts as a repository and data bank, is, then, a priority if Women's Studies is to fully understand and possibly influence the impact of external financial support on its development.

These deficiencies present several practical and methodological impediments. The insufficient data limits the researcher's ability to ask the telling questions as well as to make definitive analysis. However, existing data makes it possible to suggest some of the contours of giving patterns. Consequently, the information in this chapter is meant as a place to begin in some cases, not as a final assessment of what has or will be funded. Additionally, any assessment of funding for Women's Studies must also consider how funding initiatives shift from year to year, how world events alter the ranking of concerns, and how the political climate provides a context for allocating funds. What was true in 1979 might change dramatically in 1980. We encourage readers to use this information to investigate in greater and more specific detail potential funding sources for a particular project.

Overview

Women and money have always had an ambiguous relationship. However, this relationship becomes even more complex for working class women and women of color. Women are seen in the United States as the primary consumer of goods yet continue to suffer economic discrimination that keeps them from wielding economic influence commensurate with their numbers and labor force participation. One of the consequences of this economic disenfranchisement is that it stifles the degree to which women are free to define the terms and scope of their lives. Instead they are forced into responsive postures where they concentrate a large amount of their individual and collective energies on day-to-day survival. This has severe consequences in society where the ability to plan and strategize is ultimately a luxury linked to money and position. Compared to poor women, academic feminists are privileged indeed, yet they carry with them many of the same postures in academia that make them sometimes feel like mere survivors rather than full partners. It is, however, this determination to survive against all odds that has guaranteed the establishment of Women's Studies as a discipline.

The history of Women's Studies is a history of people operating in crisis to survive at nearly any cost while also realizing that they have both the right and the opportunity to shape the intellectual and educational contexts in which they work and in which students learn. Increasingly Women's Studies has received some of the rewards given to traditional areas of study. The history, then, is a textured one of sacrifice and reward. The preliminary research into funding sources for Women's Studies reflects a similar contradictory picture. One is both astonished by the success of this fast-growing field and surprised at its marginality even after more than two decades of institutionalized Women's Studies programs.

On the one hand, there is an impressive list of grants for research, faculty development, Women's Studies program development, scholarships, fellowships, public programming, policy studies, and collaborative programs between direct social service agencies in the community and Women's Studies in the academy. Funding agencies for such a broad range of activities include private foundations, state governments, federal government, corporations, private individuals, and educational institutions themselves. On the other hand, however, funding for women, women's issues, and Women's Studies fluctuates, sometimes dramatically, and is especially vulnerable to the political viewpoints of people in power, especially those in government.

It is a testimony to its intellectual power, institutional flexibility, and the passionate commitment of its practitioners and students that Women's Studies has continued to expand in the eighties, a decade marked by a conservative political climate that witnessed significant cut-backs in federal funding for universities and colleges, especially in the humanities, the stronghold of Women's Studies. The first Women's Studies program received institutional approval in 1969 at San Diego State. By 1977, when the National Women's Studies Association was founded, there were 276 formal programs. By 1980 the number had increased to 332; in 1989 there were 530, with every indication that the numbers will continue to increase. Recent statistics indicate that programs have become more institutionalized, especially through the undergraduate minor and the graduate minor. In 1986, there were 334 undergraduate concentrations, certificates, or minors. In 1989, that number jumped to 404. At the graduate level, the numbers increased from 23 to 55 graduate certificates, concentrations, or minors.

According to a survey by the Women's Studies faculty at the University of Alabama, most Women's Studies programs do not rely on grants from external sources to sustain their programs (*NWS Action* 1, no. 2 (1985): 1). Of the respondents, 79 percent received no outside funds; 17 percent received from 1 percent to 25 percent of funding from grants; and only 4 percent relied on grants for more than 25 percent of their budget. Women's Research Centers, by contrast, are far more dependent on external or "soft" monies to support their operations, which accounts in part for the great discrepancy in growth rates between the Women's Studies programs and Women's Research Centers. While more feminist research is done by faculty attached to Women's Studies programs, the research centers do focus singly on research. Given the higher value assigned to research over teaching, the centers as well as the scholarship done by Women's Studies faculty bring a legitimacy to Women's Studies that has earned it academic credibility.

As Women's Studies was establishing itself, its earliest years concentrated primarily on creating new courses, defining a new discipline, and producing the feminist scholarship that has been so crucial in establishing the legitimacy of the field. While such expansion was driven primarily by the dedication of its teachers, the demands of its students, and the intellectual intoxication of new knowledge that transformed the way one saw the world and one's self in it, Women's Studies also secured its institutional place because agencies beyond the university invested their money in the enterprise. According to Catherine R. Stimpson in her Ford Foundation report, *Women's Studies in the United States* (1986), some of that early financial support came from private foundations such as the Ford Foundation, Carnegie Corporation, the Rockefeller Foundation, the Rockefeller Brothers Fund, the Andrew W. Mellon Foundation, the Helena Rubenstein Foundation, the Russell Sage Foundation, the Exxon Education Foundation, the Eli P. Lilly Foundation, and the Revson Foundation. Governmental agencies included the National Endowment for the Humanities as well as its state humanities councils, the Fund for the Improvement of Postsecondary Education, the National Institute of Education, and the Women's Education Equity Act. Recent patterns of giving from some of these sources will be discussed in more detail later in the chapter.

Today, Women's Studies takes at least three major shapes in the academy. The first is found in the institutionalization of Women's Studies programs themselves, over 230 of which offer a Women's Studies major. Faculty tenure lines in Women's Studies, joint appointments, and interdisciplinary courses sponsored exclusively by Women's Studies represent the largest portion of feminist scholars and teachers. The second form of Women's Studies work is found in traditional departments where feminist scholars identify primarily with their department and do their teaching and research within the parameters of a given discipline. Courses developed for these departments by feminist faculty are typically cross-listed with most Women's Studies courses. The third and newest form of Women's Studies work is found in the efforts since 1980 to transform the curriculum by integrating the new knowledge about women across the general curriculum.

While some are campus-based and others community-based, Women's Research Centers and Women's Centers also are the locus of much Women's Studies work. The former occurs primarily in the form of research, the latter in the form of services and public programming usually for a female audience. There are some sixty-two Women's Research Centers in the United States who are members of the National Council for Research on Women. Only Spelman's Women's Research and Resource Center is based at a historically Black college. By contrast with the research centers, the Women's Centers total in the thousands. The latter affiliate with the National Women's Center Association, the National Women's Studies Association, and the National Association for Women Deans, Administrators, and Counselors.

This chapter will focus primarily on financial support for academic research, Women's Studies program development, faculty development, and curriculum transformation in higher education. It will not attempt to document the funding made available for women or women's issues in direct social services or in nonacademic settings, though both are important vehicles for doing the socially transforming work that usually makes its way into a Women's Studies classroom or affects and is affected by Women's Studies research.

Private Foundations

Private foundations that were instrumental in the early years in fostering the development of Women's Studies have remained a consistent source of financial support twenty years later. Increases in funding levels through private foundations have not been enough, however, to off-set the loss of funding through governmental sources, especially federal agencies which, under the Reagan administration in particular, drastically reduced their funding commitment to women and women's issues.

The statistics gathered here were taken from the Foundation Center's *Grants for Women and Girls* covering the years 1986–87. The total monies spent in 1986 and 1987 for women's issues in general was $87,630,205, given out in 2,086 individual grants. Of this total, $4,129,494 was given out in 62 different grants on feminist education in particular. Feminist education received, then, 2.97 percent of the number of grants funded and 4.71 percent of the total money allocated. Of the 62 grants awarded, 74.19 percent were awarded in 1987. In 1986 there were 16 grants awarded for a total of $684,895; by 1987 that number had increased to 46 grants for a total of $3,444,599.

The beneficiaries of the increase in funding were primarily international agencies outside of the United States doing research on women. In 1986, for example, only $35,800 was allocated for international research, while in 1987, $1,622,050 was spent on international research. All but one grant for $35,800 in Europe was assigned to research in Third World countries. South America received ten, the highest number of grants (16.13%), for $653,150 (15.82%); Asia came second with seven (11.29%), totalling $623,500 (15.10%). Central America received two grants (3.23%) for $124,400 (3.01%), and Africa, the largest continent in the world, received only one grant totalling $201,000 (4.87%).

Regionally the grants went disproportionately to the Northeastern seaboard. The combined tallies of New England, the Mid Atlantic, and the District of Columbia show twenty grants, which is nearly 40 percent of the total number of grants, and $1,624,677, which is just over 39 percent of the total money allocated. California and the Pacific Northwest each received less than 2 percent of the grants, the South and Southwest each received just under 5 percent, while the Midwest received 8.07 percent.

The leading private foundation, now as in the early days, is the Ford Foundation, which gave 28 of its 151 grants awarded in 1986 and 1987 for a total of $2,831,282. Ford gave 18.07 percent of its grants to feminist education. Echoing the trend in foundation giving as a whole, Ford increased the number of grants dramatically from 5 in 1986 to 23 in 1987. Ford also put more than 56 percent of that increase into funding international research. Although the figures on foundation giving used in this section stop with 1987, in 1988 Ford announced a major initiative to integrate knowledge about women of color across the curriculum and intends to invest more than a million dollars over two years in model curriculum programs. All such grants were initially awarded only to designated Women's Research Centers who worked with Women's Studies faculty and Ethnic Studies faculty to design specific grant proposals.

The greatest preponderance of grants (29) was awarded for liberal arts and social sciences research in the United States and abroad, especially in Third World countries. The next largest category was awarded for curriculum transformation and faculty development (8). Only four of the grants for research in the United States went to a project that was specifically focused on minority women. Not surprisingly, the vast majority of recipients of all the grants are also the elite universities and colleges, with a slight preference for private over public institutions. Funding continues to go to those who already have numerous privileges.

It is also important to note here that because foundations have a greater vested interest in halting social conflict, they tend to make large investments in group projects rather than individual research. Our study reveals that only five research grants were awarded to individuals for a total of $210,600. The bulk of the funding went to scholars from elite and private institutions.

One of the new private foundation funding sources for women is the Women's Funds, which total some thirty to forty. Most are regionally based and therefore reach a wider, more diverse audience than the larger national foundations. Few of the Womens' Funds award grants for research, but they are an increasingly important source for smaller grants for direct services for women.

There seems to be a trend among some private as well as public funding agencies to consider that they have "done women" and are therefore ready to move on to other "issues." Since gender is both an issue and a way of looking at everything in the world, feminist scholars and teachers will need to be increasingly creative about the rubric they use to describe what they want to have funded. Rather than coming under the primary identity as women, grants are often recast to fit as a perspective within another issue, such as children at risk, AIDS, drug abuse, teen pregnancy, family and work patterns, and environmental concerns.

Federal Funding Sources

Although limited to 1980–1984, the most complete resource about the various federal agencies is Mary Rubin's *A Declining Federal Commitment to Research about Women*, 1985, available for $6.00 from the National Council for Research on Women, 47–49 East 65th Street, New York, NY 10021. Rubin concludes that "federal funding for research about women has decreased and that the priorities for research have shifted in the funding that remains. The overall effect has been a change in the character of federally-funded research and the subsuming of research about women into areas less clearly focused on women" (Rubin, 5)

Department of Education

Within the Department of Education there are three agencies that have been major funding sources for research, curriculum, and faculty development in Women's Studies: The Fund for the Improvement of Postsecondary Education (FIPSE), the National Institute of Education (NIE), and the Women's Educational Equity Act Program (WEEA).

FIPSE. An agency that prides itself on improving education by providing solutions to emerging problems in higher education and shaping the development of postsecondary education, FIPSE was among the earliest to fund Women's Studies in the seventies. One of FIPSE's eight broad purposes is to encourage "the reform, innovation, and improvement of postsecondary education and provide equal educational opportunity for all." Not surprisingly, Women's Studies has often met this criteria. According to Rubin, between 1973 and 1975, FIPSE allocated $2.3 million in projects about women. Just under $2 million was allocated again in 1980–1981. Shifts in staffing, leadership, and funding priorities in recent years have reduced that figure, but Women's Studies projects continue to receive funding.

During 1984–1986, FIPSE itself had to battle against the administration's efforts first to slash FIPSE's budget in half, and then to eliminate it entirely. The fund has survived the assaults, however, though it has suffered a reduced budget. In 1981 it had a budget of $13.5 million that by 1984 had been reduced to $11.7 million. Since that year, its budget has remained roughly at $12 million, with $11.5 million allocated for their Comprehensive Program. One of the programs that did not survive the budget cuts was the Mina Shaughnessy Scholars programs, which allocated up to $20,000 per year to twenty educational practitioners to write about trying to achieve educational equity.

FIPSE has taken a leadership role in the curriculum integration projects, having funded the Wheaton College project in 1980–1983 that so influenced all successive projects. It also funded Smith College's Department of Afro-American Studies and the University of Massachusetts' Women's Studies Program to co-direct the first curriculum development project to bring together scholarship on Black Studies and Women's Studies. It funded one of the most important integration projects on the East Coast, the Towson State University project, that generated materials other institutions have used as models for their integration projects. In FY1989, FIPSE listed five projects they had funded that had an exclusively Women's Studies focus. The American Anthropological Association received a grant to integrate curricular material on gender into introductory anthropology courses. UCLA is integrating scholarship on Women's Studies and Ethnic Studies into humanities and social sciences, while the University of Cincinnati is doing a series of peer-directed faculty seminars looking at the effect of recent feminist scholarship on intellectual assumptions in five disciplines. The Organization of American Historians is developing materials on the role of women in Third World countries for inclusion in world civilization and area studies and testing materials at eight institutions. The fifth project funded was a three-year effort to integrate the new scholarship on women into courses at five community colleges in the Baltimore–Washington area, a project directed by Sara Coulter and Elaine Hedges, the directors of the Towson State project.

Although the full list is not available for FY 1990 projects at this writing, the National Women's Studies Association was the recipient of a three-year grant, "The Courage to Question: Women's Studies and Student Learning," which will assess what it is that students are learning in their Women's Studies courses at ten different universities, with an aim to revise the curriculum in light of the student evaluations and provide national models for both Women's Studies programs and other departments. In addition to projects with an exclusive Women's Studies focus, FIPSE has also funded projects that include women or Women's Studies as part of the grant. One such example is the grant to the Association of American Colleges for its work examining the relation of the major to the liberal arts curriculum. One of the majors included among the eleven is Women's Studies and the National Women's Studies Association has created a National Task Force to produce a report on its major.

NIE. The National Institute of Education has a general mission to support students, teachers, and administrators at various levels of education in their research, training, and dissemination of materials. Under President Carter, NIE initiated efforts to promote educational equity for girls, women, and minorities. After 1980, this special initiative was eliminated and many staff were transferred elsewhere. Its budget between 1981 and 1984 was also reduced by 25 percent. The number of grants about women and minorities fell from thirty-five in 1979 to two in 1983. Very few funds are given to individual researchers or organizations that are not directly connected to the state-based education laboratories and research centers.

WEEA. Authorized by Congress in 1974 to counter discrimination towards women and girls, the Women's Education Equity Act is designed to develop educational materials and model programs that promote educational equity for women and girls. In 1980 WEEA had as much as $10 million that it used to fund innovative Women's Studies projects both in a traditional academic setting, at the secondary and elementary levels, and in the community. Like FIPSE, WEEA was targeted for elimination under the Reagan administration but has managed to stay intact enough to continue making awards. Its budget was reduced to only $5 million by 1984, $3.351 million in 1988, and $2.949 million in 1989. According to a source within the Department of Education, it has recently chosen not to request any funding whatsoever for WEEA in its budget, which has meant that a budget is maintained only because the Congress chooses to appropriate money each year to keep WEEA alive.

In 1988 WEEA awarded thirty-two grants; in 1989 it awarded twenty-nine. Three of the grants awarded in 1989 give a sense of the range of projects that get funded. One was for "Female Educators Mentorship Project," submitted by the Panhandle Council of Women School Executives in Amarillo, Texas. Another was "Educational Equity for Women in Aviation Education," submitted by Alabama Aviation and Technological College in Ozark, Alabama. The National Black Child Development Institute in Washington, D.C. was also awarded a grant, "Exploring Career Development Options with Black Girls Project."

National Endowment for the Humanities (NEH)

NEH was established to promote scholarly and educational programs in the humanities, particularly in terms of how the humanities illuminate public issues and values. According to Rubin, during the seventies the Endowment supported projects about women in each of its six divisions. After 1979, however, "support for research projects related to women declined precipitously" (Rubin, 12). When the Endowment suffered a $20 million budget reduction, funding for women-related projects declined by one million dollars, or one-half of its former proportion, to 0.67 percent of the total budget. While the overall decline in agency funds was 14 percent, the support for women-related projects declined by 50 percent. In 1984 the number of grants awarded for research on women increased from 66 to 150. However, 63 were for $500 and 33 for less than $10,000, which meant a diversion of funding for women away from substantial financial support for long-term research.

Research on NEH from 1985 to 1987, compiled by Ellen Messer-Davidow and presented at the First Annual Meeting of the National Network of Women's Caucuses and Committees in the Professional Associations, February 24–26, 1985, confirmed the bleak picture of NEH funding for research on women. In her paper, "Monitoring the National Endowment for the Humanities," Messer-Davidow sets a context for examining NEH allocations by seeing where the government actually invests most of its research and development money. The NEH budget is, she asserts, "a mere .38% of the military R & D budget" (Messer-Davidow, 3), which according to a National Science Foundation Report is 63 percent of the total budget of $60 billion appropriated for research and development. Funding for projects on women, gender, and feminism has ranged from 5 percent to just under 7 percent of NEH's total budget.

In 1985, NEH awarded only 32 grants out of 758 to projects on women, gender, or feminism, which is just over 4 percent. While the numbers of the grants increased to 60 in 1986 and 70 in 1987, both the dollar amount and the percentage that dollar amount represents of the total NEH budget in categories counted decreased. In 1985, $2,672,541 was awarded (6.85%) and by 1987 the amount had shrunk to $1,999,183 (4.82%). As in FIPSE, the number of grants that focus on women is often masked by titles that do not indicate whether gender is considered in a study or project. It is also important to remember that those designated as women-related might not necessarily include a feminist perspective. The big picture of government funding according to Messer-Davidow is "the flow of resources away from new inquiries and into traditional ones, away from humanities and social science research and into defense-related research, away from social equity and social welfare" (Messer-Davidow).

National Science Foundation (NSF)

Mary Rubin's *Declining Federal Commitment* report includes ten pages of detailed information about NSF funding patterns from 1980 to 1984. She concludes that the funding for gender-related research peaked in 1981 at $2.3 million, which reflects the decline within NSF of the Division of the Social and Economic Sciences and the Division of the Behavioral and Neural Sciences. These had supported gender research in economics and psychology. Before 1980, according to Rubin, NSF had been an important source of funding for under-representation of women in science. During the period of her study, however, many of those programs had been seriously reduced or eliminated entirely.

In the fall of 1988, the Task Force on Women, Minorities, and the Handicapped in Science and Technology released its interim report, *Changing America: The New Face of Science and Engineering*. The new studies of the workforce have raised serious concerns in science and elsewhere about the pragmatic importance to the economy of guaranteeing educational and career equity for women and minorities. In the year 2000, 85 percent of those entering the workforce will be women and/or members of minority groups. The report also documents the estimated shortfall of scientists in 2010, which the task force clearly hopes will be avoided by aggressive action now to attract to careers in science formerly under-represented groups: women, people of color, and the disabled.

The recommendations of the task force include increasing funding for programs, research, fellowships, and education in all settings and all levels that would encourage women, minorities, and the disabled to choose science as a career. It is likely that the projected decline in U.S. scientists will become a national issue just as the poor performance of U.S. students in science and math has provoked national embarrassment. If that is the case, there should be a wide variety of science funding available in significant amounts for women, minorities, and the disabled.

Other Federal Governmental Agencies

Mary Rubin comments on several other government sources for funding during the 1980–1984 period. Since no further information was available to update material beyond her dates, readers should take note of the five other agencies who have not recently been major funders of Women's Studies but that do give away money for research and projects. The two agencies in the Department of Labor that have funded women-related grants but that now supply negligible resources are the Employment and Training Administration and the Women's Bureau. The National Institute of Mental Health has apparently reduced its funding allocation to gender research but continues to fund some proposals. The Department of Defense, not surprisingly, kept elusive data but is believed to fund more social science research than the National Institute of Mental Health. While the Department of Justice was an enthusiastic advocate for research about women in the criminal justice system in the 1970s, monies had been severely reduced by 1984. Finally, the National Institute of Aging (NIA) is a natural place for grants about women since the overwhelming percentage of older citizens are women. According to a staff member at NIA, the institute does not track its grants according to gender topics and said no data existed that would reveal funding levels within NIA on women-related research. Their total funding levels have increased, however, and the topics of interest mentioned in a recent program announcement indicate this agency would be an appropriate place for future gender research: osteoporosis, longevity, aging and bereavement, minority aging.

Curriculum Transformation Projects

Since curriculum transformation projects will continue to dominate much of the curricular reform in the next decade, it might be helpful to survey very briefly the history of funding for such projects. In the first phase of curriculum integration in the late seventies and early eighties, almost all the funding came either from private foundations, NEH, FIPSE, or WEEA. Some of the early private foundations providing resources were Ford, Mellon, Lilly, and the Rockefeller Family Fund. For a more complete description of the various projects and their funding agency, see Betty Schmitz's *Integrating Women's Studies into the Curriculum*: a Guide and Bibliography, published by the Feminist Press in 1985.

After a decade of work on transformation projects, one finds that while private foundations continue to fund some projects, a greater number are funded by state agencies, usually State Departments of Higher Education, and through the internal resources of academic institutions themselves. Longtime funding agencies are looking for a new slant on curriculum integration. Ford, for example, sponsored a million-dollar initiative to fund new projects that integrate information about women of color across the curriculum, and FIPSE funded a three-year project to integrate scholarship about women into community college courses. The Department of Education, on the other hand, funded a project to integrate Women's Studies into the undergraduate International Studies courses and to integrate an international perspective into Women's Studies courses.

The most dramatic source of funding at the state level has come from the $1.2 million project on Gender Integration funded by the Department of Higher Education in New Jersey. It is an ambitious program that has been operating since 1985 and promises to have long-range implications for education in that state. It is likely that other states will follow with some version of the New Jersey project, although every state might not be so ambitious. Other state monies are increasingly available for faculty development and curricular or instructional improvement. Once again, Women's Studies might be subsumed under a different rubric. State Humanities Councils have traditionally been sources for innovative programming and conferences that involve a broader public discussion of women-related issues. The Pennsylvania Humanities Council, for example, has among other projects funded a statewide discussion about Women's Studies in a series of forums and reading groups across the state.

The other significant shift in funding for transformation projects is the increase in the number of institutions which allocate part of their institutional budget to support curriculum projects. There has always been a certain number of institutions who have funded their own projects, but the scale of funding has altered. The University of Maryland at College Park, for instance, has invested just under $400,000 for faculty development funds over a two-year period, which does not include additional funds allocated to cover the project director's salary plus other administrative and operating expenses. The total funding, then, is a significant amount that promises to have long-term influence over the curriculum and faculty.

Strategies for Influencing Funding for Women's Studies

It is clear, then, that there are many different sources that fund programs and research about gender and even some that seek to understand the complex relationship between gender and race. The creative and shrewd grant writer has a wide variety of options. However, external funding is competitive and difficult to obtain. Those institutions that are already perceived as being elite are more likely to receive funding as are those faculty who have already achieved distinction as scholars. Funders also seem to like to award grants to people who have received previous funding. So for the outsider, the newcomer, the person at a small college with a local and not a national profile, it is less likely that funding will be secured.

It is clear, too, that as academic feminists we sometimes function as the mediator between those who have financial resources and access to power and those whose voices are unrepresented in most classrooms in the United States: the poor, the uneducated, the old, a disproportionate number of people of color in our own country, and Third World peoples. Because such a mediating relationship of power to powerlessness echoes some of the disastrous patterns of colonialism, Women's Studies academics have a responsibility to challenge the potentially crippling effects of needing to rely on a mediator. The special challenge is to expand the space in which we all stand. Some of that might be done by persuading funders to support these groups directly so that they can speak for themselves. Some of it might also be done by holding to one of the fundamental tenets of feminist research and teaching, which relies on the authority of experience and the authentic voice. If that tenet is central to the research design of grants, the mediator model will possibly empower rather than silence.

While it is pragmatic to recast one's own proposal to fit the guidelines of a funding agent, it is a process that should be done with care and thoughtfulness to be sure the integrity of one's own project is not lost. Many funders are also looking for feedback from people outside their agencies to help them anticipate where the most pressing needs are. Grant writers should consider submitting proposals that might not meet guidelines but that might help the agency perceive a need they had been unaware of previously.

Funding must be perceived in the optic growing from the feminist scholarship of the last two decades, which draws the parallel between power and the ability to speak and shape the terms of discussion in language reflective of our lives and experiences. In this context, it is very important that the language setting guidelines must be coined by both funders and Women's Studies. In addition to being rooted in gender realities, this construction must be built on race and class considerations as well.

In line with this feminist reasoning, funding must be weighed against the background of neocolonialism. In a neocolonial model, money is often used by the powerful as a fundamental tool to protect and to perpetuate power. This ability presents a real dilemma for those outside the circle of power who are seeking funding. They are faced with the paradox that while money gives one the authority to speak in our society, it also places one in a position of being silenced or coopted. How Women's Studies navigates this position in the future depends on how coalition models are built. This is particularly poignant for white feminists who face the DuBoisian duality of being both outside and inside the circle of power. For women of color in the academy who are outside of the circle because of race and gender but who are privileged by their proximity to power, the issue is whether coalitions are built on race and gender rather than on the privilege derived from being perceived as exceptional and special.

It would be foolish not to take advantage of sources for funding Women's Studies, but it would be even more foolish to forget the passionate commitment to illuminating information about women's lives and gender systems that has been at the core of our work as feminists. To a funder, women might be the initiative of the decade. To most of us involved in this process, it is a form of psychological, social, and economic survival. Our very lives and the future of the planet depend on linking the research about women of all colors, classes, and cultures to those other enterprises that seek to envision and create a world where all life can flourish.

CHAPTER 3

Private Foundation Grants to American Ethnic Studies Departments and Programs, 1972–1988: Patterns and Prospects

Katharine Bolland and John C. Walter

In the past fifteen years, private foundations have contributed significantly to the development of American Ethnic Studies departments.[1] The following brief historical analysis reveals several patterns that not only reflect the evolution of specific programs but that also suggest prospects for funding in the field.

Methodology

The sample survey of grants was drawn from the Foundation Center's *Foundation Grants Index* database. Small grants (under $5,000) do not appear in the listing. In addition, grant activity by local and relatively less affluent foundations might not appear in the data. Finally, the Foundation Center does not track grants awarded before 1972. Although the information provided by the database is selective, it is sufficiently representative to allow us to draw general conclusions about trends in foundation giving.

All grants in the study met the following criteria:

1. Only grants to Afro-American, Black, Asian American, Chicano, Latino, Hispanic, Native American, American Indian, and American Ethnic Studies departments were included

2. Only grants to institutions of higher education, including graduate and undergraduate programs, and community colleges were considered

3. Only grants specifically aimed at the establishment of a program in American Ethnic Studies (that is Black Studies, Asian American Studies, etc.) or grants funding research, scholarships or fellowships that directly aid the development of a department or program in American Ethnic Studies were

included (e.g., financial support for a conference, seminars, visiting faculty, or students directly tied to an American Ethnic Studies department)

The following grant categories were excluded from the sample:

1. Grants to departments or programs other than American Ethnic Studies (e.g., Anthropology, Sociology, Area Studies)

2. Grants for research, fellowships, or scholarships not directly tied to an American Ethnic Studies program

3. Grants to departments or programs specializing in the study of "white ethnics" (e.g., Jewish Studies or Scandinavian Studies)

A General Context

In order to evaluate the importance of the developments in foundation funding for American Ethnic Studies programs and departments, the sample selection of grants must be seen in the larger historical context of foundation philanthropy.

During the 1980s, many of the larger foundations initiated highly sophisticated investment policies. During the same period, inflation rates fell and the federal government revised laws regulating foundation grant making. In brief, the Economic Recovery Act of 1981 required foundations to pay out in grants and/or other charitable disbursements 5 percent of the market value of their assets without regard to the foundations' income; prior to 1981, foundations were required to pay out the greater of 5 percent of their assets or their adjusted net income. These three factors contributed to a rise in foundation assets in both current and constant dollars between 1981 and 1986. (Unfortunately, 1986 is the most recent year for which such aggregated information is available.) The asset growth followed several years of little change and a period of sharply falling assets between 1972 and 1975.[2]

Despite shifting asset bases, foundation total giving rose 240 percent in current dollars during the fifteen-year period 1972–1986. Adjusted for inflation, total giving rose 32 percent in constant dollars during the same period. The most substantial increase in total giving in both current and constant dollars occurred between 1981 and 1985, when it rose 29 percent and 19 percent respectively. A late 1986 surge in foundation assets suggests that the upward trend in foundation giving should continue until at least the end of the decade.[3] (See Table 1.)

The nation's educational system has benefited from the increase in total giving. The percentage of total private grant money allocated to higher education has shown a slight upward trend, peaking in 1986 at 15.9 percent. Some

Table 1

Total Grant Money Awarded to Departments and Programs in the Field of American Ethnic Studies for Development, Research, Scholarships, and Fellowships. In Constant Dollars (1967 Base Year):1972–1988

Year	For Program Development	For Program Development, Research, Scholarships, & Fellowships
1972	408,689	408,689
1973	52,313	94,557
1974	0	10,360
1975	30,380	55,168
1976	11,740	35,220
1977	23,418	51,519
1978	7,680	78,541
1979	11,270	11,270
1980	8,100	26,417
1981	9,175	37,911
1982	31,140	35,292
1983	94,135	94,135
1984	4,815	69,015
1985	25,110	87,110
1986	38,000	91,200
1987*	13,976	103,976
1988*	118,890	201,390

*Estimated

Source: Foundation Center, *Foundation Grants Index* Database

institutions enjoyed more of the fruits of the growth than others. Between 1982 and 1985, private colleges and universities noted a significant decrease in the portion of grant money received, while allocations for public institutions increased slightly.[4]

Findings

An Overview of Grant Characteristics

The Foundation Center's *Foundation Grant Index* records fifty-two grants awarded to American Ethnic Studies programs and departments during the period 1972–1988.[5] Twenty-four foundations disbursed the funds to thirty institutions of higher education. The Ford Foundation alone made twelve grants during the seventeen year period. Following Ford in rank order of the highest number of grants made are the Kimberly-Clark Foundation of Wisconsin, which disbursed six grants; and the Dolfinger-McMahon Foundation of Pennsylvania, DeRance Inc. of Wisconsin and the Southern Education Foundation of Georgia, which each awarded three grants.

Receiving the highest number of grants during the sampling period was Northland College in Ashland, Wisconsin. Also receiving multiple awards were Dartmouth College, which was awarded five grants; the University of Virginia, which received four; and Swarthmore College and Mount Senario College of Ladysmith, Wisconsin, which each received three grants.

These basic facts of foundational philanthropy mask a wide variety of funding patterns. In several cases the statistics reflect a strong relationship between an educational institution and a single foundation. A high number of awards can reflect continuing support or renewed grants. For example, the Kimberly-Clark Foundation provided five years of continuous financial support to Northland College. Similarly, Dolfinger-McMahon awarded three consecutive grants to Swarthmore College. Establishing the most lucrative of such arrangements, the University of Virginia has maintained a strong connection with the Ford Foundation, receiving three of its four grants from that source.

Foundation fund provision, however, does not always follow this pattern. Dartmouth College and Mount Senario College both diversified their funding sources. The Dartmouth Native American Studies Department received two grants from the Educational Foundation of America, one from the Lilly Endowment and one from Aetna Life and Casualty Foundation. Mount Senario College built a noteworthy funding program that should offer hope to smaller institutions. Starting with a $7,000 grant in 1979 from the local Kimberly-Clark Foundation, the College subsequently applied successfully to the national but relatively small DeRance, Inc., receiving $10,000 in 1983. One year later Mount Senario collected its largest grant to date, $15,000, from the Ford Foundation. Evidently, American Ethnic Studies departments and programs can benefit from either a continuing relationship with a single foundation or from a diversified funding program.

Funding relationships also vary according to the specific department of the program targeted. Within the field of American Ethnic Studies, different departments and programs have enjoyed various degrees of foundational support. During the sample period, Native American Studies (or American Indian Studies) received by and far the largest number of grants—twenty-seven awards, experiencing particularly strong support in the area of program/department development—nineteen grants. By comparison, Afro-American Studies (or Black Studies) departments received only eighteen

Table 2

Grants to Ethnic-Specific Programs and Departments of American Ethnic Studies for Program/Department Development Only, 1972–1988*

Year	Total	Afro-American	Latino/Chicano	Native American	AES
1972	551,500	10,800		25,000	
		16,700			
		459,000			
1973	69,658	19,658		59,000	
1974	0				
1975	49,000	49,000			
1976	20,000			5,000	
				15,000	
1977	42,500			15,000	
				27,500	
1978	15,000			15,000	
1979	24,500			7,000	
				17,500	
1980	20,000			20,000	
1981	25,000	5,000	20,000		
1982	90,000	5,000	15,000		
		25,000			
1983	281,000	5,000	248,000	10,000	
				18,000	
1984	15,000			15,000	
1985	81,000			6,000	
				25,000	
				50,000	
1986	125,000		50,000	28,000	
				47,000	
1987	46,585				46,585
1988	396,300	396,300			
TOTAL DOLLAR		991,458	330,000	441,000	46,585
TOTAL # GRANTS		10	4	19	1

*Asian American Studies departments received no grants during period according to the *Foundation Grants Index* database.

Source: Foundation Center, *Foundation Grants Index* Database

grants during the same period, only ten of which were earmarked specifically for program development.[6] Between 1972 and 1988, Chicano/Latino Studies (or Hispanic Studies) departments and programs were the recipients of six grants. One grant was awarded to a consolidated American Ethnic Studies department that includes Asian American Studies, Afro-American Studies, and Chicano Studies components.[7] No Asian American Studies programs received foundation funding during the sample period according to the Foundation Center's records. This surprising and disturbing lack of support for Asian American Studies merits detailed analysis, a project unfortunately outside the boundaries of this introductory study.

Funding relationships vary, and so do the nature and characteristics of the grants themselves. Grants to Native American Studies programs have tended to be smaller than those awarded to other departments. Despite the large number of grants received within the field, foundations awarded only $890,945 to Native American Studies. The largest grant during the period, for $275,000, was made to Harvard's program in 1988. While Native American Studies programs and departments received a substantial number of relatively minor awards, Afro-American Studies programs were the recipients of several substantial grants. During the same sample period, Afro-American Studies departments received $2,079,460. Two exceptionally large grants, $459,000 from Carnegie to California State University in 1972, and $396,300 to the University of Pennsylvania from the William Penn Foundation in 1988, account for 41 percent of the total grant money, and a full 86 percent of the funds intended for Afro-American Studies program development. On the other end of the spectrum, foundations channeled only $421,513 to Chicano/Latino Studies programs. A $248,000 J. Howard Pew Freedom Trust grant to the Eastern Baptist Theological Seminary accounts for over half of the funds disbursed to Chicano/Latino Studies.

The wide variation in monetary amounts can be summarized in terms of a simple yet revealing comparison—that is, the proportion of funds disbursed in grants of over $100,000 vs. funds awarded in grants of under $100,000. Overall, in the period 1972–1988, 90 percent of all grant money provided to Afro-American Studies departments (or eight of the eighteen awards) came in the form of grants of $100,000 or more. At the other extreme, only 31 percent of the money awarded to Native American Studies departments (or one of the twenty-seven grants) was in a grant of over $100,000. Finally, one grant of over $100,000 accounted for 59 percent of the money granted to Chicano/Latino Studies during the sample period.

Post–1983: Recent Trends in Grant Making

While clear patterns in grant making become readily apparent they must be understood from a historical perspective. Over the seventeen-year sample

Table 3

Grants to Ethnic-Specific Programs and Departments of American Ethnic Studies for Research, Fellowships, and Scholarships Only, 1972–1988*

Year	Total	Afro-American	Latino/Chicano	Native American	AES
1972	0				
1973	56,250		56,250		
1974	15,302	15,302			
1975	39,980			10,000	
				29,980	
1976	40,000			40,000	
1977	51,000			51,000	
1978	138,400	138,400			
1979	0				
1980	45,228		32,263	12,965	
1981	78,300	59,300		19,000	
1982	12,000			12,000	
1983	0				
1984	200,000	100,000			
		100,000			
1985	200,000	200,000			
1986	175,000	175,000			
1987	300,000	300,000			
1988	275,000			275,000	
TOTAL DOLLARS		1,088,002	88,513	449,945	0
TOTAL # GRANTS		8	2	8	0

*Asian American Studies departments received no grants during the period according to the *Foundation Grants Index* Database.

Source: Foundation Center, *Foundation Grants Index* Database

period, the characteristics of foundation funding of American Ethnic Studies departments and programs have changed significantly. The changing nature of foundational support for American Ethnic Studies is the result of several factors. Pressure from American Ethnic Studies scholars and advocates, change in personnel at major foundations, successful experiences funding pilot programs and Women's Studies programs, and the growing legitimacy of now solid and well-established programs and departments may all have played a role in many foundations' growing financial involvement in American Ethnic Studies.

The most noticeable shift in foundational support has been in the size of awards. The number of large grants increased significantly after 1983. According to the Foundation Center's *Foundation Grants Index*, during the decade 1972–1983 the average size of grants awarded was $43,909. When the two largest awards are disregarded, a more accurate picture of the standard grant is achieved. Excluding the Carnegie grant in 1973 and a sizeable grant from the J. Howard Pew Freedom Trust in 1983, pre-1984 grants averaged $26,218. By comparison, during the period 1984–1988 grants to American Ethnic Studies programs and departments averaged $120,926. Even discounting the two largest awards of the period, $300,000 to the University of Virginia and $396,300 to the University of Pennsylvania, the average allocation was $85,968.

The dramatic growth in the size of grants awarded to American Ethnic Studies is largely attributable to increased Ford Foundation activity in the field. Only 11 percent of the grant money allocated to American Ethnic Studies between 1972 and 1983 originated at Ford. During the following five years, Ford grants accounted for an astounding 60 percent of foundational monetary support. The specific characteristics behind the leap in funding are as impressive as the general trend. Both the number and size of Ford grants have grown. The four awards made prior to 1983 averaged $44,379. The largest grant during that period, for $59,300, went to Boston University's Afro-American Studies Department in 1981. After 1983, Ford made eight grants, averaging $135,823 a piece. The University of Virginia, alone, received three grants in the sums of $100,000, $200,000, and $300,000.

In the early 1980s, Ford commissioned the Huggins Report on the state of Afro-American Studies. Since the publication of the report, and particularly after 1985, Ford has made a major effort to fund solid, well-established American Ethnic Studies departments and programs. Also during the past couple of years, Ford has sent consultants across the nation to survey the state of the field and to select programs that, in their judgment, merit Ford support.[8]

Despite the Ford Foundation's crucial role in generating the mid-1980s funding growth, Ford alone did not account for all of the increase. Several of the nation's wealthiest foundations contributed to the post-1983 upswing in funding for American Ethnic Studies. The Lilly Endowment and Rockefeller Foundation are both ranked among the country's ten largest foundations by total giving, and both had made grants to American Ethnic Studies departments and programs prior to 1983.[9] Nevertheless, their efforts in addition to those of Ford, which is the highest ranked foundation in terms of total giving, only accounted for 21 percent of the funds awarded to American Ethnic Studies during the decade 1972–1983.[10] During the same years, the one hundred largest foundations by total giving granted 65 percent of the total funds provided by foundations to American Ethnic Studies. During the 1984–

Table 4

Percentage of Grants to American Ethnic Studies Departments/Programs by Size of Foundation [Top 10 and Top 100 by Total Giving; and the Ford Foundation (#1 by Total Giving)], 1972–1988

Year	% Ford	% Top 10	% Top 100
1972	0	0	90
1973	45	45	45
1974	0	0	0
1975	55	55	55
1976	0	0	0
1977	0	29	29
1978	0	0	90
1979	0	0	0
1980	20	20	20
1981	57	57	57
1982	0	0	0
1983	0	0	88
1984	100	100	100
1985	71	71	89
1986	17	75	91
1987	100	100	100
1988	41	41	100

Source: Foundation Center, *Foundation Grants Index* Database

1988 period, the top ten foundations, led overwhelmingly by Ford, disbursed 70 percent of the total grant money. Concurrently, and in part reflecting the activity of the top ten foundations, the top one hundred foundations significantly increased their funding of American Ethnic Studies. Ninety seven percent of the total funds granted to American Ethnic Studies came from the top 100 foundations during the five years prior to 1988.[11] (See also Table 4.)

Coinciding with the entry of the top one hundred foundations into the area of American Ethnic Studies funding, local, less well endowed foundations began a retreat from the field. The shift from smaller, often regionally focused, foundations to larger, national grant makers has significantly altered the overall makeup of foundational support for American Ethnic Studies. In general, larger foundations have placed a strong emphasis on academics and research. Historically, they have tended to be strong supporters of institutions of higher education. Smaller foundations have generally supported local community development, direct action programs, elementary and secondary schools, and the performing arts.[12] Evidently, the less well endowed, regionally based foundations' awards to programs and departments in the field of American Ethnic Studies at colleges and universities fell outside the foundations' normal purview. Thus the shift to larger foundations has significant implications for the long run as well as for short-term increases in grant frequency and size.

Regardless of their national ranking, foundations tend to favor private institutions of higher education over public ones. In this case, there is only a slight variation in behavior between small and large foundations. While the one hundred largest foundations grant approximately $2.75 to private institutions for every dollar to public institutions, smaller foundations give approximately $2.48 to private colleges and universities for every dollar to the public system. Although smaller foundations grant proportionately less money to private colleges and universities, they make more awards to such institutions. The top one hundred foundations award 60 percent of the total number of their grants to higher education to private institutions, while smaller foundations award 70 percent of their higher education grants to private institutions.[13]

Reflecting these statistics, American Ethnic Studies departments at private colleges and universities received the majority of grants listed in the Foundation Center's *Foundation Grants Index*. However, contrary to national trends, post-1983 increased grant activity by the largest foundations, particularly the Ford Foundation, has benefited several public universities. During the decade 1972–1983, public universities received only five grants while thirty-two grants were awarded to private colleges. In the following five-year period, however, public institutions received six grants almost matching the eight received by private colleges. Interestingly, in the three years prior to 1988, departments in the public system received a higher number of grants than did those at private colleges. Nevertheless, despite the smaller number of grants received, American Ethnic Studies departments at private colleges still received more money than did the parallel programs at public colleges, $699,300 and $571,585, respectively.

Again, the full significance of the statistics only becomes evident upon closer examination of the facts in historical context with an emphasis on specific grants. Thirty- four percent of grant money to American Ethnic Studies between 1972 and 1983 went to public institutions. The numbers are deceptive as they reflect the exceptionally large Carnegie endowment to California State University in 1972. By comparison, during the 1984–1988 period, 48 percent of the total funds dispensed were awarded to state-run universities. As in the earlier period, the activity of a single entity distorts the statistics. The latter percentage is almost entirely a result of the University of Virginia's successful grant-writing program. University of Virginia received

$775,000, or an astounding 43 percent of the total grant money awarded to American Ethnic Studies programs during the five-year period, and an overwhelming 93 percent of the total funds provided to such programs at public institutions.

While public institutions have received an increasingly large portion of foundation grant money, private colleges and universities administered by religious organizations have received a steadily shrinking share. During the sample period, nine religious institutions received sixteen grants for a total of $542,300. Between 1972 and 1983, 30 percent of the funds awarded by foundations to American Ethnic Studies went to religious colleges and universities. This figure is largely due to the $248,000 J. Howard Pew Freedom Trust grant to the Eastern Baptist Theological Seminary in 1983.

After 1983 only two grants and $56,000, or 3 percent of all grant money in the field, went to such institutions. The shift away from the funding of programs at religious institutions again reflects the overall movement away from smaller, regional foundations to increased grant making activity by the larger national organizations. Among the top one hundred foundations by total giving, only the J. Howard Freedom Trust and the Joyce Foundation have awarded grants to American Ethnic Studies programs at religious institutions.

Sample Grants

As has become clear in the above presentation, general trends in foundation grant making to American Ethnic Studies programs and departments are evident but must be broken down into specific grants and analyzed critically. A single grant will often affect the statistics for a year, or even, in some cases, distort the general picture for a decade. With this in mind, the following annotated sample of grants from the 1972–1988 sample period highlights several of the patterns noted above.

Proving a noteworthy exception to pre-1983 patterns, the Carnegie Corporation awarded $459,000 to California State University at San Jose for the preparation of materials for a library/repository of Black heritage. Carnegie intended the program to develop the necessary framework for those interested in exploring Black Studies.

More typical of the early 1970s was a grant made by the Southern Education Foundation to Atlanta University in 1972. The foundation earmarked the funds for support of an undergraduate Afro-American Studies Program. A few years later, DeRance, Inc. made a single $10,000 grant for scholarships for American Indian students in the University of San Diego's new Native American Studies Program.

During the mid-1970s, Northland College in Wisconsin received a series of grants from the Kimberly-Clark Foundation. Starting at $15,000, the allotments slowly increased to $20,000. Specifically targeted at programs or charitable organizations serving those areas in which Kimberly-Clark has operations, the grants supported a developing Native American Studies program.

In 1978, the Rockefeller Foundation granted $138,400 to Morehouse College to sponsor two major journals in Afro-American Studies—the *College Language Association Journal* and the *Journal of Negro History*. Three years later, the Ford Foundation awarded $59,300 to Boston University for research and seminars on the African diaspora and historical and present-day interrelations among Old and New World Africans. Both grants served the stated immediate goals and the longer-term purpose of developing the recipient departments' reputations and resources.

Three years later, the Tinker Foundation of New York made its first payment in a two year $35,000 grant to La Salle College in Philadelphia. The funds sponsored the initiation of a master's degree program in Bilingual/Bicultural Studies aimed primarily at persons who work with Latino communities.

The J. Howard Pew Freedom Trust of Pennsylvania made a three-year $248,000 commitment to the Hispanic Studies Graduate Program at Eastern Baptist Theological Seminary in Philadelphia in 1983.

Making a similar long term commitment during the early 1980s, the Dolfinger-McMahon Foundation of Pennsylvania maintained a three year funding relationship with Swarthmore College. The three consecutive $5,000 grants sponsored visiting part-time faculty to conduct Black Studies courses at the Pennsylvania school.

The Ford Foundation began large-scale funding of Afro-American Studies programs in 1983 with two $100,000 grants to the University of Virginia and Harvard University. Both grants were earmarked for fellowships and research, with a conference on current research in the field planned at UVA.

Overshadowed by Ford's activity but important nonetheless were the grant activities of smaller regional foundations during the mid-1980s. For example, the John Ben Snow Memorial Trust, which limits its activities to central New York and New York City, made two grants to Colgate University in Hamilton, New York. The foundation targeted the $53,000 award at the development of a Native American Studies program.

At the close of the sample period, large foundations and large grants dominate the record. In 1987 and 1988, respectively, Ford awarded $300,000 to the University of Virginia for fellowships in Afro-American Studies, and $275,000 to Harvard for research and student participation in Native American Studies special projects.

In the last year of the survey, the William Penn Foundation, which limits its giving to the Philadelphia, Pennsylvania and Camden, New Jersey areas, granted $396,300 to the University of Pennsylvania, School of Arts and Sciences. The three-year award will go toward the establishment of a Center for the Study of Black Literature and Culture at the university.

Conclusions

Several general conclusions can be drawn from this survey of private foundation grants to American Ethnic Studies programs and departments. A variety of factors suggest a promising future for grant writers in such departments. Coinciding with an increase in grantable funds, the nation's largest foundations, led by the Ford Foundation, are exhibiting a growing willingness to invest significant funds in academic units of American Ethnic Studies. During the 1970s, foundations disbursed many grants specifically as seed-money for new and often experimental programs. By the late 1980s, several programs had established their reputations and were thus able to attract more sizeable awards from the larger grant makers.

Unfortunately, increased activity on the part of the larger foundations seems to have coincided with a retreat from the field on the part of regional, smaller foundations. Although such a move reflects smaller foundations' general priorities, it threatens to eliminate a valuable source of support for many colleges, as lesser known private and religious institutions of higher education appear to fare better with small and regional grant makers than with nationally ranked large foundations. Both Mount Senario College and the Eastern Baptist Theological Seminary provide noteworthy exceptions to this general rule.

While public institutions have enjoyed a recent surge in grants, foundations have a long history of supporting private colleges and universities. Large public and so- called elite private schools have had the greatest success with large foundations. Leading this trend, the University of Virginia's established Afro-American Studies Program has received an impressive number of major awards. Foundations are also showing an interest in innovative programs at well- known institutions. The William Penn Foundation's decision to help underwrite a Center for Black Studies at the University of Pennsylvania exemplifies this development. A second promising indicator of some foundations' willingness to fund experimental programs is the encouraging 1987 Ford planning grant to the University of Washington's new and relatively unprecedented umbrella American Ethnic Studies Program.[14]

Unavoidably, trends in foundation giving are unpredictable. A policy change at the Ford Foundation or at another large foundation could drastically alter the grant picture. With this in mind, recent patterns suggest that American Ethnic Studies departments and programs can and should continue to seriously consider private foundations an important source of financial support.

Notes

1. The federal government's grant-making agencies do not earmark funds for specific departments. While federal funds inevitably assist American Ethnic Studies both directly and indirectly, the information is extremely difficult to obtain. Calls to officials at the Fund for the Improvement of Postsecondary Education (FIPSE) and other major federal funding agencies netted little information. There is no study of funding for Ethnic Studies comparable to Mary Rubin's *A Declining Federal Commitment to Research About Women, 1980–1984* (1985), which she did for the National Council for Research on Women. In this report, Rubin provides data showing that between 1977 and 1983 federal funding for Black Studies and "Ethnics Studies" declined 30 percent and 24 percent respectively (pp. 15–20). As it is later noted, the sample period reflects the availability of data. The Foundation Center's *Foundation Grants Index* extends back to 1972; equivalent information on prior years is not readily available.

2. Foundation Center, *The Foundation Directory, Eleventh Edition* (New York: Foundation Center, 1987), xvii–xviii.

3. Foundation Center, *Foundation Directory*, xiii–xix.

4. Ibid., xxxii–xxxvii.

5. The information provided in the following survey was compiled from a computer search conducted on 28 April 1989 on the Foundation Center *Foundation Grants Index* database. Grants that do not appear in the database do not appear in this study. Subsequent to the completion of this piece, the Ford Foundation provided information on several additional grants including $336,000 awarded to Harvard in 1988; $352,260 to Cornell in 1987, and an increase in the University of Washington's American Ethnic Studies award to total $343,800. However, in the interest of consistency and in consideration of press deadlines, information from outside the database was omitted. The paucity of existing analysis and the introductory nature of the present study make clear the need for a more complete and detailed examination of foundational support of American Ethnic Studies.

6. In part, these figures might reflect the time period for which information is available. A higher number of grants might have been awarded to Afro-American Studies departments prior to 1972.

7. The American Ethnic Studies Program at the University of Washington at Seattle is developing a comprehensive undergraduate major in which students will explore all ethnic-specific components.

8. Phone conversation with Sheila Biddle, Education and Culture Program at the Ford Foundation, 22 June 1989.

9. Foundation Center, Foundation Directory, xvi.

10. Ibid.

11. Ibid.

12. Ibid., xxxix-xl.

13. Ibid., xl-xliii.

14. As previously noted, the Ford Foundation reports expanding its initial commitment to the University of Washington's American Ethnic Studies program; the program received $343,800. See Tables I to IV for yearly funding and trends in various categories.

CHAPTER 4

Different Voices: A Model Institute for Integrating
Women of Color Into Undergraduate American
Literature and History Courses

(Originally published in
Radical Teacher, no. 37, Autumn 1989)

Johnnella E. Butler and Betty Schmitz

For one intensive week in July 1988, eighteen history and literature college faculty members from throughout the Northwest attended a residential institute at the University of Washington's Northwest Center for Research on Women to consider how to teach about American women of color. The Different Voices Institute, funded by the Ford Foundation, provided participants with theoretical frameworks, exemplary readings, and pedagogical strategies for incorporating women of color into undergraduate American history and literature courses. This institute represents one of the first projects funded by the Ford Foundation to address specifically the need to incorporate material on and by women of color in the curriculum.[1] In this chapter we review the planning assumptions, strategies, curriculum, and pedagogy of the institute itself, so that others might learn from our experience.

While the movement to transform the curriculum through the incorporation of the new scholarship on women continues to flourish, very few of these projects have incorporated ethnicity, race, culture, class, or sexual identity as more than a token litany of variables for exploring female experience. One particular problem, as has been documented by an increasing number of scholars, is the practice in Women's Studies scholarship of using gender as the primary variable in analyzing and describing female experience.[2] The white, middle-class, heterosexual bias of academic feminism pervades research and teaching about women. Curriculum transformation projects have, for the most part, perpetuated this bias. A recent evaluation of curriculum transformation projects at ten institutions concluded that few faculty had "developed new courses, changed their theoretical approaches or pedagogy, or gained administrative support for the incorporation of information concerning racial and ethnic minority women."[3]

There were, however, some important earlier models upon which to draw in designing the curriculum of the Different Voices Institute. Noteworthy projects that focused on women of color include the Black Studies/Women's Studies Project, Smith College/University of Massachusetts at Amherst; the Multicultural Women's Studies Summer Institute, University of Illinois at Chicago; the Cross-Cultural Perspectives and Women's Experience Project, Wheaton College; and the Curriculum Integration Project at the Memphis State University Center for Research on Women.[4] Leaders of these projects learned that for women and men of color and white women, attempting to work collaboratively on the shared goal of a more inclusive curriculum can be painful, divisive, and even explosive. White women and men of color often vie for the allegiance/loyalty of women of color, who repeatedly find their priorities and needs subordinated to those of these other groups. Women of color also frequently find themselves castigated by white women for acting on their cultural and racial bonds with men of color. These problems are intensified by the fact that it is almost always white women who control the resources and bring in the grants in Women's Studies and Women's Research Centers, as it is usually men of color who do so in Ethnic Studies programs and centers. In addition, differing cultural styles affect communication in these groups; hence, active attention must be paid to process as well as content. Instructors and staff of such projects must first recognize and alter the power dynamics in interracial, mixed-sex groups if they hope to model the pedagogy they intend to promote to a broader audience.

The purpose of the Different Voices Institute was to retrain faculty at selected institutions in the Northwest to teach about women of color, yet faculties and student bodies in most four-year institutions in the region are overwhelmingly white. The teaching staff of the institute would be predominantly people of color. Clearly, attention had to be paid to the ethnic, racial, and gender tensions inherent in this situation, and strategies devised to ensure a productive teaching/learning environment.

At the start of the project, a multiracially representative advisory board and resource committees representing Asian American women, American Indian women, Black American women, and Latinas were created to advise on all aspects of program planning and institute development, including the curriculum.[5] The project leadership included a Latina (Angela Ginorio), a Black woman (Johnnella Butler) and an Anglo (Betty Schmitz). All three of us knew, respected, and trusted one another prior to collaborating on this project; hence, we could speak openly about power dynamics and other issues affecting the potential success of the institute.

Early in planning we decided to limit the scope of the institute to introductory U.S. history and literature. Women's Studies and Ethnic Studies scholars have developed substantial bases of knowledge in both areas, and combining them offers significant opportunities for interdisciplinary work. Additionally, history and literature provide two primary means for inducting young people into the cultural life of this country. Finally, their study allows for the introduction of regional perspectives and resources.

We felt it essential to have a residential institute to provide a sense of community, intensity, and seriousness in the teaching/learning environment. An incentive for encouraging participation would be full room and board; the participants, or their institutions, would be required to cover travel costs. The scope of the budget only allowed for a six-day institute, a painfully short time period in which to attempt to treat the experience of Asian American women, American Indian women, Black American women, and Latinas. To make a beginning, we identified three themes or topical clusters through which to capture these differing cultures: the legal and socio-political frameworks, public and private, governing the lives of women of color; family and community contexts; and biography. One major dilemma we faced was whether to teach material cross-culturally—that is, to treat topics such as legal frameworks, family, community, identity, sexuality, and language comparatively with representative writings from each group, or whether to focus on the experience of each group separately. Because participants would lack information necessary to appreciate the comparative approach, we chose to devote one day each to American Indian, Asian American, Latina, and Black American women, and one mid-week day to curricular issues.

We devised a new strategy to achieve one of the primary goals of the institute, to encourage substantive course revision. Because previous experience of projects of this nature had shown that faculty need time to reflect on reworking the traditional frameworks of their courses, we considered it unrealistic to expect a revised syllabus at the end of one week. Setting such an expectation might, in fact, deter participants from an open exploration of the themes, approaches, and readings, and result in superficial change. We asked participants instead to keep a daily journal reflecting on the implications of the material for their teaching to use when they set out to redesign their courses. We also requested they read four or five background articles for each group of women of color prior to the institute, so that they could use the time at the institute to develop more than a superficial knowledge of themes and cultural contexts.

We knew that it was important for the faculty to have experience with curriculum transformation projects to support their goals, and to be committed to assisting white faculty members to teach about women of color. The advisory board recommended choosing eight faculty members, four historians and four literary experts, working as teams of two to focus the work on each group of women of color.[6] Three of the faculty had been board members, so there was some continuity between planning and teaching the curriculum.

In addition, one of the directors assumed the responsibility for sections of the curriculum focused on course revision. Although each faculty member received only one-day's honorarium, most generously remained for the entire week, thus allowing for development of themes cross-culturally as the week progressed.

Eighteen participants attended the institute, representing five states and all types of postsecondary institutions in the region, including state universities, community colleges, and private liberal arts colleges. Participants were experienced teachers: eleven of the eighteen had more than six years of experience, and eight had twelve or more years experience. Hence, most participants had received their formal training before the institutionalization of Women's Studies and Ethnic Studies; nevertheless, they brought considerable sophistication in teaching approaches and techniques. Ten of the participants were from English departments, four from history, three from interdisciplinary fields, and one from sociology. Three of the participants were male; there was one woman of color, and no men of color.

The first evening of the institute—Sunday—was structured to model a process of interaction among the institute leaders that demonstrated open communication across race. We were particularly concerned that neither white people nor Anglo norms dominate. As a multiethnic team, each of us had specific roles for setting the tone, conveying information, and modelling collaboration. For example, Ginorio began the session with a welcome in Spanish and a culturally specific invitation to make oneself at home (*Mi casa es su casa*). Schmitz reviewed the expectations of the institute and the rationale for its structure and content. Then, in her keynote speech, Butler underscored one of the primary objectives of the institute: encouraging participants to analyze the paradigms underlying the content they teach and the way they teach it. Presenting specific examples of how placing women of color at the center of teaching challenges the usual paradigms for pedagogy and course content, she illustrated how the now traditional feminist focus on gender does not allow an accurate description of the experience of women of color.[7] Describing the experience of women of color requires a construct reflecting the intersection and interaction among gender, race, ethnicity, and class. During the discussion that followed, participants joined actively in relating material Butler presented to expectations for the week's work.

In the days that followed, each team gave an overview of theoretical perspectives, examples of pedagogical approaches (implicitly if not explicitly), examples of texts to use in class, and bibliographies. These texts presented the range of experience of women of color, focusing not only on the pain but also on the struggle and the joyful attainment. These presentations and discussions, while expectedly revealing dissimilar content, somewhat unexpectedly revealed similar themes, concepts, paradigms, and pedagogical strategies for teaching about women of color.

Quite serendipitously, by scheduling the American Indian experience first, we began the institute with content that contrasts sharply with the Western scholarly tradition and the paradigms it has generated. Kathryn Vangen began her presentation of American Indian women's literature with the metaphor "geography of cultures" as a new way to teach American literature and history. She suggested that placing different geographical areas at the center of study necessitates alternate interpretations of history and literature that bring different cultures into prominence. She explored differences in definitions of culture and demonstrated how traditional approaches to knowledge, especially chronology, are inadequate for elucidating Indian experience. Jeanne Eder, historian, complemented this overview by presenting a historical overview of federal, tribal, and personal definitions of Indian identity and analyzing the history of federal policies affecting Indian sovereignty.

In the afternoon, Eder presented a one-person monologue, "Waheenee: Buffalo Bird Woman," recreating the historical personage of this Hitdatsa woman as an illustration of the pedagogy of Indian storytelling and the cultural role of women. Vangen presented specific examples of themes and texts that could be used with the "geography of cultures" approach. To overcome problems for teaching resulting from the diversity of Indian culture, she recommended presenting one solid cultural view as a base (Lakota and Navajo texts are the most accessible).

She also suggested a number of pedagogical strategies for teaching American Indian experiences in predominantly white classrooms that became key concepts for faculty and participants for the remainder of the week: (1) holding a question in your mind until you are ready to know the answer, that is, resisting easy answers by pulling unfamiliar experience toward the familiar; (2) developing a respectful relationship toward difference and diversity; (3) giving female experience "room to breathe" within its cultural context—that is, not imposing traditional white interpretations of gender roles on other contexts; (4) learning by accretion rather than linearly; and (5) answering a question indirectly, for example, through storytelling.

As the historical and literary traditions of Latinas, Asian American women, and Black American women were explicated in the days that followed, several necessary approaches to the study of women of color emerged. They were common to each group studied:

1. Both the lives and artistic expressions of women of color must be taught within their socio-political, cultural, and historical contexts. For example, Norma Alarcon discussed the relationship between literary aesthetics and

bilingual issues: that is, how language choice influences literary paradigms through code-switching; genre-bending; the emergence of new speaking subjects; and texts that are written in English with Spanish accentuation and cadences. In presenting aspects of twentieth-century Mexican American women's history, Vicky Ruiz commented on the complexities of intergenerational conflicts around issues of acculturation, education, and the belief in the American dream

2. Pluralism, taking into account the conflicting modes of assimilation and acculturation, provides a conceptual framework most reflective of the ethnic minority experience of juggling and merging identities. Both Stephen Sumida and Butler demonstrated the clarity that this qualified pluralism paradigm lends to understanding the differing perspectives within the Asian American and Afro-American literary traditions, respectively

3. A respectful and knowledgeable attitude toward difference and diversity must be encouraged and developed. Romanticism, nostalgia, and treating people of color as victims have often been substituted for in-depth treatment of difference. Vangen showed how the desire to teach and learn about Native Americans can result in the distortion and reduction of that culture to romanticism and victimization. Gail Nomura pointed out that often the only material taught about Asian women in Women's Studies classes deals with their sexual exploitation.

4. Gender issues and sexism must be understood within their socio-political, cultural, and historical contexts, and as they interact with race, class, and ethnicity, and their respective "-isms." Each faculty presenter in her/his own way emphasized this point. As Alarcon stated in her critique of Anglo-American feminist theorists, they "flatten out" the experience of women of color by viewing that experience solely through the lens of gender. Walter emphasized this point in his discussion of the differences between the "feminism" of white women and the "womanism" of Black women.

Participants struggled with several of these issues, particularly the last, thinking about how to incorporate new material into their teaching. It surfaced as a problem early, during the discussion about American Indian women. White women expressed a desire to present to their students a feminist critique of traditional gender roles within Indian culture as patriarchal, an approach against which both Eder and Vangen cautioned because it distorts the complex cultural contexts in which Indian women live. Thus emerged a recognition of the complexity of developing new analyses not only in "traditional" but in feminist classrooms as well.

Realizing that participants would be overwhelmed by the amount of new material, we devoted Wednesday, mid-week, to "process" and pedagogy. Participants and teaching staff all needed time to think about commonalities in the experiences of women of color and to begin planning ways to redesign their courses. Also, guided by past experience, we had allowed for time to process tensions or anger that might have developed.

In the first part of the morning, Butler and Ginorio led a discussion of issues emerging from participant daily journals, which they had collected and read. This technique elicited some important areas of concern for white faculty, as they considered the problematics of teaching about women of color in their classrooms. There was a discussion of the difference between personal experience, identity, and expertise. White faculty expressed hesitancy about teaching certain complex material because they had not experienced it first-hand. One journal entry sums up the resolution of the group on this issue:

> Can a teacher teach effectively the history, sociology, literature, whatever of a culture that she cannot claim as her own? Perhaps the question is a central one, but to keep asking it *ad infinitum* suggests that people aren't/can't/don't acknowledge that this is essentially what we do all the time if we aren't teaching the short stories or poems we ourselves/I myself/you yourself authored, unless I'm teaching the history that I've lived every moment. Between me and Buffalo Bird Woman an enormous amount occurred. Yet I am not an [Hitdatsa Woman] nor a [Sioux], not an Indian at all. I was, and with that hour encounter as part of my life history, will continue to be a learner in the presence of that experience. As such, I can also *teach* about that experience. . . . I cannot imagine that Buffalo Bird Woman or Jeanne Eder would challenge my desire to share/teach this "text" with respect and humility. . . .

A portion of the morning was devoted to discussing how to deal with racism in the classroom.[8] One healthy dynamic that began to develop from the growing confidence of the participants was their ability to think for themselves about racism, and not always to defer to faculty of color on appropriate classroom strategies. It became clear that teachers must find ways to deal comfortably with emotions in the classroom when teaching about women of color. Strategies must vary depending upon the racial mix of the classroom. For example, refraining from using the one student of color in a predominantly white classroom to serve as an example or as the assumed repository of knowledge about that ethnicity is just as important as refraining from exploiting the guilt white students may experience when learning historical facts of oppression.

One especially troubling issue for the group that was not resolved was how white faculty can deal with sensitive topics within ethnic minority cultures, such as internal racism, "oppression" of women, and lesbianism, when teaching in predominantly white classrooms. One important guiding concept that emerged from the morning session was that of discomfort—the importance, for whites especially, to live with certain kinds of discomfort long enough to get to the sources of racism, classism, and so on, and to begin to respect and perhaps know otherness.

We devoted the afternoon session to the topic of course reconstruction, beginning with an overview of feminist phase theory—how incorporating the experience of women reorients traditional course frameworks.[9] Participants then worked in small groups to design a teaching unit embodying concepts and pedagogies from the first two days of the institute. They were asked to place American Indian and Asian American women's experiences at the center of consideration and build a unit around this material, rather than beginning with their current course syllabi. Several imaginative groupings of texts emerged around unifying themes, such as place/displacement, identity, family, and culture.

In addition to the "formal" curriculum, we organized cultural activities and social events to enhance the educational experience. Participants visited the Nippon Kan theater in Seattle's International District for a presentation on Japanese bachelor societies and ate at one of the district's best Chinese restaurants; there was an evening of videos to preview for teaching purposes; and the opportunity to attend a performance of *Ma Rainey's Black Bottom*. On the last evening, *Word of Mouth: Women Reading and Singing for Peace*, a highly acclaimed multiracial performance group, presented women's texts that echoed the themes of the institute. We concluded the institute with a "give-away," an American Indian custom in which someone is honored through bestowing gifts on their family and friends in a modest way. Staff members selected items from their belongings to give to individual participants, including postcards they could use to keep in touch with one another and with the faculty.

Evaluation of the institute indicated that it provided a solid base of information for participants to restructure their courses as well as transforming the thinking of participants to see different ways of approaching their teaching.[10] In their final journal entries, the majority of the participants described plans for changes that can be described as profound, since they entail placing the experience of women of color at the center of their courses. These approaches included arranging the syllabus thematically rather than chronologically; beginning the course with a different set of definitions and concepts, such as culture, diversity, Americanization, identity; abandoning gender as the primary/sole variable for analyzing female experience. The majority of the participants listed specific texts, themes, films, and resources they would use from the materials presented at the institute.

Participants left the institute with a new sense of mission, a commitment to teaching a more inclusive body of knowledge, and with specific ideas, resources, and a network for doing so. Most importantly, they are in the vanguard of the conscious effort to ensure that the women in Women's Studies are not all white, and the women's experiences of women of color is not robbed of its complexity and beauty.

We cannot overemphasize the importance of careful and long-range planning for a program of this nature. Representative advisory groups to assist in the selection of faculty and in designing the curriculum assures greater diversity of perspectives. Directors must be informed about curriculum transformation, in particular, projects designed to incorporate the experience of women of color. It is important to know what program and courses are offered at targeted campuses. Early on, planning must include establishing trust between faculty and participants, dealing with issues of anger, pain, and guilt about racism, sexism, and other "-isms," and scheduling sessions to allow time for discussing the information and feelings.

That Butler, Ginorio, and Schmitz had worked together previously and were aware of each other's work styles, philosophical approaches, intellectual commitments, and particular strengths and weaknesses, contributed to a certain ease in planning and conducting the institute. The dedication of the institute faculty, beyond the call of duty and paycheck, allowed for a unique interchange of knowledge. They commented upon one another's presentations and drew parallels between differing experiences and approaches. This approach inspired participants as they saw faculty of color learning from one another and modifying or enlarging on their own teaching. Seeing that faculty of color did not necessarily have experience in teaching about other groups, yet were able to take concepts and incorporate them into their approaches, served as a model for the white faculty.

The institute atmosphere was also important to its success. Project directors from the start tried to convey a sense of openness and trust to the participants. The journals—which were collected in a way that assured anonymity—served as a means for participants to express their reactions to various aspects of the institute without being judged. Modifications in the schedule were made to accommodate needs for additional information or discussion. The decision not to require a revised syllabus by the end of the week freed the participants to engage the new material without the pressure of deciding immediately how to use it in their courses, hence losing some of the complexity of the material in order to "assimilate" it. The concrete suggestions of themes, texts, and approaches informed directly the plans the participants elaborated in their journals for restructuring their courses.

While we were unusually fortunate to have a group of people who genuinely wanted to learn and who were eager to tackle difficult aspects of transforming one's perspective with a certain humor and optimism, all was not perfect. The one-week institute was clearly insufficient to treat significant topics in depth. There was no time to reflect analyze, process, and test out new ideas. Participants stated that they would have appreciated more sessions

devoted to textual analysis, small group work on course redesign and pedagogical strategies, and more emphasis on the intersection of class, sexual
identity, and national origin with race and gender. Historians were less satisfied with the scope of material covered than the literature specialists. Staff and
faculty concurred that two weeks would have better served our purposes.
Greater coordination among faculty ahead of time would have improved sessions, as paralleling and converging themes could have been more succinctly
and explicitly presented. And more direct recruiting of faculty of color as
participants would have provided a more balanced institute experience. Nonetheless, what we did accomplish was the laying of groundwork for course
changes and for future projects to more efficiently continue the work of
transforming both Women's Studies and the mainstream curriculum for the
inclusion of women of color.

Notes

1. In January 1988, as part of a new initiative to encourage the integration of new
research on women of color into undergraduate liberal arts curricula, the Ford Foundation invited twenty-one Women's Research Centers to submit proposals, of which up to
ten would be funded. The foundation had previously funded projects *focused* on
women of color at Memphis State University, Spelman College, and Duke University,
and encouraged other curriculum transformation projects, such as at the Western States
Project on Women in the Curriculum at the Southwest Institute for Research on
Women, to incorporate race and ethnicity as well as gender.

2. See, for example, Johnnella Butler, "Minority Studies and Women's Studies:
Do We Want to Kill a Dream?" *International Women's Studies Quarterly* (Spring
1984):135–38; Maxine Baca Zinn et al., "The Cost of Exclusionary Practice in Wom-
en's Studies," *Signs* 11, no. 2 (Winter 1986): 290–303; Elizabeth V. Spelman, "Theories of Gender and Race: The Erasure of Black Women," *Quest: A Feminist Quarterly*
5, no. 4:36–62; Deborah K. King, "Multiple Jeopardy, Multiple Consciousness: The
Context of a Black Feminist Ideology," *Signs* 14, no. 1 (August 1988):42–72.

3. Draft of the report to the Ford Foundation, *Including Women in the Curriculum: A Study of Strategies that Make It Happen,* Formative Evaluation Research
Associates (Ann Arbor:, Sept. 1988), 10.

4. See Nancy Hoffman, "Black Studies, Ethnic Studies, Women's Studies: Some
Reflections on Collaborative Projects," *Women's Studies Quarterly* 14, nos. 1 & 2
(Spring/Summer 1986):49–53; Johnnella Butler codirected the Black Studies/
Women's Studies Project with Margo Culley and draws on their experience in this
chapter.

5. The original project proposal was written by Pamela Keating, a white woman,
then director of the Northwest Center for Research on Women. Many of the early

decisions about the scope and focus of the institute were hers. The advisory board played a very active role in shaping the institute, as did Angela Ginorio, when she assumed the directorship of the center and became principal investigator of the grant. Our use of "we" in this paper is often purposely ambiguous, since we can no longer trace the origins of specific ideas and strategies to a particular person.

6. The teaching teams were: Kathryn Vangen, Department of English, University of Washington, and Jeanne Eder, Native American Studies, Eastern Montana College; Gail Nomura and Stephen Sumida, both from the Department of Asian/Pacific American Studies, Washington State University; Vicky Ruiz, Department of History, University of California at Davis, and Norma Alarcon, Chicano Studies, University of California at Berkeley; John Walter, Department of Afro-American Studies, University of Cincinnati, and Johnnella Butler.

7. Portions of this text were drawn from Butler, "Transforming the Curriculum: Teaching About Women of Color," in *Multicultural Education: Issues and Perspectives,* ed. James A. Banks and Cherry Banks (Boston: Allyn & Bacon, 1989).

8. This session was facilitated by Carolyn Allen, Department of English, University of Washington.

9. See, for example, Mary Kay Thompson Tetreault, "Feminist Phase Theory," *Journal of Higher Education* 56 (July/August 1985):363–84.

10. We will be able to judge the impact of the institute in March 1989, when the faculty participants return to the University of Washington, in conjunction with the annual meeting of the National Association for Ethnic Studies, to report on their course changes.

PART II

The Cutting Edge of the Liberal Arts: Some Essentials in Pedagogy and Theory Building

This section demonstrates the fundamentals of a developing theory of transformation in Ethnic Studies and Women's Studies and provides examples of teaching and theory building in both fields, singly and as they relate to one another. It also presents part of the dialogue around the definition of Jewish Studies, and specifically Jewish American Women's Studies in Evelyn Torton Beck's chapter.

Butler explores the very many ways in which teaching about women of color affects the student and the teacher, and argues that this endeavor " provides a natural, pluralistic, multidimensional catalyst for transformation." Rooted in the bringing together of scholarship in Ethnic Studies and Women's Studies, she defines transformation and demonstrates the matrix-like interaction of race, class, gender, and ethnicity and provides a model for pedagogy and scholarship in viewing experience through more than simply the lens of gender or race.

Both Frankenberg and Walter explore courses in Women's Studies and African American Studies that challenge the fundamental constructs of the fields. Ruth Frankenberg, in her teaching of the course, "White Women, Racism and Anti-Racism," recounts her experience of trying to get white students (essentially white women students) to examine gender in the United States through the prism of race. She concludes that for the most part the course provided benefits other than simply a greater "awareness," for students began to conceptualize structurally and affectively and cognitively the interrelationships between feminism and race. Her work serves as a model for identifying and analyzing these structural relationships in ethnic-specific studies, Women's Studies, and singular discipline oriented scholarship.

John C. Walter describes his developing awareness of the importance of scholarship on African American women to African American history. He explains the difficulties in bringing about the desired transformation in his teaching and scholarship. Not only does he describe some of the challenges students presented to him as a Black male teaching about feminism, but he also explores one of the profound changes in scholarship that taking women seriously as actors brings about. As a result of his initial transforming efforts, he developed another course, "The History of the Afro-Amercan Woman and the Feminist Movement," and has begun to explore as a serious research interest the mislabelling of the period now called "The Era of Accommodation." Walter's work gives insight into the significance of scholarly work on women done within the interdisciplinary and comparative context of Black Studies (Ethnic Studies, in general) and Women's Studies. He shows us how the hesitancy often expressed by men and white women to engage in this type of scholarship has the possibility of becoming the scholarly and pedagogical endeavor of working through problems of location and perspective in one's own and teaching rather than the impossibility of teaching content on people of color—and here specifically African American women—well.

Johnnetta Cole demonstrates how Black Studies performs the necessary political and academic function of acting positively to change the condition of Black people in the world, and by implication bettering the condition of all. This acknowledgement of the political nature of academic work is central to the transformation of the academy to a more humane, productive environment. She reminds us, however, that Black women must be allowed a greater role in Black Studies. Drawing largely on the development of Black Studies in the Five College Consortium in western Massachusetts, she assures us that Black Studies does not simply exist for Black people to gain a larger piece of the pie, but rather to make a better pie.

As we begin to explore relationships among ethnic-specific studies and between Women's Studies and Ethnic Studies, the need for fully developing the theoretical and pedagogical constructs implicit in Ethnic Studies becomes glaringly apparent. In conceptualizing the field of American Ethnic Studies as a discipline, Rick Olguin posits that to date American Ethnic Studies has not defended its epistemology from biased and prejudiced assaults as effectively as it could have because of a paucity of faculty and students trained in philosophy and allied disciplines. Olguin challenges essentialist, cultural, and cultural/condition epistemological paradigms and uses Chicano Studies and African American Studies to "demonstrate epistemological junctures between these areas of study." He presents his views as the three elements of a rigorous epistemology transcending the subject/object dichotomy: organicism, holism, and self-reflexivity. Olguin's insistence on oppression as the defining experience for USA people of color reflects one of the argued positions in the evolution of Ethnic Studies theory.

The contradictions arising from the power of Jewish American white-skin privilege; the conflicts arising from the unclarity of the term "semitic" and of the usages of the term "anti-semitism"; the confusions resulting from the recent *merging* in some conceptualizations of the categories race, class, gender, and ethnicity in the American context; criteria for assimilation in determining who and what constitute Ethnic Studies; degrees of "othernness"; these are all issues challenging the stucturing of knowledge from the perspective of pluralism. The essays by Howard Adelman and Evelyn Torton Beck approach these issues as Jewish American scholars working in the academy, from Adelman's perspective, as a director of a Jewish Studies program, keenly aware of the American ethnic reality of American Jews, and from Beck's perspective, as a scholar in Women's Studies.

In Adelman's view, Jewish Studies indeed qualifies as Ethnic Studies in that Jewish Studies, whether considered new or old, has always passed the criteria over time as "other." In this regard Jewish Studies, like all other Ethnic Studies, offers views, values, and beliefs, indeed, a culture, as worthy as any other for intellectual or academic consideration.

Jewish women's history and culture, according to Beck, is at present not fully integrated into Women's Studies as it should be. While Jewish women hold many positions of power in Women's Studies, the problem of anti-semitism, which she views as a feminist issue, is not discussed on par with racism, classism, and sexism. While Beck combines the subjects of gender and religious prejudice, others contend that anti-semitism is a racial issue. Nevertheless, Beck concludes that the Jew "as subject in feminist discourse is given to a radical 'otherness' that is denied at the very moment in which it is being created."

Implicit in both chapters are questions about assimilation in the Jewish American experience, the double-edged sword of anti-semitism and white-skin privilege in the United States context, the merging of ethnicity and religion, as well as the confusion resulting from the centuries-long use of the racial term anti-semitism to define anti-Jewish behavior. From whence does Jewish invisibility come in the context of Women's Studies? And how do we define and analyze relative oppressions when they occur simultaneously with the enormous privilege of white skin?

Thus we have a glimpse at the politics of inclusion in Ethnic Studies and Women's Studies. As such, however, we should acknowledge that we have not reached beyond the tip of the iceberg to the incorporation of, for example, American Indian women in Women's Studies, complete with the decidely different American Indian cosmology as well as the effects of their cultural and physical genocide on all of us. Neither have we clarified the place of the study of white ethnics in the liberal arts curriculum. Implicit in this text is the call for an honest reckoning with white assimilation in contemporary American life, its appropriate inclusion in our collective history and literatures. This reckoning with assimilation in traditional disciplines is part of transformation, part of the attainment of understanding a plural wholeness in the conceptualization of our American identity. Butler offers a beginning paradigm in the "Difficult Dialogue." However, the need to constantly and consistently revise, re-vision, and restructure as we tranform Ethnic Studies and Women's Studies to transform the larger curriculum becomes fully apparent as we examine some essential questions and problems in pedagogy and theory building.

CHAPTER 5

Transforming the Curriculum: Teaching About Women of Color[1]

Johnnella E. Butler

Until very recently, teaching about women of color and incorporating material on women of color into the curriculum has been virtually ignored. At best, attention was paid to women of color from a global, culturally different perspective; however, due to various national and state efforts, race, class, gender, and ethnicity within the United States are getting serious attention. Central to this curricular revision are U.S. women of color. I see the resulting methodology and pedagogy of this cross-ethnic, multiethnic endeavor as rooted in the method of critical pedagogy developing in this country and influenced by Brazilian educator and activist Paulo Friere, and evolving from feminist pedagogy as well as the pedagogy implicit in Ethnic Studies. This chapter provides a conceptual framework, an appropriate starting point for teaching about women of color, which, I demonstrate, is at the core of transforming the curriculum.

Why "Women of Color?"

The phrase "women of color" has come into use gradually. Its use immediately brings to mind the differences of race and culture. It also makes clear that Black women are not the only women of color. In an ostensibly democratically structured society, with a great power imbalance signified by race and class privilege, labels representative of reality for those outside the realm of power are difficult to determine. This power imbalance is both cultural and political and consequently further complicates labelling. Selecting the phrase "women of color" by many women of American ethnic groups of color is part of their struggle to be recognized with dignity for their humanity and their racial and cultural heritage as they work within the Women's Movement of the United States. Furthermore, it signals a political coalescence, implying the particular sameness among U.S. women of color while still allowing for their differences. This effort of women of color to name themselves is similar to attempts by Afro-Americans and other ethnic groups to define with dignity their race and ethnicity and to counter the many stereotypical names bestowed on them. Because we tend to use the word "women" to be all-inclusive and general, we usually obscure both the differences and similarities among women.

With the decline of the Civil Rights Movement of the 1960s, the Women's Movement in the second half of the twentieth century got under way. Not long after, Black women began to articulate the differences they experienced as Black women, not only because of the racism within the Women's Movement or the sexism within the Black community, but also because of their vastly differing historical reality. One major question posed by Toni Cade's pioneering anthology, *The Black Woman*, remains applicable: "How relevant are the truths, the experiences, the findings of White women to Black women? Are women after all simply women?" Cade answers the question then as it might still be answered today: "I don't know that our priorities are the same, that our concerns and methods are the same, or even similar enough so that we can afford to depend on this new field of experts (White, female). It is rather obvious that we do not. It is obvious that we are turning to each other."2 This anthology served as a turning point in the experience of the Black woman. Previously, White males, for the most part, had interpreted her realities, her activities, and her contributions.3

Although we are beyond the point of the complete invisibility of women of color in the academic branch of the Women's Movement—Women's Studies—Black women must still demand to be heard, to insist on being dealt with from the perspective of the experiences of women of color, just as they did in 1970, as the blurb in the paperback *The Black Woman* implies: "Black Women Speak Out. A Brilliant and Challenging Assembly of Voices That Demand to Be Heard." By the latter part of the 1970s, the logic of a dialogue among women of color became a matter of course. We find, as in Cade's *The Black Woman*, women of color speaking to one another in publications such as *Conditions: Five, The Black Women's Issue*, and *This Bridge Called My Back: Writings by Radical Women of Color.*4 The academic community began to recognize American women of color who identify with the Third World, both for ancestral heritage and for related conditions of colonization; in 1980 we see, for example, the publication of Dexter Fisher's anthology *The Third Woman: Minority Women Writers of the United States.*5

The most familiar ethnic groups of color are the Asian Americans, Afro-Americans, Hispanic Americans, and Native Americans. Yet within each group there are cultural, class, and racial distinctions. These ethnic groups can be further delineated: Asian Americans consist of Chinese Americans,

Japanese Americans, Filipino Americans, and Korean Americans, in addition to the more recent immigrants from Southeast Asia. Afro-Americans consist of the U.S. Afro-American and the West Indian or Afro-Caribbean immigrants. The number of African immigrants is most likely too small to consider as a group; however, their presence should be accounted for. Hispanic Americans, or Latino Americans as some prefer, are largely Puerto Rican, Chicano, and Cuban. The American Indian is made up of many tribal groups such as Sioux, Apache, Navajo, and Chicahominy.

The phrase "women of color" helps women of all these groups acknowledge both their individual ethnicity and their racial solidarity as members of groups that are racial minorities in the United States, as well as a majority in the world. The concept also acknowledges similarity in historical experiences and political position in relation to the White American. In addition, the use of the phrase and the concept "women of color" implies the existence of the race and ethnicity of White women, for whom the word "women" wrongly indicates a norm for all women or wrongly excludes other women of color.

What We Learn From Studying Women of Color

When we study women of color, we raise our awareness and understanding of the experiences of all women either implicitly or directly. Quite significantly, because of the imbalanced power relationship between White women and women of color, information about one group tends to make more apparent the experiences of the other group. It is well known, for example, that ideals of beauty in the United States are based on the blond, blue-eyed model. Dialogue about reactions to that model ultimately reveals that White women often judge themselves by that model of beauty. White women also serve simultaneously as reminders or representatives of that ideal to women of color and, most frequently, to themselves as failures to meet the ideal.

Another way of stating this is that a way of understanding an oppressor is to study the oppressed. Thus, we come to another level of awareness and understanding when we study women of color. We see clearly that White women function both as women who share certain similar experiences with women of color and as oppressors of women of color. This is one of the most difficult realities to cope with while maintaining viable dialogue among women and conducting scholarship. White women who justifiably see themselves as oppressed by White men find it difficult to separate themselves from the effects of and shared power of White men. White women share with White men an ethnicity, an ancestral heritage, a racial dominance, and certain powers and privileges by virtue of class, race, and ethnicity, by race and ethnicity if not class, and always by virtue of White skin privilege.[6] When we study women of color, we raise our awareness and understanding of the experiences of all women, either explicitly or implicitly.

Once we realize that all women are not White, and once we understand the implications of that realization, we see immediately the importance of race, ethnicity, and class when considering gender. Interestingly, some scholarship that intends to illustrate and analyze class dynamics is blind to racial and ethnic dynamics. In similar fashion, much scholarship that illustrates and analyzes racial dynamics and class dynamics fails to see ethnic dynamics. Other scholarship gives short shrift to, or even ignores, class. We have begun to grapple with the connectedness of the four big "-isms"—racism, sexism, classism, and ethnocentrism. Much scholarship in Women's Studies, however, fails to work within the context of race, class, ethnicity, and gender and their related "-isms," which modulate each other to a greater or lesser extent. Elizabeth V. Spelman illustrates how the racist equating of Blackness with lustfulness in Western culture modulates sexism toward Black women.[7] One resulting stereotype is that the Black woman has a bestial sexuality and, as such, deserves or expects to be raped. This racism is also modulated by an ethnocentrism that further devalues the Black woman, thereby justifying the sexism. Classism may also modulate this sexism if the perpetrator is of a higher class status than are most Black women. However, if this cannot be claimed, racism, ethnocentrism, or both will suffice. Nonetheless, each is operative to some degree. Lower-class Whites or Whites of the same economic class as Blacks can invoke skin privilege to differentiate within the common denominator of class. The categories of race, class, ethnicity, and gender are unified; likewise their related "-isms" and their correctives.

Attention to race makes us aware of the differing perspectives that women have about race and skin color—perceptions of what is beautiful, ugly, attractive, repulsive: what is ordinary or exotic, pure or evil, based on racist stereotypes; the role that color plays in women's lives; and the norms by which women judge themselves physically. Attention to race also brings us to a realization that White women too are members of a race with stereotypes about looks and behavior. These realizations lead us to more sophisticated analyses of institutional racism. Attention to race in women's lives, with the particular understanding that race has a function for White women and within the context of the connectedness among women due to the playing out of the varying gender roles, as well, reveals the oppression of racism, both from the point of view of one oppressed and of one who oppresses or participates in oppression by virtue of privilege.

Attention to class reveals, among other things, that because of different historical experiences, class means different things to different groups. Not necessarily measured by financial status, neighborhood, and level of education, class status frequently is measured by various ways in which one approximates the Anglo-American norm of middle to upper class. Our society encourages such behavior to a great extent, as shown by the popularity of the Dynasty model, the Yuppie, and the Buppie. Simultaneously, our society insists on formally measuring class status by economic means. Yet for the woman of color, as for the man of color, the dynamic of social class becoming a measure for success is particularly insidious, threatening to destroy the affirmation and utilization of ethnic strengths. Chinese Americans who have reached a high education level may move from Chinatown, feel compelled to adhere to Anglo-American norms that dictate certain dress, foods, and lifestyle, and embrace the cultural imperative of the superiority of the Anglo values. This, in turn, may threaten or seriously distort the sense of a sustaining identity that can recognize and negotiate racism and ethnocentrism. Ties to family and friends may be questioned, and the very historical reality and understandings that provided the source of strength for coping in the White world may be devalued and discarded. Poverty, for example, quickly becomes shameful, and the victim is easily blamed for not being a rugged enough individual.

Ethnicity, as a category of analysis, reveals the cultural traditions, perspectives, values, and choices that shape women's lives and their position in society, ranging from hairstyles and jewelry adornment to modes of worship and ways of perceiving a divine force, from moral values to the perception of women's and men's roles. Ethnicity, our cultural and historical heritage, shapes our perception of race and racism, sex, sexism and heterosexism, class and classism.

The element of power or lack of power has a great deal to do with the benefits or deficits of race and ethnicity. Similar to the example regarding classism, ethnic traditions, kinships, and values that are sustaining in the context of an ethnic group that is a minority, and thus, powerless, may become deficits when interacting with the majority or dominant society. On the other hand, when one becomes secure in one's ethnic identity, deficits of powerlessness and the moves to various levels of success (access to limited power) can be negotiated through variations on those strengths. Kinship networks, for example, are of primary importance to people of color for cultural reasons and for survival. Women's friendships have particular significance, specifically friendships of younger women with elder women. The structure of the larger American society does not make allowances for such friendships. Most of us do not live in extended families or in neighborhoods near relatives. Women of color frequently insist that they maintain such relationships over great distances. Time spent with family, especially extended family, must have priority at various times during the year, not just for tradition's sake but for maintaining a sense of rootedness, for a dose of shared wisdom, a balanced perspective of who you are, and often, simply for that affirmation that Momma or Aunt Elizabeth loves you. Ethnicity tells us that women of color celebrate who they are and where they come from, that they are not simply victims of ethnocentrism and other "-isms."

Ethnicity is important in women's lives. Most importantly, ethnicity reveals that besides the usually acknowledged European American ethnic groups, White Anglo-Saxon Protestants are an ethnic group. Even though it is an ethnicity that boasts a defining dominance that makes it unnecessary to name itself, it is an ethnicity. That it is an ethnicity to which many Whites have subscribed, rather than one to which they belong by birth, frequently is cause for confusion. However, it is no less an ethnicity for this reason.

The presence of Anglo-American ethnicity within the ethnicity of ethnic groups of color is often cause for confusion. Nonetheless, American ethnic groups of color manifest ethnicities that constantly balance, integrate, and synthesize the Western European Anglo-American, with what has become, with syncretism over the years, Chinese American, Japanese American, Afro-American, Chicano, American Indian, and Puerto Rican American. In a similar fashion, the English who came here syncretized with the values that emanated from being on this continent and became English Americans. They maintained a position of power so forceful that other Europeans syncretized to their English or Colonial American culture and eventually began to be called Americans. The assumption that people living in the United States are called Americans and that those living in other nations in the hemisphere are Latin Americans, Caribbean Americans, or Canadians attests to this assumed and enforced position of power.

Religion is closely related to ethnicity. Its values are sometimes indistinguishable from ethnic values. Ethnicity as a category of analysis therefore reveals sources of identity, sources of sustenance and celebration, as well as the cultural dynamics that shape women's experience. It makes even more apparent the necessity of viewing women pluralistically.

Gender roles may assume differing degrees of importance. By virtue of the modulation of the other categories, women may see gender or sexism to be of lesser or greater importance. Furthermore, the kind of gender roles or sexism may vary according to the influence of other categories. Attitides towards homosexuality are most frequently shaped by ethnicity (and by religion, which is closely tied to it), as is the depth and form of homophobia.

Gender roles for women of color are more apparently designated, determined, or modulated by ethnocentrism, racism, and sexism. It should not be surprising that women of color argue that racism most frequently assumes primary importance as an oppressive force with which to reckon. The Black woman, harassed in the workplace because she wears her hair in intricate braids and wears clothes associated with her African heritage, receives harsh treatment because of racism, not sexism. Racism also caused Black women to be denied the right to vote after White women gained suffrage rights. The sexism experienced by women of color within their communities is frequently tied to the racist, classist, and ethnocentrist power relationships between men of color and White America. The sexism experienced in the larger society is affected by this relationship as well as by racism, classism, and ethnocentrism directed specifically to the woman of color.

Women of Color: The Agent of Transformation

In dealing with the commonalities and differences among women, a necessity in teaching about women of color, I am reminded that the title of Paula Gidding's work on Afro-American women is taken from Anna J. Cooper's observation: "When and where I enter, then and there the whole . . . race enters with me."[8] Repeated in many forms by women of color, from the nineteenth-century struggle for the vote to the present-day Women's Movement, this truth ultimately contains the goal of transformation of the curriculum: a curriculum that reflects all of us, egalitarian, communal, non-hierarchical, and pluralistic. Women of color are inextricably related to men of color by virtue of ethnicity and traditions as well as by common conditions of oppression. Therefore, at minimum, their struggle against sexism and racism is waged simultaneously. The experiences and destinies of women and men of color are linked. This reality poses a special problem in the relationship between White women and women of color. Moreover, in emphasizing the commonalities of privilege between White men and women, the oppressive relationship between men of color and White men, women of color and White men, and men of color and White women—all implied in Anna J. Cooper's observation—the teaching about women of color provides a natural, pluralistic, multidimensional catalyst for transformation.[9] As such, women of color are agents of transformation.

This section defines transformation and provides the theoretical framework for the pedagogy and methodology of transformation. The final section discusses aspects of the process of teaching about women of color, which, though closely related to the theoretical framework, manifest themselves in very concrete ways.

A review of feminist pedagogy over the past fifteen years or so reveals a call for teaching from multifocal, multidimensional, multicultural, pluralistic, interdisciplinary perspectives. This call, largely consistent with the pedagogy and methodology implied thus far in this chapter, can be accomplished only through transformation. Although many theorists and teachers now see this point, the terminology has still to be corrected to illustrate the process. In fact, we often use the words "mainstreaming," "balancing," "integration," and "transformation" interchangeably. Mainstreaming, balancing, and integration imply adding women to an established, accepted body of knowledge. The experience of White, middle-class women has provided a norm in a way that White Anglo-American ethnicity provides a norm, and all other women's experience is added to and measured by those racial, class, ethnic, and gender roles and experiences.

Transformation, which does away with the dominance of norms, allows us to see the many aspects of women's lives. Understanding the significance of naming the action of treating women's lives through a pluralistic process— transformation—leads naturally to a convergence between Women's Studies and Ethnic Studies. This convergence is necessary to give us the information that illuminates the function and content of race, class, and ethnicity in women's lives and in relation to gender. In similar fashion, treating the lives of people of color through a pluralistic process leads to the same convergence, illuminating the functions and content of race, class, and gender in relation to lives of ethnic Americans and in relation to ethnicity.

We still need to come to grips with exactly what is meant by this pluralistic, multidimensional, interdisciplinary scholarship and pedagogy. Much of the scholarship on, about, and even frequently by women of color renders them systematically invisible, erasing their experience or part of it. White, middle-class, male, and Anglo-American are the insidious norms corresponding to race, class, gender, and ethnicity. In contrasting and comparing experiences of pioneers, White males and females, when dealing with American Indians, for example, often speak of "the male," "the female," and "the Indian." Somehow, those of a different ethnicity and race are assumed to be male. Therefore, both the female and the male Indian experience is observed and distorted. They must be viewed both separately and together to get a more complete view, just as to have a more complete view of the "pioneer" experience, the White male and White female experiences must be studied both separately and together. Thus, even in our attempts to correct misinformation resulting from measurement by one norm, we can reinforce measurement by others if we do not see the interaction of the categories, the interaction of the "-isms," as explained in the previous section. This pluralistic process and "eye" is demanded in order to understand the particulars and the generalities of people's lives.

Why is it so easy to impose norms, effectively erasing the experience of others? I do not think erasing these experiences is always intentional. I do, however, think that it results from the dominance of the Western cultural norms of individuality, singularity, rationality, masculinity, and Whiteness at the expense of the communal, the plural, the intuitive, the feminine, and people of color. A brief look at Elizabeth Spelman's seminal work, "Theories of Race and Gender: The Erasure of Black Women," explains the important aspects of how this erasure comes about.[10] A consideration of the philosophical makeup of transformation both tells us how our thinking makes this erasure happen and how we can think to prevent it from happening.

Spelman gives examples of erasure of the Black woman, similar to the examples I have provided. She analyzes concepts that assume primacy of sexism over racism. Furthermore, she rejects the additive approach to analyzing sexism, an approach that assumes a sameness of women modelled on the White, middle-class, Anglo-oriented woman. Spelman shows that it is premature to argue that sexism and racism are either mutually exclusive, totally dependent on one another, or in a causal relationship with one another. She discusses how women differ by race, class, and culture or ethnicity. Most important, she demonstrates that Black does not simply indicate victim. Black indicates a culture, in the United States the African-American culture. She suggests, then, that we present Women's Studies in a way that makes it a given that women are diverse, that their diversity is apparent in their experiences with oppression and in their participation in United States culture. To teach about women in this manner, our goal must not be additive, that is, to integrate, mainstream, or balance the curriculum. Rather, transformation must be our goal.

Essentially, transformation is the process of revealing unity among human beings and the world, as well as revealing important differences. Transformation implies acknowledging and benefiting from the interaction among sameness and diversity, groups and individuals. The maxim on which transformation rests may be stated as an essential affirmation of the West African proverb, "I am because we are. We are because I am." The communality, the human unity implicit in the proverb, operates in African traditional (philosophical) thought in regard to human beings, other categories of life, categories of knowledge, ways of thinking and being.[11] It is in opposition to the individualistic, difference-is-deficit, European, Western pivotal axiom, on which integration, balancing, and mainstreaming rest (as expressed through the White, middle- class, Anglo norm in the United States): "I think; therefore, I am," as expressed by Decartes.

The former is in tune with a pluralistic, multidimensional process; the latter with a monolithic, one-dimensional process. Stated succinctly as "I am we," the West African proverb provides the rationale for the interaction and modulation of the categories of race, class, gender, and ethnicity, for the interaction and modulation of their respective "-isms," for the interaction and modulation of the objective and subjective, the rational and the intuitive, the feminine and the masculine, all those things that we, as Westerners, see as either opposite or standing rigidly alone. This is the breakdown of what is called variously critical pedagogy, feminist pedagogy, or multifocal teaching, with the end result being the comprehension of and involvement with cultural, class, racial, and gender diversity; not working simply toward tolerance, but rather toward an egalitarian world based on communal relationships within humanity.

To realize this transformation, we must redefine categories and displace criteria that have served as norms in order to bring about the life context (norms and values) as follows:

1. Non-hierarchical terms and contexts for human institutions, rituals, and actions

2. A respect for the interaction and existence of both diversity and sameness (a removal of measurement by norms perpetuating otherness, silence, and erasure)

3. A balancing and interaction between the individual and the group

4. A concept of humanity emanating from interdependence of human beings on one another and on the world environment, both natural and human-created

5. A concept of humanity emanating from a sense of self that is not abstract and totally individually defined (I think, therefore, I am), but that is both abstract and concrete, individually and communally defined (I am we; I am because we are; we are because I am).

Such a context can apply to pedagogy and scholarship, the dissemination and ordering of knowledge in all disciplines and fields. Within this context (the context in which the world does operate and against which the Western, individualistic, singular concept of humanity militates) it becomes possible for us to understand the popular music form "rap" as an Americanized, Westernized version of African praise singing, functioning, obviously, for decidedly different cultural and social reasons. It becomes possible to understand the syncretization of cultures that produced Haitian voodoo, Cuban santeria, and Brazilian candomble from Catholicism and the religion of the Yoruba. It becomes possible to understand what is happening when a Japanese American student is finding it difficult to reconcile traditional Buddhist values with her American life. It becomes possible to understand that Maxine Hong Kingston's *Woman Warrior* is essentially about the struggle to syncretize Chinese ways within the United States, whose dominant culture devalues and coerces against syncretization, seeking to impose White, middle-class conformity.

Thinking in this manner is foreign to the mainstream of thought in the United States, although it is alive and well in American Indian traditional philosophy, in Taoist philosophy, in African traditional philosophy, and in

Afro-American folklore. It is so foreign, in fact, that I realized that in order to bring about this context, we must commit certain "sins." Philosopher Elizabeth Minnich suggested that these "sins" might be more aptly characterized as "heresies," since they are strongly at variance with established modes of thought and values.[12] The following heresies challenge and ultimately displace the ways in which the Western mind orders the world.[13] They emanate from the experiences of people of color, the nature of their oppression, and the way the world operates. Adopting them is a necessity for teaching about women of color. The conceptualization and the emerging paradigms implied in these heresies surface when we study women of color and lead naturally to the transformation of the curriculum to a pluralistic, egalitarian, multidimensional curriculum.

Heresy 1: The goal of interaction among human beings, action, and ideas must be seen not only as synthesis, but also as the identification of opposites and differences. These opposites and differences may or may not be resolved; they may function together by virtue of the similarities identified.

Heresy 2: We can address a multiplicity of concerns, approaches, and subjects, without a neutral or dominant center. Reality reflects opposites as well as overlaps in what are perceived as opposites. There exist no pure, distinct opposites.

Heresy 3: It is not reductive to look at gender, race, class, and culture as part of a complex whole. The more different voices we have, the closer we are to the whole.

Heresy 4: Transformation demands an understanding of ethnicity that takes into account the differing cultural continua (in the United States, Western European, Anglo-American, African, Asian, Native American) and their similarities.

Heresy 5: Transformation demands a relinquishing of the primary definitiveness of gender, race, class, or culture and ethnicity as they interact with theory, methodology, pedagogy, institutionalization, and action, both in synthesis and in a dynamic that functions as opposite and same simultaneously.

A variation on this heresy is that although all "-isms" are not the same, they are unified and operate as such; likewise their correctives.

Heresy 6: The Anglo-American, and ultimately the Western norm, must be seen as only one of many norms, and also as one that enjoys privilege and power that has colonized, and may continue to colonize, other norms.

Heresy 7: Feelings are direct lines to better thinking. The intuitive as well as the rational is part of the process of moving from the familiar to the unfamiliar in acquiring knowledge.

Heresy 8: Knowledge is identity and identity is knowledge. All knowledge is explicitly and implicitly related to who we are, both as individuals and as groups.

Teaching About Women of Color

The first six heresies essentially address content and methodology for gathering and interpreting content. They inform decisions such as the following:

1. Not teaching Linda Brent's narrative as the single example of the slave experience of Afro-American women in the nineteenth century, but rather presenting it as a representative example of the slave experience of Afro-American women that occurs within a contradictory, paradoxical world that had free Black women such as Charlotte Forten Grimke and abolitionist women such as Sojourner Truth. The picture of Black women that emerges, then, becomes one that illuminates their complexity of experiences and their differing interactions with White people.

2. Not simply teaching about pioneer women in the West, but teaching about American Indian women, perhaps through their stories, which they have "passed on to their children and their children's children . . . using the word to advance those concepts crucial to cultural survival." The picture of settling the West becomes more balanced, suggesting clearly to students the different perspectives and power relationships.

3. Not choosing and teaching separate biographies of a White woman, an Asian American woman, and an Afro-American woman, but rather finding ways through biography, poetry, and storytelling to introduce students to different women's experiences, different according to race, class, ethnicity, and gender roles. The emphases are on the connectedness of experiences and on the differences among experiences, the communality among human beings and the interrelatedness among experiences and ways of learning.

The last two heresies directly address process. After correct content, process is the most important part of teaching. Students who learn in an environment that is sensitive to their feelings and supports and encourages the pursuit of knowledge will consistently meet new knowledge and new situations with the necessary openness and understanding for human development and progress. If this sounds moralistic, we must remember that the stated and implied goal of critical pedagogy and feminist pedagogy, as well as of efforts to transform the curriculum with content about women and ethnicity, is to provide an education that more accurately reflects the history and composition of the world, that demonstrates the relationship of what we learn to how we live, that implicitly and explicitly reveals the relationship between knowledge and social action. Process is most important, then, in helping students develop ways throughout their education to reach the closest approximation of truth toward the end of bettering the human condition.

The key to understanding the teaching process in any classroom in which teaching about women of color from the perspective of transformation is a goal, is recognizing that the content alters all students' perceptions of themselves. First, they begin to realize that we can never say women to mean all women, that we must particularize the term as appropriate to context and understanding (for example, White middle-class women, Chinese American lower-class women, or Mexican-American middle-class women). Next, students begin to understand that using White middle-class women as the norm will seem distortingly reductive. White women's ethnic, regional, class, and gender commonalities and differences soon become apparent, and the role in oppression of the imposed Anglo-American ethnic conformity stands out. Student reactions may range from surprise, to excitement about learning more, to hostility and anger. In the volume *Gendered Subjects*, Margo Culley details much of what happens. Her opening paragraph summarizes her main thesis:

> *Teaching about gender and race can create classrooms that are charged arenas. Students enter these classrooms inbued with the values of the dominant culture: they believe that success in conventional terms is largely a matter of will and that those who do not have it all have experience a failure of will.* Closer and closer ties between corporate American and higher education, as well as the "upscaling" of the student body, make it even harder to hear the voices from the margin within the academy. Bringing those voices to the center of the classroom means disorganizing ideology and disorienting individuals. Sometime, as suddenly as the fragments in a kaleidoscope rearrange to totally change the picture, our work alters the ground of being for our students (and perhaps even for ourselves). When this happens, classrooms can become explosive, but potentially transformative arenas of dialogue.[14]

"Altering the ground of being" happens to some extent on all levels. The White girl kindergarten pupil's sense of the world is frequently challenged when she discovers that heroines do not necessarily look like her. Awareness of the ways in which the world around children is ordered occurs earlier than most of us may imagine. My niece, barely four years old, told my father in a definitive tone as we entered a church farther from her home than the church to which she belongs, "Gramps, this is the Black church." We had not referred to the church as such; yet, clearly, that Catholic congregation was predominantly Black and the girl's home congregation predominantly White. Her younger sister, at age three, told her mother that the kids in the day school she attended were "not like me." She then pointed to the brown, backside of her hand. Young children notice difference. We decide what they do with and think of that difference.

Teaching young children about women of color gives male and female children of all backgrounds a sense of the diversity of people, of the various roles in which women function in American culture, of the various joys and sorrows, triumphs and struggles they encounter. Seeds of awareness of the power relationships between male and female, and among racial, ethnic, and class groups are sown and nurtured.

Teaching about women of color early in students' academic experience, thereby bringing the voices of the margin to the center, disorganizes ideology and ways of being. Furthermore, however, it encourages an openness to understanding, difference and similarity, the foreign and the commonplace, necessary to the mind-set of curiosity and fascination for knowledge that we all want to inspire in our students no matter what the subject.

Culley also observes that "anger is the energy mediating the transformation from damage to wholeness," the damage being the values and perspectives of the dominant culture that have shaped opinions based on a seriously flawed and skewed American history and interpretation of the present.[15] Certain reactions occur and are part of the process of teaching about women of color. Because they can occur at all levels to a greater or lesser extent, it is useful to look for variations on their themes.

It is important to recognize that these reactions occur within the context of student and teacher expectations. Students are concerned about grading, teachers about evaluations by superiors and students. Frequently fear of, disdain for, or hesitancy about feminist perspectives by some students may create a tense, hostile atmosphere. Similarly, fear of, disdain for, or hesitancy about studying people different from you (particularly by the White student) or people similar to you (particularly by the student of color or of a culture related to people of color) also may create a tense, hostile atmosphere. Student expectations of teachers, expectations modulated by the ethnicity, race, class, and gender of the teacher, may encourage students to presume that a teacher will take a certain position. The teacher's need to inspire students to perform with excellence may become a teacher's priority at the expense of presenting material that may at first confuse the students or challenge their opinions. It is important to treat these reactions as though they are as much a part of the process of teaching as the form of presentation, the exams, and the content, for indeed they are. Moreover, they can affect the success of the teaching of the material about women of color.

Specifically, these reactions are part of the overall process of moving from the familiar to the unfamiliar. As heresy #7 guides us, "Feelings are direct lines to better thinking." Affective reactions to content, such as anger, guilt, and feelings of displacement, when recognized for what they are, lead to the desired cognitive reaction, the conceptualization of the facts so that knowledge becomes useful as the closest approximation to the truth. As Japanese American female students first read accounts by Issei women about their picture bride experiences, their reactions might at first be mixed.[16] Raising the issue of Japanese immigration to the United States during the late nineteenth century may challenge the exotic stereotype of the Japanese woman or engender anger toward Japanese males, all results of incomplete access to history. White students may respond with guilt or indifference because of the policy of a government whose composition is essentially White, Anglo-oriented, and with which they identify. Japanese American male students may become defensive, desirous of hearing Japanese American men's stories about picture bride marriages. Afro-American male and female students may draw analogies between the Japanese American experience and the Afro-American experience. Such analogies may be welcomed or resented by other students. Of course, students from varied backgrounds may respond to learning about Issei women with a reinforced or instilled pride in Japanese ancestry or with a newfound interest in immigration history.

Teacher presentation of Issei women's experience as picture brides should include, of course, lectures, readings, audiovisuals about the motivation, the experience, the male–female ratio of Japanese Americans at the turn of the century, and the tradition of arranged marriage in Japan. Presentations should also anticipate, however, student reaction based on their generally ill-informed or limited knowledge about the subject.[17] Discussion and analysis of the students' initial perspectives on Issei women and of how those perspectives have changed, given the historical, cultural, and sociological information, allows for learning about and reading Issei women's accounts to become an occasion for expressing feelings of guilt, shame, anger, pride, interest, and curiosity, and for getting at the reasons for those feelings.

Understanding those feelings and working with them to move the student from damage, misinformation, and even bigotry to wholeness sometimes becomes a major portion of the content, especially when anger or guilt is directed toward a specific group—other students, the teacher, or perhaps even the self. Then it becomes necessary for the teacher to use what I call pressure-release sessions. The need for such sessions may manifest itself in many ways. For example,

> The fear of being regarded by peers or by the professor as racist, sexist or "politically incorrect" can polarize a classroom. If the [teacher] participates unconsciously in this fear and emotional self-protection, the classroom expe-

rience will degenerate to hopeless polarization, and even overt hostility. He or she must constantly stand outside the classroom experience and anticipate such dynamics. . . . "Pressure-release" discussions work best when the teacher directly acknowledges and calls attention to the tension in the classroom. The teacher may initiate the discussion or allow it to come about in whatever way he or she feels most comfortable.[18]

The hostility, fear, and hesitancy "can be converted to fertile ground for profound academic experiences. . . . 'Profound' because the students' knowledge is challenged, expanded, or reinforced" by a subject matter that is simultaneously affective and cognitive, resonant with the humanness of life in both form and content.[19] Students learn from these pressure-release sessions, as they must learn in life, to achieve balance and harmony in whatever pursuits; they learn that paradoxes and contradictions are sometimes resolved and sometimes stand separately yet function together (recall heresy #1).

Teaching about women of color can often spark resistance to the teacher or cause students to question subject veracity. Students often learn that the latter part of the nineteenth century and the turn of the century was a time of expansion for the United States. Learning of the experiences of American Indian and Mexican women who were subjected to particular horrors as the United States pushed westward, or reading about Chinese immigrant women whose lives paralleled those of their husbands who provided slave labor for the building of the railroads, students begin to realize that this time was anything but progressive or expansive. Teaching about Ida Wells-Barnett, the Afro-American woman who waged the anti-lynching campaigns at the end of the nineteenth century and well into the twentieth century, also belies the progress of that time. Ida Wells-Barnett brings to the fore the horror of lynchings of Black men, women, and children; the inhuman practice of castration; the stereotyped ideas of Black men and women, ideas that were, as Giddings reminds us, "older than the Republic itself—for they were rooted in the European minds that shaped America."[20] Furthermore, Wells-Barnett's life work reveals the racism of White women in the suffragist movement of the early twentieth century, a reflection of the racism in that movement's nineteenth-century manifestation. The ever-present interaction of racism and sexism, the stereotyping of Black men and women as bestial, the unfounded labelling of Black men as rapists in search of White women, and the horrid participation in all of this by White men and women in all stations of life, make for difficult history for any teacher to teach and for any student to study. The threat to the founding fathers and Miss Liberty versions are apparent.

Such content is often resisted by Black and White students alike, perhaps for different reasons, including rage, anger, or shame that such atrocities were endured by people like them; indifference in the face of reality because "nothing like that will happen again"; and anger, guilt, or shame that people of their race were responsible for such hideous atrocities. Furthermore, all students may resent the upsetting of their neatly packaged understandings of U.S. history and of their world. The teacher must know the content and be willing to facilitate the pressure-release sessions that undoubtedly will be needed. Pressure-release sessions must help students sort out facts from feelings, and, most of all, must clarify the relevance of the material to understanding the world in which we live and preventing such atrocities from recurring. Also, for example in teaching either about the Issei women or about the life of Ida Wells-Barnett, teachers must never let the class lose sight of the vision these women had, how they dealt with joy and sorrow, the triumphs and struggles of their lives, the contributions to both their own people and to U.S. life at large.

In addition to variations on anger, guilt, and challenges to credibility in learning about women of color, students become more aware of the positive aspects of race and ethnicity and frequently begin to take pride in their identities. As heresy #8 states, "Knowledge is identity and identity is knowledge. All knowledge is explicitly and implicitly related to who we are, both as individuals and as groups." The teacher, however, must watch for overzealous pride as well as unadmitted uneasiness with one's ethnic or racial identity. White students, in particular, may react in a generally unexpected manner. Some may predictably claim their Irish ancestry; others may be confused as to their ethnicity, for they may come from German and Scottish ancestry, which early on assumed Anglo-American identity. Students of Anglo-American ancestry, however, may hesitate to embrace that terminology, for it might suggest to them, in the context of the experiences of women and men of color, an abuse of power and "all things horrible in this country," as one upset student once complained to me. Here, teachers must be adept not only at conveying facts, but also at explaining the effects of culture, race, gender, and ethnicity in recording and interpreting historical facts. They also must be able to convey to students both the beautiful and the ugly in all of us. Thus, the Black American teacher may find himself or herself explaining the cultural value of Anglo-American or Yankee humor, of Yankee precision in gardening, of Yankee thriftiness, and how we all share, in some way, that heritage. At whatever age this occurs, students must be helped to understand the dichotomous, hierarchical past of that identity, moving toward expressing their awareness in a pluralistic context.

Now that we have explored the why of the phrase "women of color," identified the essence of what we learn when we study women of color, discussed the theory of transformation, and identified and discussed the most frequent reactions of students to the subject matter, we will now focus more on the teacher.

Teaching about women of color should result in conveying information about a group of people largely invisible in our curricula in a way that encourages students to seek further knowledge and ultimately begin to correct and reorder the flawed perception of the world based on racism, sexism, classism, and ethnocentrism. To do so is no mean feat. Redefining one's world involves not only the inclusion of previously ignored content, but also the revision, deletion, and correction of accepted content in light of missing and ignored content. As such, it might require a redesignation of historical periods, a renaming of literary periods, and a complete reworking of sociological methodology to reflect the ethnic and cultural standards at work. This essay, then, is essentially an introduction to the journey that teachers must embark on to begin providing for students a curriculum that reflects the reality of the past, that prepares students to deal with and understand the present, and that creates the basis for a more humane, productive, caring future.

The implications of teaching about women of color are far-reaching, involving many people in many different capacities. New texts need to be written for college-level students. Teacher education must be restructured to include not only the transformed content but also the pedagogy that reflects how our nation and the world are multicultural, multiethnic, multiracial, multifocal, and multidimensional. College texts, children's books, and other materials need to be devised to help teach this curriculum. School administrators, school boards, parents, and teachers need to participate and contribute to this transformation in all ways that influence what our children learn.

For college professors, high school and elementary teachers, and those studying to teach, the immediate implications of a transformed curriculum can seem overwhelming, for transformation is a process that will take longer than our lifetimes. Presently, we are in the formative stages of understanding what must be done to correct the damage in order to lead to wholeness. I suggest that we begin small. That is, decide to include women of color in your classes this year. Begin adding some aspect of that topic to every unit. Pay close attention to how that addition relates to what you already teach. Does it expand the topic? Does it present material you already cover within that expansion? Can you delete some old material and still meet your objectives? Does the new material conflict with the old? How? Is that conflict a valuable learning resource for your students? Continue to do this each year. Gradually, other central topics will emerge about men of color, White men, White women, class, race, ethnicity, and gender. By beginning with studying women of color, the curriculum then will have evolved to be truly pluralistic.

Once embarked on this journey, teachers must be determined to succeed. Why? Because all the conflicting emotions, the sometimes painful movement from the familiar to the unfamiliar, are experienced by the teacher as well. We have been shaped by the same damaging, ill-informed view of the world as our students. Often, as we try to resolve student conflicts, we are simultaneously working through our own. Above all, we must demand honesty of ourselves before we can succeed. The difficulty of the process of transformation is one contributing factor to the maintenance of the status quo. Often we look for the easiest way out. It is easier to work with students who are not puzzled, concerned, overly romantic, or angered by what they are studying. Teachers must be willing to admit that while we do not know everything we do know how to go about learning in a way that reaches the closest approximation of the truth. Our reach must always exceed our grasp, and in doing so we will encourage the excellence, the passion, the curiosity, the respect, and the love needed to create superb scholarship and encourage thinking, open-minded, caring, knowledgeable students.

Notes

1. A version of this chapter originally appeared in *Multicultural Education: Issues and Perspectives*, ed. James A. Banks and Cherry M. Banks (Boston: Allyn and Bacon, 1989), 145–65. Reprinted with permission.

2. Toni Cade, *The Black Woman: An Anthology* (New York: New American Library, 1970), 9.

3. The Moynihan Report of 1965, the most notable of this scholarship, received the widest publicity and acceptance by American society at large. Blaming Black social problems on the Black family, Moynihan argues that Black families, dominated by women, are generally pathological and pathogenic. In attempting to explain the poor social and economic condition of the Black lower class, Moynihan largely ignores the history of racism and ethnocentrism and classism in American life and instead blames their victims. His study directly opposes the scholarship of Billingsley and others, which demonstrates the organizational differences between Black and White family units as well as the existence of a vital Afro-American culture on which to base solutions to the social problems Moynihan identifies. see Daniel Moynihan, *The Negro Family* (Washington, D.C.: U.S. Dept. of Labor, 1965); Joyce Ladner, ed., *The Death of White Sociology* (New York: Vintage, 1973); Andrew Billingsley, *Black Families in White America* (Englewood Cliffs, N.J.: Prentice-Hall, 1968); Harriet McAdoo, ed., *Black Families* (Beverly Hills, Calif.: Sage Publications, 1981).

4. *Conditions: Five, The Black Woman's Issue* 2, no. 3 (Autumn 1979); Cherríe Moraga and Gloria Anzaldua, eds., *This Bridge Called My Back: Writings by Radical Women of Color* (Watertown, Mass.: Persephone Press, 1981).

5. Dexter Fisher, ed., *The Third Woman* (Boston: Houghton Mifflin, 1980).

6. See "On Being White: Toward a Feminist Understanding of Race and Race Supremacy," in *The Politics of Reality: Essays in Feminist Theory*, by Marilyn Frye

(Trumansburg, N.Y.: The Crossing Press, 1983), 110–27. Also see "Understanding Correspondence Between White Privilege and Male Privilege Through Women's Studies Work," unpublished paper presented by Peggy McIntosh at the 1987 National Women's Studies Association Annual Meeting, Atlanta, GA. Available through Wellesley Center for Research on Women, Washington St., Wellesley, Mass., 02181. These works illuminate race and class power relationships and the difference between race and skin privileges. They emphasize not the rejection of privilege but the awareness of its function in order to work actively against injustice.

7. Elizabeth V. Spelman, "Theories of Gender and Race: The Erasure of Black Women," *Quest: A Feminist Quarterly* 5, no. 4 (1982): 36–62. Also see Renate D. Klein, "The Dynamics of the Women's Studies Classroom: A Review Essay of the Teaching Practice of Womens' Studies in Higher Education," *Women's Studies International Forum* 10, no. 2 (1987):187–206.

8. Paula Giddings, *When and Where I Enter: The Impact of Black Women on Race and Sex in America* (New York: William Morrow, 1984).

9. See Lillian Smith, *Killers of the Dream* (New York: Norton, 1949, 1961). Smith provides a useful and clear description of the interaction between racism and sexism and its legacy.

10. Elizabeth V. Spelman, "Theories of Gender and Race," 57–59.

11. See John Mbiti, *Introduction to African Religion* (London: Heineman, 1975); Basil Davidson, *The African Genius* (Boston: Little, Brown, 1969). For a discussion and explication of Western cultural imperatives, see George Kent, *Blackness and the Adventure of Western Culture* (Chicago: Third World Press, 1972).

12. I began to conceptualize this framework while doing consulting work with college faculty to include Black Studies and Women's Studies content in their syllabi at The Conference on Critical Pedagogy at the University of Massachusetts, Amherst, in February 1985. The concept of heresy here implies a reworking of the way that Westerners order the world, essentially by replacing individualism with a sense of communality and interdependence.

13. See also Paulo Friere, *Pedagogy of the Oppressed* (New York: Seabury, 1969); *Education for Critical Consciousness* (New York: Seabury, 1973).

14. Margo Culley, "Anger and Authority in the Introductory Women's Studies Classroom," in *Gendered Subjects: The Dynamics of Feminist Teaching*, ed. Margo Culley and Catherine Portugues (Boston: Routledge and Kegan Paul, 1985), 209.

15. Ibid., 212. See also in same volume, Butler, "Toward a Pedagogy of Everywoman's Studies," 230–39.

16. "Sei" in Japanese means "generation." The concepts of first-, second-, and third-generation Japanese Americans are denoted by adding a numerical prefix. Therefore, Issei is first generation; Nisei, second; and Sansei, third. Most Issei immigrated to the United States during the first quarter of the twentieth century to provide cheap,

male, manual labor, intending to return to Japan after a few years. However, their low wages did not provide enough money for them to return. In 1900, out of a total of 24,326 in the United States, 983 were women. Through the immigration of picture brides by 1920, women numbered 38,303 out of a population of 111,010. Because of racist, anti-Japanese agitation, the U.S. government helped bring these brides to the United States. For a complete discussion, see the Introduction and "Issei Women" in Nobuya Tschida, ed., *Asian and Pacific American Experiences: Women's Perspectives* (Minneapolis: University of Minnesota Press, 1982).

17. An important rule in the scholarship of critical pedagogy is that the teacher should build on the ideas and feelings that students bring to a subject, helping them understand how they might be useful, in what ways they are flawed, correct, or incorrect. Sometimes this simply means giving the student credit for having thought about an idea, or helping the student become aware that he or she might have encountered the idea, or aspects of material studied, elsewhere. Generally this process is referred to as moving the student from the familiar to the unfamiliar.

18. Butler, "Toward a Pedagogy," 236.

19. Ibid.

20. Giddings, *When and Where I Enter*, 31.

CHAPTER 6

Teaching "White Women, Racism and Anti-Racism" in a Women's Studies Program[1]

Ruth Frankenberg

Abstract

In 1988 I developed and taught the course, "White Women, Racism and Anti-Racism" for the Women's Studies Program at the University of California, Santa Cruz. Here I explain the institutional context that made possible and appropriate a course focused on white women as racially positioned actors, as well as something of the personal history and research experience that prepared me to teach it. The greater part of the chapter discusses the questions the course set out to explore, and how and why it did so. Like many Women's Studies courses, this one was interdisciplinary; as is also often the case in Women's Studies, participants' ability to work a range of registers—historical, sociological, political, experiential, emotional—was equally crucial. My discussion of students' and teaching assistants' interaction with the course will include exploration of the difference race and ethnicity made to the meaning of the course for participants. Finally, I will speculate on the course's effects on the Women's Studies Program more broadly.

Introduction

Women's Studies is a field of learning which, in the words of feminist historian Joan Kelly-Gadol, seeks to "place women at the center" of substantive and analytical attention.[2] It is also a body of ideas, institutions, practices, and practitioners that is ultimately inseparable both from the movements for social change that gave it birth and from the structures of political, social, and institutional domination in context of which it must do its best to survive and to mature. The 1980s have been a chastening time for many white feminists, but also a challenging one. In the context of a thorough-going critique of racism and ethnocentrism in feminist discourse, undertaken mainly by feminist and radical women of color, we have been urged to examine the ways in which we, as participants in Women's Studies and in the feminist movements of western Europe and North America, have replicated aspects of those very systems of domination that we have sought to challenge.

The challenge of women of color "in and against" feminist movement is too multidimensional and broad in scope to be discussed in detail here. Centrally at issue is the way in which much of feminist (and Women's Studies) thinking and practice has placed only some women at the center, while marginalizing others. The institutions of Women's Studies and feminism have, for the most part, been white-dominated.[3] Thus, analysis (for example, of the effects of family structures on women, or of women's relationship to wage labor) has, in unspoken and often unintended ways, universalized white, middle-class women's experience, thereby making such analysis irrelevant, even contradictory, to the needs of those who are non-white and non-middle class.[4] The critique of Women' Studies as "eurocentric" refers, again, to the replication of patterns of centrality and marginality. Here white cultures remain in center stage of feminist discourse, whether as objects of criticism, reform, or celebration (for example, a discussion of "women and the Christian religion" discusses white women's struggles for ordination into the Christian churches, but does not ask how an examination of Black women's role in the church or of "liberation theologies" might transform an overall sense of "religion" as "oppressive"). In a further twist of ethnocentrism, the "westernness" of much feminist discourse and Women's Studies teaching is seen to intersect with its "whiteness," as feminists unthinkingly take over anthropological and colonial images of women in the Third World.[5] Finally, feminism and Women's Studies have frequently emphasized gender difference as the central axis of domination in all societies, and as concomitant, the possibility of unity amongst women on the basis of our "equality under patriarchy."[6] As such, they have failed to thematize both the "simultaneity" of the impact of race, class, and gender oppression on the majority of women of color, and the intersection of multiple axes of privilege and oppression in the lives of many white women, feminists included.[7]

In a Women's Studies movement being challenged for its white-centeredness, a course on racism addressed primarily to the dominant racial group in a sense begs the question of its own legitimacy. One might ask whether a course whose stated concern is with "White Women, Racism and Anti-Racism" merely perpetuates in a new guise the same old white-centered focus. However, I would argue for the value of such a course, while emphasizing the importance of context in determining the appropriateness of its inclusion in Women's Studies programming.

Context for the Course

The Women's Studies Program at the University of California, Santa Cruz is one that, since the early 1980s, has in many ways made manifest a real commitment to multiracial curriculum content. This is evident, for example, in the program's "Introduction to Feminism," "Feminist Methods," and "Women's Culture" courses, and in "Feminist Theory." My course was thus by no stretch of the imagination the first to address questions about race, racism, and cultural diversity in women's lives, nor the first to explore with students the issue of racism in the feminist movement.

On the other hand, all of the permanent faculty in the program were white. (This situation has since been modified somewhat with the appointment of one woman of color to a full-time faculty position. At press time, a search is underway for at least one more women of color for a full-time position.) In addition, the majority of Women's Studies students were and are white. This reflects rather than departs from the student profile across the whole campus. In the two or three years prior to my teaching the "White Women, Racism and Anti-Racism" course, the Women's Studies Program had been offering annually a course on "U.S. Women of Color," taught by women of color appointed on a visiting or part-time basis.

I proposed and taught "White Women, Racism and Anti-Racism" as a part-time lecturer, in the winter quarter of 1988. The course ran simultaneously with the "Women's Culture" and "Feminist Methodology" courses mentioned above, and preceded two courses taught by a feminist woman of color, hired as a Distinguished Visitor for spring quarter, including one on "Women of Color in the United States."

I would argue that it is primarily alongside these other "disturbances" to the white-centeredness of Women's Studies—on the one hand general Women's Studies courses with multiracial content, and on the other hand specialized courses formulated specifically from the standpoint of women of color—that a course such as mine becomes both appropriate and productive. It should be emphasized, however, that my sense of its validity is not based on any kind of a simple "equal shares" argument. Rather, the course seems to me to have been appropriate because, among other things, it set out to teach white women to better comprehend their historical, social, and epistemological positioning with respect to race. As such, it had the potential to offer white women skills to function more effectively in relation to a developing multiracial curriculum and program. By contrast, in a context where no such multiracial curriculum is offered, a more urgent priority might be the creation of curriculum with a multiracial scope, and/or the employment of women of color faculty.

At the time I taught the course, I was close to finishing dissertation research on white women, race, culture, and racism.[8] The research, involving life history interviews with white women, had given me the chance for detailed contemplation of the racial structuring of white women's experience, as well as providing the context for theoretical and historical study of race and culture. Equally important, I had been active since 1980 in personal and political work against racism, in community and university settings. These kinds of intellectual, political, and personal activities (and the support networks they generated) constituted my preparedness to offer the course on "White Women, Racism and Anti-Racism."

Thirty students enrolled in the course, all women. Of these, twenty-six were white, of Jewish and non-Jewish heritage, one was African-American, one was Chicana, and two were Japanese American. Except for two Swiss women, all the students were either U.S.-born or long-standing U.S. residents. I will return to a discussion of the significance of all these differences, below.

The Structure of the Course

Over a ten-week quarter, the course addressed six interlocking themes related to racism as a national and global system with structural, discursive, and individual dimensions; the impact of that system on all women and the inflection of gender and sexuality by race and class; and the rethinking of feminism, by women of color and white women, in the context of issues of racism. (The syllabus is reproduced in full in Appendix I, and the course bibliography in Appendix II). The six segments of the course were introduced in the syllabus as follows:

1. meanings of "race" and "racism"

2. the experiences of white women and women of color, as racially positioned members of society

3. the transformation of these positionings into standpoints for theory and action by feminists, white and of color, in the present "second wave" of feminism

4. the context and voices of anti-racist white women, prior to the second wave of feminism

5. the relationship between the Civil Rights Movement and feminism; the lessons offered to white feminists by Black and white civil rights activists

6. "new struggles, new dialogues": building a white anti-racist consciousness; models of work towards coalition and solidarity, across race and class lines

In beginning the course (segment 1), it was important to establish a common ground in relation to the meanings of "race" and "racism." I used a lecture and readings (Gould; Omi and Winant [see Appendix II for full reference]) to propose a nonessentialist and nonbiological understanding of "race," as a category that is historically, socially, and politically determined, and that shifts over time. Exploration of the term "racism" began by means of an interactive process over two sessions. In it, the group was invited to contribute to wall chart listings, headed "racism," "white people's relationship to racism," and "feminism and racism." This process enabled the beginning of discussion and had the advantage of asking students to view themselves as knowledgeable and concerned about racism, rather than as outsiders to the set of issues under consideration. Needless to say, the meanings and dimensions of racism were explored continuously through the course.

The second segment of the course (weeks two and three) asked students to examine the impact of racism on women's daily lives, and to explore the notion that the lives of all women, *including white women*, must be understood in relation to the racial structuring of society (Glenn; Pesquera; Pearce; Buss; Davis; Segrest; Frankenberg; Pratt; Cameron; Smith and Smith). Readings emphasized the intersection of gender and sexuality with race and class in shaping the life experiences of women, signalling (although not fully surveying) the range of ways in which race, class, and culture have inflected the experience of being female in U.S. society. These readings also made manifest the visibility of racial oppression as a factor in the conscious experience of women of color, in contrast with the structured invisibility of the salience of race privilege in much of white experience. (It was expected, given other course offerings in the Women's Studies Program, that students would already be familiar with some of these ideas. Here, the goal was to set the context for the course by reminding students of women's different, yet connected, experiences of living in a racially unequal society. This course was *not*, however, a survey of "race, class, and gender in the United States"—to mistake it for one would indeed have been a reinstatement of "white-centeredness" in a new guise.)

One of my goals in this segment of the course was to invite students to view themselves as historically and socially positioned subjects in U.S. society, and to examine their relationship to racism in historical and social, rather than only individual, terms. The readings by white women (Segrest;

Pratt; Frankenberg) were drawn out of the recent efforts by some white feminists to explore whites' positioning as members of the racially dominant
group—a project that, it was hoped, white students in the class would also
take on as their own.

The second segment of the course also set the scene for the third, which
was to be an exploration of feminist standpoints and the question of racism.
First, it provided the backdrop for making the argument that if women's lives
differed because of their racial, class, and cultural positionings, we should not
be surprised if their feminist agendas differed also. Further, the readings and
discussions of the second segment suggested a social and material basis for
the ignoring of race in most white feminist work.

In the third segment, articles by Hartsock and Zavella invited students to
look specifically at the relationship between women's experience and the
construction of feminist standpoints and agendas. Sandoval, and Zinn et al.
drew students' attention to the impact of racism, class inequality, and white-
centeredness on the institutional structures of feminism. The work of Trinh
and Mohanty moved the discussion of white feminist racism beyond the
questions of invisibility and exclusion of people of color to that of distorted
visibility, in the form of the racist and colonial discourses that shape white and
Western people's senses of "Other" and of self.

At this point in the course, the first assignment, a four-to-five-page paper
on "autobiography through a new prism" asked students to

> Explore an aspect of your life—childhood, community, family, sexuality,
> the trajectory of your family over several generations, being conscious of the
> patterning of experience with respect to structures of race (while also not
> forgetting class and gender—but the focus for this time should be race).

(A complete description of the assignment appears in Appendix III).

In the fourth and fifth segments of the course (weeks five, seven, and
eight) we shifted focus away from contemporary feminism to its context in
recent history. One of my goals in asking students to examine the voices of
white women prior to the 1960s (Smith; Halsey; Stalvey) was to emphasize
that the women of the second wave of feminism were not the first to "discover" white racism; a second was to explore models of white anti-racist consciousness that, in contrast with 1980s feminism, did not draw exclusively on
"identity politics." A third goal was to suggest to white students the possibility of a female, anti-racist heritage upon which to draw in constructing themselves as anti-racist white feminists. In addition, however, students read these
earlier voices critically, looking for their traces of patronage, colonial discourse, anti-communism, and homophobia.

Discussion of the legacy of the Civil Rights Movement (segment five) similarly served multiple purposes. First, I hoped students would begin think-ing about the present feminist movement in relation both to its indebtedness to the social movements of the late-1950s to 1960s and to its struggles against the sexism of those movements (Omi and Winant; Evans). Second, discussion of the emergence of a women's liberation movement in the late 1960s, on the heels of the Civil Rights struggles, occasioned exploration of the circum-stances in which the former ultimately took on the white-centered shape against which we continue to struggle today (Evans; Giddings). Discussion of Civil Rights offered a sense of the importance of an older generation of Black women as role models for younger Black *and* white activist women. And finally, it added to the notion of a white, female, anti-racist heritage, begun through class discussions of Lillian Smith and others (Deming; Blumberg).

The sixth and final segment of the course explored the immediate strug-gle towards a feminism that is integrally anti-racist. This discussion had in fact begun in a very powerful way in the sixth week of the course; I had raised funds from several departments of the university to enable a four-day visit to the campus by Mab Segrest, a white lesbian feminist active in North Carolina in full-time political work against racist, religious, and homophobic violence. In addition to discussing with students her own trajectory and family history, implicated as it was with racism in the South, Segrest drew students' attention to neo-Nazi and extreme right racism as a Californian as well as a Southern phenomenon and provided resources for those who wanted to think about becoming activists for the first time.[9]

Weeks nine and ten completed this segment of the course. Here, we explored modes and philosophies of interracial coalition, both within femi-nism (Bulkin, Pratt, and Smith; Reagon) and outside it (Braden). Secondly, there was further discussion of what the struggle to build interracial coalitions might demand of activists as individuals, white and of color, including will-ingness by white people to accept leadership from people of color, ability to operate outside of one's own cultural environment, willingness to sacrifice feelings of familiarity and personal safety (Bulkin et al; Reagon; Braden; Frankenberg and Martens). A second guest speaker, Terry Berman, presented to the group her own trajectory as a political activist who has been involved in a number of multiracial, coalition-based struggles, and her changing con-sciousness of self as a white, Jewish, lesbian feminist. At this point in the course there were also discussions of the relationship between racism and anti-semitism, and lectures and discussions on the relationship between per-sonal and political issues in the construction of anti-racist stances within feminism.

The choice of topic for final papers or projects was left open to students; these were consequently broad in scope. Several students focused on the impact of racism in specific areas of life (for example, women and sports,

colored contact lenses, standards of physical beauty, the *Roe v. Wade* decision), academia (for example, art history) or feminism (for example, feminist
theory, the Wiccan Movement). Some students discussed their own experiences of anti-racist work (for example, as a class project one student organized an "unlearning racism workshop" for her college dormitory, seeking a
leader for the workshop, fundraising, publicizing the event, and so on; another more experienced activist described a nearby town's struggle to redraw
electoral boundaries in order to combat racism institutionalized in the electoral system). Students had the option to present their work to the class; about
ten students offered slide-shows and brief lectures, and one, an art student,
presented and discussed her sculpture representing racism and the struggle
for social change. Also in this context, Ekua Omosupe, one of the two
teaching assistants for the course, presented on behalf of her discussion section the results of a group project on defining and combating racism (see
Appendix V).

A third, impromptu class project took place towards the end of the
quarter, when I received from the university administration copies of white
supremacist literature that had been circulating on one of the other University
of California campuses. Amongst the literature, a cartoon story attributed to
the "White Students' Union" (WSU) told the story of race conflict in a
desegregated high school, in such a way, not surprisingly, as to parade a range
of racist and fascist myths and stereotypes and to argue the necessity for a
"white students' union." It had happened in the third week of class that our
discussions of "race and the social geography of childhood" had occasioned,
above all other topics, many white students' talking about unresolved, confused, and painful memories about their experiences of school desegregation.
The appearance of the WSU cartoon thus provided an opportunity for students
to explore the issue once again. In this context, they were able to see clearly
the need to take an explicitly anti-racist stand and support school desegregation. Drawing in part on skills developed during the course, they were able to
identify and analyze the racist moves made in the cartoon, and to think about
the importance of generating non-racist narratives about school desegregation, for themselves if not for any kind of public circulation. I gave students
my own detailed analysis of the cartoon at the end of class, but in the
meantime the group had independently identified all the points in it, and
more.

The Role of Teaching Assistants (TA's)

The involvement of the teaching assistants who worked with the course
was invaluable. Of the two women one, Ekua Omosupe, was a graduate

student and was paid for her participation. The other, Rosa Maria Villafañe-Sisolak, was an undergraduate and received academic credit. As their names suggest, both are women of color. Given the focus of the course and the predominance of white enrollees, the question of the racial and ethnic identities of its instructor and teaching assistants is not a neutral one.

One issue of concern here is the possible imposition on women of color of being asked to educate a largely white group of students about racism, a pattern that, as women of color have pointed out in recent years, is frequently replicated in feminist circles. However, it is worth remembering in the present context that the two TA's came to the course by their own choice, although in rather different ways. Rosa Maria and I were longstanding friends and Rosa had expressed interest in gaining the experience of leading discussion sections. Ekua had, in fact, originally expected to act as TA to the "U.S. Women of Color" course. However, when that course was postponed by a quarter, she and I discussed the "White Women, Racism and Anti-Racism" course, and she expressed interest in working on it.

Both women brought to the course a strong commitment to teaching and a willingness to share with the group both their perspectives on issues and aspects of their life experiences. In these ways they at times provided a useful counterpoint to my standpoint as a white analyst; at other times their own memories were very important in helping white students see other sides to contexts they had experienced as whites.

Depending on the size of the course and the allocation of funding, I had originally hoped that it would be possible to have access both to white TA's and TA's of color, so that all students, white and of color, could choose whether to participate in same-race or mixed-race discussion groups. An additional concern in not providing white students access to a white TA was that they might be inhibited in discussions, particularly of their own internalization of racist ideas. By the same token, as important as those discussions are, it also seemed unfair to impose on students or TA's of color the experience of witnessing or participating in discussions of that nature. However, on this occasion what was ultimately more important than the race of the individuals leading the discussion groups was their clarity of analysis of racism, and their sensitivity and commitment as teachers in relation to the issues at hand.

Student Participation

As noted above, of the thirty students enrolled in the course, twenty-six were white, some Jewish and some not. Of the four women of color enrolled, one was Black, one was a Chicana, and two were Japanese American. The course was an elective and drew fewer students than the other two core

Women's Studies courses offered concurrently. This, it seems to me (and here I draw in part on conversations with one of the enrolled students) may have resulted from the popularity of the full-time faculty member teaching courses the same quarter, as well as from the challenging character of the question of white women and racism. But this selective enrollment meant that those white students who *did* take the class were very serious in their determination to come to grips with the questions about racism addressed in the course, and that there were few of the problems of anger, hostility, or "proto-backlash" that might have emerged under other circumstances. (The absence of men in the class probably merely reflected the usual ratio of men to women students in Women's Studies courses at UCSC—roughly one man to every thirty women.)

Given its objectives and structure, the course, although by no means irrelevant to the interests of women of color, must presumably have tapped into a greater sense of urgency for white students. This was reflected in the predominance of white students in the class. As should be clear, while the course was not exclusively about white women, amongst its primary foci were a set of issues of immediate importance to white feminists. These included the development and critique of white feminist standpoints, and the history and future of white contributions to an anti-racist feminism.

However, these questions were addressed in the context of a broader set of discussions of interest and concern to white women *and* women of color. These included the history and sociology of racial oppression and privilege and their particular impact on women, and the recent history of movements for social change. In addition, the course drew extensively on the perspectives and voices of people of color as well as those of white people. Thus the construction of the agency and identity of women of color was also in some senses on the agenda. The course also was of relevance to women of color *and* white women as people concerned with the structure of society and with social change. In addition, at least one of the women of color made it clear during the quarter that, as the daughter of Japanese and white parents, questions about whiteness were of personal as well as intellectual concern.

The course called upon students to achieve a delicate balance of personal and intellectual engagement with the issues at hand and, similarly, to remain attentive to the present moment in feminism while comparing and contrasting it with other times and other movements.

On one hand, my hope was to shift the ground from the (arguably) excessive focus on the interpersonal dimension of racism that seems often to characterize *both* dominant cultural and white feminist discussions of racism. Given this, discussions of racism and the social structure and of the history of racism and anti-racism were key.

On the other hand, I did not want to lose hold of the crucial feminist insight that political and social structures are made manifest in personal life, shaping life experience and consciousness—an insight that challenges us to remember that we always work from within, not outside or above, the social relations we seek to change. And it requires us to explore and work against racism on multiple levels, within and outside ourselves, as members of dominant or dominated racial groups. With regard to the issue of white people's internalization of racist ideas and the emotional aspects of confronting oneself as the inheritor of membership in the racially dominant group, it must be emphasized that those students who were able to participate in an "Unlearning Racism Workshop," benefited tremendously from doing so.[10] Access to such workshops is, it seems to me, an extremely valuable adjunct to a course like this one.

Impact of the Course

The impact of any course is difficult to assess in any final way, particularly as an insider to it. In terms of students' responses, the high quality of their engagement with the material, and the caliber of their written work, the course was certainly successful. I would also take to heart some of their major criticisms, and my own retrospective assessment, and would hope in repeating the course to address more fully the relationship between racism and anti-semitism, and to explore more adequately the political involvement of other women of color besides Black women in the social movements of the 1960s, as well as their relationships to the present wave of feminism in its early years.

One measure of the impact of the course came in the form of reactions of those white students who had been enrolled in "White Women, Racism and Anti-Racism," to participation the following quarter in the "U.S. Women of Color" course, which has over the years frequently been a site of tension between white women and women of color. Those white women who had taken the former course reported themselves more aware of the political context for the latter course than other white students. They saw themselves as less apt to want to use the course to resolve their own relationships to racism and more cognizant of the possibility of white students inadvertently replicating the patterns of the dominant culture by "colonizing" the discursive space in the classroom. This suggests that the course on white women had been successful in enabling students to examine their own positioning, both in Women's Studies classrooms and in the racial structuring of the United States, and to begin finding ways to act with an awareness and sensitivity to their location.

As suggested earlier, it seems to me that a course such as this one is an important component in meeting Women's Studies need for a fully multiracial curriculum, but can by no means be viewed as meeting that need in its entirety. The course does not, for example, seek to survey, compare, or analyze the impact of racial inequality on women across the lines of race, in the United States or globally. Nor does it place at the center of attention, although it clearly asks students to learn from, the ways in which women of color have begun reformulating feminist agendas so as to pay attention to the intersection of gender and sexuality with race and class in women's lives. Rather, drawing on a comparative perspective, the course looks at how white women in particular fit into an analysis of the United States viewed as a racially structured environment. It asks white women to consider how feminism, and their own experiences in the world, look different once the United States *is* viewed through the lens of race. It asks students to examine the meaning and experience of race privilege and its intersection with other axes of privilege and oppression. It explores, as we have seen, the ways in which feminism has been shaped by its location within the relations of racism, as well as the ways in which white women have at times been activists against racism, both within and outside feminist contexts.

One of the benefits of a course such as "White Women, Racism and Anti-Racism" is that it locates white women *inside* the question of racism; by making clear the ways in which racism is not simply an issue for feminist women of color to address while white feminists look on, it may help to clarify the extent to which a truly integrative approach to Women's Studies involves not only making additions to the field but also transforming it in ways that will deeply affect how all of us see our studies, and ourselves.

Appendix I
Course Syllabus

Women's Studies 143
Ruth Frankenberg
Teaching Assistants:
Ekua Omosupe,
Rosa M. Villafañe-Sisolak

Winter 1988
Mon–Wed–Fri 12:30–1:40 P.M.
Applied Sciences 152

White Women, Racism and Anti-Racism

Course Description

The course will explore the following:

1. meanings of "race" and "racism"

2. the experiences of white women and women of color, as racially positioned members of society

3. the transformation of these positionings into standpoints for theory and action by feminists, white and of color, in the present "second wave" of feminsim

4. the contexts and voices of white, anti-racist women, prior to the second wave of feminism

5. the relationship between the Civil Rights Movement and feminism; the lessons offered to white feminists by Black and white civil rights activists

6. "new struggles, new dialogues"; building a white anti-racist feminist consciousness; models of work towards coalition and solidarity across race and class lines.

Requirements

Attendance at lectures and weekly discussion sections; 4–5 page paper, due in section, Friday, 29th January; 12–15 page research paper on a topic related to course themes and materials, due last class meeting.

Required Readings

Course Reader
Mab Segrest, *My Mama's Dead Squirrel: Lesbian Essays on Southern Culture*, (1985).
Michael Omi and Howard Winant, *Racial Formation in the U.S., From the 1960s to the 1980s*, (1986).
Elly Bulkin, Minnie Bruce Pratt, and Barbara Smith, *Yours in Struggle: Three Feminist Perspectives on Racism and Anti-Semitism*, (1984).
Lillian Smith, *Killers of the Dream*, (1978).

Week I: January 6 & 8 Definitions of Race and Racism

Patty di Rosa, "Dynamics of Racism—Basic Assumptions"
Omi and Winant, Introduction, pp. 1–6
Stephen Jay Gould, "Human Equality is a Contingent Fact of History"
Statistics: State of California, UCSC and UC System—Racial and Ethnic Inequality

Week II: January 11–15 The Material Experiences of Race, Class, and Gender— Women's lives

Evelyn Nakano Glenn, "The Dialectics of Work: Japanese American Women and Domestic Service, 1905–1940"

Beatriz M. Pesquera, "'Having a Job Gives You Some Sort of Power': Reflections of a Chicana Working Woman"
Diana M. Pearce, "The Feminization of Ghetto Poverty"
Fran Lepper Buss, ed., *Dignity*—"Helen: I've Been with the Best and the Worst"
Angela Y. Davis, *Women, Race and Class*—"The Legacy of Slavery: Standards for a New Womanhood"

Week III: January 18–22 The Social Geography of Childhood—White, Black, and Native American Perspectives

Mab Segrest, *My Mama's Dead Squirrel*—"Mama, Grandma, Carrie, Bell: Race and Class, A Personal Accounting," pp. 146–176
Ruth Frankenberg, "Growing Up White: Feminism, Racism, and the Social Geography of Childhood," manuscript
Minnie Bruce Pratt, in *Yours in Struggle*—"Identity: Skin, Blood, Heart," pp. 11–20
Barbara Cameron, "Gee, You Don't Seem Like an Indian from the Reservation"
Barbara Smith and Beverley Smith, "Across the Kitchen Table: A Sister-to-Sister Dialogue"

Week IV: January 25–29 The Construction of Theory

Nancy Hartsock, "The Feminist Standpoint: Developing the Ground for a Specifically Feminist Historical Materialism"
Patricia Zavella, "The Problematic Relationship of Feminism and Chicana Studies" (draft manuscript)
Chela Sandoval, "Women Respond to Racism"
Maxine Baca Zinn, Lynn Weber Cannon, Elizabeth Higginbottom, and Bonnie Thornton Dill, "The Costs of Exclusionary Practices in Women's Studies"
Trinh T. Minh-ha, "Difference: 'A Special Third World Women Issue'"
Chandra Talpade Mohanty, "Under Western Eyes: Feminism and Colonial Discourse"

ASSIGNMENT DUE JANUARY 29
4–5 pages: Autobiography through a new prism—Explore an aspect of your own life—childhood, school, the trajectory of your family over several generations, being conscious of the patterning of experience in relation to structures of race, class, gender.

Week V: February 1–5 Voices of White Women Against Racism, Before the Second Wave of Feminism

Lillian Smith, *Killers of the Dream*
Part I chapters 1–3, pp. 25–73

Part II chapters 1, 3, 4, pp. 83–98; 114–55
Part III chapter 1, pp. 174–79
Margaret Halsey, *Color Blind*—"Color Conscious," "Up From Apathy," "Would You Like Your Daughter to Marry One?" "The Care and Feeding of Bigots"
Lois Mark Stalvey, *The Education of a WASP*, pp. 1–80
Recommended: Lillian Smith, *Strange Fruit* (available, Bay Tree Bookstore)

Week VI: February 8–12 Mab Segrest: Confronting Racism, Sexism, and Homophobia in the 1980s

Monday, February 8, Mab Segrest, Guest Lecture

Omi and Winant, *Racial Formation in the United States*, pp. 109–35
Mab Segrest, *My Mama's Dead Squirrel*, chapters to be announced

Week VII: February 15–19 The Lessons of the Civil Rights Movement: Anti-racism and Feminism

Sara Evans, *Personal Politics: The Roots of Women's Liberation in the Civil Rights Movement and the New Left*, chapters 2,3,4
Barbara Deming, "Give us this Day"; "In the Birmingham Jail"; "Notes after Birmingham"; "Excerpts from the Prison Notes"
Rhoda Lois Blumberg, "Careers of Women as Civil Rights Activists"; "White Mothers in the American Civil Rights Movement"
Possible guest speaker, to be announced

Week VIII: February 22–26 Civil Rights and the "Great Transformation" in Social Movements

Omi and Winant, *Racial Formation in the United States*, chapters 1–6
Possible guest speaker, to be announced

ASSIGNMENT: one-page proposal for final project, due Friday, 26 February

Week IX: February 29–March 4 New Struggles, New Dialogues, Racism and Anti-Racism in 1980s U.S. Feminism

Bulkin, Pratt and Smith, *Yours in Struggle*

Week X: March 7–11 New Struggles, New Dialogues, Continued—Coalitions and Solidarity

Bernice Johnson Reagon, "Coalition Politics—Turning the Century"
Anne Braden, "Un-doing Racism: Lessons for the Peace Movement"
Ruth Frankenberg and Janet Martens, "Racism: More than a Moral Issue"
Possible guest speaker, to be announced

Week XI: Monday, March 14 only

Conclusions . . .

ASSIGNMENT DUE IN CLASS: 12–15 page paper

Appendix II
Course Bibliography

Books

Bulkin, Elly, Minnie Bruce Pratt, and Barbara Smith. *Yours in Struggle: Three Feminist Perspectives on Racism and Anti-Semitism.* New York: Long Haul Press, 1984.

Omi, Michael, and Howard Winant. *Racial Formation in the United States: From the 1960s to the 1980s.* New York: Routledge and Kegan, 1986.

Segrest, Mab. *My Mama's Dead Squirrel: Lesbian Essays on Southern Culture.* Ithaca: Firebrand Books, 1985.

Smith, Lillian. *Killers of the Dream.* New York: W.W. Norton, 1978.

Articles and Selections

Blumberg, Rhoda Lois. "Careers of Women Civil Rights Activists." *Journal of Sociology and Social Welfare* 7, no. 5 (September 1980).

Braden, Anne. "Un-Doing Racism: Lessons for the Peace Movement." *The Non-Violent Activist* (April-May 1987).

Buss, Fran Leeper. "Helen: I've Been with the Best and the Worst." In *Dignity: Lower Income Women Tell of their Lives and their Struggles.* Ann Arbor: University of Michigan Press, 1985.

Cameron, Barbara. "Gee, You Don't Seem Like an Indian from the Reservation." In *This Bridge Called My Back: Writings By Radical Women of Color*, ed. Cherrie Moraga and Gloria Anzuldua. Watertown, Mass.: Persephone Press, 1981.

Davis, Angela Y. "The Legacy of Slavery: Standards for a New Womanhood." In *Women, Race and Class.* New York: Random House, 1981.

Deming, Barbara. *We Are All Part of One Another.* Edited by Jane Meyerding. Philadelphia: New Society Publishers, 1984 (selections).

di Rosa, Patty. "Dynamics of Racism: Basic Assumptions." Simmons School of Social Work, Boston, Mass.

Evans, Sara. *Personal Politics: The Roots of Women's Liberation in the Civil Rights Movement and the New Left.* New York: Random House, 1979 (selections).

Frankenberg, Ruth. "Growing Up White: Feminism, Racism and the Social Geography of Childhood." In *The Third Wave: Feminist Perspectives on Racism*, ed. Alarcon et al. New York: Kitchen Table Women of Color Press, forthcoming.

Frankenberg, Ruth, and Janet Martens. "Racism: More than a Moral Issue." *Trouble and Strife* 5 (Spring 1985).

Giddings, Paula. *When And Where I Enter*. New York: Bantam, 1985 (selections).

Glenn, Evelyn Nakano. "The Dialectics of Work: Japanese American Women and Domestic Service, 1905–1940." *Feminist Studies* 6:3.

Gould, Stephen Jay. "Human Equality is a Contingent Fact of History." In *The Flamingo's Smile*. New York: W.W. Norton, 1985.

Halsey, Margaret. *Color Blind*. New York: Simon and Schuster, 1946 (selections).

Hartsock, Nancy. "The Feminist Standpoint: Developing the Ground for a Specifically Feminist Historical Materialism." In *Discovering Reality*, ed. Sandra Harding and Merrill B. Hintikka. Dordrecht: D. Riedel, 1983.

Mohanty, Chandra T. "Under Western Eyes: Feminist Scholarship and Colonial Discourses." *Boundary* 2 (Spring-Fall 1984).

Pearce, Diana M. "The Feminization of Ghetto Poverty." *Society* (November–December 1983).

Pesquera, Beatriz M. "Having a Job Gives You Some Sort of Power: Reflections of a Chicana Working Woman." *Feminist Issues* (Fall 1984).

Reagon, Bernice Johnson. "Coalition Politics: Turning the Century." In *Home Girls: A Black Feminist Anthology*, ed. Barbara Smith. New York: Kitchen Table Women of Color Press, 1983.

Sandoval, Chela. "The Struggle Within: Women Respond to Racism." Center for Third World Organizing Occasional Papers, Oakland, Calif., n.d.

Smith, Barbara, and Beverly Smith. "Across the Kitchen Table: A Sister-to-Sister Dialogue." In *This Bridge Called My Back: Writings by Radical Women of Color*, ed. Cherrie Moraga and Gloria Anzaldua. Watertown, Mass.: Persephone Press, 1981.

Stalvey, Lois Mark. *The Education of a WASP*. New York: Morrow, 1970. (selections)

Trinh, Minh-ha T. "Difference: A Special Third World Women Issue." *Discourse* (Fall-Winter, 1986–87).

Zavella, Patricia. "The Problematic Relationship of Feminism and Chicana Studies." University of California at Santa Cruz, manuscript.

Zinn, Maxine Baca, Lynn Weber Cannon, Elizabeth Higginbotham, and Bonnie Thornton Dill. "The Cost of Exclusionary Practices in Women's Studies." *Signs* 9:2 (1986).

Appendix III
Assignment

Autobiography through a new prism
4–5 pages (typed)—due Jan. 29, in section

Explore an aspect of your own life—childhood, community, family, sexuality, the trajectory of your family over several generations, being conscious of the patterning of experience in relation to structures of race (while also not forgetting class and gender—but the focus for this time should be race).

Each of you has your own stories to tell . . . and for all of us the "personal accounting" changes, as our conceptual apparatus changes, shifts, and grows. Each of you has your stories to tell about race and racism, whether your racial identity is that of a member of a racially oppressed group, or a (the?) racially dominant one. Even if you grew up in a racially homogeneous environment, that doesn't mean racism was not present.

Also—what were the other dynamics operating in your life? Issues of sexuality, gender, sexism, class, culture, religion, ethnicity—and how did/do they intersect with race/racism?

Issues: "Watershed" moments in history . . . or in your life, with respect to race and racism: Many of you may have been unborn, or babies, when Martin Luther King or Malcom X were assassinated, or when the Civil Rights Movement began. But some of you were alive and alert. Some of you may have experienced school desegregation programs. And what were/are the moments of intensity with respect to racism, in your own or your family's life?

You can address the past or the present; an hour, a lifetime, or several generations. What I'd like for you to do is to use race, racism, and race difference as the lens or prism through which you order your thoughts—but at the same time not to toss all the other lenses out the window.

Appendix IV
Anti-Racism

1. Admit you are a racist.

2. Recognize stereotypes that are associated with non-white people, question and deconstruct them.

3. Examine your own assumptions, "knowledges" about people who are not "white." Admit to yourself how you are complicit in the perpetuation of these "knowledges." Are you complicit? Honestly ask yourself how you can make a difference both personally and collectively.

4. You must do your own research. Do not expect people who are not white to "teach" you about their oppression.

5. Question universal "truths": What is normal? What is white? What is superiority? What is Third World? What is Feminism? What is problematic about these labels?

6. Recognize that white guilt keeps one from effectively working against racism; it perpetuates denial and continued complicity.

7. Speak out against behaviors that perpetuate prejudice, invalidation of people who are non-privileged (non-white). Intentionality is not the issue.

8. You must claim your ethnic/cultural/"racial" identification and find pride in yourself. With this comes responsibility. With this also comes the recognition of the wholeness of other people (regardless of sex, "race," and ethnicity), the importance of validation, and the connection of integrity and humanity.

Authored by Ekua Omosupe and members of class, "White Women, Racism and Anti-Racism," University of California, Santa Cruz, January–March 1988.

Our Weapons Against Addiction and Co-Dependency

1. Education (not necessarily in the traditional sense)

2. Literacy (how to read the texts, the world, and ourselves within these contexts and outside them)

3. Voice (speak up and out; what you see, what you hear, what you interpret is necessary to forming your own speech)

4. Revision (learning takes place within each second, you are allowed to change your mind, to modify, to recreate. Life and experience are not static)

5. Have a point of view (we all come from different places, different perspectives, different experiences. They are all valid)

6. Challenge (nothing is written in stone. Moses broke the tablets)

7. "Civil Disobedience" (Thoreau did it and he was a "white" male)

8. Resist (you have your chance everyday. Everything costs something. What are you willing to pay?)

9. Tell our stories (they did happen, will continue to happen, and happen everyday)

10. Be angry for the cause: this will give you courage to fight whenever and however you have to

11. Have hope and faith (neither is any good if you don't work)

12. Maintain your traditions (if they are oppressive, create new ones)
customs
language (if you don't know it, find a way to learn it)
herstories/histories
your own stories (make it up if you can't remember or if you disagree with
what anybody–somebody told you)

Authored by Ekua Omosupe and members of class, "White Women, Racism, and
Anti-Racism," University of California, Santa Cruz, January–March 1988.

Notes

1. This chapter is dedicated with gratitude to Rosa Maria Villafañe-Sisolak; Ekua
Omosupe; the students enrolled in the class, "White Women, Racism and Anti-
Racism"; and to Helene Moglen and the Women's Studies Program at the University of
California, Santa Cruz. It was first presented as a paper at the National Association for
Ethnic Studies Annual Conference, Seattle, Washington, March 2–5, 1989.

2. Joan Kelly-Gadol, "The Social Relations of the Sexes: Methodological Implications of Women's History," *Signs* 1 (Summer 1976): 809–825.

3. See, for example Maxine Baca Zinn, Lynn Weber Cannon, Elizabeth Higginbotham, and Bonnie Thornton Dill, "The Cost of Exclusionary Practices in Women's
Studies," *Signs* 11, no. 2 (1986): 290–304.

4. See for example, Hazel V. Carby, "White Woman Listen! Black Feminism and
the Boundaries of Sisterhood," *The Empire Strikes Back: Race and Racism in '70s
Britain* (London: Hutchinson, in association with the Centre for Contemporary Cultural Studies, University of Birmingham, 1982); Angela Y. Davis, *Women, Race and
Class* (New York: Random House, 1981).

5. Mohanty, Trinh, (see Appendix II).

6. There is always the danger of over-simplifying in such a brief recounting of ten
years of (often heated and passionate) struggle. Here, it must not be forgotten that
Marxist and socialist feminists have often been much clearer than most radical feminists about inequalities between women, especially inequalities based on class. However, what radical, Marxist, and socialist feminists have shared throughout most of
their history has been their lack of attention to racism.

7. Combahee River Collective, "A Black Feminist Statement," in *Capitalist Patriarchy and the Case for Socialist Feminism*, ed. Zillah R. Eisenstein (New York:
Monthly Review Press, 1979); Patricia Zavella (see Appendix II).

8. Ruth Frankenberg, "White Women, Race Matters: The Social Construction of
Whiteness," Dissertation, History of Consciousness, University of California at Santa
Cruz, June 1988.

9. The visit involved the cooperation of several departments and units; in addition to speaking to my own class, Mab Segrest's lecture schedule included presentations to literature and community studies classes, and the campus women's center.

10. "Unlearning Racism" refers to a format for workshops on systems of oppression developed by Ricky Sherover-Marcuse, "Unlearning Racism Workshops," 6501 Dana Street, Oakland, CA 94609. Its value lies in part, I believe, in the fact that it provides a safe environment, and conceptual tools, for exploring the affective and psychological dimensions of racism in consciousness, both for oppressed and oppressor class members.

CHAPTER 7

Gender and the Transformation of a Survey Course in Afro-American History

John C. Walter

When I began teaching for the first time as an instructor in 1970 I inherited a survey course in Afro-American history from a professor who had taught it for a number of years. The course was entitled "The Black Man in America." At the time the title seemed perfectly normal to me, for at no time in two graduate schools had anyone raised the question of the appropriateness of such a title. Neither had I, at any time, given the appropriateness of such a title any conscious consideration requiring conclusion, or decision. Also, I suspect I never gave the title much thought because apart from its apparent normality, I as a mere instructor was too busy trying to learn "everything." To critically examine the title of a course and its implications was beyond my capacities. After all, I was still a student, and there was also the dissertation to be finished so that the exalted rank of assistant professor could be achieved. This, I was determined, had to be done within a year.

In retrospect, it seems odd that no student between 1970 and 1976 challenged the title or the content of the course. Neither was there a challenge regarding the role and activities of Black women from anyone in any of the other courses, such as "The Harlem Renaissance" or "Twentieth Century America." In Afro-American courses such as "The Harlem Renaissance" and "The Civil Rights Era," the activities and "contributions" of the most outstanding Black women were automatically described and discussed, but there were no deep-delved, self-conscious examinations of Black women's activities. I never sought to find out what these women's thoughts were on the activities in which they were engaged, never considered the disadvantages they encountered even in working with men of their own race, and when Shirley Chisholm attempted to gain the Democratic nomination for president of the United States in 1972, I did not take her seriously either. Looking back now, it is clear that there were two powerful influences on my outlook and approach to teaching Afro-American and American history at that time.

111

First, I faithfully reproduced most of the postures and views of my graduate school mentors. After all, I wanted to be a good student and a good professor. I believed that these people knew a lot more than I did, which of course they did, and although I argued with them on a number of issues, the history of women was certainly not one of them, because the subject was never broached.

Second, as a beginning professor one had to navigate carefully, of necessity, the treacherous waters of academe. Consequently, even if I had thought a great deal about women's history I would not likely have done much about it; the early 1970s was still the "civil rights era" to me and there was the larger battle to fight, the incorporation of *more* courses on Afro-American history and Black Studies into the curriculum. In Black Studies and Afro-American history I passionately believed, and I did suffer severe setbacks in my "career" because of my unrelenting advocacy of increased Black Studies and Afro-American history offerings. I *knew* about the importance of Black Studies and Afro-American history and was ready to risk tenure in their advocacy, but certainly not for women's history or Afro-American women's history. The fact is, I was not well informed.

In 1976 I changed jobs and once again inherited a course taught by a white male. Apparently tradition was being preserved because the course was entitled "The Black Man in American Society Since 1865." This time I knew the title was inappropriate and that the syllabus also would be severely flawed, which indeed it was. I knew this because I had been busy since 1970. I had obtained the Ph.D. one year after A.B.D., had published and had obtained the rank of associate professor, and more importantly had been able to read a great deal on my own. I had delved deeper into Afro-American history, reading books such as Mary Church Terrell's *A Colored Woman in a White World* (1940), Gerda Lerner's *Black Women in White America: A Documentary History* (1972), Lowenberg and Bogin's *Black Women in Nineteenth Century American Life* (1976), and Toni Cade's *The Black Woman* (1970). Books such as these greatly stimulated my interest in Black women's history, but I was unable to read as much as I desired about them because there were other more urgent tasks to be completed. At this time I decided to examine also what white women were saying. I had begun with Betty Friedan's *The Feminine Mystique* (1963). White and Black women colleagues urged me to do this and so I did. From that "non-scholarly" work I proceeded to, among others, Lois W. Banner's *Women in Modern America: A Brief History* (1974), and J. Stanley Lemons *The Woman Citizen: Social Feminism in the 1920s* (1973).

By 1976, then, I knew something of women's history and resolved that I would not at this stage simply accept another professor's hand-me-down. I restructured the course entirely and argued the case with the professor who was my senior. That argument he never forgot or forgave, and later our disagreement had deleterious consequences for me. Yet the new course I presented in 1976 was no model. Although I included "women" in my lectures much more so than in 1970, and lectured on why the course could no longer be called "The Black Man," and so on, it had no readings by or about Black women. (See syllabus in Appendix A.)

This state of affairs lasted until 1981. In that year professors Johnnella Butler and Margo Culley, of Smith College and the University of Massachusetts, respectively, obtained a Fund for the Improvement of Postsecondary Education (FIPSE) faculty development grant that they called "Black Studies/Women's Studies: An Overdue Partnership." I was accepted to participate because both directors felt that I had done more in my courses to include the history of women than most historians in our vicinity, an initiative they wished to encourage further. I was very amenable because I had never been in a group of Women's Studies scholars before, and I was intrigued by the prospect of Black Studies and Women's Studies faculty working together. Furthermore, I thought I could learn a lot in the projected seminar, although I knew that nearly all the "women scholars" would be concerned with white women. This was of small consequence, however, for white women's history interested me also. I had by now read books such as William Chafe's excellent *The American Woman: Her Changing Social, Economic and Political Roles, 1920–1970* (1972), and Mari Jo and Paul Buhle's *The Concise History of Woman Suffrage* (1978), among others. Such books were, of course, very helpful. One readily extracted the methodologies used and the unorthodox questions asked. But critical reading of these books, though very helpful, would not be as urgently informative and stimulating as an open seminar of professors from five different colleges, including two women's colleges. Indeed, this two-year seminar proved the major turning point in my education.

From the twenty people who met bi-weekly on Thursday nights from 7:30 to 9:30 P.M., I learned more than I could have anywhere imaginable. There were moments of frustration and annoyance, but always there was the feeling that we were engaged in an important journey of exploration and discovery. In the end I emerged from that seminar with the assurance I lacked before, and with the confidence that I could now restructure and transform all my courses to reflect a more comprehensive presentation and analysis of Afro-American history, and of American history. As soon as the seminar was finished I restructured the survey course (see Appendix B), and while it will always be in transformation it will never be transmogrified. That seminar made it possible also for me to introduce a course I had contemplated for some time. In 1980 I had sketched out a course entitled "The Afro-American Woman and the Feminist Movement," but thought then that I needed more "seasoning." The seminar provided it, and at the end of the first year of my participation I felt nearly ready.

As a Black man intending to teach a course dealing with Black women and feminism from the early nineteenth century to the present, I knew life would not be easy. I had noted the bristling body and verbal language of some white female professors in our seminar, who should have known better, when the obvious racism of Susan B. Anthony and other white feminists were commented upon. Therefore, it would have been naive of me to expect any less belligerent behavior from female students at my Seven Sisters woman's college to whom the likes of Carrie Chapman Catt and Alice Paul were heroes. To prepare myself for the expected attack, I used the $1,500 summer stipend provided by the seminar to develop the course for the 1982–83 academic year. Almost immediately after the course was announced, the expected fireworks began.

I recall with great clarity the first encounter of the angry kind. There was a knock on my door and in strolled a female student who angrily demanded to know who did I think I was as a man to be offering a course in women's history. When I responded that I believed I knew more than she did about the subject, that I had spent a whole summer putting the course together, and that I had been thinking about the course and reading various sources prior to the summer, her response was that she was going to take the course only because none other was now offered at the college. Her parting words were "We will see!" She was mild compared to the one who followed. This student began by asking a number of questions, gleaned, I suspected, from a women's literature course she had taken. When I passed the examination with flying colors, which I think infuriated her, she angrily leaned over my desk so far that it necessitated balancing herself with one knee on the edge of my desk, and asked, "As a *Black* man, do you really believe you can teach such a course? And how do you expect me to believe you are not going to use this course to trash white women?" Noting the anger and condescension, I decided against argument and invited her to take the course. I calmly suggested that if she found the course wanting, she would then have an excellent opportunity to "trash" me. That did it! She departed stiffly with the by now expected refrain "We will see!"

There were a few others with aggressive and hostile postures, while most of the rest wanted to know "where I was coming from." Sometimes I would say "nowhere," which caused blank stares tinged with what appeared to be annoyance. On other occasions I would say "I am coming from Jamaica, West Indies," which was indeed true. That one worked after they had put my accent and answer together. Who can be against a fellow whose very presence evokes fond memories of tropical skies, sun and surf, and the sighs of the cooling Trade Winds? Indeed, the ploy worked!

It was odd that no Afro-American student came to complain about the course. I have not yet determined why. Apparently the Afro-American women in the course were quite comfortable with an Afro-American man teaching their history. In contrast, a significant number of white females were at the outset uncomfortable with a man dealing with the history of white women, and a Black one at that. Ultimately, the course was a success. About thirty-eight students attended class the first week and by the end of the second week there were, if I am not mistaken, forty-two enrolled. This number remained constant throughout the semester. Ironically, I received from this class the best student evaluation in my career at this college, and the next year the demand was so high that enrollment had to be limited.

I have briefly chronicled the development of the course, "The Afro-American Woman and the Feminist Movement," because its nascence and maturation had an important effect on the "Survey of Afro-American History" course. Consider, for example, the period 1875–1915. In the ordinary history textbook this span of forty years is divided into two periods called the Gilded Age, and the Progressive Era. This same period is known in Afro-American history as the Era of Accomodation. I am uncertain of when this view of the period began, but it was already current in my graduate school years, 1966 to 1970. Perhaps it began with the publication of August Meier and Elliott Rudwick's *From Plantation to Ghetto*,[1] which was immediately greeted as a work of high scholarship, and which today is seen as a classic, as well as with August Meier's earlier work *Negro Thought in America, 1880–1915*.[2]

In *From Plantation to Ghetto*, Meier and Rudwick conclude that the period following the demise of Radical Reconstruction and preceding World War I was characterized by Black accomodation. In order to substantiate their argument, the authors, while acknowledging the number of protest leaders and radical movements, emphasized the activity and power of Booker T. Washington. The centrality of Washington to their thesis is seen in the title of the chapter devoted to the period in *From Plantation to Ghetto*: " 'Up' from Slavery: The Era of Accomodation." Although the authors acknowledge the activity of the Afro-American Council (p. 223) and the Niagara Movement (p. 226), and mention in passing "the noted antilynching crusader Ida Wells-Barnett" (p. 224), they conclude that "the chief opposition to accomodation came from a small group of Northern intellectuals" (p. 224).

Booker T. Washington's behind the scenes activities are also discussed in the Third Edition.

> Overtly he might urge blacks to acquiesce in the separate-but-equal doctrine; privately he had entree to white social circles in the North and abroad that few Southern whites could enter, and secretly he aided the fight against railroad segregation. . . . He hired a lobbyist to defeat legislation that, if passed, would have encouraged segregation on interstate trains in the North. . . . Behind the scenes he was the most influential politician in the history of American Negroes and surreptitiously fought the disfranchisement laws. . . . he clandestinely spent thousands of dollars financing the fruitless

test cases taken to the Supreme Court against the Southern disfranchisement amendments. (p. 222–23)

The authors also recognize that the philosophies of self-help, racial solidarity, and assimilation to white middle-class values often went hand in hand:

> On the one hand, this cluster of ideologies functioned as an accomodation to the system of segregation and discrimination; in fact, in contrast with the 1950s when this viewpoint was held by militant protest leaders like Frederick Douglass, in the expression of Southern leaders it now became explicitly identified with a program of conciliation and accomodation. On the other hand, this way of thinking also functioned as a means of inculcating group pride and self-respect. (p. 213)

Despite the ample evidence of ever-present resistance to white racism, Meier and Rudwick assert their basic thesis, that the period can be characterized as the "Age of Accommodation," because:

> Protest, agitation, political action had failed. There had been a definite trend in the direction of accommodation in the 1880s and 1890s, and at the turn of the century certain prominent protest leaders, who would later be among Washington's most prominent critics, in their despair thought that his method might be of some help. (p. 229)

In his earlier text, *Negro Thought in America, 1880–1915*, Meier explores in greater depth the thought and policies of Booker T. Washington and his contemporaries. In chapter 5, entitled "Protest and Accomodation," he acknowledges the existence of strong currents of protest. He cites the 1885 formation of the Baltimore Brotherhood of Liberty, which pledged to "use all legal means within our power to procure and maintain our rights" (p. 70); and which successfully "obtained additional school facilities, agitated on lynching, and served as a legal redress society" (p. 70). Another example provided is that of T. Thomas Fortune who "in 1883 urged that Negroes put off first-class coaches should defend themselves; one could not be killed in a better cause" (p. 73). In January 1890, Fortune delivered an even more militant address:

> He defended agitation, even revolution, as necessary for progress and the preservation of rights. . . . He excoriated the nation for betraying the Negro who must "fight fire with fire. . . . It is time to face the enemy and fight inch by inch for every right he denies us." (p. 129)

Nevertheless, Meier concludes that:

As the century drew to a close, support for Washington increased. W.E.B. DuBois later recalled that criticism, at first widely voiced, largely disappeared. In those dreary years the advancing tide of segregation and disfranchisement made protest seem futile, and even some who, like the Grimke brothers, were later numbered among the Tuskegeean's most distinguished opponents, supported his program (p. 171).

In order to arrive at his conclusion, Meier avoids exploring the strong stand taken Ida B. Wells-Barnett at the 1889 Afro-American Council convention. He notes that:

> In her talk on mob violence she charged that Washington was greatly mistaken in thinking that Negroes would gain their rights merely by making themselves a significant element in the nation's economy and criticized President McKinley for failing to give attention to the matter of the race's rights. (p. 172)

He moves quickly, however, from Wells-Barnett's assertion to Washington's assumption of control of the council.

Meier does avoid oversimplifying Washington's position. He examines Washington's covert activity and provides "an interpretation" of Washington's infamous Atlanta Exposition, explaining that "careful reading of the address indicates that it could also be interpreted as including ultimate goals more advanced than white Southerners could possibly support" (p. 101). Nevertheless, he focuses on Washington's "accomodative" ideology, and his constant deprecation of protest and agitation, noting that "As conditions grew worse Washington became more rather than less conciliatory" (p. 107), although after 1895 he argued that "separate but equal facilities would be satisfactory" (p. 108). Documenting the brutality of the regressive post-Reconstruction period, Meier notes:

> Increasingly, as disfranchisement grew and office holding decreased, Negroes became disillusioned with politics and placed more and more emphasis on economic and moral development as a substitute for and as a prerequisite to political activity. In fact economic improvement was primarily regarded as a temporary accommodation to realities, and an indirect technique for achieving political rights. (p. 35)

Examining the decline of Washington during the early twentieth century, Meier remarks

> Probably nothing Washington could have done would have prevented the rise of the NAACP. For the continued deterioration of conditions during the

period of his ascendancy led to ideological disillusionment with his program, and this fact, coupled with the reform spirit of the Progressive Era, encouraged the rise of protest organization. (p. 184)

Had Meier examined the activities of Afro-American women more closely he might have recognized the strong current of protest that had continued throughout the period between the demise of Radical Reconstruction and the start of World War I.

In both texts, the authors, perhaps due to the tenor or the times, paid relatively little attention to the activities of Afro-American women. Had they examined the lives, publications, and other activities of Black women, they might not have concluded as comfortably that the period was indeed the "Age of Accommodation."

It is useful to note the earlier quote in *Negro Thought in America* that "Washington's critics consisted of a minority of the intellectual and professional men." What appears obvious is that the emphasis is on the role of men, and that women who were opposed to Washington and staunch non-accommodationists were not given equal attention. Close examination of the period reveals that there were a significant number of women who opposed Washington, and who consistently displayed in this period no accommodationist behavior of any kind. The conclusion in *From Plantation to Ghetto* is also predictable, because one searches in vain in its index for the names of these women. One does not find, for example, Victoria Earle Matthews, an outstanding writer and civil rights advocate of the era, and a complete militant. Neither is Frances E. W. Harper, the outstanding writer and author of *Iola Leroy*, in evidence. In addition, one looks in vain for the name of Pauline Hopkins, a strong opponent of the accommodationist ideas of Booker T. Washington and his cohorts.

Of course Ida Wells-Barnett is discussed for her role in the anti-lynching campaign of the late nineteenth and early twentieth century. One does not find the name of Mary Church Terrell in the index, but Robert H. Terrell, her husband, is listed and discussed. Yet the case could easily be made for the inclusion of Mary Church Terrell. In fact, she was a far more active person than her husband in Negro affairs during her lifetime. She was an early member of the NAACP and eventually became the president of the Washington D.C. branch. Previously, she served as president of the National Association of Colored Women. Indeed her activities with the NAACP so angered Booker T. Washington that he complained to her husband. Meier notes this in *Negro Thought*, but not in *From Plantation to Ghetto*, where the "accomodation" thesis is presented.

There were quite a number of other Black women, all effective non-accommodationists. For example, there was Anna Julia Cooper, regarded then and now as an outstanding educator, who lectured widely and wrote the outstanding book, *A Voice From the South* (1892). There was also Fannie Barrier Williams, who spoke up tirelessley against the smear campaigns of bigots who branded Black women as immoral.

It is understood that not all these women could be dealt with in a brief book expected to be used in a survey course in Afro-American history. But the fact that they are not mentioned at all means that the student who takes a one-semester course to satisfy in part a liberal arts curriculum requirement, and who will not be pursuing a degree in history, will be left with the impression that Black women in this period did very little, made very few contributions, and that nearly all important activities were conducted by men.

For those who consider the years 1877 to 1915, or to World War I, an accommodationist era, the problem lies in what activities by individuals or by a people are considered important. The argument is often made by the misinformed as well as the uninformed that the African-American influence and contribution to the American national experience could not have been great, because Black people have never weilded great political power. As a result, the argument goes, they made no important decisions affecting national life as did white people. As crude and rude as this view is, it still exists, albiet in refined variations among scholars. It is a reason why on many campuses today, African-American history is still viewed with a jaundiced eye. This same attitude prevails towards women's history, and more so towards Black women's history. In neglecting Black women's experience in the period under discussion, the picture that results is incomplete. This incompletion becomes problematic when a label is ascribed to a period, a label that is a direct result not so much of the exclusion of women, but moreso because the criteria used in deciding who and how many should be included are based on a perception of values historically characterizing male activities. Thus, the "Era of Accomodation" is a gross misnomer.

Jacquelyn Jones has pointed out in her book, *Labor of Love, Labor of Sorrow: Black Women, Work and the Family, From Slavery to the Present*, that:

> After emancipation, schooling of Black chldren continued to have sinister connotations in the minds of white Southerners. . . . Consequently, teachers as a matter of course performed their duties with a certain racial self-consciousness, and it is not surprising that the period's outspoken, national Black female leaders (among them Fanny Jackson Coppin, Lucy Laney, Charlotte Hawkins Brown, and Fannie Barrier Williams) began their careers with life long service as southern elementary school teachers.[3]

Jones demonstrates the value of this kind of activity as historical fact to the full comprehension of the Black American historical experience. Along the same lines, she also points out an even more subtle contribution of Black women in the resistance to oppression that is clearly non-accomodating. She writes: "The preservation of family integrity served as a political statement to the white south. To nurse a child, send a daughter to school, feed a hungry family . . . these simple acts of domesticity, acquired special significance" (p. 107–08).

Professor Jones is correct in reaching this conclusion, but it is not the prevailing view among American historians that preservation of family integrity is a political act on the part of Black women. It does not rank with fiery speeches from the pulpit, or with the leadership of civil rights organizations. As a result, the history of Black women has been slighted and the history of Afro-American people distorted and will remain so until the criteria for judging worth in all spheres, political and otherwise, change. When this change becomes noticeable, the syllabi of courses in Afro-American Studies will change noticeably.

I have used the period from 1877 to 1915 to illustrate the importance of the inclusion of Black women in Afro-American history, for even today, despite pressure from the various Ethnic and Women's Studies programs, many professors simply attach material on previously neglected groups to the end of their syllabi, in the name of curriculum revision, balancing, or integration. If the scholars were to stop and to listen to the new included voices, however, they would find that more than addition is required; rather a complete transformation is required. My experience in teaching and revising an African American history course that covers the so-called Age of Accommodation revealed the depth of change necessary. The inclusion of texts and lectures on the experience and activities of African American women during the period of 1877 to 1915 required a fundamental rethinking of basic assumptions about the period in question, and indeed the labelling of the period. In my case it ended with radical restructuring of the course, and the beginning of research on African-American women during this period.

Appendix A*
Afro-American History Survey: Fall 1977

*All courses in the appendices represent gradual change. They now are more fully transformed as the scholarhip has become avilable.
This is an introductory course on the history of Black people. No prerequisites are required except a willingness to work hard and to THINK.

FORMAT:

Lectures, readings, and discussion.

A brief paper is required for this course. *A 15-MINUTE QUIZ MAY BE EXPECTED ON ANY TUESDAY!* These quizzes count toward the final grade and will be based heavily, but not exclusively, on your readings. *BE PREPARED!* There will be two (2) 1¹/₂ hour examinations and one final examination that will last three (3) hours. Grading is "progressive." Please see me about this.

TEXTS:

1. Leslie Fishel and Benjamin Quarles, *The Black American* (Glenview, Ill.: Scott Foresman, 1976).

2. E. L. Thornbrough, *Black Reconstructionists* (Englewood Cliffs, N.J.: Prentice Hall, 1972).

3. Joel Williamson, *The Origins of Segregation* (Lexington, Mass.: D.C. Heath & Co., 1968).

4. Dan T. Carter, *Scottsboro* (Fair Lawn, N.J.: Oxford University Press, Inc., 1971).

5. Charles W. Chestnutt, *The House Behind the Cedars* (New York: Oxford University Press, 1971).

6. Nathan Huggins, *Harlem Renaissance* (New York: Oxford University Press, 1971).

7. W. E. B. DuBois, *The Autobiography of W.E.B. DuBois* (New York: International Publishers, 1968).

8. Martin Luther King, *Why We Can't Wait* (New York: Signet Books, 1964).

9. E. David Caronon, *Black Moses: Marcus Garvey* (Madison: University of Wisconsin Press, 1969).

10. James Baldwin, *The Fire Next Time* (New York: Dell Publishing Co., 1962).

WEEK I
Introduction

WEEK II
A. American Society after the Civil War: The Northern Catalyst and the Southern Substrate.
READINGS: Fishel and Quarles: pp. 258–80
B. The Black Condition after the Civil War: The Interface.
READINGS: Thornbrough: *Black Reconstructionists*

WEEK III
  A. & B. The role and Legacy of Blacks in Reconstruction.
  READINGS: *Reread* Thornbrough: *Black Reconstructionists*

WEEK IV
  A. The Beginnings of Black Peonage.
  READINGS: Fishel and Quarles: pp. 280–93
              DuBois: Chapters 6–9
  B. The Death of Reconstruction and the Coming of Jim Crow.
  READINGS: Fishel and Quarles: pp. 293–305

WEEK V
  A. From Black Republicanism to Populism: The Peculiar Extension of Black
     Political Life.
  READINGS: Fishel and Quarles: pp. 306–50
              DuBois: Chapters 10–12
  B. FIRST HOUR EXAMINATION

WEEK VI
  A. The Death of Douglass and the Capitulation to "Accomodation"?
  READINGS: Chestnutt: *The House Behind the Cedars*
  B. Bishop Turner, Thomas Fortune et al. and the Origins of Twentieth-Century
     Black Nationalism.

WEEK VII
  A. The Progressive Era or The Conservative Era? Black Progressivism in a
     Regressive Era: Urban League, etc.
  READINGS: Williamson: *The Origins of Segregation*
              Fishel and Quarles: pp. 374–93
              DuBois: Chapters 13–15
  B. The Black Immigrant Impulse in Black Progressivism.
  READINGS: Fishel and Quarles: pp. 394–401

WEEK VIII
  A. & B. The Geopolitics of the Harlem Renaissance. The Cultural Dimensions
         of the Harlem Renaissance.
  READINGS: Fishel and Quarles: pp. 402–46
              Huggins: *Harlem Renaissance*

WEEK IX
  A. Communism, Socialism, the Depression, and Black Nationalism.
  READINGS: Carter: *Scottsboro*
              DuBois: Chapters 16–17
  B. Blacks and the New Deal.
  READINGS: Fishel and Quarles: pp. 446–67
              DuBois: Chapters 18–19

WEEK X
A. Review and Discussion.
B. SECOND HOUR EXAMINATION.

WEEK XI
A. Prelude to Black Revolution: A. Philip Randolph and Black Political Protest Movements in World War II. James Farmer and the C.O.R.E.
READINGS: Fishel and Quarles: pp. 467–89
B. Origins of The Civil Rights Movement: The Texas White Primaries and *Brown v. The Board.*
READINGS: Fishel and Quarles: pp. 490–518
Dubois: Chapters 20–24

WEEK XII
A. Blacks in the New Frontier: The Civil Rights Act of 1964–1965.
READINGS: Fishel and Quarles: pp. 518–35
B. Dr. King, Non-Violence, and Black Progress.
READINGS: King: *Why We Can't Wait*

WEEK XIII
A.& B. Black Power, or Black and White Power—R.A.M., Panthers, Muslims, and Others.
READINGS: Fishel and Quarles: pp. 536–74

WEEK XIV
A. The Decline of Black Power—Rap Brown, Huey Newton, and Eldridge Cleaver—Where are They?
READINGS: Fishel and Quarles: 575–94
B. Retrospect and Black Prospects.
READINGS: Reread King: *Why We Can't Wait*
Dubois: Chapters 1–5

READING PERIOD

WEEK XV *EXAMINATIONS*

**Appendix B
Department of Afro-American Studies
History of the Afro-American People
Syllabus (1981)**

This course is an examination of the broad contours of the history of Afro-Americans in the United States. Students will consider the cosmology of the West African, American slavery systems and the Black American's resistance; the rise of Jim Crow;

W. E. B. DuBois's, Booker T. Washington's, and Marcus Garvey's philosophies of protest; the tactics of Martin Luther King, Jr., A. Philip Randolph, and Malcolm X.

Course Format: Lectures, discussions, brief paper, and if available, a film or two. There will be two 1 1/2-hour exams and a scheduled final exam.

Grading: 25–25–50

Required Texts: Quarles, Benjamin. *The Negro in the American Revolution.*
Blassingame, John. *The Slave Community.*
Stampp, Kenneth. *The Era of Reconstruction: 1865–1877.*
Davis, Angela. *Women, Race and Class.*
Meier, August. *From Plantation to Ghetto.*
Boles, John. *Black Southerners.*
Sitkoff, Harvard. *The Struggle for Black Equality.*
Genovese, Eugene. *From Rebellion to Revolution: American Slave Revolts in the New World.*

Course Outline

WEEK 1
1. The uses of the Afro-American past.
2. Africa on the eve of European slavery.
3. Myths and realities of the African past.
READINGS: M & R: Chapter 1
Boles: Introduction & Chapter 1

WEEK 2
1. The inception and legal institutionalization of slavery.
2. The colonial mind and colonial slavery.
3. Blacks on the eve of the American Revolution.
4. The free Negro.
READINGS: M & R: Chapter 2
Boles: Chapter 2
Davis: Chapter 1

WEEK 3
1. Blacks in the American Revolution.
2. Slavery ends in the North; Mr. Walter's Thesis.
3. Slavery as a Southern "phenomenon."
4. Mr. Elkins's Thesis.
5. The Southern slave and the free community.
READINGS: Quarles: *Entire Book*
Blassingame: *Entire Book*

WEEK 4
1. Slave and Indian relations.

2. Slave rebellions.
3. Abolitionism, emigration, and colonization.
4. The role of the free Negro and the Black church.
READINGS: Boles: Chapters 3 & 4
M & R: Chapter 3
Davis: Chapters 2 & 3
Genovese: *Entire Book*

WEEK 5
1. Did slavery pay?
2. Why the Civil War?
3. The "Black Factor" in the Civil War.
READINGS: M & R: Chapter 4
Boles: Chapters 5 & 6

WEEK 6
1. Review.
2. First "hour" exam.

WEEK 7
1. The Black community after the Civil War.
2. The role of women.
3. The role and legacy of Blacks in Reconstruction.
4. The Civil Rights Act of 1870–1875; the beginning of the end.
READINGS: Stampp: Chapters 1–6
Boles: Chapter 8
David: Chapters 4–5

WEEK 8
1. The death of Reconstruction, and
2. The coming of Jim Crow.
3. From Black Republicanism to Populism.
4. Black women and suffragism.
READINGS: Stampp: Chapter 7
David: Chapters 6–7

WEEK 9
1. SPRING BREAK

WEEK 10
1. The death of Frederick Douglass and the capitulation to "accomodation."
2. Bishop Turner and the origins of twentieth-century Black Nationalism.
3. Black women and the campaign against lynching and
4. The Progressive/Regressive Era; accomodation?
READINGS: Davis: Chapters 8–9
Sitkoff: Chapter 1

WEEK 11
1. The Black immigrant impulse in Black Progressivism.
2. The Harlem Renaissance: Black women writers in the Harlem Renaissance Era.
READINGS: M & R: Chapter 5
          Sitkoff: Chapter 2

WEEK 12
                         All Papers Due
1. Communism, Socialism, and the New Black Nationalism.
2. Blacks in the Depression and New Deal.
3. Prelude to Black Revolution; A. Philip Randolph and the M.O.W.M.
4. Black women and communism.
READINGS: M & R: Chapter 6
          David: Chapter 10

WEEK 13
1. The legal origins of the Civil Rights Movement. The Texas White Primaries through *Brown v. Board of Education*.
2. The Black Revolt.
3. The Civil Rights Acts, 1964, 1965, and 1968.
4. Title VII and women's rights.
READINGS: M & R: Chapter 7
          Davis: Chapters 11–13
          Sitkoff: Chapters 3–4

WEEK 14
1. The Black Power ideology.
2. Black Panthers, Black Muslims, SNCC, and others.
3. The decline of Black Power.
4. The decline of the American State.
READINGS: M & R: Chapter 8
          Sitkoff: Chapters 5–7

WEEK 15   Final Exam—as scheduled

Appendix C
Afro-American Studies
History of Afro-American Women and the Feminist Movement (1987)

This course is a survey of the development of the "Feminist Movement" from the early nineteenth century to the present. It will treat the relationship between Black and white women in their struggle for independence, at times together and at times apart. The reasons, process, and results of collaboration as well as opposition will be delineated and discussed. Recent and contemporary attempts at cooperation will be examined and assessments made of their viability.

This is a survey course: There are no prerequisites, although a survey course in American or Afro-American History would be useful.

Possible Texts

1. Mansbridge, Jane J. *Why We Lost the ERA.* Chicago: University of Chicago, 1986.

2. Brent, Linda. *Incidents in the Life of a Slave Girl.* New York: H. B. J., 1978.

3. DuBois, Carol Ellen. *Feminism and Suffrage, 1848–1869.* Ithaca: Cornell, 1978.

4. Lerner, Gerda. *The Majority Finds Its Past.* New York: Oxford, 1979.

5. Evans, Sarah. *Personal Politics.* New York: Vintage, 1980.

6. Hooks, Bell. *Feminist Theory: From Margin to Center.* Boston: South End Press, 1984.

7. Giddings, Paula. *When and Where I Enter.* New York: Morrow, 1984.

8. Banner, Lois W. *Women in Modern America.* New York: H.B.J., 1984.

WEEK 1
    a. Introduction
    b. Feminism. What is it?
    c. 18- & 19th-century views on women.
    d. Feminist consciousness and the muted voice of the Black woman.
    READINGS: Brent: Entire Book
                Lerner: Pages 1, 54, 150–64

WEEK 2
    a. Abolitionism and Feminism: Practical experience in protest, propaganda, and organization.
    b. The Seneca Falls Convention.
    READINGS: DuBois: Introduction and Chapter 1
                Lerner: pp. 54–92

WEEK 3
    a. From Seneca (1848) to Kansas (1968).
    b. The Rejection of Black women.
    c. Black women's perspectives after the Civil War.
    d. Black and White Feminism (1869–1890)

READINGS: DuBois: Chapters 2-6
Lerner: pp. 92-122

WEEK 4
a. The White Woman's Club movement
b. The Black Woman's Club movement.
c. Attempts at "Integration," 1896-1920.
READINGS: Giddings: Chapter 1-6
Lerner: pp. 437-72

WEEK 5
a. Review.
b. *EXAM.*

WEEK 6
a. The successful crusade for White women's suffrage, 1900-1920.
b. The disfranchisement of Blacks and the response of Black women.
READINGS: Giddings: Chapter 7
Lerner: pp. 122-50

WEEK 7
a. The 19th Amendment and the legacy for Black and White women.
b. The decline of social feminism, 1920-1960.
c. The rising tide of Black Women 1920-1960.
READINGS: Giddings: Chapters 8-12
Lerner: pp. 479-526

WEEK 8
a. The long-awaited intersection.
b. Women's Rights and Civil Rights, 1954-1968.
READINGS: Giddings: Chapters 13-15
Evans: *Entire Book*
Lerner: pp. 563-85

WEEK 9
a. From "Mystique" to Second Wave.
b. Are Black women in this ocean?
READINGS: Giddings: Chapters 16-20
Hooks: Chapters 1-4
Lerner: pp. 585-614

WEEK 10
a. Feminism or Black solidarity?
b. Retrospect and prospect.
READINGS: Hooks: Chapters 5-12
Mansbridge: *Entire Book*

WEEK 11   *Final Examination*

Notes

1. August Meier and Elliott Rudwick, *From Plantation to Ghetto*, 3d ed. (New York: Hill & Wang, 1976).

2. August Meier, *Negro Thought in America, 1880–1915* (Ann Arbor: University of Michigan, 1973).

3. Jacquelyn Jones, *Labor of Love, Labor of Sorrow* (New York: Vintage Books, 1985), 114.

CHAPTER 8

Black Studies in Liberal Arts Education

Johnnetta B. Cole

As an African American and as an educator, I turn with you to a critical assessment of Black Studies in liberal arts education.[1] I dare to do so not in conflict with but rather in concert with of other scholars and activists in this process. The Curriculum Development Project of the Institute of the Black World; the Howard University FifteenYear Assessment of Black Studies Conference; the symposium on Black Studies and Women's Studies entitled "An Overdue Partnership" organized by Smith College's Afro-American Studies Department and the University of Massachusett's Women's Studies Program; and the ongoing work of the National Council of Black Studies are only a few of the many organized discussions of the state and potential of Black Studies. Thus my comments and analysis should be viewed as a part of this widespread and ongoing discussion.

This discussion of Black Studies is limited to liberal arts curricula in predominantly white institutions of higher education, but not because what takes place in Black colleges, elementary schools and high schools, and in community settings is unimportant. It is simply that clarity and conciseness require that we place some limitations on the boundaries of this discussion.

The History of Black Studies One More Time

"Any attempt to discuss the question of what has come to be called Black Studies . . . outside of a political perspective is futile"[2]. This is very obviously the case for the late 1960s surge for Black Studies. It is equally so when we review the prolonged history of what is the minimal call of Black Studies: "the inclusion of our point of view and our cultural heritage in educational curricula on a basis of equality . . . "[3] A political perspective is essential to an understanding of the most comprehensive meaning of Black Studies: the development of a fundamentally new way for Black people to look at themselves and be looked at by others; and a fundamentally new way for Black people to be actively involved in affecting positive changes in their condition, and thus in their society and in the world.

African American concern about their formal education and their role in that process goes back at least to the creation of the Freedman Schools at the end of the Civil War. During the period of Reconstruction, when there was blatant white control of segregated Black educational institutions, Afro-Americans spoke out passionately for "a stronger, even a controlling voice in the process and institutions of education for our people".[4] Such was the view of C. E. Becker, expressed in a letter to Henry L. Morehouse, dated November 17, 1882:

> . . . we are willing to return thanks to the many friends who have assisted us in educating ourselves thus far, but we have now reached the point where we desire to endeavor to educate ourselves, to build school houses, churches, colleges, and universities, by our own efforts . . . ere we sacrifice our manhood.[5]

Today we would refer to our peoplehood, but the sentiment of this statement remains:

> . . . the desire to establish curricula to serve the needs of our people—to provide skills training, to transmit our values, to pass on a dignified version of our history and culture in a world in which our very persons were met (and are met) almost without exception with condescension, scorn, and hostility.[6]

When we turn to the most recent expression of the long-standing drive for Black Studies, that which began in the late sixties, the importance of placing the issue in a political context is extraordinarily clear. For as Julius Lester puts it:

> Black Studies carries the burden of its beginning. It was not invited into the curricula of colleges and universities because it was thought to have something new and vital to offer the humanistic body of knowledge. Indeed, it was not invited into curricula at all. It fought its way in through demonstrations in the sixties and seventies. Black studies was born because a man named King was assassinated.[7]

During the late sixties and early seventies, there was a substantial increase in the numbers of Black youths in American colleges and universities, two-thirds of whom were at white universities.[8] Their presence on college campuses was clearly related to the demands of the Civil Rights and Black Power movements of that period.

In ways unprecedented in our history, these young Afro-Americans forced us to confront the relationship between what was going on "in the streets" of America and what was going on, and in their view should go on, in the classrooms of U.S. educational institutions. These Black students recognized a relationship between their lives and the lives of the masses of Black people who were expressing their anger and frustration in the burnings and lootings of urban rebellions.

Black scholars, few in numbers on white campuses, joined with their students. In Vincent Harding's words: "When the students rose on the campuses and demanded our presence, or pressed for greater visibility and recognition for our work, we claimed, with them, indissoluble bonds to the heaving life of the Black masses."[9]

Black Studies must be understood as a part of that Black Student Movement—"the takeovers of computer centers, academic buildings and student unions; the creation of Black Student Unions and Black Cultural Centers; [and] the emergence of Black nationalist ideology within the potential Black petty bourgeois stratum."[10]

A full understanding of the rise of Black Studies also requires an appreciation of the influential interaction between the Black Student Movement and the general student movement of the sixties and seventies, and between the student movements and the resistance and revolt of the "anti-war movement".

The Five Challenges of the Black Studies Critique

The beginnings of Black Studies in liberal arts institutions is usually dated with the establishment of an Afro-American Studies Department at San Francisco State College in 1968. However, programs in Afro-American Studies existed at other white institutions before 1968; for example, Cornell University had a functioning program in 1967. Intimately tied to the Black Student Movement, and fueled by the Civil Rights and Black Liberation movements, Black Studies is fundamentally a critique of educational institutions in American society, and a set of proposals for beginning the long and difficult process of change in those institutions.

The Black Studies critique explicitly addresses shortcomings, omissions, and distortions in liberal arts curricula and institutions as they affect Afro-Americans. It also charges that the liberal arts curricula falls far short of what is required to correctly educate white youth.

The Black Studies critique has taken the form of volumes of written and spoken words: explained before white faculties and administrators, written in the paragraphs of proposals for initiating programs and departments, analyzed in scholarly journals and popular articles, and debated in the string of conferences and symposia that took place all over the United States.

I suggest that the major points of the Black Studies critique can be summarized in terms of five challenges. Black Studies challenges *what* is taught in the liberal arts curricula of America's colleges and universities; *to whom* and *by whom* it is taught; *how* it is taught; and *why* it is taught. These challenges represent a sweeping critique, followed by plans, proposals, curricula, and projects designed to begin to correct certain fundamental problems in American higher education.

What is Taught

Scholars and activists of Black Studies argue that a profound chasm separates the claim and the reality of what is taught in America's liberal arts institutions. The claim, simply put, is that liberal arts education is an objective, value-free exploration of the range of human history, activity, knowledge, and creativity. The reality is that this education is based on a Eurocentric perspective of the world, reflecting a racial, gender, and class bias that distorts African and African American experiences.[11] "The history of America looks very different viewed from a cotton patch."[12]

There is no shortage of examples of these biases in mainstream scholarship. Among the examples frequently referred to are the notion in mainstream scholarship that Black culture is either nonexistent or merely a deviation from middle-class Euro-American culture; and the Moynihanian concept of the Black matriarchy. Another familiar example is the litanies of great classics that always refer to Mozart but never to Coltrane, to Conrad but not to Achebe, to Virginia Woolf but not to Margaret Walker, and to John Stewart Mill, but never to W. E. B. DuBois.

The problem with the notions of "objectivity" and "value-free science" is that these sacred fetishes of Western scholarship are in reality, as Lewis King notes, " . . . a metaphor of the collective subjectivity of a particular group in history and the abstract representations of a singular race, sex and economic class".[13] Thus Black Studies argues for a corrective approach that would negate the myths and distortions inherent in traditional "White Studies" construction of Black people and indeed the world; explore all of history (and herstory as well); consistently address racism; and institutionalize a Black presence in American education.

Black Studies challenges what is traditionally taught, and introduces a different curriculum.

> By its very nature Black Studies begins with the life and culture of Blacks, and in the American context that means a race of people brought into this country for one purpose and one only: to be slaves (I would not be in America if not for slavery, or if one of my ancestors had missed the boat). Thus the vantage point of Black Studies is qualitatively different from that of the traditional disciplines. Black Studies does not begin with the conquering

of kingdoms, the decrees of monarchies, or the rhymed lines of a sonnet. It begins in a group experience of suffering and agony, of struggle and survival. When such is the crux of experience, definitions of life are vastly different.

Black Studies is not only the study of the history, culture, and lives of Blacks. It is the point of view that comes from a reality so tenuous that one did not own even the very breath of his or her life. This reality is the heart of Black Studies. As W. E. B. DuBois said almost 50 years ago: Instead of the university growing down and seeking to comprehend in its curriculum the life and experience, the thought and expression of the lower classes, it almost invariably tended to grow up and narrow itself to a sublimated elite of mankind.[14]

By Whom and To Whom

Black Studies during the 1960s and 70s took a critical look at the participants in American higher education. The ideal, often purported to be a reality, is that institutions of higher education choose professors because of their intellectual strengths and ability to contribute to the educational enterprise. Similarly, students are presumably selected because of their demonstrated abilities and intellectual potential. If this is indeed the case, Black Studies proponents ask, then why are almost all professors white male Ph.D.s of a middle-class mind-set if not origin, who have been trained by scholars of a similar background? If intellectual potential really matters in the selection of students, and not simply demonstrated ability as indicated by culturally biased test scores and good grades in well financed middle class white schools, then why are there so few Black and other Third World students in America's colleges and universities? The truth, say the advocates of Black Studies, is that the overwhelming majority of the participants in liberal arts institutions reflect and reinforce the very streams of thought that dominate the curriculum: white, male, and middle class.

The reality of who teaches and who is taught in liberal arts institutions has led the proponents of Black Studies to make demands for a substantial increase in the number of Black faculty. They also ask that colleges and universities consider some individuals without academic degrees but with a wealth of practical and scholarly experience for faculty positions. Black Studies activists demand changes in admissions criteria, increases in financial aid, and expanded academic and other support services to give more Black students a fighting chance to go to college. Finally, advocates of Black Studies often fight for academic offerings for community residents to be held in community settings.

The call is very simply to bring about a Black presence in liberal arts institutions, such that Black students will have Black role models among their faculty and staff and all students will have the possibility to learn experientially about peoples, cultures, histories, and ideas that differed from their own.

How What is Taught is Taught

The Black Studies critique of liberal arts education also addresses questions of pedagogy. In short, not only is there a need to change what is taught, to whom and by whom, but also to qualitatively overhaul methods of teaching and learning. Thus Black Studies argues for a number of far-reaching reforms. There should be a greater emphasis on student participation in the teaching/learning process, rather than the banking process where the teacher deposits knowledge into students' heads and periodically (at exam time) makes withdrawals. There should be a closer relationship between the academy and "the outside world," in contrast to the traditional model of the academy as an isolated ivory tower. Thus students should be encouraged to engage in field projects and practicums that place them in dynamic interactions with communities. The competitive atmosphere that is so deeply embedded in the American educational process is also challenged. Black Studies proposes that students should be encouraged to engage in more cooperative learning experiences. Finally, the loyalty to disciplines over knowledge, the territoriality of departments, and the sanctity of specialized, indeed professional versus general education, are questioned. The call is for far greater dependence on an interdisciplinary approach. Julius Lester, a professor of Afro-American Studies, exemplifies this approach:

> . . . Black Studies cannot concern itself with the University as an apprenticeship system. This does not mean discouraging a student who wants to be a specialist in the field. However, it does not focus its energies on this student, [or] find its raison d'etre here. The mission of Black Studies is to invite and guide students into human experience as it has affected the lives of Blacks and to examine the variety of ways in which Blacks have responded.

> I am not interested, therefore, in creating intellectuals or for that matter in even teaching potential intellectuals. I am interested in that student who will leave the university and go into life, who will, in all likelihood, end up with a job rather than a career. Instead of demanding that this student write a critical analysis of *Native Son,* I ask soemthing harder. I ask the student to learn what he or she feels freedom to be. What is instructive is how often the students have to be convinced that what they think matters. [15]

No discipline has a monopoly on understanding of what freedom is. The best theoretical formulation of freedom is sterile if it is not understood in practice. Finally, freedom, like effective education, is achieved most often when groups of human beings cooperate with each other, not when lone individuals compete against all others.

Why Teach What is Taught

It is perhaps on this last point that the perspectives of Black Studies and the tradition of liberal arts education are at greatest odds. The issue is very simply that of purpose—the raison d'etre of education in our colleges and universities.

The dominant view is that the purpose of liberal arts education is to assist individuals, especially youth, to gain an understanding of the world in which they live. This is a process said to involve an understanding of how the world came to be as it is (history), its physical and natural elements (the sciences), the development and functioning of individuals and societies (the social sciences), and the creative expressions that are unique to the human species (the arts). As they engage in this process, to whom or to what are members of the academy accountable? The dominant view is that scholars are accountable to an abstract notion called "*TRUTH*," or more concretely, to an intellectual community. Professor Mike Thelwell further explores the issue:

> Scholarly objectivity is a delusion that liberals (of both races) may subscribe to. Black people and perceptive whites know better. The fact is that the intellectual establishment distinguishes itself by its slavish acceptance of the role assigned to it by the power brokers of the society. It has always been the willing servant of wealth and power, and the research done in the physical sciences, the humanities and social sciences has been, with very few honorable exceptions, in services to established power, which has, in this country, always been antithetical to the interests of Black people. The goals of the research undertaken, the questions asked, the controlling assumptions governing it, and consequently, the results obtained have always fitted comfortably into a social consensus which has been, by definition, racist.[16]

Black Studies, the intellectual arm of the Black Power Movement, articulates a very different perspective from that of the "intellectual establishment." Why study? Not simply to take a place in the world but to understand the world and to actively participate in helping to change it. To whom are scholars and students accountable? Black Studies advocates respond that Black teachers and students should be accountable to Black people as they struggle for a place of dignity, integrity, and equality in American society. By extension, they argue that all scholars and students must be accountable to the best interests of humankind.

A scholarship that is accountable to human interests is fraught with problems. Who defines these interests? How does one resolve conflicting notions of "best interest"? But on the question of racism, Black Studies advocates are absolutely positive that the perpetuation of this destructive system is not in the interest of any but a small elite.

Black Studies advocates argue, like C. Wright Mills, that we should strive to be objective, but we should not seek to be detached. Education, they argue, is one means by which Black youth could be prepared to play a significant role in the improvement of the conditions of Black communities. For these reasons, Black Studies proponents call for a strong activist component in the curriculum, and a close and dynamic relationship between the academy and African American communities.

Black Studies in Liberal Arts Education: An Assessment

Who has heard the critiques first voiced by the founders of Black Studies twenty years ago? Which Black Studies proposals have reached fruition? What is the best course of action for Black Studies advocates in the 1980s? How should we interpret the fact that the number of Black Studies programs and departments has declined over a twenty year period?

Our experiences over the past twenty years and the present realities in our country serve as a sobering context for an assessment of Black Studies. The times have changed. Since the inception of Black Studies programs and departments, governmental support of education and all other social services has markedly decreased. In a parallel and related development, North American society has become far less responsive even with token gestures to the needs of Black people. While the African Americans struggle has not ceased, the definitive turn to the right in American politics and the severity of economic conditions are among the factors that have made our struggle less public, and less national in scope than it was during the late 1960s.

Today, more than in the 1960s, there is a sense of the relationship between the struggle of African Americans in the United States and Third World peoples in other areas of the world. But there is also today the possibility of a shared doom among all peoples. Nuclear bombs are not designed to selectively destroy based on color, gender, or class coding. Clearly, our conditions today are not the same as those that reigned when Black Studies began.

We recall that Black Studies began during a period in which the Black Panther Party was organizing nationally, and claiming to be a genuine challenge to the ruling power structure. It was a time of rapid increase in the number of Black students and faculty, largely due to Black students' pressures on administrators. It was also a time of rapid increase in the number of Black faces in industry, social service agencies, and government.

In the excitement of the late sixties and early seventies, many Black

Studies participants acted as though these programs and departments would not only endure but also maintain access to resources, autonomy, and decision-making power within white liberal arts institutions. This stance was in some ways functional. By assuming the role of secure, confident administrators with power and financial commitments, many Black administrators and faculty were able to gain a degree of "legitimacy" for their programs. But such a stance clearly involved political myopia.

The euphoria of that period of rapid growth of Black Nationalism, the Black Student Movement, and Black Studies did not last. The systematic and violent repression of political groups such as the Black Panther Party and the assassination of national Black leaders tempered early optimism. Also contributing to the disillusionment were a decline in government programs for poor and minority people and the lessening of guilt-induced efforts by white institutions and individuals.

There has been a definitive decline in the number of Black Studies programs and departments. Today, according to the National Council for Black Studies, there are approximately 375 programs and departments of Black Studies, compared with about 800 in the early 1970s. Among Black Studies faculty, it is generaly known that many of the programs and departments continue to exist under considerable strain. Budget cuts, denial of tenure and promotion, lack of academic support counselors, and in some cases, active counseling against Black Studies, all take their toll.

A new emphasis on vocationalism in American education has caused many Black as well as white students to question the "usefulness" of Black Studies, as compared to courses and majors in business, engineering, and computer science.

Twenty years after the first Black Studies department was founded, many academicians are still questioning the necessity and relevance of Black Studies. It is particularly interesting to note that similar doubts are not so freqently raised about area studies: American Studies, Middle Eastern Studies, East European Studies, African and Latin American Studies.

It is clear that Black Studies differs from area studies in several fundamental ways. In Black Studies, the scholars are, for the most part, of the same group as the people studied. They not only claim identity with the people being studied but, indeed, feel accountable to them. Such identity and accountability are less prevalent in area studies programs. Unlike Black Studies, area studies programs have access to sizeable research funds, faculty positions, and government contacts. In addition, the United States government frequently turns to area studies for information and advice.

Black Studies thus differs from area studies in certain fundamental ways, yet it is often judged by the same standards and expectations used to judge area studies programs. Obviously, Black Studies falls short.

In contrast to area studies, Women's Studies has fared more like Black Studies. Both Black Studies and Women's Studies were "granted" by university administrators in response to demands that were made during the sixties and seventies. Both had to overcome the traditionalists' self-fulfilling prophecy that since there were few readily available resources or qualified personnel, the focus on Black Studies and then on Women's Studies did not warrant expenditure of resources or the stamp of academic legitimacy. These issues, the traditionalist said, could be handled adequately within the regular liberal arts curricula and departments. Yet it was precisely because the traditional departments and curricula failed to deal adequately with issues of racism and sexism, and consistently demonstrated an unwillingness to hire Black or women staff, that a need for Black Studies and Women's Studies arose.

Thus the two programs exist on the fringe or periphery of the "regular" liberal arts curriculum. Many often perceive the departments as existing mainly to provide their clientele with psychic support, while relieving the pressure for more fundamental, university-wide curricula change.

The points made here concerning Black Studies and Women's Studies also hold for Comparative American Ethnic Studies programs and departments, such as Native American Studies, Chicano Studies, Puerto Rican Studies, and Asian American Studies.

Despite changes in American society and in liberal arts institutions that have not been conducive to the growth of viable Black Studies, many Black Studies programs and departments have survived. Survival is not necessarily a sign of the fittest. Neverthless, there are concrete indices of healthy development in some Black Studies programs and departments. There are also important "by-products" of the ongoing Black Studies movement. Among the concrete accomplishments of Black Studies are a steady rise in the number of dissertations, books, and journal articles in Afro-American Studies, and a growing number of scholarly journals and professional organizations in Black Studies.[17] Black Studies has also had some effect on the concepts, theories, and methodology of the traditional areas in the liberal arts curriculum.

The question of Black culture provides a specific example of the influence of Black Studies on social science. Charles Valentine, in a publication, *Black Studies and Anthropology: Political and Scholarly Interests*, defines the importance of Black Studies in correcting the position in anthropology (sociology and psychology, political science, history, and education as well) that Black folks have no culture. Prior to the publication of Melville J. Herskovits' *Myth of the Negro Past*, in 1941, the only position articulated within the ranks of established social science was the notion that Black folks were stripped of their culture before coming to the New World. According to this view, any remnants of African culture that reached these shores were wiped away by the brutality of the slavery experience.[18] Within mainstream scholarship this position was articulated in its modern version by scholars such as Gunner Myrdal (*An American Dilemma*); E. Franklin Frazier (*The Negro Family in the United States*: The Negro Church in America, etc.); and Glazer and Moynihan (*Beyond the Melting Pot*). Glazer and Moynihan declare: "It is not possible for Negroes to view themselves as other ethnic groups viewed themselves because—and this is the key to much in the Negro world—the Negro is only an American and nothing else. He has no values and culture to guard and protect."[19] The contrary position to that articulated by Glazer and Moynihan was presented by Herskovits in his carefully documented *Myth of the Negro Past*. Despite detailed evidence of the retention of African cultural traits in the music, dance, folklore, religion, language, and social organization of New World Black folks, mainstream scholars insisted that Afro-Americans are simply imitators of white American ways.[20] Gunnar Myrdal put it bluntly in the summary statement to a series of chapters, "The Negro Community as a Pathological Form of An American Community." Myrdal said "American Negro culture is not something independent of general American culture. It is a distorted development, or a pathological condition, of the general American culture."[21]

In the new version of Glazer and Moynihan's book, *Beyond the Melting Pot*, they explicitly state that Black Studies has been a source which corrected the theory of Black folks as "cultureless." And yet, the way they phrase their "change of heart" is an indication of the tenacity of their original view. Valentine, critically analyzing Glazer and Moynihan writes:

Students of the changing scholarly scene may be interested to find that in a second edition of their book, Glazer and Moynihan have edited the quoted statement to soften it somewhat without changing its basic message. Elsewhere in the new version of their book, these resourceful authors present a lengthy footnote on the same subject which is a small masterpiece of academic doubletalk. First they say they didn't really mean what they said in their original statement. Then they admit they made a mistake but blame it on "authoritative scholars, among them E. Franklin Frazier." Their mistake, as they see it, was to ignore "African survivals," and they give credit to "Afro-American and Black Studies" for challenging this, although they also condemn this field for "separatism." Eventually they conclude that, "Out of American origins, one can create a distinctive subculture. . . This has certainly happened as a result of 300 years of Black American history, and could ("could", not "did") serve as a sufficient basis for strong organization, regardless of the contribution of African origins. All this can surely be seen as a sign of the times, a tribute to effectiveness of the young field of Black Studies. Yet is is also a sharp reminder that the essential message of the traditional view remains intact and continues to be dominant outside Black Studies".[22]

There are other examples of the influence of Black Studies on mainstream attitudes, assumptions, and even theories. To note only a few, the pioneering work of Herbert Aptheker on slave revolts has received increased attention and has "become more possible as truth" as a result of widespread use of his material in Afro-American Studies and the dissemination of those ideas into communities outside the universities.

The Moynihan thesis on Black families has been severely challenged by Black Studies faculties and students; in fact there are few programs or departments that do not use the Moynihan theory as a teaching device for educating Black students about the convergence of "scholarly" and "ruling class political interests." The fact that Moynihan has become a known name in many Black communities is in some measure a result of the work of Black scholars associated with Black Studies.

Black Studies brought to the social sciences a different perspective, a perspective of the oppressed, the view of those without power, the view from the cotton patch.[23]

Black Studies and Liberal Arts Education: Where do we go from here?

Many of the scholars and activists who helped found Black Studies programs and departments seriously critique what has transpired over the past twenty years. Joined by younger colleagues, students, and "drylongso" African Americans in communities throughout the United States, these scholars offer direction for the future of Black Studies.[24] These advocates of Black Studies openly criticize the continuing resistance to Black Studies by white administrators and faculty. They deplore the ways in which the financial hard times facing academic institutions and the conservative hostile environment in the United States adversely affect Black Studies. With no less honesty, these proponents of Black Studies turn inward and openly discuss those parts of the problem for which we ourselves may have the solutions.

Some of the points of discussion and debate are relatively new issues, others have been up for discussion since the very inception of Black Studies. For example, the issue of technology and African America is relatively new. How will various sectors of African American communities be affected by this society's increasing dependence upon high technology and information as a product as well as a method of communicating? Given the potential for uneven access to high technology and for existing racial as well as gender and class inequalities, what should be the stance of Black Studies? Concretely, should Black Studies curricula take on instruction in computer and information science? Or should the Black Studies curricula continue to focus on the areas more traditionally covered in the liberal arts?

The question of race versus class as the focal point of Black Studies has been openly, indeed heatedly discussed and debated since the inception of Black Studies. What is new, and encouraging, is the growing rejection of the very formulation of a dichotomy such that it is either race *or* class that is *the* key concept for Black Studies: Black Nationalism *or* Marxism that is *the* correct perspective.[25]

To illustrate this dynamic of critical assessment within Black Studies, I choose an example that is particularly appropriate to this volume—the woman question within Black Studies.

The Woman Question Within Black Studies

Black women as scholars and teachers, and Black women as an area of scholarship, appear to be caught between a rock and a hard place, that is, between the racial and ethnic bias of much of Women's Studies and the gender bias in much of Black Studies.

The situation in almost all of the Women's Studies programs and departments, where Black female professors are indeed rare, is summarized by Arlene Avakian in these terms:

> . . . most of the white women teaching and doing research in Women's Studies do not see Black and Third World women. Until very recently only the exceptional Women's Studies course included any women of color in its syllabus. Even rarer was any discussion at all of racism as a force in all of our lives. . . . Women of color are seldom included in our classes, journals or conferences, and when they are it is as if they are another species tacked on to the end of the course. It is rare to find women of color and their concerns fully integrated into a Women's Studies class or conference. And when Black and Third World women speak to this issue at conferences, the attitude of white women is generally one of annoyance, because their conference has been disrupted.[26]

The figures that confirm Avakian's point are found in the pages of *Who's Who and Where in Women's Studies*.

> . . . between 1970 and 1973, courses which concerned minority women or which considered race and class in addition to gender comprised only 4 percent of women's studies courses. Three years later, within the 15 "mature" women's studies programs, only 11 percent of the courses were devoted to considerations of race and class, or to minority women's experiences. Within that number, there were some courses that specifically addressed the experiences of Black women; some of these were, in fact, jointly sponsored

by Black studies and women's studies programs. Proportionately, however, they still "wouldn't fill a page".[27]

In 1978, not a single Black Studies program in a western land-grant college offered an independent course on Black women. Until 1982 and 1983, none of the few existing textbooks on Black Studies included specific discussions on Black women. The issues of Black women, when mentioned, are included under the topics of the Black family and traditional African societies. It is important to note that the most recent publication of *People's College* does include a fuller discussion of Black women's issues. This inclusion was clearly in response to criticisms raised by Black Studies scholars, especially women. Also, until recently, the course syllabi for Black Studies courses have drawn almost exclusively on male authors (Black and white) and the material of the syllabi rarely distinguishes Black women's experiences from those of Black men.

The paucity of scholarly attention to Black women within Black Studies is matched by the paucity of Black women as colleagues in these programs and departments. This is particularly important to note because within Black Studies, as in American society as a whole, there is a myth of Black female dominance. The reality is that there are very few Black women in leadership positions in Black Studies. The Black women who are involved in these programs and departments face very clear problems of gender inequality.

Professor Monica Gordon and I did a series of telephone interviews with Black women involved in Black Studies in the New England region. While we clearly did not conduct a rigorous study, nonetheless the women to whom we spoke articulated many of the same problems. The women interviewed believe that the inequities in promotion and salary experienced by Black women are a consequence of the myth that women are a "risk" because they will leave the workforce to have babies. The women deplored the insinuation that Black women who do hold positions in Black Studies gained them because they granted sexual favors (a variant on the myth that Black women have only advanced, since slavery because they "give in" sexually to males). Some of the women we interviewed said that they are simply not taken seriously as scholars and as teachers. Finally, some of the women indicated that they are criticized within their Black Studies programs or departments and charged with divided loyalties because of their involvement in women's issues and Women's Studies. The reality is that most if not all Black women have differences with segments of the Women's Movement and with Women's Studies—both of which have been historically bound by middle-class white perspectives and values. But a rejection of those values does not eliminate the genuine concerns that Black women have *as women*.[28]

Until recently, Black Studies scholars and activists did not openly discuss these issues and concerns. In part, they did not raise these issues fearing that to do so would be divisive when cooperation between Black men and women is a prerequisite for the success of Black Studies. In addition, raising "the woman question," it was feared, would give the impression that there is only conflict or dissension between Black men and women in Black Studies when, in fact, there are many areas of cooperation. But ignoring or refusing to talk about problems rarely if ever makes them simply go away.

The issue of Black women in Black Studies has been brought out into the open. In Atlanta at the Institute of the Black World curriculum development conferences, and at the Howard University fifteen Year Assessment of Black Studies Conference, the issues of Black women as colleagues and as subject matter in Black Studies were openly addressed. Similarly, at recent Women's Studies conferences these issues are receiving attention. The criticisms raised by Black women, and often by Black men as well as by white colleagues in Women's Studies, may well be heard and acted upon to the point that "more Black is put into Women's Studies, and more women are put into Black Studies".[29]

Without Conclusion

The "no conclusion" to this review of the beginnings, development, and current state of Black Studies in liberal arts institutions is that the Black Studies challenge remains, and the struggles it embodies continue. What can be said is captured in these words:

> Black studies offers a challenge to higher education far beyond the inclusion of black subject matter in the curriculum. Its challenge is how we view human existence itself. The question is, whose lives do we value? Black studies begins with the lives of black people and reaches out to all humanity. How many times I have had white students say to me at the end of a course, "I didn't know I would learn so much about myself by studying black literature."
>
> I knew, because within black literature, history and culture lie truths about America that can be found in no other place. I knew because universal truths lie within the black experience as certainly as these truths reside in the experiences of any people. Unfortunately, white academicians resist growing down into the black experience because to do so means an inevitable confrontation with the underside of America—racism. Yet, what more appropriate place for such a confrontation than the classrooms of universities and colleges.[30]

Notes

1. A stipend from Oberlin College made it possible for Elizabeth H. Oakes to serve as my research assistant for this chapter.

2. Mike Thelwell, "Black Studies: A Political Perspective," The Massachusetts Review, Vol. 10(4): 703.

3. Eugene Terry, "Introduction," Quadrennial Review of the Undergraduate Curriculum, W.E.B. DuBois Department of Afro-American Studies, University of Massachusetts at Amherst.

4. Ibid., 2.

5. Ibid.

6. Ibid.

7. Julius Lester, "Growing Down," *Change Magazine.* (1979): 34.

8. In 1950, about 4.5 percent of the Black youth between the ages of eighteen and twenty-four attended U.S. colleges. By 1970, 15.5 percent of Black youth of this same age group were in colleges and universities. Only five years later, 20 percent of Black males and 21 percent of Black females between eighteen and twenty-four were in institutions of higher education. A decline began in 1976, reflecting the brutal attacks upon educational opportunities for African Americans. See Manning Marable, "Afro-American History: Post Reconstruction." Review Essay. Black Studies Curriculum Development Course Evaluations, Conference I: History and Political Economy, October 1–3, 1981, Institute of the Black World, Atlanta, Georgia. p. 3.

9. Ibid., 4.

10. Ibid.

11. While the focus of this chapter is Black Studies and the African American experience in higher education, the Eurocentic perspective similarly misrepresents the experience of other people of color and non-Western people.

12. Lester, "Growing Down," 37.

13. Lewis King, "The Future of Mental Health Research of the Black Population: Outline of an Alternative Deep Structure." *Research Bulletin*, Vol. 1, no. 1.

14. Lester, "Growing Down," 35–36.

15. Ibid., 37.

16. Mike Thelwell, "Black Studies: A Political Perspective," 709.

17. Abdul Alkalimat, "Research and Evaluational Empirical Trends of Professional Devlopment and Productivity in Black Studies," Delivered at "Symposium on Black Studies: A Fifteen Year Assessment," Howard University, December 1–2 1982.

18. Although established social science argued the absence of Black culture, many Black scholars and writers have proclaimed a unique, and sometimes a superior way of life. For a detailed discussion of this point see Herbert Aptheker's *Afro-American History: The Modern Era* (New York: The Citadel Press, 1971): 68–80.

19. Nathan Glazer and Daniel Patrick Moynihan, *Beyond the Melting Pot.* Cambridge, Massachusetts: M.I.T. Press, 1970.

20. Frances S. Herskovits, ed., *The New World Negro* (Bloomington: Indiana University Press, 1966); Melville J. Herskovits, *The Myth of the Negro Past* (New York: Harper, 1941); J. C. Moore, "Religious Syncretism in Jamaica," *Practical Anthropology* 12 (1965) :63–70; Vera Rubin, ed., *Caribbean Studies: A Symposium*, University of Washington Press, 1957, Seattle; George E. Simpson, "The Belief System of Haitian Vodun," *American Anthropologist* 47 (1945): 35–59; Lorenzo D. Turner, *Africanisms in the Gullah Dialect* (Chicago: University of Chicago Press, 1949); Richard D. Waterman, "African Influence on the Music of the Americas" in *Acculturation in the Americas*, Sol Tax, ed.,(Chicago: University of Chicago Press, 1952); Norman E. Whitten and John F. Szwed *Afro-American Anthropology* (New York: The Free Press, 1964).

21. Gunnar Myrdal, *An American Dilemma*, London: Routledge & K. Paul, 1958.

22. Charles Valentine, *Black Studies and Anthropology: Scholarly and Political Interests in Afro-American Culture* (Reading, Mass.: Addison Wesley).

23. Scholars of other Third World groups have made similar contributions. For example, the rise in Native American consciousness led to the work of Vine Deloria and others, in which the view of Native Americans presented is very different from that of the Bureau of Indian Affairs and many Euro-American anthropologists.

24. In his book, *Drylongso: A Self Portrait of Black America* (New York: Random House, 1980), anthropologist John L. Gwaltney uses the term to refer to the vast majority of Afro-Americans in the U.S.—regular, everyday people.

25. James B. Stewart, "Toward Operationalization of an 'Expansive' Model of Black Studies." Paper presented for the Black Studies Curriculum Development Project Administered by the Institute of the Black World, Atlanta, 1982.

26. Arlene Voski Avakian, "Women's Studies and Racism," *New England Journal of Black Studies*, 1981: 33.

27. Charles P. Henry and Frances Smith Foster, "Black Women's Studies: Threat or Challenge," *The Western Journal of Black Studies*, 1982: 16.

28. "Rape cannot be a 'white' woman's issue when 60 percent of all women raped in the U.S. are Black. The issue of jobs and equal pay for equal work is not a white feminist issue, not when the median income of Black women is only 94 percent of that of white women, 73 percent of that of Black men, and 54 percent of that of white men" (Cole and Gordon, New England Journal of Black Studies 1981: 7).

29. Johnnetta B. Cole, "Black Studies, Women's Studies: An Overdue Partnership." Luncheon Address at the Conference on "Black Studies, Women's Studies: An Overdue Partnership." University of Massachusetts at Amherst, 1983.

30. Lester, "Growing Down," 37.

CHAPTER 9

Towards an Epistemology of Ethnic Studies: African American Studies and Chicano Studies Contributions

R. A. Olguin

Towards an Epistemology of Ethnic Studies

A question that divides american Ethnic Studies scholars, and that forms the central concern of this chapter, is the extent to which we reject objectivity as the epistemological root of our discipline. Basically put, to what extent is the need for a separation of american Ethnic Studies from the traditional disciplines based on political arguments about autonomy as the only way to ensure voice, and to what extent is such a need driven by the inadequacy of objectivity as a way of knowing?

This chapter will explore these issues by examining work in the areas of Chicano and African american Studies.[1] American Ethnic Studies is a discipline only partially comprised of African american and Chicano Studies. Asian american Studies and Native american Studies also contribute to the development of a more encompassing intellectual activity, which can be institutionally housed as a department of american Ethnic Studies. This is not true simply because scholars in these areas at times publish in the same journals and attend the same meetings.

One of the purposes of this essay is to demonstrate the epistemological junctures between these areas of study. Space limitations, however, require that the argument be made about these two fields. One hope is that this chapter will initiate discussion of the applicability of this analysis to other areas of study. The specific focus will be upon work from the period 1965–1975, which was the period when the various fields within american Ethnic Studies began to demand their right to exist as self-defining disciplines. The rhetoric of the period demanded "autonomy," defined as the establishment of distinct departments or colleges with decision-making power to be vested in the "community."

As a consequence, american Ethnic Studies scholars were involved in more than the long-standing effort to document the conditions of their peoples. They were also seeking insight into what modifications of U.S. society would be required in order to end racial and ethnic inequality. The university, or the knowledge factory, was one social institution, and it happened to be the one with which most scholars were most familiar. As a consequence of this expertise, the production of knowledge became one of the earliest social institutions to be thoroughly criticized.

This chapter will examine this critical analysis in two steps. First will be presented a brief sketch of the issues underlying our criticism of the idea of objectivity as the defining trait of the academic community. Having established this point of departure, I will then present what I believe to be the three main tenets of an american Ethnic Studies epistemology: organicism, holism, and self-reflexivity. The ultimate conclusion is that these three elements constitute a rigorous epistemology that transcends the subject/object dichotomy.

Objecting to Objectivity

Scholars in american Ethnic Studies during the late 1960s were in a position to carry out this criticism of the academy in several ways. One possible route was to continue documenting actual conditions among minority communities. These findings could then be compared to the expectations and results of mainstream scholarship in a demonstration of its inadequacy. What was and is left unquestioned by this kind of work is the source of these biases and errors. Why have the traditional disciplines tended to produce findings about the Chicano and African american community that do not correspond to the reality of these peoples?

A second aspect of this period, then, was criticism of the theoretical structures that "misguided" the questionable research. This work, in the period covered, focused primarily on the issue of objectivity. The pioneers of american Ethnic Studies questioned the capacity of scholars to provide objective knowledge about different cultures, especially when those cultures were related by structures of domination and exploitation. At its deepest level, pioneering efforts in the american Ethnic Studies fields called into question the very ideal of objectivity.

Chicano anthropologist Octavio Romano is an early pioneer of this two-step analysis of the dominant discourse on race and ethnicity. He saw linkages between the empirical inaccuracies and the conceptual shortcomings he investigated. Romano argued that the previous depictions of the Chicano as "passive, lazy, fatalistic and traditional" were empirically false.[2] Romano calls attention to the long history of militancy and organization that characterized

Anglo-Mexicano relations in the Southwest. Romano argued that Chicanos were, and are, more assertive and historically creative than presented in previous research conducted by Anglo historians.

Romano further claimed that these errors were not just the result of poor research or sampling techniques, but instead due to the use of the faulty concept of "traditional culture."[3] Romano argues that the major problem with the accepted notion of culture is that it is a-historical. By this, Romano means that the notion of traditional culture ignores the historical record.

> Actual history itself reveals this formulation to be a grand hoax, a blatant lie. . . . Social scientists have never asked themselves why such massive militant action was necessary. . . . To ask themselves this question would be to acknowledge history, a history of constant confrontations brought about by elements of the same "traditional culture" which they have repeatedly described as virtually stagnant and actionless.[4]

Romano's work presents a springboard for subsequent empirical investigations of Chicano history and culture. The effort to refute inaccurate descriptions of a culture continues, and is still linked to the goal of sociopolitical empowerment. By highlighting the active role people of color have played in the formation of U.S. history, scholars in american Ethnic Studies hoped to provide motivations to action. By emphasizing the confrontational nature of this history, these scholars have also hoped to increase the solidarity of such action by using history as vehicle for defining the enemies of the community.

However, the work of the 1960s also attempted to transcend previous writing via theoretical revision. Romano criticizes the notion of traditional culture in two aspects. First, it connotes a unilinear scale of historical development that places Anglo-European culture at the end of a process of development through which other cultures will eventually pass on their road to modernity. This stages-of-growth model thus utilizes the cultural structures and practices specific to one historical experience as a standard for describing and evaluating alternative cultures. Anglo-European culture is thus illegitimately reified into an "ideal type."

The consequence of this reification is misrepresentation of the history of oppression and resistance, which has been the overriding characteristic of interracial relations in this country. As noted above, the model is invalid because it ignores the self-assertive role played by people of color in the creation of their cultural worlds. Just as the minority's efforts at self-assertion are ignored, the dominant strata's imposition and appropriation are also forgotten. This combination allows the impression that Chicanos or Afro-americans are generally passive except for periodic and inexplicable outbursts of inarticulate violence and rage.

In sum, then, early work in the field of american Ethnic Studies argued that anthropology, sociology, and psychology all suffer from the same "ideological" and methodological flaws in discussing race and ethnicity. There is the tendency to place the responsibility for social inequality on the shoulders of the less equal, and to deny the conflictual and oppressive history of race relations in this country. This clears the way for analyses of various groups as if they had a similar experience of America.

Since the objective experience is "held constant," analysis concludes that outcomes are predicates of group differences. As a result, those who flourish in the status quo are exonerated of responsibility for the plight of their fellows, and are thus alleviated of the responsibility to use their advantages to ameliorate these conditions. The field of american Ethnic Studies thus sees the canon of objectivity as one that has the function of defending the status quo.

Ethnic Studies Perspectives on Method

In formulating itself as a discipline, american Ethnic Studies has gone beyond simple opposition and revisionism. This positive activity is not yet completely, formally and rigorously articulated, so the remainder of this chapter will lay out the three fundamental epistemological tenets of american Ethnic Studies. These three canons are organicism, holism, and self-reflexivity.

Organicism

The principle component of the american Ethnic Studies approach to critical theory is organicism.[5] This concept is universally shared in the field, albeit in varied forms, and serves as a definition of what theory is. Organicism is a descriptive, rather than a narrowly prescriptive, approach to theory. From this empirical judgement that social theory and social science are social institutions flow the two prescriptive aspects of the american Ethnic Studies perspective on theory: holism and self-reflexivity.

In rejecting previous analyses of race and ethnicity as being ideological in nature, scholars in american Ethnic Studies are not making what Raymond Geuss would call a genetic criticism of these works.[6] Traditional studies are not said to be flawed by virtue of their origin rather than their technique. At its crudest, Geuss' argument criticizes a body of work, or an individual work, because those who created it have certain ascriptive traits.

Such a method for adjudicating the validity of a piece of research is seriously flawed. First, it is a recapitulation of the destruction of reality by prejudice, which american Ethnic Studies set out to repudiate. Any discourse that does what it claims ought not to be done is clearly problematic at best. Further, this sort of thinking provides no useful method for mediating intragroup disagreements, as it focuses on the researcher rather than on the research. Both the African american and Chicano populations are too diverse to allow the blackness or brownness of an author to be the criterion of an idea's adequacy.[7]

Except when involved in polemic, most scholars in american Ethnic Studies do not put this simple genetic argument to work for them. It is rather, as we have seen, the functional aspects of research that form the basis for indictment and criticism.[8] The issue is similar to Bakhtin's notion of voice.[9] To speak for someone is either to utter their sentiments for them, or it is to put words in their mouth. Either course is fraught with peril, especially when speaker and spoken-for are members of groups involved in competitive or conflictual social relations. The study of ethnicity in america is intellectually trickier than the study of "foreign" cultures, since domestic ethnic groups must mutually create a polity. The rules that determine what knowledge is valid, therefore, cannot be drawn from the beliefs of only one group. For if one party to a conflictual situation can determine and define what it is that is meaningful to say, then the views of other parties to the conflict will be ruled meaningless *a priori*.

The real point of contention is the objectivity of social scientific practice, and not the possibility of individual value-neutrality. Having indicted the key concepts in the traditional disciplines as rationalizations for European americans' racial stereotypes, the question remains as to the inherence of such problems. Having shown the myth of the passive, fatalistic Chicano to be just that, can we reconstitute the theoretical structure of these disciplines so that it does not matter who applies them?

The epistemic rejection of social scientific objectivity is a rejection of the principal of objectivity itself. Na'im Akbar argues that "the objective approach does not preclude values because objectivity is a value. When an observer chooses to suspend from his or her observations certain levels of reaction, this is a value judgement."[10] The value judgement implicit in a commitment to objectivity is one that posits the superiority of a set of culturally specific ideas about the nature of cognition appropriate to social action.

The argument runs as follows. Objectivity is an outgrowth of the philosophical tradition of the West, and is dependent on the conceptual separation of mind and body. "The concept of objectivity is impossible without a corresponding belief in man's ability to separate his mind not only from his body, but also from all of his ecological surroundings, whether or not these ecological surroundings are human or physical."[11] This belief, according to Romano, has two ramifications. First, social science incorrectly defines emotion and reason as separate mental faculties. This false dichotomy is then incorrectly applied both to the research and the subject's mental activities.

Researchers, by posing a distinction between reason and affect, are led to the false conclusion that purging cognitive procedures of affective bias will assure the objectivity of their results.[12] Subjects are then studied in terms of their rationality or their emotions. This dichotomy lays the ground for false debate, partial definition, and artificial distinctions between the quality of thought of subjects and researchers.

The second ramification of this dualism, which according to Romano and Akbar belies the notion of objectivity, is the tendency to objectification. Objectification is the "externalization and systematic articulation of a thought or theoretical construct the parts of which are *seemingly* interrelated and *seemingly* coherent."[13] What is being argued is that the notion of a mind separate from a material essence allows the false impression of a transcendant reason, which in turn allows the impression that the concepts produced by this reason are not spatially or temporally bounded. This impression is held to be false in that theoretical concepts are "influenced, modified and limited by forces that are extraneous to the theoretically pure process of objectification itself."[14]

With respect to american Ethnic Studies, the myth of objectivity allows social science to defend its particularistic depictions of race via *a priori*, generic argument about the objectivity of technique. Particular notions about race, which are drawn from the ideological interpretation of social reality, are presented as objective constructs or empirical heuristic. Their refutation thus entails not just a presentation of facts, as the facts are partially responsible for the shape of the construct.

What is also necessary, therefore, is organization and presentation of facts by a voice that says "I am not that."[15] The specific "that" which is to be rejected is the self separate from its ecological surroundings, or a self capable of objectivity through reason alone.[16] Rejecting objectivity, then, requires that we call into question the Western conception of the self, which means positing an ontology distinct from that of the Enlightenment.

By positing the existence of a self-consistent ontology and epistemology distinct from that of the Enlightenment, Romano asserts the strongest possible refutation of the idea of a value-free social science. Yet aside from the argument that Chicanos are willing, historical actors who self-consciously perceive themselves tied into the web of life, Romano himself provides little insight into what is culturally specific about Western social science.[17]

Psychologist Na'im Akbar has carried this strong position further by arguing that an Afrocentric social science would have two distinguishing traits. First, it would replace the epistemological emphasis on individualism with a holistic one. By rejecting the mind–body split, an Afrocentric method would replace the individual abstracted from all social connections with the community as the ontological foundation for observation. In so doing this approach "does not deny 'uniqueness,' but it does deny the isolated notion of individualism."[18]

Second, an Afrocentric paradigm would rejoin affect and reason in an effort to understand human psyche and behavior. Furthermore, according to Akbar, spirituality would also be redefined as a relevant aspect of the human experience. As such, it would be not only a subject of investigation but also an integral part of theory building. For Akbar, spirituality is an aspect of humanity's essentially moral nature.[19] Morality is thus essential for any consideration of human thought, so that the "values made explicit in the Afrocentric approach are implicitly present in the Eurocentric approach."[20] Akbar's argument that an Afrocentric approach simply renders explicit the moral significance of all social research is important. The contention that social theory is inevitably organic means that these scholars do not see their work as differing from that of the mainstream in form, but rather in the level of self-awareness. "Our" work is no less ideologically driven and loaded than is "their" work. "We" are simply more aware than are "they" about the ways in which power constrains the act of knowing whether we like it or not.[21]

When reduced to its fundamental level, the argument claims that persons of color from cultures basically communalistic have an epistemology that rejects dualism as a foundation for cognition. An Afrocentric social science would differ from that derived from the Enlightenment tradition by "not allowing social processes to be dichotomized into inevitably opposing and conflicting qualities."[22] This difference is said to result from an "African Epistemological tradition."[23]

Johnnella Butler calls this the "both/and" approach, which she distinguishes from the "either/or" approach of European epistemology.[24] As voiced by individual scholars, the American Ethnic Studies rejection of objectivity is founded on the idea that epistemologies are culturally specific. Dualism, objectivity, and the attendant rationalism are held to be specific to the West. The non-Western view is said to be oriented toward communal action in the world, to be holistic (dialectical?), and is concerned with the notion of the self-generating subject.

The problem is not the coherence of this alternative, since it is as coherent as any other rejection of empiricism or positivism. One problem with the presentation of the argument is the multiple claims to its unique origins. Some scholars claim Africa and pre-Columbian America as the "primordial" home of this more appropriate and accurate conception of knowledge.[25] Feminist theorists have also made an essentializing claim to this epistemology.[26]

That this both/and epistemology is claimed by a number of groups does not imply that it is inadequate. What is being questioned is the grounding for these epistemological claims. If African americans, Native americans, Chicanos, and women, qua women, all share this epistemology it cannot flow from some trait essential to any one of them. It instead either flows from some common aspect of the lives of these groups, such as oppression, or it flows from a different characteristic of each group's life. In either event, the multiplicity of claims to this anti-objectivist epistemology reminds us to avoid essentialist arguments about the nature of ideas.

Beyond this confusion is another, more insidious, weakness in the strong argument: The dichotomy between Western and non-Western thought is inconsistent with the "both/and" epistemology being advocated. Four-hundred years of Western colonial depredation has surely led to the colonization of all alternative epistemic systems. The idea that there exists a world view not affected by the Liberal idea of knowledge contradicts the description of cultural history put forth in american Ethnic Studies. The "correct" approach is not the romanticizing of a unique form of thought that no longer exists; it is instead the understanding of how these two competing world views have been synthesized in the bicultural experience of African americans, and Chicanos.[27]

The Political Rejection of Objectivity

This is the project of scholars who put forth the "political" rejection of objectivity. Here the issue is not the genesis of an epistemological position but rather its function.[28] Like the strong view there is in this work an acceptance of the proposition that theories are outgrowths of experience. This epistemological relativity, however, is tempered by an ontological objectivism that holds that all theories must and do connect with an objectively "real" historical/material situation. This reality may not be open to cognition or articulation. Or such articulation may only be partial at best, but in any event the reality can be invoked as a loose check against the tendency of relativity to degenerate into relativism.

This use of historical reality to assess the ideological validity of a theory is not falsification or any other form of positive objectivism. For knowledge is rooted not only in personal experience but is also structured by the social functions it is ordained to play. Both of these limits to objectivity provide at once both a limit to the claims to valid knowledge that are possible and also means for ascertaining the validity of any such claim put forth.

In order to understand this two-directional notion of validity, it is crucial to grasp the concept of an organic group. For the political rejection of objectivity begins with the notion of society as composed of groups of people involved in social intercourse. Social theory or science, by extension, is a project of groups involved not only with the material world, but with other groups as well.[29] The emerging epistemology "sees consciousness-raising and change in the political, economic and social order as the fundamental concepts of Black Studies in the same way as an artist sees beauty, the educator sees knowledge or the anthropologist sees culture as fundamental concepts in their disciplines."[30] The community of which the scholar is a part is supposed to provide the motive force and subject matter for research.

If one seeks to study a community of which one is not a member, the same strictures apply. For the needs and goals of the community, rather than intellectual structures, should provide the ordering principles for the discipline.

> When one attempts to comprehend a field of study, there is no better method than to draw questions and concepts from the action source. . . . It is people and groups of people, their successes and disappointments, their mores and values, their thoughts and actions, their institutions and their environment which affect progress in Black Studies.[31]

This approach is thus more than a call for the study of a population by its members.[32] It is an orientation to the activity of scholarship that firmly bases it in the liberation and empowerment of the community.

The substantial subject of research would be much the same in a non-objectivist epistemology as it has always been: the obviously inferior social conditions of the African american or Chicano community. But the orientation differs in terms of how the problem is conceived and in how the notion of solution is postulated. So, for example, "the study of the Black family is a legitimate concern of Black Studies, but only when it is understood from the perspective of its relevance to the survival and prosperity of the Black people, and not as a social problem for the White community."[33] What has changed is that the research object is no longer desubjectified; its voice is actively sought out and listened to. In political terms, the research object is no longer subjected; it is liberated and empowered.

This idea of the survival and prosperity needs of the community is important because it provides a necessary anchor for critical research: a positive concept of what scholarship and education are about. These activities are not just instrumental activities in which a student's head is filled with knowledge. They are intended, in Boniface Obichere's words, "to impart to students, as human beings, the best possible education for living."[34]

Ethnic Studies and Holism

Making the community the rock upon which american Ethnic Studies is built does not banish all validation problems, because an action oriented researcher has his or her own perspectives on the community itself. The action oriented researcher must, like any community member, be able to define the extent of the community. The needs and wants of this entity are also in need of determination.[35] Since these issues are subject to debate by the community itself, they do not provide univocal guidelines to those who would speak *with* and *for* the community.

We have rejected the essentialist criticism as a technique for mediating competing claims among the groups. All who claim to be organic intellectuals will claim that their perspective is functional for the community. Thus we still need an epistemology that will allow the community to sort out such competing claims.

Therefore, if the organicism can help us create better scholarship, it must be because this conception of theory provides guidelines for theory validation. The notion of organic theory provides american Ethnic Studies with two keys: holism and self-reflexivity. These two claims about theory/science are derived from the ontological reality of the minority experience of america. Any scientific or other theory that does not use a holistic and self-reflexive approach cannot, therefore, be said to be epistemologically valid. This is because such theories are not in conformity with the ontological status of the subject.

Holism

Holism is the first methodological prescription that can be drawn from a commitment to the organic nature of social theory. Holism is a concept with two moments, both of which are necessary aspects of a valid theoretical structure. These two aspects are ontological and epistemological. We will now turn to the analysis of each of these aspects of holism in turn.

Ontological Holism

Ontology deals with the nature of being or existence. It is a branch of philosophy that derives its name from the Greek words for the verb "to be" (onto), and the "word" or "way" (logos). The ontological holism found in the american Ethnic Studies method maintains that an "adequate explanation of social phenomena necessitates statements which are not reducible to statements about individuals."[36] This is a result of the fact that individual persons are born into concrete social situations that give shape and structure to their cognition and behaviors. Individual persons, therefore, depend upon socially constructed situations, as opposed to mere existence, in order for their thoughts, words, and actions to have meaning.[37]

As Mandlebaum notes, such an ontology does not deny the existence of individuals as necessary for the possibility of the existence of groups. The argument is less expansive, and holds that facts about groups are not necessarily identical with facts about the persons who comprise the group.[38] At another level, however, the argument is even more destructive of ontological individualism. For the very concept of the self as an individual is itself held to be socially determined. Infants develop, and are not born with, a sense of the self as separate from others, thus the cognitive content of this sense of self is learned through social interaction. This means that the enlightenment fetish of the autonomous self, which underlies the individualist ontology, is itself a contingent, social fact.

The application of this to issues of race and ethnicity is quite straightforward. People are born into groups that predate their birth. These groups are involved in relations with one another and part of these relations are ones of mutual definition and material exchange. Individuals, therefore, are born into groups that have identities that constrain the possible self-identities of members of the group. Even though the existence of the Black community in the United States is a predicate of the existence of persons with black skins, their identification as Black or African american is itself irreducibly predicated on a socially constructed distinction between black and non-black.

Social constructions are like the forces analyzed by physics: They can be presumed to exist without being open to our sensory organs. A socially constructed distinction, such as race, can be evaded at the level of consciousness. They may also fail to manifest themselves in behaviors. However, examination of the social being of groups will reveal their reality.[39]

As an indication of the implications of this view, consider the notion of racism. A holistic interpretation of this phenomenon would argue that it is not reducible to statements about individual racists. Carmichael and Hamilton thus distinguish between individual racism and institutional racism.[40] The former is impossible without the latter, for without a set of institutions that separate white and black in an unequal fashion there is no ground upon which individuals with notions of racial superiority can base their claims. In such a situation, there would be no manifest inequalities that required explanation, and therefore no need to create doctrines holding that such and such a group is subhuman.[41]

Aside from this logical defense of holism, there is a second reason for advocating this ontology. This is an argument based on the nature of the organic groups in question. One of the issues involved in such a project is the indictment of the cultural specificity of individualistic rationalism. The idea of a Third World epistemology entails positing the non-individualistic content of African and pre-Columbian thought, which embraces a both/and epistemology.

I argue that the non-dichotomous way of knowing comes from our status as oppressed peoples. Our communities exist because they have been generated by the imperial contradiction of colonizer and colonized. Hispanics exist

R. A. Olguin

only because the census defines the category. *Yo soy Chicano*. My father was Mexican, my brother-in-law is Mexican American, and a family who lives down the street is Puerto Rican and looks African. The state categorizes us as Hispanics, and we respond (*En Espanol*) "*somos Latinos.*" Both abstract categories, Hispanic and Latino, are created from political contact with a universalizing other; both are simultaneously real and illusory.

Our very existence as peoples created out of oppression and conflict renders us multivocal. We can say that two things are the same but that they are different, without feeling contradiction. We resist when we can and submit when we must, but we do not assume our submission to indicate assent. This lived reality must surely give rise to a non-dichotomous way of knowing.

Epistemological Holism

The second major conception of holism in american Ethnic Studies is epistemological, and flows from our ontology. Epistemology is the branch of philosophy that studies the nature of knowledge and derives its name from the Greek words for "understanding" (episteme) and "word" (logos). The epistemology of american Ethnic Studies is consistent with its ontology. We hold social facts are real and irreducible at an ontological level, so our epistemology must take this into account.

There are two arguments advanced in support of a holistic epistemology. The first argument is a functional defense of holism, while the second is a political defense. These two arguments of holism are based on a definition of the problems facing minorities in the United States, and in the heterogenous nature of minority populations. Both of these arguments grow out of the notion that theory is organically related to corporate experience, since both arguments are founded on a conception of the nature of minority communities.

Basically put, the first argument contends that our work will be ineffective if research is broken down along traditional disciplinary lines. If one accepts that the underlying problem facing ethnic communities is the legacy of racism, it is clear that this vexatious issue is present in economic, political, sociological, and psychological institutions and practices.[42]

An adequate solution to the legacy of racial domination must, therefore, be one that can analyze the problem in its completeness. Large amounts of information may require specialization, but theoretical work must always take place in a cross-disciplinary setting. This speaks to the establishment of a separate discipline, as this would facilitate such cross-fertilization.

A negative defense of epistemological holism is found in the indictment of research carried out from a narrow disciplinary perspective. To break down the problem of racial prejudice is said to subvert the problem-solving capacity of social science.[43] The set of social relations that are called prejudicial are analyzed in many social sciences, precisely because the problem is real in itself.

In other words, social prejudice is not a subject constituted by the sciences that study it but is a real phenomenon that is subsequently *reconstituted* by the theoretical traditions of specific disciplines. Since traditional disciplines are defined by theory or method rather than by substantive problems, their research is not bound to an organic conception of relevance. This allows such research to be more motivated by the sociology of the university department than by its human consequences.

> This approach . . . leads to a selection of research problems on the basis of what is currently fashionable in the discipline rather than on the basis of concrete human problems. One result is a kind of "endless chain" procedure in which each study gives rise to methodological and theoretical problems which then become the topic of future "studies."[44]

As a result, the needs of professional advancement may dominate the nature of prejudice itself in the process of reconstitution.

The final argument for a holistic perspective is also grounded in the nature of ethnic communities. Here, however, it is the real diversity of these groups that speaks to a multidisciplinary and multiperspective paradigm. One of the earliest criticisms of mainstream social science was that it tended to stereotype ethnic peoples. Part of the process of stereotyping is the reduction of intragroup differences. In refuting these stereotypes, one of the elementary steps has been a refutation of the assumption of homogeneity underlying them.

The internal division of any population provides, as we have seen, one of the stumbling blocks to an organically validated theory. Once again the answer is not a retreat into principles of monistic truth, but full commitment to diversity. The multiplicity of the African american community, for example, calls for the development of ways to evaluate competing proposals from within this community.[45] This diversity also speaks to a pluralist theoretical structure that will allow all to discuss, compare, and mediate their disparate views.[46]

The crucial implication of this commitment to intellectual pluralism is that it works to prevent scholars from reifying their particular ideas. A commitment to pluralism is *not* a commitment to relativism. It is instead a commitment to an openness of judgement that does not seek to suspend one's capacity for individual criticism.[47] Barrera suggests that scholars must use their skills and training to formulate their own notions of the community's interests while recognizing their limits and imperfections: "rather than imposing our conceptions on others we must be able to engage in dialogue with other elements of the community, constantly reformulating our ideas in light of that dialogue."[48]

The appropriate relation between leader and led, expert and lay-person, is not susceptible to simple formulation, so that Barrera's observation may seem a bit facile. But his commitment to an open dialogue with the community is a more promising foundation for the construction of a democratic discourse than a monistic notion of truth.

Democracy is irrelevant in a world of social problems with objective solutions awaiting discovery. The construction of social truth is contingent, and should therefore be a democratic affair. Therefore our methodological rules for truth creation must themselves be democratic. This aspect of a commitment to organic theory brings us to the second prescription for method found in american Ethnic Studies: self-reflexivity.

The Need for Self-Reflexive Social Science

Self-reflexivity is presented as a useful criterion of theoretical adequacy, and combined with a holistic perspective the result is a powerful standard of validity. Like holism, self-reflexivity has received a large number of definitions in the literature, not all of which are equally cogent. These cumulative implications of self-reflexivity are: revelation of bias, theoretical consistency, and pedagogic adequacy.

Self-reflexivity, in its least sophisticated form, is presented as autobiography. This statement of where the researcher is "coming from" is intended as a corrective for some of the ideological excesses that are possible in a highly politicized research program. Having criticized mainstream social science for hiding its values and social functions behind a veil of objectivity, scholars in american Ethnic Studies are open to the charge that their activity is equally ideological.[49] This charge is not without substance. Many scholars in american Ethnic Studies see their role precisely as the creation of counter myths that their communities can use to combat the hegemony of Anglo "stereotypes."[50]

But even at this level one can still differentiate between the presentation of myths as truths and their presentation as myths. The latter approach is no less ideological except in its not presenting itself as an objective truth.

At any rate, more process-oriented scholars recognize that the juxtaposition of two mythologies is no exit from the ideology trap. Those who hold one mythology can always reject a competing myth. Theory is intended to provide a common language that will allow meaningful communication across such mythic gulfs. By rejecting scientific notions of objectivity, american Ethnic Studies requires some alternative. Barrera argues that the rejection of value freedom is not a rejection of objectivity, but merely a commitment to "avoiding obvious distortions of data." This is to be accompanied by an open statement of "one's values and concerns."[51]

The problem is that much of the bias revealed by "deconstructive" work in american Ethnic Studies is subtle rather than obvious. The statement of one's commitments does provide the reader with a warning, so there is a "fair-labelling" argument at work here. The question nonetheless remains as to how such a simple statement of one's values works to prevent non-obvious distortions? Further, what does one do with this statement of bias? Is it to be placed in a footnote and then forgotten? Is it to form the subject of an obligatory autobiography to accompany each presentation of one's research? Or is it intended to provide both a motor for the research as well as a warning to the reader?

This last possibility brings us closer to other notions of self-reflexivity. The second, and more sophisticated, idea underlying this stricture is that theories must be able to criticize themselves in a manner consistent with their criticism of competing theories. Such theories should be held accountable for analyzing themselves.

Once again there is a straightforward logic in support of this position. Accepting the axioms that theory is a reflection of the experience of the theorizer, and that theory is a collective enterprise, allows us to conclude that theory building is like any other institution: a social activity. Any and all social theories, to the extent they claim to explain social institutions, must be able to explain themselves. This means that american Ethnic Studies takes on the full burden of critical theory: the construction of a self-referential theory of theory.[52] The idea that theory must be self-referential is supported not by reason alone but also by the intellectual needs of ethnic communities for a positive self-understanding. If theory is a process of clarifying the nature of our action as subjects, then it is imperative that theory provide a concrete analysis of the subjects' condition, both external and internal. A Chicano perspective, for example, must be able to know itself as it is known by others, and be able to know others as it knows itself.

In the case of a community whose identity has been suppressed and distorted, this self-reflexive element of theory is even more important. For here our work must assist in the process of sorting out a multiple identity. The american Ethnic Studies epistemology does not, because it cannot, present us with a unified, integrated self. This way of knowing instead seeks to bring the various aspects of our self-hood into discourse with one another.

This is the most elaborate conception of self-reflexive theory. This conception refers to the effects of the theory upon those who are to learn from it. Unlike studying a foreign culture where one confronts subjects as objects, the study of one's own culture places one in the position of seeking an understanding of the self as a subject. Thus "Chicano history involves more than the creation of a new discipline or area of study. . . . It involves the *self-definition* of a people."[53]

Conclusions

The discipline of american Ethnic Studies has emerged from an encounter with the discourse of intellectual colonialism, which was a part of the larger process of material colonialism. This encounter has yielded a cultural relativization of the idea of objectivism and a rejection of the dichotomy between subject and object. These claims are bold indeed, and lead to the critical revision, if not outright abandonment, of many of the epistemological underpinnings of Western philosophy. Chief among these casualties is the idea that objectivity flows out of individual rationality rather than organically collective discourse.

The standards of self-reflexivity combine with holism to provide a powerful and rigorous epistemological alternative. By forcing theory to be consistent with itself and the needs of its users, the standard of self-reflexivity serves to prevent theory from becoming pure ideology. By promoting a standard of authenticity, we prohibit the use of theories that are justified solely upon their capacity to "further the aims and goals of a particular group, cause or movement."[54] Education for living should teach students "independence of mind, initiative, intellectual curiosity and an interest in life."[55]

Such a conception places the field of american Ethnic Studies in a position such that its practitioners are calling for a partial return to the traditions of humanism.[56] This call to emphasize human beings rather than individuals as the starting point for knowledge is consistent with the commitment to human liberation that grows out of the effort at racial liberation. The idea of the human being differs from that of the individual in its emphasis on the real traits of persons, rather than abstracting them into an intellectually tractable but nonexistent quantity.[57]

In american Ethnic Studies there are emerging proposed standards of good and bad theory: holism and self-reflexivity. If work reflects a holistic perspective that is self-reflexively applicable, we can consider it as having engaged in the discourse of this discipline. This does not mean the findings or interpretations advanced are "true," but simply that they are authentic. That is, that they open the knowing self to the possibility of being transformed by the act of knowing.

Despite the powerful perspective on theory that has developed in american Ethnic Studies, the discipline has only begun to explicitly state and defend its epistemology. This lacuna is based on the paucity of faculty and students trained in philosophy and allied disciplines, which may be a function of a not unwarranted suspicion of abstract formalization. Yet, if american Ethnic Studies is to succeed in establishing itself as a discipline coequal with Sociology, English, or History, we must continue to disprove the contention that the field is "devoid of logical or conceptual systems."[58]

Notes

1. The adjective american is not capitalized as the author feels that this concept is a fiction imposed by colonialism. America did not exist until it was invented. Further, the "americanness" of the groups discussed is frequently challenged in this colonial discourse.

2. Octavio Romano-V., "The Anthropology and Sociology of the Mexican American," *El Grito, A Journal of Contemporary Mexican Thought*, (Berkeley: CA: Quinto Sol Publications, 1971, pp. 44–46.

3. Ibid., 47.

4. Ibid., 55.

5. Boniface I. Obichere, "The Significance and Challenge of Afro-American Studies," *Journal of Black Studies* 1, no. 2 (1970):170.

6. Raymond Geuss, *The Idea of a Critical Theory: Habermas and the Frankfurt School* (Cambridge: Cambridge University Press, 1981), 35.

7. The traits of an actor are important in understanding the origins and consequences of his or her thoughts and actions, but this is different from using such traits as a measure of worth.

8. Geuss, *Idea of Critical Theory*, 39.

9. Jean Bakhtin, *The Dialogic Imagination* (Austin, Tex.: University of Texas Press, 1981); Jean Bakhtin, *Rabelais and his World*, trans. Helene Iswolksy (Cambridge: Cambridge University Press, 1968).

10. Na'im Akbar, "Afrocentric Social Sciences for Human Liberation," *Journal of Black Studies* 14, no. 4 1984:396.

11. Octavio Romano-V. "Social Science Objectivity and the Chicanos," 30–31; see also, Akbar, "Afrocentric Social Sciences," 399.

12. Romano, "Social Science Objectivity," 36–37; Akbar, "Afrocentric Social Sciences," 402.

13. Romano, "Social Science Objectivity," 37.

14. Ibid.

15. Ibid., 38.

16. Ibid., 40.

17. Ibid.

18. Akbar, "Afrocentric Social Sciences," 407.

19. Ibid., 409.

20. Ibid.

21. It should not be surprising that the oppressed are more aware of the effect of power and the existence of constraint than are the privileged.

22. Semmes, "Foundations," p. 8.

23. Akbar, "Afrocentric Social Sciences," 409.

24. Johnnella Butler, *Black Studies: Pedagogy and Revolution: A Study of Afro-American Studies and the Liberal Arts Tradition Through the Discipline of Afro-American Literature*,(Washington D.C.: University Press of America, 1981), 41.

25. See Francisco Vasquez, "Aztec Epistemology," *El Grito*, 1972.

26. Charlotte Bunche, "Beyond Either/Or: Feminist Options," In *Building Feminist Theory: Essays from Quest*. Charlotte Bunche (New York: Longmans Press, 1981), 44–56.

27. W. E. B. DuBois, *The Soul of Black Folks* (New York: Fawcet, 1961); Gerald Jackson, "The Origin and Development of Black Psychology: Implications for Black Studies and Human Behavior," *Studia Africana* 1, no. 3, 1979:281; Ronald Walters, "The Social Construction of Black Political Reality," *The Black Scholar* (April 1976), p. 36; Arturo Madrid-Barela, "In Search of the Authentic Pachuco," *Aztlan* 4, no. 1 39–59; 39–59; Eliu Carrana, "The Gorkase Mirror," in *The Chicanos*, ed. Edward Ludwig and James Santibanez (Baltimore: Pelican Press, 1976); Butler, *Black Studies Pedagogy and Revolution: A Study of Afro-American Studies and the Liberal Arts Tradition Through the Discipline of Afro-American Literature* (Washington D.C.: University Press of America, 1981).

28. Alfredo Mirande, "Chicano Sociology: A New Paradigm for Social Science," *Pacific Sociology Review* 21, no. 3: July 1978: 303.

29. Robert Staples, "Race and Ideology: An Essay in Black Sociology," *Journal of Black Studies* 3, no. 4 1973:397; Robert Staples, "Race and Colonialism," in *The Death of White Sociology*, ed. Joyce Ladner (New York: Random House, 1973), 168.

30. Phillip T. K. Daniels, "Theory Building in Black Studies," *The Black Scholar* (May/June 1981), p. 32.

31. Ibid., 33.

32. Donald Henderson, "What Direction Black Studies?" in *Topics in Afro-American Studies*, Henry J. Richards, ed. Buffalo: Black Academy Press, 1971), p. 17.

33. Semmes, Foundations 9; Joseph Scott, "Black Studies and Nation Building," in *The Death of White Sociology*, ed. Ladner, 290.

34. Obichere, "Challenge of Afro-American Studies" p. 164; see also Paulo Friere, *Pedagogy of the Oppressed* (New York: Seabury Press, 1970).

35. Raymond Plant, "Community: Concept, Conception and Ideology." *Politics and Society*, 8, no. 1, 79–105, for a useful discussion of the various uses of the idea of community in social theory.

36. Maurice Mandlebaum, "Social Facts," in Alan Ryan, ed. *The Philosophy of Social Explanation*. (Oxford: Oxford University Press, 1973), p.107.

37. To understand this distinction, consider the adage about a tree falling in the forest. Without anyone there to hear, the tree would certainly bring a noise (air vibrations of a specific frequency) into existence, but the noise would have no meaning.

38. Mandlebaum, p. 111.

39. See J. P. Sartre, *Jew and Anti-Semite*, for a premier ontological examination of racism.

40. Stokely Carmichael and Charles Hamilton, *Black Power*, (New York: Vintage Books, 1967), 4.

41. Robert Staples, "Race and Ideology: An Essay in Black Sociology," *Journal of Black Studies*, 12: 3, pp. 248–251.

42. Robert Staples, "Race and Colonialism," *Black Scholar*, June 1976, p.44.

43. Carlos Muñoz, "Politics and the Chicano: On the Status of the Literature," *Aztlan*, 5, no. 1; Daniels, p. 33.

44. Mario Barrera, "The Study of Politics and the Chicano," *Aztlan*, 5, no. 1, 15.

45. Jones, p. 9–11.

46. Maxine Baca-Zinn, "Sociological Theory in Emergent Chicano Perspectives," *Pacific Sociological Review*, 24, no. 2, p. 268; Barrera, p. 17; Rutledge M. Dennis, "Science Knowledge and Values: A Responseto Mack Jones," *Review of Black Political Economy*, 7, no. 4, p. 246.

47. Staples, "Race and Colonialism," p. 168.

48. Barrera, p. 20; Daniels, p. 31.

49. Alfredo B. Cuellar, *A Theory of Politics: The Idea of Chicano Revisionism* (Ann Arbor: University of Michigan Microfilms, 1977), p.34.

50. James S. Turner, "Sociology of Black Nationalism," in ed. Ladner, p.240.

51. Barrera, p. 14.

52. Geuss, p. 27; James S. Turner and Eric Perkins, "Towards a Critique of Social Science," Black Scholar, April 1976, pp. 6 & 10.

53. Juan Gomez-Quinones, "Toward a Perspective on Chicano History,"Aztlan Fall 71, pp. 2 & 39.

54. Rocco, p. 171.

55. Obichere, p. 165.

56. Eliu Carranza, *Pensamientos on Los Chicanos: A Cultural Revolution* (Berkeley: California Book Co., 1969), pp. 13–15; Raymond C. Roco, "The Role of Power and Authenticity in the Chicano Movement: Some Reflections," *Aztlan*, 5, no 1 & 2, pp. 395–414.

57. Karl Marx, *The German Ideology* (New York: International Publishers,1972), p. 43.

58. Daniels, p. 32.

CHAPTER 10

Is Jewish Studies Ethnic Studies?

Howard Adelman

Introduction[1]

The history of Jewish Studies has not yet been written. Scholars engaged in this field, however, are beginning to subject it to searching analysis. Pertinent articles have appeared that offer two extreme positions on the development of Jewish Studies: One sees the increase in Jewish Studies as a result of heightened Jewish self-awareness during the late 1960s because of the Six-Day War, growing interest in the Holocaust, and the influence of rising African American and ethnic consciousnesses that resulted in the establishment of academic programs and a move toward the diversification of the curriculum. The other, usually a reaction to the first view, argues that the study of Hebraica and Judaica has held an ancient and honorable place in the traditional university curriculum.

This chapter will trace the history of Jewish Studies, by which is meant the critical study of the history, literature, and thought of the Jewish people since the biblical period, and will indicate some of the features that undermine both of the positions mentioned above. Thus it will be demonstrated that the status of Hebraica and Judaica has not always been ancient or honorable and that the academic field has roots other than the consciousness-raising events of the late 1960s. These observations are offered with the hope that an outline of the development of Jewish Studies will suggest interdisciplinary discussion about the origins and development of other fields of study. When suggesting a comparison of different fields, it is hoped a level of discourse can be established that transcends the use of comparison as a foil for elaborating the strengths of one's own predilections. It is for this reason that Ethnic Studies cannot be narrowly defined but must be used in the general sense of any field that attempts to study a particular community, often neglected by the general curriculum. Jewish Studies are ethnic, and considering them as such is necessary not only for purposes of obtaining cooperation from administrators and mutual support of colleagues, but also for the creation of acadamically sound disciplinary and methodological approaches.

I.

Although Jewish scholarship can be traced uninterruptedly from the first century to the present, academic interest in the study of Hebrew was motivated by Christian missionary concerns. In 1311–1312 the Spanish Dominican Raimon Lull (c. 1235–1315) elicited a declaration from the Council of Vienne calling for instruction in Hebrew, Arabic, Syriac, and Greek for purposes of conversion. Hebrew instruction was soon instituted at universities such as Paris, Oxford, Bologna, Salamanca, and Alcala, and perhaps even earlier in Naples and Salerno. Jews were not involved in these programs of study; Christians or apostate Jews taught Christian students.

It is unlikely that Jews were allowed to attend universities at all until the fourteenth and fifteenth centuries in Italy, when they became involved in the study or the teaching of medicine.[2] Information about these early Jewish university students is available because for them to graduate and to practice, special dispensations had to be granted them by the popes.[3] Fear of the temptations to which Jewish students at Christian universities were exposed prompted Italian Jews in the fifteenth and again in the sixteenth century to propose a university under Jewish auspices where Jews could study Jewish and secular studies without distraction, pursuing degrees in medicine, law, philosophy, and rabbinics.[4] Nothing came of these plans at that time.

In Italy there were a few Jews who served as university Hebrew instructors in Ferrara, Pisa, Padua, and Bologna.[5] At Padua, the Jewish scholar Elijah del Medigo (c. 1460–1497) regularly lectured, although not as an official member of the faculty. (As a tribute to his contribution to the humanism of the period, his portrait was included among the great scholars of the time in a fresco by Gozzoli in the Palazzo Ricardi in Florence.) Most academic instruction in Hebrew was still offered by Christians. These courses were sporadic and not a regular feature of the curriculum. For example, in Bologna, Ionnes Faminius is listed as "*Ad Litteras hebraicas et caldeas*" from 1521 till 1526; the position is then listed until 1523 with no incumbent. After that it is dropped from the rolls.[6] The relationship between the study of Hebrew and medicine was particularly close during the Renaissance because many of the standard Greek and Arabic medical and philosophical texts were being reintroduced to Christian Europe through Latin translations made from Hebrew versions. By the end of the fifteenth century, Christian interest in Hebrew books also turned to kabbalistic works. These proved the truth of Christianity according to some of the leading figures of the Renaissance, such as the humanist Pico della Mirandola (1463–1494), who had studied with Elijah del Medigo.

In 1490, after a meeting in Florence with Pico, the German scholar Johannes Reuchlin (1455–1522) devoted himself to the study of Kabbalah and Hebrew. On his return to Germany, Reuchlin was appointed to the chair of Hebrew at Ingolstadt and then at Tuebingen. He was able to prevent the Talmud, which was being printed for the first time, from being burned at the instigation of the apostate Johannes Pfefferkorn (1469-c.1512). This controversy and Reuchlin's work in Hebrew stimulated a strong interest in the study of Hebrew literature in Europe, including Poland.[7] From 1525 to 1530, rabbinic studies received much Christian attention when they took on practical and political importance. Because of conflicting interpretations of several verses in Leviticus that were relevant to the validity of his marriage with Catherine of Aragon, Henry VIII of England sought rabbinic support in Italy for its annulment. In the wake of this controversy, Henry VIII established Regius Charis of Hebrew at Oxford and Cambridge, and Hebrew became a required subject. As was the case elsewhere, these positions were filled by Christians and apostates—Jews were not even allowed to live in England.

Interest in Hebrew and Kabbalah also spread to France, another country in Europe that had no Jews. In 1538, Guillaume Postel (1510–1581), a Christian Hebraist, taught Hebrew in Paris. One of the first practicing Jews invited to teach Hebrew at a European University was Elijah Levita (c. 1468–1529), a German Jewish Hebrew scholar and Yiddish writer who lived in Italy and worked for the Hebrew publishers there. Since there were no other Jews in France, and it would have been difficult if not impossible for him to continue to live as an observant Jew, he did not accept the position.

With the coming to Europe of the Reformation at the beginning of the sixteenth century, positions in Hebrew and Semitic languages flourished at the leading universities such as Jena, Leipzig, Heidelberg, Strasbourg, Basle, and Wittenberg. The early Protestant incumbents showed strong interest not only in biblical Hebrew, but also in rabbinic writings in order to advance their arguments against the interpretations and practices of the Catholic Church. From the sixteenth to the eighteenth centuries, these Protestant Hebraists devoted themselves to writing Hebrew grammars and translating into Latin sections of the Mishnah (c. 200), the Mishneh Torah—Moses Maimonides' (1135–1204) code of Jewish law, or the biblical commentaries of Solomon ben Isaac (Rashi, 1040–1105), Abraham ibn Ezra (1089–1164), or Isaac Abravanel (1437–1508). During the Council of Trent and the Catholic Restoration, even after the Catholic Church confirmed its commitment to the Latin canon of the Bible, many Catholic scholars continued to turn to post-biblical rabbinic literature and produced significant bibliographic catalogues, manuscript collections, and philological works.[8] Hebrew libraries, to which Jews were usually denied access, were developed by nobles, cardinals, bishops, and popes. As late as 1865, the Vatican Library, a major treasure-trove of Hebrew manuscripts, was closed to all Jews, prompting one Jewish scholar to urge the people of Italy to overthrow the Pontifical State for the sake of humanity—and Jewish scholarship.[9]

During the seventeenth century, Protestant scholars in many cities, such as Amsterdam, Utrecht, Leiden, and Altdorf, continued to exhibit interest in post-biblical Judaism. Typical of this generation of scholars was Johann Wagenseil (1633–1705) of Altdorf, who knew Yiddish, Hebrew, and Aramaic. Wagenseil defended Jews against the blood libel, translated rabbinic tractates, collected Jewish writings, and prepared polemics that he hoped would help convert the Jews. Another Dutch Protestant Hebraist, who not only read the Bible regularly in Hebrew but who was able to write letters in Hebrew, was Anna Maria van Schurman (1607–1678), an artist, poet, and student of Semitic languages, for whom a special loggia was built so that she could hear the lectures of Gysbertus Voetius (1589–1676) at the new University of Utrecht.[10] Between 1603 and 1611 at Oxford and Cambridge, Protestant scholars not only worked on translating the Bible for King James, but also were able to translate post-biblical texts such as the Mishnah and Maimonides' Code, and to correspond in Hebrew with Italian Jews. From 1647 to 1649 John Drury (1596–1680) proposed a college at the University of London for Jewish Studies for Protestant students, "For Conversions or correspondency of Jews and advancement of Oriental Language and Learning." Drury's published proposal also indicated that he felt that knowledge of Semitic tongues and Jewish mysteries was a key component of education for Protestants. Drury himself would later play a role in advocating the readmission of the Jews to England. There were also attempts by Hugh Broughton (1549–1612) to translate the New Testament into Hebrew for the benefit of Jews who had requested such a work from him.[11]

Although Christian Hebraists took Jewish literature seriously, maintained friendships with Jewish scholars, and devoted their lives to producing works that continue to be of value for Jewish Studies today, their material was often marred by their attempts to cast aspersions on Jewish practices, to justify Christian beliefs, and to win converts to Christianity. By 1700, Christian Hebrew scholars began to produce works that were even more hostile to Judaism. For example, Johannes Eisenmenger (1645–1704), a professor of Semitic languages at Heidelberg who had studied Talmud and Midrash with Jews for nineteen years under the pretense that he wanted to convert, wrote *Entdecktes Judentum*, "Judaism Unmasked," a collection of distorted translations of rabbinic texts designed to stigmatize Judaism. In this work, the professor gave credence to the blood libel and to the accusations that Jews poisoned wells. Nevertheless, Christian scholars continued to produce substantial works in Jewish Studies. *The History and Religion of the Jews from the Time of Jesus Christ to the Present*, the first major synoptic history of post-biblical Jewish life, was written by Jacques Basnage (1653–1725), a French Protestant who lived in exile in Holland after the revocation of the Edict of Nantes. Although Basnage's historicism did much for the presentation of Jews in nondogmatic terms, he still felt that the Jews had been rejected because they rejected Jesus.

II.

During the seventeenth century, Jews and Jewish Studies reached the new colleges in the American colonies. Hebrew was required at Harvard from the university's beginning; many students wrote theses about Hebrew and attempted to prove that it was the original language. Nevertheless, to teach Hebrew at Harvard, Judah Monis (1683–1764), a rabbi of obscure origins, had to convert before he could receive his appointment in 1722.[12] In the sermon he preached on the occasion of his public acceptance of Christianity, he used Kabbalah and the Hebrew scriptures to prove the truth of Christianity.[13] Ezra Stiles (1725–1795), a minister who had studied Hebrew and Kabbalah with an itinerant kabbalist, made Hebrew a required subject at Yale when he was president there from 1778–1795.[14] Chairs in Hebrew were established at Princeton and the schools that would later be called Columbia and the University of Pennsylvania. These classes were taught primarily for Christian divinity students by Christian instructors. Despite these early efforts, the study of Hebrew began to wane because as colleges shifted from training clergy to providing general education for the young men of the new nation they had become more practical and less classical. In 1787 Hebrew became an optional sujbect at Harvard and the professor of Semitic languages switched to teaching English. The swan song for colonial Semitics study was the last Hebrew oration delivered at the Harvard commencement of 1817.[15]

In the early nineteenth century, Jews first began to attend German universities in large numbers. For a few years (1812 to 1822), when Prussian authorities allowed Jews to hold academic posts, Jewish intellectuals in Europe turned to the *Wissenschaft des Judentums*, "the science of Judaism," calling for the modern, objective, critical study of Jewish history, Bible, rabbinics, literature, theology, law, and even contemporary statistics. This was a movement that attracted young Jewish intellectuals, primarily students at the new University of Berlin, whose feelings towards their own people had been awakened by contemporary criticism, popular anti-Jewish movements, and the indifference, estrangement, or apostasy of many young Jews. Noting the positive contributions made by Christians to the study of Judaism, they hoped that the "purely scholarly" study of the Jewish past, especially as embodied in Hebrew literature, would awaken in Jews a sense of pride; produce educational, communal, and religious reform; help foster Jewish survival; and cause non-Jews to have a more favorable opinion of Jews.[16] The pioneers of *Wissenschaft* included Leopold Zunz (1794–1886), Eduard Gans (1798–1839), and Hayyim (later Heinrich) Heine (1797–1856). By 1824, however, having published only three numbers of their *Zeitschrift*, their organization had disbanded and, ironically, soon afterwards Gans, Heine, and some of the others converted to Christianity. Heine noted later in life that *kugel* (noodle pudding) had done more to preserve Judaism than all three numbers of the *Zeitschrift fuer die Wissenschaft des Judentums*. Nevertheless, Zunz as a private scholar continued to pursue research that changed the nature of Jewish Studies and influenced, among others, Abrahim Geiger (1810–1875), a leader of Reform Judaism, Zacharias Frankel (1801–1875), a leader of what would become Conservative Judaism, and Solomon Rapoport (1790–1867) and Samuel David Luzzatto (1800–1865), who were traditionally religious scholars.[17]

These scholars hoped that *Wissenschaft* would be accepted as part of the curriculum of at least one European university, but this did not happen.[18] Instead *Wissenschaft* was fostered by Jewish scholars who served as rabbis, Jewish teachers, or businessmen. They communicated with each other in letters and made their findings known through articles that appeared in Jewish journals. In 1854 the Jewish Theological Seminary in Breslau, headed by Zacharais Frankel, became the first institution devoted to *Wissenschaft*. Other seminaries that followed this pattern soon opened in Berlin, Vienna, Paris, London, Budapest, and Italy. The rabbis who led these schools usually held doctorates in Semitics from the leading universities in Europe. Some monographs, critical editions, multivolume histories, and scholarly journals devoted to *Wissenschaft* began to appear.

It was in America that the first Jewish scholar with modern training was appointed to a university position in Semitics. Around 1835, Isaac Nordheimer (1809–1842), the first avowedly Jewish professor in the United States, taught, for no salary, at the new New York University from 1836 to 1842, in addition to Union Theological Seminary, inaugurating a long tradition of Semitic study there.[19] It has been suggested that he flirted with Christianity,[20] but this can neither be demonstrated in the tendentious reminiscences of a Christian colleague used for proof of such an assertion,[21] nor in accounts of his life written by other Christian contemporaries.[22] Finally, several Jews received appointments in Hebrew, Semitics, or rabbinics at European universities, beginning, appropriately, with Julius Fuerst (1805–1873), a Polish Jew who had studied at the University of Berlin with Hegel and at the Universities of Breslau and Halle with the prominent Semitic philologist Heinrich Gesenius (1786–1842). Fuerst taught Hebrew, Syriac, and Aramaic grammar and literature at the University of Leipzig and by 1864 he was appointed a full professor. Other Jews received positions teaching Talmud and rabbinics in Paris, Heidelberg, Strasbourg, Berlin, and Oxford and Cambridge soon after Jewish students were admitted.

For the most part, Christian Hebraists of the nineteenth century tended to concentrate more on the Hebrew Scriptures than post-biblical literature. Nevertheless, some Christians continued to teach Jewish subjects at major universities. Even the most committed scholars at this time, such as Franz Delitzsch (1813–1890), who wrote the first history of Hebrew poetry, and Hermann Strack (1848–1922), a prolific scholar of rabbinic literature, also engaged in missionary work among the Jews. These were the philosemites. There were also anti-semitic Semitic scholars such as Paul de Lagarde (1827–1891), a professor at Goettingen, who considered the Jews "a repulsive burden with no historical use."

In Europe *Wissenschaft* did not fulfill its goals. Indeed, its goals made it impossible for it to succeed. The attempt to use Jewish scholarship to create a sense of pride for Jews opened the door for some to use Jewish scholarship for other purposes. Not only were Jewish Studies open to anti-semites and missionaries, but much of the material produced by Jewish scholars was marked by ideological tendentiousness and denominational biases.[23] *Wissenschaft* also attracted "younger rabbis . . . who find their consolation in deciphering manuscripts and publishing books, when it is impossible to decipher the faith and convictions of their people . . . they work among the libraries rather than among the ignorant and superstitious."[24] By the end of the century, one of *Wissenschaft's* last and most famous practitioners, Moritz Steinschneider (1816–1907), lamented: "We have only one task left: to give the remains of Judaism decent burial."[25]

III.

In the United States, the last quarter of the nineteenth century was a period of institutional consolidation and rapid expansion for the American Jewish community. This was also a period of growth for American universities, for the involvement of Jews in university life, for renewed interest in Semitics, and for the creation of the first American graduate schools.[26] In 1871 Abram Isaacs, an alumnus of New York University and a rabbi who had received further training in Breslau, was appointed to teach at his alma mater, rising to the professorship of Semitics in 1889. Ironically, by this time the library of the abovementioned Paul de Lagarde had become the main corpus of the New York University Semitics collection. In 1874 the newly opened Cornell University hired Felix Adler (1851–1933), the son of a prominent New York Reform rabbi, as a professor of Hebrew and Semitic languages. At the time, this arrangement, financed by members of his father's synagogue, was unique for an American college. When, a few years later, Adler left academics to become the founder of the Ethical Culture Society, Jewish Studies would remain divided between Christian Hebraists (usually clergymen) at the universities and European-trained Jewish scholars (also usually clergymen) at Jewish community institutions. In 1875 Isaac Mayer Wise (1819–1900), once offered the help of Senator Daniel Webster to secure a position teaching at Boston University in 1849, founded Hebrew Union College in Cincinnati to train Reform rabbis, and in 1885 Sabato Morais (1823–1897) opened the Jewish Theological Seminary in New York to train more traditional rabbis. These seminaries would attract many European Jewish scholars and rabbis to the United States.

At the end of the nineteenth century some American Jews who had earned doctorates in Europe, who for the most part came from the Reform movement, and who were often the sons of the leading pulpit rabbis, had begun to teach Semitics and rabbinics at major American universities.[27] These men, who sometimes taught for no pay or for a subsidy provided by the Jewish community, attracted both Jewish and Christian students, but they did not produce any widespread dissemination of Jewish Studies on American campuses.

The important work in Jewish Studies was done at institutions developed by the Jewish community. In 1888 the Jewish Publication Society of America was founded to help publish basic Hebrew texts, English translations of important works, and new scholarship. In 1892 the American Jewish Historical Society was established to promote research in American Jewish history. From 1901 to 1905, *The Jewish Encyclopedia*, the first systematic presentation of Jewish scholarship, was published in the United States by Dr. Isaac Funk, a distinguished Christian minister. A key collaborator in the work of the Jewish Publication Society and the *Jewish Encyclopedia* was Henrietta Szold (1860–1945), who would go on to a distinguished career as a leader of zionist educational and philanthropic organizations.

In 1902–1903, three men who would do much to promote Jewish Studies in America received appointments at important institutions. As president of the Jewish Theological Seminary, Solomon Schechter (1847–1915) would gather some of the finest Jewish scholars in America and Europe. Similarly, as president of Hebrew Union College, Kaufmann Kohler (1843–1926) assembled a very distinguished faculty. George Foot Moore (1851–1931), as professor of Religion at Harvard, developed the academic study of religion by combining German scientific standards with an American openness for Jews and the study of Judaism.[28]

During this period of expansion in the field, Dropsie College, an institution devoted exclusively to post-graduate study of Hebrew, Semitics, and rabbinics, opened in Philadelphia in 1907. Moses Dropsie (1821–1905), a child of a mixed marriage who accepted Judaism at the age of fourteen, made provisions in his will for this institution and required that there would be "no distinction on account of creed, colour or sex in the admission of students." Significantly omitted from most accounts of his largess is the fact that members of the faculty and the board had to be Jewish.[29] In 1906, the year between Dropsie's death and the year the college opened, the executors of his estate solicited opinions from the leading figures in higher education concerning how the school should be run. The replies provide wide-ranging views about the nature and purpose of graduate education in general and Jewish higher education in particular.[30] The considerations ranged from the "ethical" to the employment prospects of the graduates—positions as heads of orphan asylums with enough time for scholarly research. Also under discussion during that period was whether the college would include a center for Jewish education or whether this would violate the nonsectarian spirit of Dropsie's will.[31] The mantle of Jewish scholarship unofficially passed from the old world to the new in 1910 when the *Jewish Quarterly Review* moved from England to Dropsie College.

Institutions devoted to Jewish Studies continued to emerge in the United States. Local Hebrew colleges in many major cities offered preparatory programs for high school students and courses for college credit. Important Judaica and Hebraica collections were developed at the Library of Congress, Jewish Theological Seminary, Hebrew Union College, Yale, and the New York Public Library. In 1915, the Alexander Kohut Memorial Foundation was established to support the publication of Jewish scholarship. In 1916 Bernard Revel, a Dropsie graduate and head of the Rabbi Isaac Elhanan Theological Seminary (later Yeshiva University), tried to establish a Society of Jewish Academicians of America with the announced provision that ". . . scientific truth will have to be sacrificed to tradition."[32] Revel's plan was opposed by the leading scholars and it came to naught. Shortly afterwards, in 1920, the American Academy of Jewish Research was established to promote Jewish scholarship in the United States. Drafts of the articles of its incorporation show that Revel's name was crossed out, perhaps indicating continued tensions over the nature of Jewish scholarship.

Despite the slow acceptance of Jews into the ranks of American faculties, Jewish Studies continued to emerge at secular colleges, and prominent scholars in areas of Jewish Studies received appointments.[33] In 1924 David

Blondheim (1884–1934), a pioneer in the study of Judeo-Romance dialects, including the French glosses in Rashi's commentaries, began to teach Romance languages at Johns Hopkins. In 1925 a chair in Jewish Studies at Harvard was established by Lucius N. Littauer, a member of the Jewish community of New York; until 1958 this position was occupied by Harry A. Wolfson (1887–1974), a student of Moore's who had been teaching Jewish Studies at Harvard since 1915. In 1930 a chair in Jewish history was endowed at Columbia. It was held until 1968 by Salo Baron (b. 1895). Wolfson and Baron produced graduate students who would determine the contours of the field for a long time. A major boon to the furtherance of Jewish collegiate life and the teaching of Jewish Studies was the establishment between 1923 and 1925 of the Hillel movement, a national organization that helped provide rabbis, leaders, and program material for local campus Jewish organizations.

Jewish Studies continued to develop abroad. When the Hebrew University in Jerusalem opened in 1925, a secular setting had been established that would support many departments for specialization in Jewish Studies and encourage the development of Hebrew as a living language for Jewish scholarship. In Europe, Jewish academicians found positions not only at seminaries in Germany, England, Poland, Italy, Hungary, and France, but also at universities such as Warsaw, Frankfurt, and Padua.

In the United States, influenced by the renaissance of Hebrew language and literature in Eastern Europe and Palestine, there was a growing interest during the 1930s in the study of Hebrew. (Some themes in Hebrew literature unique to the United States were Native American motifs and descriptions of the plight of the African Americans.[34]) As a result, during the early 1930s Hebrew was introduced in the New York City public high schools. This movement soon reached the colleges, and in 1934 New York University (the institution that had the largest Jewish student body in the world but not a single Jewish instructor until 1930) began to offer modern Hebrew in the division of General Education.[35] Similarly, although there had been a course in Jewish history since the 1930s, Hebrew was not introduced at City College until 1948. By the 1940s about a dozen colleges offered modern Hebrew, in addition to the seventy-seven colleges and forty-seven seminaries that taught biblical Hebrew. Some of the schools that introduced modern Hebrew included standard bastions of Semitics such as Pennsylvania, Hopkins, Chicago, Harvard, Columbia, and Yeshiva as well as large universities often with sizeable Jewish enrollments such as Buffalo, Boston, Brooklyn, Colorado, Missouri, Wayne State, and Houston.

At least one small liberal arts college with relatively few Jews also offered courses in Modern Hebrew and Jewish Studies during the 1930s and 1940s. This was Smith College, a prominent women's college in Northampton, a small town in western Massachusetts. Smith catalogues show that beginning in 1938 Margaret Breckenbury Crook (1886–1972), who had been at Smith since 1921, taught a Hebrew course in the Department of Religion and Biblical Literature that included "readings from Modern Hebrew school-books." For a year or two this course was taught by a young Jewish visiting lecturer in the department, Cyrus Gordon (b. 1908), who was at Smith to study its famous collection of cuneiform tablets. Beginning in the academic year 1940–41 there was also a course called "Contemporary Judaism," described as "An Analysis of Judaism, its religion and social background; Dispersion; the Jew in Europe and in America; Judaism's contribution to Christianity and to democracy. Present forces influencing Jewish Christian relations." The instructor was S. Ralph Harlow (1885–1972), a Christian scholar and activist who travelled regularly in Palestine (and India), lectured in synagogues, protested the persecution of Jews, and invited rabbis to speak to his class. Harlow also organized regular field trips to New York City each year, and the itineraries included going to Harlem to listen to "negro music," touring the Lower East Side, visiting the Spanish Portuguese Synagogue, and attending Sunday morning services at Riverside Church to hear Harry Emerson Fosdick preach.[36] The work of Harlow, following the pattern established by Moore at Harvard, shows clearly how Jewish Studies began to enter some colleges in the United States. Believing that religion is a major force in the world that has to be understood in its own terms, Harlow and his department hoped that by teaching about all religions greater understanding between all peoples would be fostered.[37] As he and his colleagues began to teach about Eastern religions, it was only natural that attention would be given to developments in Judaism after the Bible. In recognition of his accomplishments, Harlow was awarded an honorary degree from Hebrew Union College, bringing the relationship between secular colleges and Jewish institutions full circle.

IV.

Although by 1945 some schools had let their Semitics programs lapse, there were now about a dozen full-time positions around the country in Jewish Studies.[38] After the establishment of the State of Israel in 1948, Jewish Studies, especially courses on Israel and Hebrew, were introduced at schools with both large and small Jewish enrollments. Also at this time, Brandeis University, opened in 1948 as a secular university supported by the American Jewish community, developed a department of Near Eastern and Judaic Studies under the leadership of Simon Rawidowicz (1896–1957). Courses in Jewish Studies were still mostly taught by Hillel directors, leaders of Jewish educational agencies, and special appointees.[39] By 1956, 48 colleges and universities offered modern Hebrew, and 133 colleges and 112 seminaries taught biblical Hebrew, an interesting increase since the language of the Bible had not changed much in a decade. In 1958 the National Defense Education Act gave added impetus to the study of foreign languages, including modern Hebrew. Continuing to reflect the changing status of Jewish Studies on the national level, in 1963 Smith College hired Jochanan Wijnhoven (1927–1988), a specialist in Kabbalah and medieval Jewish religious philosophy who had degrees from the Hebrew University and Brandeis, to teach in the Religion department. The course in contemporary Judaism became a year-long survey of Jewish thought. An introductory course in biblical Hebrew led to a sequence of courses in post-biblical Hebrew religious texts. By 1966, throughout the country, there were fifty-four professors and thirty-four Hillel directors who offered Jewish Studies at 92 colleges and universities.[40]

In 1966, observers were aware of the growth of Jewish Studies. They explained that the phenomenon was due in part to pride in the State of Israel and (growing) concern over the losses of the Holocaust. They saw the Jewish Studies programs as a sign of the new acceptance of Jews and Judaism in the colleges and universities of the United States after World War II. Part of the reason for the expansion of Jewish Studies during the 1940s and 1950s was attributed to basic changes in the curriculum of higher education, which allowed for interdisciplinary studies, more flexibility, and a broader range of courses. Finally, the Jewish community often backed Jewish Studies programs and supported what was considered to be one of the few opportunites for serious study in modern Jewish life. Jewish students, however, were not turning out in large numbers for the courses and non-Jewish participation was dismissed as "negligible." Because there were more positions than trained candidates, questions were raised about the qualifications of many people who were hired to teach during this period of expansion. It is significant to note that at this time on the undergraduate level the number of women students equalled or exceeded that of men; however, most of the graduate students and faculty were men, and when writing about the growth of Jewish Studies writers routinely referred to faculty members as "men."

Thus, before the Six-Day War and the public recognition of African American and other American Ethnic Studies, Jewish Studies had already developed as a field that enjoyed some success but also suffered from many problems. Of course, these later events did inspire many Jews on the faculties, in the student bodies, in alumni organizations, and in the community to turn to Jewish Studies and the number of programs continued to rise. In 1969, the year the Association for Jewish Studies was established, there were 80 full-time positions and another 200 part-time appointments. According to some estimates, at least 600 students were majoring in Jewish Studies in 1969. During the 1970s, interest in the study of modern Hebrew continued to grow while national trends indicated decreased participation in language courses.[41] During the 1980s, after a period of recession in university growth, many schools in the country have some offerings in Jewish Studies and it is easy to find programs in modern Hebrew. New chairs in Jewish Studies are still being established, most recently at several of the Seven Sisters such as Mount Holyoke, Wellesley, and Smith. More chairs in Jewish Studies are now occupied by women scholars.

In conclusion, the analysis of Jewish Studies reveals several paradoxes. On the one hand, the field has had a long history; on the other, Jewish Studies surely has had an erratic pattern of growth and, even after their establishment, these courses have been dispensable. The appearance of Jewish Studies seems to correlate more with the needs of the practitioners, Christian or Jewish, than with what schools have considered to be their essential curricular needs. Although making substantial academic contributions, medieval and colonial Christian pioneers in Hebraica, Judaica, and rabbinica pursued their work for the furtherance of Christianity, often at the expense of Judaism. The early pioneers of "the Science of Judaism" had an agenda that would now be categorized as ethnic—Jewish survival and pride. The failure of Jewish Studies to find acceptance at universities until the twentieth century is as much an indication of the nature of the field as it is of the universities themselves. Having developed in other contexts (most notably rabbinical seminaries and Jewish communal institutions) Jewish Studies has acquired contours that still make it difficult for it to fit into the secular collegiate curriculum. The burden of adjustment, however, does not fall exclusively on Jewish Studies. One of the essential aspects of Jewish Studies is a challenge to the nature and structure of Western higher education. One of the reasons for interest in Jewish Studies and other Ethnic Studies is that the basic university curriculum not only excludes materials relevant to the lives of many students, but there is, according to many, little room conceptually for anything but "an un-self-conscious, Western, white, Christian, male view of the world," which is often considered "universalistic." One of the unstated tensions present as new fields emerge is whether they or the traditional curriculum are in fact ethnic. Is it the regular departments or the new programs that really represent parochial concerns? Practioners of Jewish Studies and other Ethnic Studies need not feel any shame that students are motivated to take their courses out of a sense of personal interest, that they themselves entered the field because of specific communal or personal concerns, that growth in their field correlates with the arrival of large numbers of their group on a given campus, that their group is using the university to recognize its concerns and validate its position, and that their field does not conform to the standard curricular rubrics. Ironically, writers on Jewish Studies want to distance their field from the label of "ethnic," which often evokes partisan associations, while at the same time they list all the benefits the Jewish community derives from the academic study of Judaism. They argue that Jewish Studies should not be a partisan enterprise but overlook the fact that the academic process has always been committed to fostering particular values, whether they are nationalistic, religious, sexual, or racial. The ultimate defense against ideological forays into the classroom is the academic process itself, which is based on rigorous disciplinary and methodological questioning of all data, assumptions, and conclusions. If such tests are not applied—and, even before the development of Ethnic Studies, they have not always been—the fault does not lie with the particular field but the academic process itself. The task before Jewish Studies and Ethnic Studies, therefore, is, on the one hand, not the repression of identity, community, or social concerns, but the creation of a methodology that will help these matters find expression among many disciplines and departments on campus. On the other hand, traditional courses, offering what they do in terms of content, method, depth, and coverage, cannot try to accomodate all that every ethnic perspective brings to academic study. To be sure, the experiences of the minority, any minority, can only be understood in light of the influence on it by the majority of its culture, just as the majority culture must be seen as influenced by many different traditions. Questions for the future include how to coordinate Ethnic Studies with traditional disciplines and with new fields of inquiry, such as Women's Studies, and different ethnic fields with each other, such as Jewish Studies and Latin American Studies or Jewish Studies and African American Studies.[42]

The articulation of Jewish or ethnic considerations in the curriculum is an opportunity not only for those involved an academics, but also for those committed to the ethnic community as well. Indeed, the academic study of the Jewish people is the only opportunity to challenge tendentious, polemical, and self-serving interpretations of the Jewish experience. Thus, Jewish Studies is a valuable way to invigorate a sense of cultural creativity and to develop critical thinking in the Jewish community. Jewish and Ethnic Studies will succeed not because they serve the needs of a particular constituency, but because they offer a methodologically sound perspective for all students, contribute to the advancement of larger disciplines, and aid the overall intellectual development of each student.

Notes

1. I would like to thank John Walter and Johnnella Butler for their encouragement in preparing this chapter; Benjamin Ravid, Leonard Ehrlich, Arnold Adelman, and Cynthia Smith for their suggestions; and Jonathan Sarna of the American Jewish Archives and the staff of the Smith College Archives for their assistance. This chapter

was originally presented as a paper at the National Association for Ethnic Studies and prepared for publication in *Explorations in Ethnic Studies* 11, no. 2 (March 1988). A brief version appeared in *The Chronicle of Higher Education* (3 August 1988), p. A36.

2. Emilia Veronese Ceseracciu, "Ebrui laureti a Padova nel Cinquecento," *Quaderni per la storia dell'Universita di Padova* 13 (1980):151–68; Felice Momigliano, "Un ebreo professore di medicina all'Universita di Perugia nelle sconde meta del secolo xiv," *Il Vessillo Israelitico* 66 (1918):384–87.

3. Cecil Roth, "The Medieval University and the Jew," *The Menorah Journal* 19 (1930–1931):128–41; Vittore Colorni, "Sull'ammissibilita degli ebrei alla laurea anteriormente al secolor xix," *La Rassegna Mensile di Israel* 16 (1950):202–16.

4. Jacob Marcus, *The Jew in the Medieval World* (Cincinnati: The Union of American Hebrew Congregations, 1938), 381–88.

5. F. Servi, "Studii orientali in Italia," *Il Vessillo Israelitico* 24 (1876):408–10.

6. Umberto Dallari, *I rotuli dei lettori legisti e artisti dello studio bolognese dal 1384 al 1799* (Bologna: Regia tip. dei Fratelli Merlani., 1889), 32–69. On the study of Hebrew in Pavia during the fifteenth century, see Shlomo Simonsohn, *The Jews in the Duchy of Milan* 2 (Jerusalem, 1982), nos. 2275, 2276, 228s.

7. Witold Tyloch, "Hebrew Studies in Poland—Warsaw University," *Hebrew Studies* 26 (1985): 131–35.

8. Giuliano Tamani, "Gli studi ebraici a Padova nei secoli xvii-xx," *Quaderni per la storia dell'Universita di Padova* 9–10 (1976–1977):215–28.

9. Nahum Glatzer, "The Beginnings of Modern Jewish Studies," in *Studies in Nineteenth Century Jewish Intellectual History*, ed. Alexander Altmann (Cambridge: Harvard University Press., 1964), 31.

10. On Anna Maria van Schurman, see Dame Una Birch Pope-Hennessy, *Anna Van Schurman: Artist, Scholar, Saint* (London: Longman's, Green and Co., 1909); Paul Tschackert, *Anna Maria von Schuermann: der Stern von Utrecht* (Gotha: Friedrich Andreas Perthes., 1876); and Anna Margaretha Hendrika, *Anna Maria Van Schurman en de Studie der Vrouw* (Amsterdam:, H. J. Paris 1924). An English translation of this fascinating woman's autobiography, *Eucleria sue melioris pratis electio* (Alton, 1673), remains a desideratum. Originally written in Dutch, it has been translated into German (1783) and Latin (1782). The *History of Women* (microfilm series) has micro-filmed her autobiography and a collection of her letters (New Haven:, Research Publications, Inc. 1975) see reel 77, nos. 494–95. Schurman also wrote a tractate on the education of women, *De ingenii muliebris ad doctrinam et meliores litteras aptitudine* (Leiden: ex officiana Elseviriana., 1641). On other female Christian Hebraists, see Meyer Kayserling, "A Princess as Hebraist," *Jewish Quarterly Review* o.s. 9 (1897):509–14. I am indebted to Jochanan Wijnhoven for this information.

11. see Richard Popkin, "The First College for Jewish Studies," *Revue des Etudes juives* 143 (1984):351–64.

12. On Monis, see Milton M. Klein, "A Jew at Harvard in the Eighteenth Century," *Proceedings of the Massachusetts Historical Society* 92 (1985):135–45.

13. On the conversionary aspects of Christian Kabbalah, see my "Rabbi Leon Modena and the Christian Kabbalists," in *Renaissance Rereadings: Intertext and Context*, ed. Maryanne Cline Horowitz (Urbana: University of Illinois Press.?, 1988): 271–86.

14. Eisig Silberschlag, "The Primacy of Hebrew in Early America," *Hebrew Studies* 26 (1985):123–30; Robert Pfeiffer, "The Teaching of Hebrew in Colonial America," *The Jewish Quarterly Review* n.s. 45–46 (1954–1956):363–73.

15. William Rosenau, "Semitic Studies in American Colleges," *Central Conference of American Rabbis Yearbook* 6 (1896):99–113.

16. For a selection of important documents about *Wissenschaft des Judentums*, see Paul R. Mends-Flohr and Jehudah Reinharz, *The Jew in the Modern World* (New York: Oxford University Press., 1980), 182–213.

17. Jacob Haberman, "Some Changing Aspects of Jewish Scholarship," *Judaism* 35 (1986):186–87.

18. Salon Baron, "Jewish Studies at Universities: An Early Project," *Hebrew Union College Annual* 46 (1975):357–76.

19. Lewis S. Feuer, "Stages in the Social History of Jewish Professors in American Colleges and Universities," *American Jewish History* 81 (1982):432–65.

20. Harold Wechsler and Paul Ritterband, "Jewish Learning in American Universities: The Literature of a Field," *Modern Judaism* 3 (1983):260.

21. H. Neil, "Reminiscences of I. Nordheimer," *New Englander and Yale Review* 33 (1874):506–12.

22. Edward Robinson, "Biographical Notices of Gesenius and Nordheimer," *Bibliotecha Sacra* (New York: self-published, 1843), 379–90; Jonathan D. Sarna, *Jacksonian Jew: The Two Worlds of Mordecai Noah* (New York: Holmes & Meier, 1981), 128 and 202.

23. Gershom Scholem, "The Science of Judaism—Then and Now," in *The Messianic Idea in Judaism and Other Essays in Jewish Spirituality* (New York: Schocken Books., 1971), 304–17; Michael Meyer, "Jewish Religious Reform and *Wissenschaft des Judentums*: The Positions of Zunz, Geiger, and Frankel," *Leo Baeck Institute Yearbook* 16 (1971):19–41.

24. A. S. Isaacs, 1881, cited by Harold S. Wechsler, "Pulpit of Professoriate: The Case of Morris Jastrow," *American Jewish History* 74 (1985):338.

25. Scholem, "The Science of Judaism," 307.

26. Feuer, "The Stages," 433, suggests that apart from a few appointments in Jewish or Semitic Studies, Jews usually entered new academic fields.

27. Wechsler, "Pulpit or Professoriate," 338–55; for names of individuals and institutions involved in every stage of the development of Jewish Studies in the United States, consult my article, "Jewish Studies at American Colleges and Universities," *Encyclopaedia of Jewish-American History and Culture*, ed. Jack Fischel and Sanford Pinsker (New York: Garland Press, 1990).

28. Solomon Zeitlin, "Jewish Learning in America," *Jewish Quarterly Review* n.s. 45–46 (1954–1956):582–616.

29. Cyrus Adler, *I Have Considered the Days* (Philadelphia: The Jewish Publication Society of America., 1941), 274.

30. Meir Ben-Horin, "Scholars' 'Opinions': Documents in the History of Dropsie University," *Salo Wittmayer Baron Jubilee Volume* (New York: distributed by Columbia University Press. Published by Jerusalem: American Academy for Jewish Research., 1974), 167–208.

31. Herbert Parzen, "New Data on the Foundation of Dropsie College," *Jewish Social Studies* 28 (1966):131–47.

32. Ira Robinson, "Cyrus Adler, Bernard Revel and the Prehistory of Organized Jewish Scholarship in America," *American Jewish History* 69 (1979):502.

33. Feuer, "The Stages," estimates that there were less than one-hundred Jewish liberal arts faculty members by the mid-twenties.

34. Eisig Silberschlag, "Hebrew Literature in America," *Jewish Quarterly Review* 45–46 (1954–1956): 413–33.

35. Feuer, "The Stages," 455–56.

36. Based on materials on Harlow in the Smtih College Archives.

37. Based on a telephone discussion with Professor Virginia Corwin Brautigam, a retired member of the Smith College Department of Religion and Biblical Literature.

38. Abraham Katsh, "The Status of Hebrew in American Colleges and Universities," *Jewish Education* 13 (1941):108–09, 142.

39. Abraham Katsh, "The Teaching of Hebrew in American Universities," *The Modern Language Journal* 30 (1946): 575–86; idem, "Growth of Hebrew in American Colleges and Universities," *Jewish Education* 21 (1950):11–16.

40. Arnold Band, "Jewish Studies in American Colleges and Universities," *American Jewish Year Book* 67 (1967):3–10.

41. David Rudavsky, "Hebraic and Judaic Studies in American Higher Education," *Congress Bi-Weekly* 41 (1974):8–20.

42. For an example of the integration of Jewish Studies and Women's Studies, see Judith Baskin, ed., *Jewish Women in Historical Perspective* (Detroit: Wayne State University Press, 1990).

CHAPTER 11

The Politics of Jewish Invisibility in Women's Studies

Evelyn Torton Beck[1]

Like these, my despised ancestors, I have become a keeper of accounts
— *Bashert,* Irena Klepfisz

The task of integrating Jewish women's history and culture into the feminist project has been only partially successful, in spite of the many different kinds of writings produced by Jewish feminists in the last decade and the variety of papers and workshops on Jewish themes presented at the National Women's Studies Association conferences. Not even the presence of a strong and visible Jewish Women's Caucus, which in 1986 organized a highly successful plenary revealing the strength and diversity of "Feminist Jewish Women's Voices," has assured Jewish themes a recognized place in the feminist classroom or within feminist theorizing.[2]

For this reason, delighted as I am by the publication of three excellent new resources in Jewish Women's Studies, which will be of enormous help to those who wish to engage in research or teaching about Jewish women, I can no longer simply celebrate the appearance of these books as if I believed their availability would really make a major difference in the emerging discipline of Women's Studies. In truth, I see no reason to believe that these new books will be any more successful than were the books and essays that preceded them and that these texts document and annotate.[3] Because Jewish women's lives continue to remain so conspicuously absent from the majority of introductory Women's Studies texts as well as most feminist and lesbian feminist anthologies—even those purporting to represent a spectrum of difference—it is difficult not to believe Jewish themes are being systematically excluded.[4] A few texts that do mention Jewish women, marginally, often focus exclusively on the patriarchal aspects of the Jewish religion, fail to mention feminist transformations of Judaism, and fail to speak of the diversity Jewish women themselves represent. Nor do they develop a conceptual framework that would provide an analysis of anti-Semitism.

Let me clear that I am not speaking of the exclusion of writings *by* Jewish women. Many of those who have produced feminist theoretical writings are, in fact, Jewish, though it may be unadvisable to call attention to that fact since Jews have historically and stereotypically (on more than one occasion even within the feminist movement) been accused of "taking over" and "grabbing power."[5] Let me be clear, therefore, that I am not talking about an exclusion of Jews *per se* either from the institutions, the presses, or from positions of power within Women's Studies. I am talking about the absence of writings *about* Jewish women from feminist texts and the conspicuous absence of Jewish women's culture from feminist "multicultural" events or those focusing on "minority" women.[6] But most especially, I am writing of the silence surrounding the recognition that *anti-Semitism*, whose shadow continues to fall on Jewish women's lives, is, or ought to be, a feminist issue.

An unwillingness within the Women's Movement to recognize anti-Semitism as appropriate to the feminist agenda is not new in the history of feminism. In "American Feminism and the Jewish Question, 1890–1940," a revealing essay that ought to become required reading in a number of Women's Studies courses (especially American women's history and feminist theory), Elinor Lerner demonstrates persuasively "that Jews have been essentially discounted in the history of American feminism" throughout the twentieth century.[7] She shows how the reluctance of native-born white American feminists to talk explicitly about Jews or to deal with rising anti-Semitism in the early decades of this century made Jewish support for feminism invisible, and further, allowed feminists to neglect issues that were specifically Jewish. As a result, the Women's Joint Congressional Committee, an umbrella group formed in 1920 to lobby for women's issues (to which the National Council of Jewish Women belonged), refused to take any formal position against the persecution of Jews in Europe, although it took a stand on a wide variety of other social concerns not focusing specifically on women, such as peace issues, anti-lynching legislation, internationalism, and home rule for the District of Columbia. While Lerner also documents some clear acts of overt anti-Semitism and Jewish stereotyping within the suffrage movement, she concludes that "More common than open, anti-Jewish statements was anti-Semitism by neglect: the non-recognition of Jewish existence." I find it deeply troubling that, with only a little modification, Lerner's words can be used to describe the contemporary period of feminism as well.

Some aspects of historical neglect are uncomfortably reminiscent of NWSA's initial reluctance to include anti-Semitism among the "-isms" it opposes, a position NWSA ratified in the early 1980s only after considerable debate, when it went on record as "opposing anti-Semitism against Arabs and

Jews." While this compromise is clearly a better solution than non-inclusion, it seems a transparent effort to protect the organization against the interpretation that if it is unqualifiedly against "Jew-hating," it will be viewed as being "for Israel." A stronger stand would have left anti-Semitism its integrity of meaning, and would have added "anti-Arab discrimination" as an act of greater inclusivity and specificity.

In 1982 I wrote, *"Jewish invisibility is a symptom of anti-Semitism as surely as lesbian invisibility is a symptom of homophobia."*[8] This statement has an even stronger resonance in the conservative political climate of the late 1980s, a time when Jews have a high negative visibility because of the ways in which the media has perpetuated the false myth that all Jews approve of Israel's foreign and domestic policies. While it is true that a number of conservative American and Israeli Jews do continue to defend Israel's hard-line policies, many others are in sharp disagreement. While some hesitate to criticize Israel because of historic anti-Semitism and a misplaced sense that to criticize Israel is to betray it, there are many thousands of Jews in the United States and Israel who are protesting Israel's actions and issuing a call for immediate negotiations for a peace in the Middle East that will recognize the rights of both Jews and Palestinians to a homeland.[9]

In the United States and Europe, anti-Semitism is also being fueled by the growth of neo-Nazi white supremacists, neo-conservative Christian fundamentalists, and extremists in Farrakhan's Nation of Islam. The increasing tendency of many members of the political Left to oversimplify Middle Eastern politics has resulted in the easy elision of "Jew" with "Israel," which has made Jews the world over targets for anti-Israeli sentiments that are often expressed by violent acts of Jew-hating.[10]

Because patriarchal world politics also enters the feminist arena, this is the context in which we must analyze the reluctance of many Jewish women to write about Jewish themes. On the whole, it has not felt safe to bring Jewish issues into feminist discourse. First, there is the fear of attack that produces a protective silence; second, is the fear of being perceived as too "demanding," "pushy," or "politically incorrect." Third, and possibly more important than any other factor, the fear of being excluded keeps Jewish women silent. Speaking and writing about explicitly Jewish themes (or even including them substantially) raises the worry that the work will be perceived as marginal, and therefore not as widely read and discussed. In short, in writing as a Jew the feminist takes the risk of losing her place. I have long believed that it is the centrality of Jewishness to her writing that has kept the brilliantly evocative poetry of Irena Klepfisz from being more widely known.[11] There is also a fourth factor: the confusion that many Jewish feminists experience in trying to bring together Jewish and feminist (or lesbian feminist) identities and agendas. Just how unsafe it can be is demonstrated by Jenny Bourne's virulent

attack on such efforts in which she singles out *Jewish* women's struggle for
identity as particularly reactionary: "Nowhere has the reversal of political
priorities in feminism been more evident than amongst Jewish women."[12]
While this particular debate is occurring in Great Britain, it has its resonance
in the United States and has, I believe, discouraged some feminists from
speaking out as Jews.[13]

The responses of Jewish women to the 1986 NWSA plenary are particularly instructive. Many reported that they felt equally elated by the positive
reception to the session and relieved that there had been no negative response.
A number of women who only marginally identified as Jews were especially
moved and encouraged by this public support to identify themselves as Jews
in a non-Jewish space for the first time in their adult lives.

In the last decade, Jewish women have also been increasingly intimi-
dated by the virulent attacks upon them that have taken the form of a vicious
stereotyping commonly known as "JAP" ("Jewish American Princess") bait-
ing.[14] This most recent embodiment of anti-Semitism (promoted by greeting
cards, T-shirts, jokes, books, cartoons, and in common speech) has become
shorthand to designate all that is despicable in American culture, framed in
anti-Semitic terms and projected onto the body of the Jewish woman. In fact,
the term "JAP" (many foolishly deny that the "J" for "*Jewish* American
Princess" is of any significance) has become the female embodiment of all the
evils previously cast upon Jewish men—she is shown to be greedy, manipula-
tive, parasitic, crude in speech (she has a New York accent), vulgar in dress,
ugly (like the hooked-nosed Jews of old, she needs a "nose job"), materialis-
tic, ostentatious, unfeeling, and sexually unreliable. This attack comes not
only from the dominant culture, but has also been perpetuated by the misogyny of some Jewish men. As a result, those Jewish women who have
internalized this anti-Semitism as a form of self-hatred also use the term. The
existence of these stereotypes serves to make Jewish women feel especially
vulnerable and keeps them from identifying as a Jew in environments where
that "safety" is even more questionable.

In this connection, an anthology like Carole S. Vance's *Pleasure and
Danger: Exploring Female Sexuality* provides a good example of a missed
opportunity, for this book's theorizing about female sexuality would have
been more complete and more complex if it had included the experiences of
Jewish women. Vance leads one to expect inclusivity and a deeper level of
self-reflection, since she is fully aware of the ways in which some feminist
theories have replicated the false universalizing of white males by assuming
"that women are white, middle- or upper-class, heterosexual, able-bodied,
and moderately youthful, or that the experiences and perspectives of these
women are shared by all."[15]

But Vance's book reveals that she herself does not yet recognize the presumption of a shared Christian (or non-Jewish) background as an equally unspoken norm within feminist theorizing and within her own text. When she amplifies the "self-criticism of feminist parochialism in recent years," she lists only anthologies by lesbians or women of color. No Jewish texts are named or recognized as having made a significant contribution; in fact, the word *Jewish* barely appears in this text. Yet Jewish women have a particular history of sexual projections placed upon them, in which, in the contemporary period, the Jewish woman is said to be both a nymphomaniac and frigid, accused of using sexuality to maintain control over her (male) partner.[16] An analysis of the residue of traditional Jewish attitudes toward women and sexuality and their effects on Jewish women who may not themselves be Orthodox would have strengthened the anthology and would have provided a point of dialogue with Hortense Spiller's analysis of the sexuality of Black women.

The list of supposedly inclusive anthologies from which Jewish themes are absent is long, and I do not intend to document them all here. But when Jewish women are left out of texts focusing on women and religion (that form of Jewish life most easy for non-Jews to comprehend), then we know we are up against strong forces that would exclude Jews. *Women in the World's Religions: Past and Present* contains not a single essay on the Jewish religion, but mentions Judaism, when it does, very much in passing, only *negatively*.[17] This negative attention is the reverse side of invisibility and represents yet another form of anti-Semitism, which occurs not only in texts but also in some conference sessions that otherwise exclude any mention of Jews. In, for example, a 1987 NWSA plenary focusing on coalition politics (the year after the successful Jewish plenary!), Jews were not represented, but Barbara Macdonald, in presenting examples of ageism, found it necessary to single out Ruth Geller's portrait of her Jewish grandmother in her 1984 novel, *Triangles*. I believe this criticism was misplaced and that Macdonald clearly did not understand the cultural context of this lovingly humorous portrait; the insidiousness of this kind of negative inclusion often escapes notice and should not be allowed to continue without comment.

The ignoring of Jewish texts can also distort our research. In historical accounts of women's autobiographies, I have nowhere seen reference to one of the earliest autobiographical texts, *The Memoirs of Gluckl of Hameln*, written between 1689 and 1719 in Yiddish, a Jewish woman's language. This text presents a fascinating view of the public/private intersection in Jewish women's lives at a certain moment in history.[18] Other kinds of exclusions can be personally harmful to both Jewish and Gentile women. A recent self-help book for lesbian couples discusses how racism can affect interracial couples but does not even mention the difficulties Jewish/Gentile couples might encounter, especially in the charged atmosphere surrounding Christmas. Even

more odiously, Dell Richard's *Lesbian Lists* (1990) which exists purportedly
to "put lesbians into history," is completely silent about the very existence and
contributions of Jewish lesbians.

One of my purposes in this chapter is to sensitize the Women's Studies
community to the ways in which Jewish women's lives are left out of the
feminist project and to suggest the contexts in which they should be included.
Because theory builds on itself, one omission frequently prepares the way for
the next. In this respect, I find the silence surrounding anti-Semitism (except
as a marginal aside) in two recent feminist texts, which I expect will be widely
adopted for classroom use, particularly disturbing. In *Racism and Sexism: An
Integrated Study*, Paula Rothenberg defines the parameters of her analysis so
that Jews, by definition, do not belong to her study (because they are "white,"
though this is not explicitly stated either); yet she undertakes the analysis of
"discrimination" and "prejudice" against ethnic minorities in ways that make
the omission of any consideration of anti-Semitism a travesty against the very
real anti-Semitism to which Jews have been subject.[19] What must have been a
deliberate decision not even to mention the existence of Jews as an "ethnic"
minority (not even in a chapter focusing on ethnicity), calls forth the words of
Tsvetan Todorov, who is here commenting on a similar omission of Jews from
a text entitled "Race, Writing, and Difference." He writes, "I was surprised,
not to say shocked, by the lack of any reference to one of the most odious
forms of racism: anti-Semitism. . . . Its absence from the volume suggests
that the authors chose to '*actively ignore*' it."[20] If anti-Semitism is not more
appropriately analyzed as a form of racism, it nonetheless has its own specificity, which needs to be named and analyzed.

Another particularly disturbing example of active omission is provided
by Teresa de Lauretis's *Feminist Studies/Critical Studies*, which was based on
papers presented at a conference entitled, "Feminist Studies: Reconstituting
Knowledge," in Milwaukee in 1985. The absence of any discussion of anti-
Semitism in this volume is all the more troubling because the issue *was* raised
at the conference, in a paper which first met with silence, then with hostility
and overt verbal attacks that repeated many of the most obvious anti-Semitic
assaults on Jews. The fact that this paper was not included in the body of the
text, nor the episode recorded or analyzed by the editor, serves to obscure the
existence of anti-Semitism within contemporary feminism.[21] I take this omission particularly seriously because this anthology seems likely to be a text that
will, in the words of Catharine R. Stimpson, "do nothing less than to create
the next stage of feminist thought." If it succeeds in so doing, it will also
succeed in keeping Jewish themes out of the feminist agenda.

Having said that, it seems important to try to figure out how to proceed
differently. I would like to believe that neither malice, deliberate anti-
Semitism, nor complete indifference is the cause of these continuing omis-

sions. While some of these factors no doubt do serve to keep Jewish themes out of feminist theorizing, there are also other factors to explore. I believe that a significant portion of the problem stems from our initial conceptual framework, which established (and quickly *fixed*) the interlocking factors of "sex, race, and class" as *the* basis for the oppression of women. While such a framework has allowed us to stretch "sex" into "sexual difference" and "race" into "ethnicity," it failed to allow us to account for the *Jew*, who cannot be made to fit into the pre-existing categories.[22] "Jew" describes a variety of factors (including, but not limited to, the intersection of religious identification, historical, cultural, ethical, moral, and linguistic affinities). Clearly then, if the concept "Jew" does not fit the categories we have created, then I suggest we need to rethink our categories. This is what feminists have said to the builders of patriarchal theories into which women do not fit, and it is what lesbians have said to feminist theorists who excluded lesbian identity—"not *we*, but your theories are inadequate." The unwillingness to rethink the adequacy of our categories, which in any case have become somewhat formulaic, suggests a refusal to consider the politics behind our namings and a refusal to face the implications of our questioning.

One of the results of perpetuating these categories is the invisibility of Jews, and an exclusion, a non-consideration that inevitably leads to the "benign" anti-Semitism of indifference and insensitivity that has allowed the "JAP" stereotype to flourish unchecked. The result, the Jew as subject in feminist discourse, is given a radical "otherness" that is denied at the very moment in which it is being created. This denial is especially schizophrenic if you are a member of the group that is actively being made invisible at the very moment that "difference" is becoming increasingly central to feminist discourse and is now considered essential to the appropriate further development of feminist theory. If Jews do not fit, it is quite likely that other groups may not fit into the conceptual framework we have constructed. My own experience of working in the feminist project is that one opening almost always leads to another; this is a path that leads toward the expansion and transformation of our theories in ways that we cannot yet know but could nonetheless take pleasure in moving toward.

Notes

1. This article first appeared in *NWSA Journal* I:1 (1988):93–102. Republished with permission of Ablex Publishing Corp. With thanks to L. Lee Knefelkamp for her thoughtful editorial work and unflagging encouragement.

2. A tape of this session is available for $6.95 from the National Women's Studies Association, University of Maryland, College Park, MD 20742. These tapes include

the stories of Jewish women who are secular and religious, Ashkenazi and Sephardi, rural and urban, American-born and Holocaust survivors, and those who represent different class backgrounds.

3. These are: Sue Levi Elwell, ed., *The Jewish Women's Studies Guide*, 2d ed. (Lanham, Md.: University Press of America, 1987); Aviva Cantor, ed., *The Jewish Woman, 1900–1985: A Bibliography*, 2d ed. (Fresh Meadows, N.Y.: Biblio Press, 1987); Joan Scherer Brewer, *Sex and the Modern Jewish Woman: An Annotated Bibliography* with essays by Lynn Davidman and Evelyn Avery (Fresh Meadows, N.Y.: Biblio Press, 1986). The first edition of Aviva Cantor's *Bibliography* was published as early as 1979; the first edition of *The Jewish Women's Studies Guide* appeared in 1982. Major anthologies about Judaism and feminism appeared as early as 1976, for example, Elizabeth Koltun, ed., *The Jewish Woman: New Perspectives* (New York: Schocken Books, 1976), some of whose essays were in print as early as 1970.

4. Johnnetta Cole's anthology, *All American Women: Lines That Divide, Ties That Bind* (New York: Free Press, 1986) is a welcome exception to this generalization. Cole's text not only includes substantial information about Jewish women, but the complexity of that information is reflected in the index. Edith Blicksilver's anthology on *The Ethnic Woman: Problems, Protests, Lifestyle* (Dubuque, Iowa: Kendall/Hunt, 1978) is also exceptionally inclusive, though Jewish lesbians are not mentioned in either text.

5. See, for example, Letty Pogrebin, "Anti-Semitism in the Women's Movement," *Ms.* 12 (June 1982): 45–49, 62–75; Pogrebin, "Going Public as a Jew," *Ms.* 16 (July/August 1987): 76–77, 194–195; Selma Miriam, "Anti-Semitism in the Lesbian Community," *Sinister Wisdom* 19 (1982): 50–60; Evelyn Torton Beck, *Nice Jewish Girls: A Lesbian Anthology* (Watertown, Mass.: Persephone Press, 1982; revised and expanded edition, Boston: Press 1989.); Beck, "Between Invisibility and Overvisibility: The Politics of Anti-Semitism in the Women's Movement and Beyond," Working Paper in Women's Studies, no. 11 (Madison: University of Wisconsin, 1984); Melanie Kaye/Kantrowitz, "Anti-Semitism, Homophobia, and the Good White Knight," *off our backs* 12 (May 1982): 30–31; and Kaye/Kantrowitz and Irena Klepfisz, eds., *The Tribe of Dina: A Jewish Women's Anthology* (Montpelier, Vt.: Sinister Wisdom Books, 1986; revised and expanded edition, Boston: Beacon Press, 189).

6. The strange removal of Jews from categories of "minority" and "ethnicity" probably has its origins in the fact that Jews no longer constitute an "under-represented minority" in the professions and are thus not included in the Civil Rights Act of 1964. The reality is that Jews still only represent a small minority in the United States and have never exceeded 3.7 percent of the total population; thus, the exclusion of Jews from these namings can only be a political decision that distorts and ultimately obliterates the existence of Jews.

7. David A. Gerber, *Anti-Semitism in American History* (Urbana: University of Illinois Press, 1986), 305–28. Many of the other essays in this anthology would also prove to be useful for Women's Studies theorizing about marginality; Gerber's intro-

ductory essay, "Anti-Semitism and Jewish-Gentile Relations in American Historiography and the American Past" provides a good overview of how deeply implicated the dominant American culture has been in anti-Semitism.

8. Beck, *Nice Jewish Girls*, (1989), xvii.

9. In the United States, New Jewish Agenda, a progressive political organization, has staged vigils in front of the Israeli embassy protesting Israeli policies and has recently launched a petition campaign calling for negotiations and an international peace conference that would include the PLO as representative of the Palestinian people. New Jewish Agenda is located at 64 Fulton St. #1100, New York, N.Y. 10038. The "Jewish Women's Committee to End the Occupation of the West Bank and Gaza" holds vigils to protest the occupation in dozens of cities across the United States and in Israel. For further information contact JWCEO an ask for a free copy of the *Jewish Women's Peace Bulletin* at the Agenda address.

10. In 1987 overt acts of anti-Semitism in the United States rose by 23 percent. On November 9–10, 1987, the eve of the anniversary of *Kristallnacht*, Jewish-identified shops and synagogues were vandalized, windows smashed, swastikas and "Jews Die!" painted on walls in dozens of communities across the United States. These acts clearly mirror the events of that night in 1938 when seven thousand Jewish shops were destroyed and synagogues throughout Germany burned down by state-sanctioned pogroms. During the first 4 1/2 months of 1988, the Anti-Defamation League reported 443 anti-Semitic incidents—88 percent of them had a politically related anti-Israel component. Anti-Semitic acts have also risen sharply on college campuses across the country, especially where there are visible Jewish student populations.

11. Recently, she has begun to receive more attention. See Klepfisz, *A Few Words in the Mother Tongue: Poems Selected and New (1972–1990)* and *Dreams of an Insomniac: Jewish Feminist Essays, Speeches and Diatribes* (Eighth Mountain Press; Portland, OR., 1990).

12. "Homelands of the Mind: Jewish Feminism and Identity Politics," *Race & Culture* 29 (Summer 1987):1–24. While this essay is poorly argued, its effects may nonetheless be critical, especially as it appeared in a widely read journal. For a response, see Francesca Klug, "Jewish Feminists Answer Back," *The Jewish Socialist* 12 (Winter/Spring 1988):12–14.

13. Letty Pogrebin was attacked when she wrote about anti-Semitism in *Ms.* (June 1982); see especially the responses to her article in the June 1982 *Ms.*

14. A major portion of the Fall 1987 issue of *Lilith: The Jewish Women's Magazine*, no. 17, focuses on harmful effects of still-flourishing stereotypes of Jewish women. See especially the essays by Sherry Chayat, Judith Allen Rubinstein, and Susan Weidman Schneider. This topic was discussed in December 1987 on National Public Radio and has become the focus of educational projects by many Jewish women's organizations. See also, Evelyn Torton Beck, "From 'Kike' to 'J.A.P.': How Anti-Semitism, Misogyny and Racism Construct the 'Jewish American Princess',"

Sojourner: the Women's Forum 14: 1 (September 1988), 18–23 and Beck, "Therapy's Double Dilemma: Misogyny and Anti-Semitism," _Jewish Women and Therapy_, eds. R. J. Siegel and Ellen Cole, in press 1991.

15. Vance, _Pleasure and Danger_ (Boston: Routledge and Kegan Paul, 1984), 17.

16. For an excellent analysis of this phenomenon, see Susan Weidman Schneider, "In a Coma! I thought She was Jewish! Some Truths and Speculations about Jewish Women and Sex," _Lilith: The Jewish Women's Magazine_ (Spring/Summer 1977), 5–8.

17. Ursula King, ed., _Women in the World's Religions: Past and Present_ (New York: Paragon House Press, 1987). Represented in individual chapters are several different forms of Christianity, Buddhism, Krishna worship, African religions, and Goddess worship. In the index under "Judaism," we find only three references: "patriarchal in nature," "monotheism based on male dominance," and "masculine aspects of God." Rosemary Radford Ruether and Rosemary Skinner Keller, eds., _Women in Religion in America: The Colonial and Revolutionary Periods: A Documentary History_ (New York: Harper and Row, 1983) has quite a comprehensive focus on the religions of American Indian women, Spanish American, Colonial French, New England, Southern, Black American, and Utopian groups but does not even mention Jews, though Jews were present among the first settlers of the "New World."

18. _Memoirs of Gluckl of Hameln_ (rpt. New York: Schocken Press, 1977).

19. Rothenberg, _Racism and Sexism_ (New York: St. Martin's Press, 1988).

20. Henry Louis Gates, Jr., ed. _Race, Writing, and Difference_ (Chicago: University of Chicago Press, 1986), 377. The collection contains the essays that appeared originally as "'Race,' Writing, and Culture," _Critical Inquiry_ 12 (Autumn 1985) and 13 (Autumn 1986).

21. Teresa de Lauretis, ed., _Feminist Studies/Critical Studies_ (Bloomington: Indiana University Press, 1986). Because such events are rarely talked about, I would like to record the basic outlines of that episode, which I am in a position to do since I was the speaker in question. First, the moderator did not allow questions in response to my talk because "time did not permit," while she allowed time for several questions for the paper following mine. When I objected to this differential treatment, one woman in the audience shouted words to the effect that "Jews control the media, which is why the Holocaust is getting so much attention, while the Middle Passage is ignored." In response to a reminder about the gassing of Jews in the concentration camps in World War II, this same woman answered, "Yes, but you Jews have it so good until they come get you!" Another panel member made fun of this episode by quipping, "I can't possibly be anti-Semitic; I was married to 'a nice Jewish boy.'" Following this episode she ended her presentation by calling for solidarity with Palestinian women out of any context that would have made that appropriate. The audience, for the most part, seemed to be paralyzed and only one or two women came to the defense. By my count, about one-third of the audience was Jewish.

22. Alison M. Jaggar and Paula S. Rothenberg, *Feminist Frameworks: Alternative Theoretical Accounts of the Relations Between Women and Men*, 2d ed. (New York: McGraw-Hill, 1984) set up "frameworks" that completely box us in and allow no room for the consideration of how Jews might fit into the analysis.

PART III

The Cutting Edge of the Liberal Arts: Some Implications for Scholarship

Elizabeth Spelman argues that any feminism ignoring the intricate inter-sections of race, gender, class, and ethnicity and their corresponding "-isms," is seriously defective. Spelman suggests that feminism should be a transform-ing enterprise, engendering a fairer and more equitable community. This article, which originally appeared in her book, *Inessential Woman: Problems of Exclusion in Feminist Thought*, is critical of the views of Nancy Chodorow, on which much of feminist thought and practice is based. Spelman persua-sively contends that "while Chodorow's work is compelling, it ought to be highly problematic for any version of feminism that demands more than lip service to the significance of race and class, racism and classism in the lives of the women on whom Chodorow focuses." Once we take race and ethnicity seriously, we see how they modulate and moderate gender and class.

Chin et al. excoriate the portrayal of Asian Americans in the arts and seek to reclaim and re-present their past and present in their own authentic way. The authors contend, between justifiable spasms of outrage, that present images of Asians are demonic and nightmarish, the product of white Ameri-can fears. The pervasiveness of stereotypes distorts scholarship and classroom content. They represent an aspect of the re-visioning of scholarship and con-tent so crucial to transformation.

In "The Sign in Sidney Brustein's Window: Toward a Transformative Aesthetic," Butler shows how Lorraine Hansberry's concept of the social value of art results in an aesthetic that is pluralistic, non-hierarchal, capable of incorporating that which seems diametrically opposed. She demonstrates the emergence of this aesthetic from a particular African American sensibility, rooted in a non-linear concept of time and connectedness, and in the concept of non-antagonistic of opposites that may be traced to the African roots of African American culture. This aesthetic is in concert with the philosophical conceptualization of transformation, and suggests its broad and deep dimensions.

The epistemological shifts inherent in transformative scholarship sug-gested in Butler's piece on Hansberry are further discussed in the American

Indian context by Kathryn Shanley. Shanley, in presenting ways in which mythic time functions in American Indian life and literature, argues that in literature the Indian use of mythic time is far from being simply a literary device but is an essential element of Indian cosmology and epistemology. Shanley's essay insists upon the necessity of recognizing a literature and its aspects *within* the context of its culture. Chin et al., along with Butler and Vangen, show us ways in which the American literary aesthetic must radically expand and change—be transformed.

Finally, Armenian women, have not, according to the "first word" of research by Arlene Avakian, assimilated. As such their experience as white, unassimilated ethnic women differs significantly from that of the white, assimilated Euro-American women. Avakian delineates, describes, and analyzes the culture of first-generation Armenian women in America. She shows a culture undergoing the rapid erosion towards the American mainstream as the aging first-generation women search for their roots and seek to sustain and maintain their heritage, but with gender equality. The mode and costs of assimilation are strikingly akin to experiences of Americans of color, and yet, the paradigms implicit in studying Euro-Americans prove to vary considerably as well due to race and ethnicity.

CHAPTER 12

Gender in the Context of Race and Class*

Elizabeth V. Spelman

It is theoretically significant for any feminist analysis of gender and of sexism, if statements that appear to be true about "men and women" clearly aren't true when we specify that we are talking about men and women of different races and classes. For example, it would be deeply misleading to say simply that Aristotle thought men were superior to women. For though he thought free men were by their very nature superior to free women, he clearly did not think that those men whom he considered by their very nature to be slaves were superior to those women whom he thought were not "by nature" slaves. Similarly, it would be a gross distortion of the ideology and the reality of life in the ante-bellum United States to say simply that men were regarded as the superiors of women—as if Black male slaves were thought to be the superiors of white women of the slave-owning class. If gender identity were isolatable from class and race identity, if sexism were isolatable from classism and racism, we could talk about relations between men and women and never have to worry about whether their race or class were the same or different. If gender were isolatable from other aspects of identity, if sexism were isolatable from other forms of oppression, then what would be true about the relation between any man and woman would be true about the relation between any other man and any other woman.

Much of feminist theory has proceeded on the assumption that gender is indeed a variable of human identity independent of other variables such as race and class, that whether one is a woman is unaffected by what class or race one is.[1] Feminists have also assumed that sexism is distinctly different from racism and classism, that whether and how one is subject to sexism is unaffected by whether and how one is subject to racism or classism.

The work of Nancy Chodorow has seemed to provide feminist theory

* From Chapter 4 of *Inessential Woman: Problems of Exclusion in Feminist Thought*, Elizabeth V. Spelman, (Beacon Press, 1988)

with a strong foundation for these arguments. It has explicitly and implicitly been used to justify the assumption that there is nothing problematic about trying to examine gender independently of other variables such as race, class, and ethnicity. Though Chodorow's writings have received sometimes scathing criticism from feminists, more often they have been seen by feminist scholars in many different disciplines as providing a particularly rich understanding of gender.[2] Indeed, Chodorow offers what appears to be a very promising account of the relations between gender identity and other important aspects of identity such as race and class. For while she treats gender as separable from race and class, she goes on to suggest ways in which the sexist oppression intimately connected to gender differences is related to racism and classism.

I hope to show that while Chodorow's work is very compelling, it ought to be highly problematic for any version of feminism that demands more than lip service to the significance of race and class, racism and classism, in the lives of the women on whom Chodorow focuses. The problem, as I see it, is not that feminists have taken Chodorow seriously, but that we have not taken her seriously enough. Her account points to a more complicated understanding of gender and the process of becoming gendered than she herself develops. She tells us to look at the social context of mothering in order to understand the effect of mothering on the acquisition of gender identity in children; but if we follow her advice, rather than her own practice, we are led to see that gender identity is not neatly separable from other aspects of identity such as race and class. They couldn't be if, as Chodorow insists, the acquisition of gender occurs in and helps perpetuate the "hierarchical and differentiated social worlds" we inhabit.

I.

According to *The Reproduction of Mothering*, there are systematic differences between girls and boys, between women and men, that are biological; but there also are systematic differences in behavior and in what some psychologists refer to as "intrapsychic structures."[3] The latter differences cannot be accounted for by the biological differences. But neither can they be explained by reference to learning to behave in certain ways, whether by exposure to role models, ideological messages, or coercion. Neither account enables us to understand the psychological investment girls and boys come to have in becoming women and men and the psychological investment women and men have in reproducing girls and boys. In particular, we have to understand the different "relational capacities" and "senses of self" in girls and boys, women and men. These differences are produced by the sexual division of labor in which women, and not men, mother; and that division of labor is in turn reproduced by these differences. The sexual division of labor can reproduce itself because through it are produced women and men who "develop personalities which tend to guarantee that they will get gratification or satisfaction from those activities which are necessary to the reproduction" of the sexual division of labor (p. 173).

In short, we can't adequately describe gender differences without focusing on the different senses of self women and men have that are linked to their thinking or not thinking of themselves in ways that prepare them for mothering; at the same time, neither can we explain how these gender differences come about without focusing on the fact that it is women and not men who mother. For it is the mothering of girls and boys that women do that explains why girls and boys develop different relational capacities and different senses of self—why girls in turn go on to mother and boys not only do not mother but demean mothers and mothering.

Our becoming girl-gendered or boy-gendered, then, is a process mediated by our mothers:

> An account of the early mother–infant relationship in contemporary Western society reveals the overwhelming importance of the mother in everyone's psychological development, in their sense of self, and in their basic relational stance. It reveals that becoming a person [girl or boy] is the same thing as becoming a person in relationship and in social context. (p. 76)

But mothering itself is a mediated activity. "Women's mothering does not exist in isolation" (p. 32). It is an intricate part of the sexual division of labor; it is part of a "social organization" that "includes male dominance, a particular family system, and women's dependence on men's income" (p. 21). It is "informed by [the woman's] relationship to her husband, her experience of financial dependence, her expectations of marital inequality, and her expectations about gender roles" (p. 86).

Chodorow believes that "all societies are constituted around a structural split . . . between the private, domestic world of women and the public, social world of men" (p. 174). There is a division of labor between the public, "nonrelational" sphere (p. 179), where men have their primary location, and a private "relational" sphere, where women have their "primary social and economic location" (p. 11, 13). Mothering in such a context is a process geared to producing girls who will be fit denizens of the private sphere and boys who will participate in the public world—the "capitalist world of work" in Western society (p. 180–81). How does this happen?

In answering this, Chodorow is trying to carry out the promise contained in the subtitle of the book: "psychoanalysis and the sociology of gender." Her focus on the social context of gender and mothering makes use of Freud and object-relations theorists. Briefly, mothers see their daughters as "more like and continuous with" themselves than their sons are (p. 166). Girls are not called upon to individuate themselves, to see themselves as distinct from their mothers, as early, as firmly, or as finally as boys are. A girl's sense of self is not as threatened by her ties to her mother as a boy's is; the resolution of his oedipal stage means he must give up his mother in a way his sister does not have to. At the same time, because a girl learns what it is to be a woman by identifying with her mother (p. 175), and because the asymmetrical organization of parenting means the mother is present, this process of identification takes place in the context of a personal relationship. However, part of the asymmetrical organization of parenting is that the boy's father is not present in the way the mother is; learning what it is to be masculine hence happens not in the context of a personal relationship but "through identification with cultural images of masculinity and men chosen as masculine models" (p. 176). Because of the context in which mothering takes place, mothers have different kinds of relationships with their daughters than they do with their sons. And these different kinds of relationships produce different psychic configurations in girls and boys—configurations that prepare the growing girls and boys to come to find satisfaction in the very same division of labor in the context of which mothering occurs.

According to Chodorow, then, the most significant difference between girls and boys, women and men, is in terms of the degree to which they see themselves as related to and connected with others. "The basic feminine sense of self is connected to the world, the basic masculine sense of self is separate" (p. 169). This is the psychological counterpart of the roles women and men are expected to play: "Women in our society are primarily defined as wives and mothers, thus in particularistic relation to someone else, whereas men are defined primarily in universalistic occupational terms" (p. 178). As long as it is only women who mother, in the social context in which they do, these differences in women and men will continue to exist. If we want to change or to put an end to such differences, the institution of mothering has to change.

Chodorow says in a later article in the feminist journal *Signs* that any feminist ought to want to eliminate those kinds of differences between men and women, because "a treating of women as others, or objects, rather than subjects, or selves" not only adversely affects women but "extends to our culture as a whole."

> The boy comes to define his self more in opposition than through a sense of his wholeness or continuity. He becomes the self and experiences his mother as the other. The process also extends to his trying to dominate the other in order to ensure his sense of self. Such domination begins with mother as the object, extends to women, and is then generalized to include the experience

of all others as objects rather than subjects. This stance, in which people are treated and experienced as things, becomes basic to male Western culture.[4]

Here Chodorow elaborates on a quotation from Levi-Strauss she placed at the beginning of her 1979 article, "Gender, Relation, and Difference in Psychoanalytic Perspective":

> I would go so far as to say that even before slavery or class domination existed, men built an approach to women that would serve one day to introduce differences among us all.[5]

Though Chodorow does not take it upon herself to explain or defend these points in any more detail, it seems fairly clear that she takes sexism to be independent of racism and classism but at the same time to be both the model for them (the domination of male over female is adapted for the purposes of other forms of domination) and the cause of them (if men weren't so insecure about their sense of self vis-a-vis their mothers, they wouldn't need to define anyone else as Other).

II.

As mentioned earlier, Chodorow's feminist critics have not been shy about pointing to what they take to be particularly vulnerable aspects of her account of gender acquisition: her reliance on some of the more troubling aspects of Freud, her uncritical use of the distinction between "public" and "private" spheres, her assumption of women's heterosexuality.[6] Though I share her critics' concerns, I want to focus on aspects of her work that have not received sufficient attention. But first I shall describe what I take to be some of the questions she leaves unanswered.

Perhaps the most politically significant part of Chodorow's account is her reminder that mothering occurs in a particular social context. It is informed, she notes, by the mother's relation to her husband, her economic dependence on him, her experience of male dominance. But why does Chodorow focus on only these elements of the larger social context? After all, most societies— including that of contemporary North America, about which she is most concerned—are also characterized by other forms of dominance, other sorts of hierarchies. Women mother in societies that may be racist and classist as well as sexist and heterosexist. Are we to believe that a woman's mothering is informed only by her relation to a husband or male lover and her experience of living in a male-dominated society, but not by her relation to people of other classes and races and her experience of living in a society in which there are race and class hierarchies? Chodorow wants us to think about the "specific implications of the actual social context in which the child learns" (p. 47). But if I do that, then it does not seem accurate to describe what my mother nurtured in me, and what I learned, as being simply a "girl." I was learning to be a white, middle-class Christian and "American" girl. Chodorow rails against the view that "feminine biology shapes psychic life without mediation of culture" (p. 149). But does only one part of the culture mediate mothering?

"Families," Chodorow says, "create children gendered, heterosexual, and ready to marry" (p. 199)—or anyway they are supposed to. But do families have no racial or class or ethnic identity? Do they create children prepared to marry anyone, no matter the person's race, class, ethnicity, religion? Is the creation of children in the ways Chodorow lists the only thing families are supposed to do? As Chodorow herself so usefully points out, the socialization that must take place in order for the society to continue to reproduce itself "must lead to the assimilation and internal organization of generalized capacities for participation in a hierarchical and differentiated world" (p. 32). Families are organized so as to produce new beings who will "get gratification or satisfaction from those activities which are necessary to the reproduction of the larger social structure" (p. 36–37). But is this true for only certain elements of that larger social structure? If children are said to be prepared to participate in a sexually unequal society (p. 173), why aren't they also said to be prepared to participate in a society where there are racial, class, and other forms of inequality?[7]

As we've seen, Chodorow certainly is not unaware of forms of domination other than sexism, and undoubtedly she would acknowledge that the raising of children contributes in some ways (and presumably in different ways in different families) to the perpetuation of racism, classism, and other forms of oppression. She probably would respond to the questions above by saying that the production of gender identity in families is separate from, even if at some point in tandem with, the production of other aspects of identity such as race or ethnicity or class. But let us look in more detail at what she means by "gender" and see whether what she tells us about gender indeed means that it can or must be specified independently of elements of identity such as race and class.

Chodorow refers to a "core gender identity" that, along with a sense of self, is established in the first two years. This core gender identity is a "cognitive sense" of oneself as male or female.[8] As we saw above, according to Chodorow the distinction between a "basic feminine sense of self" and a "basic masculine sense of self" involves seeing oneself as connected to or seeing oneself as separate from the world (p. 169). But she also describes gender in more specific terms:

> I am using *gender* here to stand for the mother's particular psychic structure and relational sense, for her (probable) heterosexuality, and for her conscious and unconscious acceptance of the ideology, meanings and expectations that go into being a gendered member of our society and understanding what gender means. (p. 98)

Part of gender ideology is that men are superior to women, for male superiority is built "into the definition of masculinity itself" (p. 185). Gendered senses of self have to be politically loaded, since they prepare girls and boys to enter a world in which there is a sexual division of labor that is itself politically loaded: male domination couldn't continue, Chodorow reasons, unless gender differentiation included gender hierarchy. Whether or not Chodorow thinks that the engendering of baby humans *causes* sexual domination, she clearly thinks that coming to be and think of oneself as masculine or feminine involves assuming one's place (and having a sense of one's place) in a world in which masculine beings dominate feminine ones.[9] Mothering in a sexist context reproduces sexism insofar as it creates young humans well-adapted psychologically to take their places in a sexist world.

Chodorow begins her book with the claim that "women's mothering is one of the few universal and enduring elements of the sexual division of labor" (p. 3). She means by this that no matter how else cultures and subcultures differ with respect to the division of labor along sexual lines, the work of mothering is always done by women. At the same time Chodorow says that mothering "is not an unchanging transcultural universal" (p. 32). By this she seems to mean that as the world into which children enter changes over time, so the responsibilities of women preparing children for entry into the world change. For example, "the development of industrial capitalism in the West entailed that women's role in the family become increasingly concerned with personal relations and psychological stability" (p. 32). Together these two claims suggest that while it is women who everywhere mother—that is, who not only feed and clean infants but provide them with "affective bonds and a diffuse, multifaceted, ongoing personal relationship" (p. 33)—the kind of development they unconsciously and consciously encourage in their children will depend on the particular requirements of the world in which they live and for which they must prepare the children. To learn one's gender identity is among other things to learn what work one is supposed to do and also to want to do that work (at least not *not* want to because it isn't the kind of work one is supposed to do).

There are, then, according to Chodorow, two universals: a sexual division of labor and, within that division, the assignment of mothering to women. Two things are not universal: the particular tasks (other than mothering) that are assigned along sexual lines and the content of mothering. Indeed, Chodorow says that class differences within a society—below she is speaking of modern capitalist societies—are reflected in "parental child-rearing values":

> Working-class parents are more likely to value obedience, conformity to external authority, neatness, and other "behavioral" characteristics in their children; middle-class parents emphasize more "internal" and interpersonal characteristics like responsibility, curiosity, self-motivation, self-control, and consideration (p. 176).

Whether or not Chodorow's descriptions of class differences are accurate, it is important to note that she does think class may make an important difference to mothering. "We know almost nothing" about effects of class differences on mothering, she cautions, and admits that "all claims about gender differences gloss over important differences within genders and similarities between genders" (p. 215). Moreover, in a later response to critics, she says that among the things she would stress more than she did in her book is

> how women's mothering and early infantile development is tied to the treatment of people as things and rigid self–other distinctions that characterize our culture and thought. That is, I would examine the link between what seems exclusively gender related and the construction of other aspects of society, politics and culture [and also would encourage study of] class and ethnic differences, differences in family and household structure, differences in sexual orientation of parents, and historical and cross-cultural variations in these relationships.[10]

From this further foray into Chodorow's account of gender, several things emerge: that according to her analysis, sexual hierarchy is built into definitions of masculine and feminine, and that we know little about the effect of class differences on the mothering practices that reproduce gender identities. But if she says these things about gender, it makes it harder rather than easier to show that gender is isolatable from other elements of identity.

First of all, what kind of difference could the study of class and ethnic differences make to the study of gender identity and the role of mothering in its production and reproduction? Unless Chodorow thinks they might make a significant difference, she presumably will not think it important to investigate any further. Her own theory reveals something of her answer to this question. One of the major functions of families, she told us, is to produce beings who will "get gratification or satisfaction from those activities which are necessary to the reproduction of the larger social structure" (p. 36–37). But investigation of ethnicity and class and race within that social structure might make us consider the possibility that what one learns when one learns one's gender identity is the gender identity appropriate to one's ethnic, class, national, and racial identity. Understanding gender, Chodorow told us, includes understanding "the ideology, meanings, and expectations that go into being a gendered member of our society" (p. 98). But if, for example, masculine identity is rich enough to include the notion of male superiority, as Chodorow says it is (p. 185), then we are not barred from asking whether it doesn't also include notions of class or race superiority. In a racist society such as the United States, is the ideological content of masculinity the idea that any man is superior to any woman?

At this point we may usefully recall the scope of Aristotle's claim about the natural superiority of men to women: he clearly did not think this applied in the case of slave men and slave women nor in the case of slave men and free women. The ideology of masculinity in the United States hardly includes the idea that Black men are superior to white women. So if gender is supposed to include ideology, and if learning one's gender identity prepares one for what is expected of a person gendered in the way one is, then we can't describe masculinity as including simply the notion that men are superior to women. If a poor Black boy in the United States thinks that being "masculine" entitles him to dominate white women, since he's male and they are female, he's not been prepared well for the society into which he's been born (and as we shall discuss below, it is highly unlikely that his mother would be unaware of this). This is not to say that he may not wish to dominate white women (along with Black women), but rather to remind us that if Emmet Till had been white, he wouldn't have been murdered by white men for talking to a white woman, nor would his murderers have been acquitted.[11]

III.

Chodorow invites us to consider the difference class makes to parenting and suggests that the sexism built into the context of early psychological development has some role to play in the maintenance, perhaps even in the creation, of racial and class hierarchies. Her account thus raises some very crucial methodological questions for anyone who thinks that a complete feminist analysis of sexism ought to include at least some examination of the relation between sexism and other forms of oppression. The methodological questions have to do with where and how issues about race and racism, class and classism, enter into the analysis. As we have seen, Chodorow herself suggests at least two places they might intersect. Starting with her suggestions and thinking of other points of entry, we can generate a fairly long list of the ways we might begin to examine connections between issues of race and class and those of gender:

1. Does race or class identity affect gender identity? For example, are there elements of race and class in notions of masculinity and femininity? Isn't the idea of superiority built, as Chodorow affirms, into the notion of "masculinity" understood to apply only under certain conditions? Does the ideology packed into the notion of masculinity include the notion that any man is superior to any woman? Does the ideology packed into the notion of femininity include the notion that any woman is inferior to any man, that all women are inferior in just the same way to all men?

2. Does a child's sense of self include a conscious or unconscious sense of race or class? (This is closely connected to question 1.)

If we are looking for an account of psycho-social development that explains how children come to be psychologically and socially prepared for the positions set for them in a hierarchically ordered political and social and economic world, we might do well to ask what it is to be men or women of their race, class, ethnicity.

3. What are the hierarchies in the world into which children are born and socialized? Is sexual privilege or domination affected by the race and class of the men and women in question?

The world into which the children enter is one in which race and class identity cuts across gender identity (men can be Anglo- or Afro-American, women can be upper class or working class, and so on), and racism and classism cut across sexism (there are significant differences in the situations of highly educated well-to-do women with tenured jobs and poor women on welfare). It would be much easier to account for how children are prepared for entry into such a complex world if what they learned when their gender identity was being formed was not simply that they were boys or girls but something more complicated—for example, that they were white male or female, Black male or female, and so forth.

4. What are the ways in which sexism might be related to other forms of oppression? For example, is sexism a support for or cause of racism or classism? Or is it in some sense more closely intertwined with them?

Perhaps we can begin to account for the reproduction of racism by taking our task to be not simply to explain how men have come to think of themselves as superior to women, but rather to explain how children learn that the superiority built into "masculine" is meant to be the prerogative of a certain group of men; and to explain how it is possible for a group of women thinking of themselves as inferior to "men" to also think of themselves as superior to some men and some women.

IV.

Chodorow's work (and the work she draws on) suggests some obstacles to the kind of inquiry I am proposing, for it seems to be a fairly universal phenomenon that people do not become conscious of their racial, class, ethnic, religious, or national identity until long after they have a sense of their gender identity. How can their gender identity be intertwined with other aspects of their identity if they can be conscious of the former but not of the latter?

This question echoes Descartes's famous argument about the separation of self (that is, he says, of mind) from body. In the *Meditations*, Descartes insisted that while he had grounds for doubting whether he had a body (since he had reasons for doubting the evidence of his senses), he knew for certain that he existed. The "I" that I know to exist cannot be a body, for how could the "I" that I know to exist be a body if I can doubt that there is a body but not doubt that this "I" exists?

How can gender identity have anything to do with racial or class identity if a person can have a clear sense of their gender identity while simultaneously having no particular awareness of their racial or class identity?

The response that has often been made to Descartes goes something like this: It doesn't necessarily follow that because you can doubt whether x exists, while being certain that y exists, x is not the same as y. I can doubt or feel that it is impossible to know whether Marian Evans existed, while feeling certain that George Eliot existed, but this hardly shows that Marian Evans cannot be George Eliot.[12]

Similarly, it can hardly follow from the fact that I describe my gender identity as "woman" that there are neither racial nor class dimensions to my understanding of "woman"—anymore than if I described what I learned in college and graduate school simply as "philosophy" it would follow that there are no Western cultural dimensions to my understanding of philosophy. Just because some people don't think of themselves as having any class identity doesn't mean that they have none. Indeed, under certain circumstances the very lack of awareness of elements of one's identity is a significant reflection of that identity. For example, my being and having a sense of myself as white in this society can be said to be reflected in the fact that it does *not* occur to me to note it, nor am I required by convention to note it: the conventions about self-description allow me to refer to myself simply as "woman." But if I were a Black woman, people would think I was withholding important information if I did not qualify "woman" with "Black." One therefore cannot argue, from the fact that someone is conscious of her gender identity but not conscious of her racial identity, that her gender identity has nothing to do with her racial identity.

But perhaps Chodorow's point is that gender identity is so basic that it is not really conscious; that the most significant effects of girls' and boys' relationships to their mothers (and fathers) occur long before children are conscious of either their gender identity or their race or class identity. What we develop at such an early stage is a general relational stance; girls see themselves in relation to their mothers and as connected to the world; boys see themselves as separate from and in opposition to their mothers and as separate from the world. And this supposedly is true no matter the race or class of the mother and children.

However, there are at least two major problems with this representation of Chodorow's views about gender identity. First of all, as noted several times above, Chodorow describes masculine gender identity as including the belief in male superiority (p. 185). That is a fairly sophisticated notion to be packed into a preconscious sense of oneself. Second, Chodorow needs a fairly rich picture of gender identity in order for her claims about the relation between gender identity and the readiness to occupy one's appropriate place in the world to make sense. We live in a world in which gender differentiation is thoroughly intertwined with gender hierarchy, and one can't learn the one without learning the other (even if there might be some society, in the past or in the future or even right now, in which differences between genders did not have built into them the notion that one gender is better than the other).[13] Learning gender identity would not be the important thing Chodorow believes it to be unless learning it explained why men and women are so well prepared for living in and reproducing a hierarchical social world. Chodorow can't have it both ways. She can't have a notion of gender identity that is devoid of significant conscious content and also use that notion to explain what she thinks it explains: hence her insistence that the sense of masculinity that boys acquire includes not simply the general notion of being separate from women but the notion of being superior to them. But—to repeat a point made several times above—if what children learn in acquiring gender identity is rich enough to explain how they are so psychically ready to assume their place in a hierarchical world, how can it not include an understanding of gender identity appropriate for one's race, class, ethnic group? For I learn that my place in the established hierarchies of the social world is not determined simply by whether I am male or female but also by whether I am white or Black, rich or poor. In the society in which my mother, and then I, grew up, the differences between white and Black, middle and working class, Christian and Jew, were no less differences than the one between girl and boy.

V.

If we take seriously Chodorow's insistence on the social context in which mothering and the acquisition of gender takes place, we might then take note of concrete examples of "senses of self" in specific social contexts. Because mothering may be informed by a woman's knowledge of more than one form of dominance, the development of gender occurs in a context in which one learns to be a very particular girl or boy, and not just simply a girl or boy. If we look at biographical and autobiographical literature by and about women of various races and classes, we get a much more complicated picture than Chodorow's account gives us of the world in which mothers mother. It is indeed a "hierarchical and differentiated social world"—as Chodorow says—but differentiated and ranked not only along gender lines. For example, Mary Burgher has described how,

> in her autobiography or in her daughter's, the Black mother's knowledge and endurance of America's racial hostility and violence are envisioned as strengthening and motivating tools with which she prepares others of her race for self-sufficient and productive lives.[14]

How do some women of color in the United States take to the suggestion that awareness of race and racism was absent from, or anyway not an important consideration in, their mothers' or their own minds as children, or that the learning of gender identity was separable from the learning of race identity? Here's Nikki Giovanni:

> It's great when you near your quarter-century mark and someone says "I want an experience on how you came to grips with being colored." The most logical answer is, "I came to grips with Blackdom when I grabbed my mama"—but I'm told on [TV] that we don't necessarily know our mothers are colored, and you can win a great big medal if you say it loud.[15]

And Barbara Cameron:

> One of the very first words I learned in my Lakota language was *wasicu* which designates white people. . . . During my childhood . . . my moth-er . . . explained the realities of being an Indian in South Dakota.[16]

None of this is to say that mothers are never ambivalent about the racial or ethnic identity of their children, only that they are keenly aware of it. Cherrie Moraga has described the role of her mother in her learning what it means to be a "fair-skinned" Chicana:

> Everything about my upbringing . . . attempted to bleach me of what color I did have. . . . To [my mother], on a basic economic level, being Chicana meant being "less." It was through my mother's desire to protect her children from poverty and illiteracy that we became "anglocized"; the more effec-tively we could pass in the white world, the better guaranteed our future.

Work done in the social sciences also reveals how Black women's or Chicanas' raising of their children is informed by a kind of awareness of and wariness about the world that goes beyond an awareness of "male dominance" or "gender role expectations." As Gloria Joseph has pointed out, a theory about relationships between mothers and children could hardly be complete "without a consideration of racial relations and racism."[18] In concrete terms, such considerations remind us that

> the Black mother has a more ominous message for her child and feels more urgently the need to get the message across. The child must know that the white world is dangerous and that if he does not understand its rules it may kill him.[19]

Insofar as a Black mother's mothering is informed by and takes place in a social context in which there is racism, it cannot be said that she is preparing her male child to assume his appointed superior place among the "men," as Chodorow argues. In fact she is preparing him "for his subordinate place in the world"[20]—or are we to assume that his maleness will be recognized by his mother, his father, his sister, himself, and everyone else, as something separable from his Blackness?

Dorcas Bowles has addressed head-on the question of the conditions under which a Black female's sense of self (and indirectly a Black male's sense of self) develops.[21] Her work makes us think about the ways in which Black mothering is different from white mothering in terms of the knowledge mothers have about how their children will be greeted by a racist society. This knowledge of difference, and this difference in knowledge, may be connected with differences in what a mother's love or nurturing means. Chodorow tends to write as if the kind of care mothers provide is everywhere the same—despite her acknowledgment of the likelihood of cultural differences on this score. There is indeed no reason to presuppose that what counts as "mother's love" will not vary from culture to culture, from subgroup to subgroup.[22] Daryl Dance recounts a story by John Williams about the confusion two Black children feel about their mother's treatment of them. On the one hand, they remember the treatment with considerable hostility; on the other, they begin to wonder about how love might be expressed by a Black woman in a racist society:

> Love? What is that? Giving love to children was a luxury she couldn't afford and when she could, she had got out of the habit. I don't mean that she didn't have the feeling. Love? You know, that's whipping the crap out of your children so that they don't crack their heads against the walls that make up the labyrinth and if they don't they might live and make out somehow. That's a kind of love, isn't it?[23]

But it is not just the mothering of Black women or other women of color that is informed by knowledge of racial distinctions and racial hierarchies. In *Killers of the Dream*, Lillian Smith describes the childhood lessons she learned from her Southern white parents, especially her mother:

> I do not think our mothers were aware that they were teaching us lessons. It was as if they were revolving mirrors reflecting life outside the home, inside their memory, outside the home. . . . We learned from this preview of the world we were born into, what was expected of us as human creatures.
>
> We were taught in this way to love God, to love our white skin, and to believe in the sanctity of both.[24]

Smith goes on to explain ways in which lessons about whiteness were intertwined with lessons about sex and one's body: They were told, she says,

> Parts of your body are segregated areas which you must stay away from and keep others away from. These areas you touch only when necessary. In other words, you cannot associate freely with them any more than you can associate freely with colored children.[25]

At the same time, they were also taught that

> though your body is a thing of shame and mystery, and curiosity about it is not good, your skin is your glory and the source of your strength and pride. It is white, [which] proves that you are better than all other people on this earth.[26]

Smith also explores the different kinds of relationships white male infants had with their own mothers and their Black nurses, and the likely effects of those relationships on their adolescent and adult sense of themselves as well as on their sense of white women and Black women. In light of these reflections, it seems positively bizarre for Chodorow to suggest that the only part of the social context that informs a woman's mothering is her sense of gender differences and gender inequalities. Chodorow does point—in a footnote—to the phenomenon of Black slave women's mothering of white slaveowners' children, but only to say that it seems to support her view that good mothering (such as the Black women were said to have provided for their owners' children) cannot be explained merely by reference to coercion (p. 33). She does not seize the opportunity to reflect on what this phenomenon might tell us about the social context of mothering.

Is the situation Smith describes too peculiar, too unusual, too atypical, to be used to challenge Chodorow's views? My mother was white, and a Christian, but she didn't tell me not to play with Black children or with Jewish children; indeed, both my parents stuck to what they perceived to be Christian principles of all people being one in the sight of God, even when other members of their church refused to. However, that doesn't mean my mother's mothering was not informed by awareness of her family as white and other families as Black, or her family as Christian (nay, Episcopalian) and others Jewish. My brothers and sisters and I may have learned different lessons about the difference between being white and being Black than Lillian Smith and her siblings did, but we surely did learn such lessons and they were inextricably tied to what we learned about being girls and boys—or if they weren't so tied, we have not learned from Chodorow's account on what grounds they can be excluded.

VI.

Once we begin to look at the social context of mothering, and hence at the social context of gender, we have to think about what it means to say that women possess the same gender. For if it is true that gender identity is not separable from other aspects of identity, then, as the examples discussed above suggest, one's sense of oneself as a "woman" is not separable from one's sense of oneself as, say, Chicana, Black, or white; one is known as and knows oneself as Chicana, Black woman, or white woman. Or are we in our entirety divisible into parts? Can I point to the "woman" part, then to the "white" part? Would it be desirable to be able to do so? No doubt we have linguistic habits that suggest we are so divisible: "We say things like, "As a woman, I think that . . . , while as a Jew, I think that. . . ." We say things like, "Daily, we feel the pull and tug of having to choose between which parts have served to cloak us from the knowledge of ourselves."[27] We sometimes ask ourselves where and with whom we feel most ourselves—with other women, with other lesbians, other Blacks, other Hispanas, other Jews? What do such habits and grammatical possibilities tell us?

One thing they tell us is that there are a lot of different ways of sorting human beings. If we look at that variety, we of course see that sorting along one dimension cuts across another. The dimension "women" cuts across race and class and nationality; the division "race" cuts across sex and class. Any given individual will be included in any number of divisions, and no individual will be included in only one. Why there are the sortings there are depends, among other things, on the goals of the sorters and the point of the sorting. Is there some sorting that is more fundamental in some sense than any other? Are some principles of sorting somehow built into the nature of things, while others are more conventional and hence, it would seem, more subject to change? Can a person change any of the ways in which she is sorted? Can she disguise any of these ways? Do answers to these two questions have implications for what is more "fundamental"? These are rather metaphysical concerns—with political consequences if not political presuppositions. We can't begin to go into these questions here but we can say that the experience and meaning of being sorted out along one dimension of human identity is very much influenced by the experience and the meaning of being sorted out along another dimension. This means that even if you are sorted out along one dimension with others, your experience is nevertheless likely to be different from those others insofar as you are not sorted together along another dimension. For example, socialist feminists have shown us why accounts of living under conditions of class oppression cannot be the same for men and for women because of the invidious sorting also done along the lines of sex and gender identity.[28] By the same token, accounts of living under conditions of sexual oppression cannot be the same for women of all classes. And this, I think, tells us that while in one sense women are all of the same gender, what it means to be a "woman" depends on what else is true about oneself and the world in which one lives. All women are women, but there is no being who is only a woman. For different reasons and on different occasions, being a woman may be, both in the eyes of others and in the eyes of a woman herself, the most important fact about her. But it is not the only fact about her, and the meaning of that fact about her—to herself and to others—will depend on other facts about her. Thus it has been suggested that great differences between the lives of affluent and working-class women in Victorian England, as well as great differences between the ideologies about their lives, meant that "it was as if there were two different human species of females."[29] How many different "species" there are depends on how crucial other variables are in giving shape and meaning to women's experiences at any particular time and place.

All this is perfectly compatible with the well-founded feminist desire to focus on the fact of a certain and a very large number of humans being women. It is very important and very useful to be able to do this. But there is great variety in what it means to be a woman—both to outsiders and to us ourselves—and it is precisely that variety that feminism explores (even when it claims to be doing something more "universal" about "women in general") and from which feminists act. It is the burden of Chodorow's work and the work of those influenced by her to tell us about how gender identity is constructed and maintained by societal institutions, and how gender identity might be different if institutional arrangements, such as asymmetrical patterns of parenting, were different. But once we begin to think of gender identity, as opposed to sexual identity, as part of a society's conventions—even as part of every society's conventions—then we can't assume that what it is to be, and to be thought of as, a "woman" will always and everywhere be the same.[30] The process of becoming a girl, and then a woman, occurs, as Chodorow herself tells us, in a social context. But attention to that context seems to tell us how inextricably intertwined that process is with the acquisition and the meaning of other parts of our identity.

VII.

According to Chodorow, we recall, girls and boys, women and men, are distinguished from each other in terms of their "relational sense," that is, the degree to which their sense of self incorporates an understanding of oneself as basically connected with others or as fundamentally distinct from others. This fits them either for women's work, which increasingly has involved affective ties with others, or for men's work, which increasingly has had no room for affect. This does not mean, and presumably Chodorow wouldn't say it means, that men have no relation to others or that men are free of affective states. Nevertheless, she sometimes tends to talk as if the "private sphere" women are said to occupy is one in which people are connected and see themselves that way, while people in the "public sphere" are separate, not only from those in the private sphere but also from each other.

Yet she also contrasts the spheres by saying that in the private sphere the "exercise of influence" is in "face-to-face, personal contexts," while the public sphere is a context "defined by authority" (p. 180). "Male superiority," Chodorow says, "is built into the definition of masculinity itself" (p. 185). But if the public, masculine sphere is in large part defined by authority, then it is a sphere involving people in relation to one another, for surely authority is a relation. Moreover, it is hard to imagine how male domination works—for those for whom it works—unless men see themselves as related to other men. Chodorow herself hints at this when she says early on that "public institutions, activities and forms of association . . . tie men to one another apart from their domestic relationships" (p. 9). Capitalism as Chodorow describes it requires (though does not necessarily succeed in getting) workers to see themselves "in relation," even if it is not a relation that seems very positive (p. 186 and passim).

Perhaps men deny their relation to others, but denial of connection is not the same as absence of connection. Indeed, on some views, denial of connection is not only compatible with but perhaps even evidence of the presence of connection. Chodorow attends to this to a certain extent, but she does not really note the discrepancy between the ideology of men as separate and highly individuated and the reality of their relationships. Such ideology discourages us from seeing that while not all relations may be the kind we think of when we think about mothers and children, that doesn't mean they aren't relations. Similarly, not all "affections" may be the kind we are encouraged to think of when we think about nurturing children, but that doesn't mean they aren't affections. Fear, pride, and anger are affects just as much as love and motherly caring (which itself of course is not free of fear, anger, pride, or jealousy). What Chodorow describes as the public world (or sphere) of work is teeming with affect—whether it be boredom, pride, anger, jealousy, hope, contempt, or fear.[31]

Chodorow really doesn't say very much in detail about what she means by the presence or absence of affect and affective ties, but she might insist that a highly organized, bureaucratized work world requires those who are in it to repress affect—thus a worker might be bored, or angry, but can't show it; a corporation vice-president might be proud but had better not strut. In the domestic sphere, however, women's mothering, even if it is merely adequate, requires the expression of certain feelings, such as a constant concern for the welfare of the child.

However, one might respond in reply that factory workers would not be able to perform routine and boring work day after day unless they had a fairly high level of fear or anxiety that without this work they would be without income. In a capitalist economy of the kind Chodorow describes, how much is the willingness to work in a low-level, low-paying job sustained by the hope of rising through the well-marked ranks? Chodorow herself indicates how important the creation of appropriate affect is among those who work in the "public sphere" as well as in the "private sphere," arguing that any adequate account of why women mother and why men do not has to describe and explain why women and men seek out and find satisfaction in the activities prescribed for them by the sexual division of labor. We need, she insists, to focus on the rather good fit between the psyches of women and men and the social roles they are expected to play. Just as there couldn't be such a fit if women were not affectively prepared for their work, so there wouldn't be if men were not affectively prepared for theirs. Men have pulled one over on us if we believe that they are without emotion; they have been able to describe their emotional states as the absence of emotion and women's as the presence, when in fact perhaps there are just different sets of emotions. This is parallel to white Anglo-Saxon Protestants believing that only Italians, Hispanos, Jews, Chinese, and others have "ethnic" identities. Of course men have emotions, and Chodorow's own theory points us to that very fact. Their work requires them to have certain emotions just as women's does. Paradoxically, it may require them to fear showing emotion, or to take pride in not showing it.

It is thus not the absence of affect that characterizes the public world, but perhaps it is an absence of affective ties. Men have feelings, but not the kind that reflect relations with other people—if they fear, it is for themselves; if they feel pride, it is in themselves. But Chodorow implicitly argues against this when, for example, she says that in highly placed jobs workers have to make the "goals and values of the organization for which they work . . . their own" (p. 186). Men's "affective ties" with one another in such circumstances may be strictly contained, and may exclude the forms of affection thought proper only for the domestic realm, but that does not mean there are no such ties. Again, are we to believe that male domination is a significant factor in our lives, and that men typically feel superior to women, without believing that this signals the presence of some important kinds of affective ties among men?

If Chodorow sometimes tends to ignore or underrate the strength of affect and affective ties in the public sphere, she also tends to exaggerate and misrepresent the strength of affect and affective ties in what she calls the private sphere. Late in the book, she remarks that "women tend to have closer personal ties with each other than men have, and to spend more time in the company of women than they do with men" (p. 200). This is misleading because it fails to note that there are phenomena such as racism, classism, ethnocentrism, heterosexism, anti-Semitism, and so on, that shatter the cozy image of easy womanly alliance suggested by Chodorow's remark. Is it clear that women tend to have closer personal ties with women of different classes or races than they do with men of their own class and race? Once again we have to ask Chodorow to be more specific about women's senses of themselves as "women," of the nature of their "personal ties" with each other, of the real extent of their identification with each other.

Indeed, part of Chodorow's claim about the separability of gender from other aspects of identity comes out in her statement that girls, in learning to identify with their mothers, learn also to identify with "women in general" (p. 77,137,175). What Chodorow seems to mean by this is that a girl learns to think, feel, and act like a woman, to have feelings about her mother and other women, and to have the kind of sense of self that women have through her relationship to her mother and other women in her immediate community. That is how she "learns what it is to be womanlike" (p. 175).

But Chodorow's claim that a girl comes to identify with "women in general" goes against her own view that the development of girls' sense of self involves a very concrete relationship while that of boys involves a much more abstract one. As we asked earlier: Is a girl only aware of her mother's being a woman, and not of her mother's being Black or white? Does a girl learn who and what she is and is not only be reference to her difference from boys and men? Is she taught that her difference from the boys and men of her own race and class is the same as her difference from the boys and men of other races and classes?

Finally, is it really possible to learn about or identify with "women in general"? There are multitudes of persons all correctly referred to as "women," but it doesn't follow that there *must* be something we all have in common that explains what "women in general" means, nor does it follow that if we learn something essential about one woman we thereby learn it about all women. If there is something women have in common, it surely is not something we can come to know by extrapolation from our own case and the cases of those like us. It is not something a girl can come to know through interactions among members of her family constellation—no matter how she feels and no matter how she describes that feeling. And if it were true that in learning to become girls and women we really learned to "identify" with women in general, how do we explain the failure of women who have enjoyed race and class privilege to see as fellow women those to whom such privilege does not accrue? Seeing another as a woman no doubt is different from seeing another as "sister," but Chodorow tends to conflate the two when she talks about girls identifying with women and having a strong relational sense. She is right to point to the social context in which mothering, and the development and learning of gender, take place. But in that context we know that it is an achievement for women of one class or race or nationality to "identify" with women of another class or race or nationality—it is hardly a given, and it is surely not something that comes automatically with the acquisition of gender identity.

What is the connection between Chodorow's implicit claim that gender is isolatable from other elements of identity and her claim that a central difference between feminine and masculine gender identity has to do with the degree to which one is, and sees oneself as being, in relation to and connected with others? The first claim, unlike the second, says nothing about the content or substance of gender identity, and someone could agree with Chodorow about the first but disagree about the second, placing some other quality or personality trait or disposition at the heart of a gender identity. Hence a criticism of one of her claims does not entail a criticism of the other. I have reasons for questioning both claims. While I have been especially concerned about the first—that gender is an independent variable of human identity—I have also raised questions about the second, which involves Chodorow's concept of relatedness. For if the first claim gives us an unwarranted sense of the shared *identity* of women across lines of race, class, and ethnicity, the second promotes an unwarranted sense of a shared *community* of women across such lines. Our actual histories, rich with the differences and marked by painful divisions among us, tell us that such identity and community do not follow, when they do come about, merely from the fact of our having become women.

VIII.

It is a general principle of feminist inquiry to be sceptical about any account of human relations that fails to mention gender or consider the possible effects of gender differences: for in a world in which there is sexism, obscuring the workings of gender is likely to involve—whether intentionally or not—obscuring the workings of sexism. We thus ought to be sceptical about any account of gender relations that fails to mention race and class or to consider the possible effects of race and class differences on gender: for in a world in which there is racism and classism, obscuring the workings of race and class is likely to involve—whether intentionally or not—obscuring the workings of racism and classism.

For this reason alone we may have a lot to learn from the following questions about any account of gender relations that presupposes or otherwise insists on the separability of gender, race, and class: Why does it seem possible or necessary to separate them? Whatever the motivations for doing so, does it serve the interests of some people and not others? Does methodology ever express race or class privilege—for example, do any of the methodological reasons that might be given for trying to investigate gender in isolation from race and class in fact serve certain race or class interests?

These questions are not rhetorical. For very good and very important reasons, feminists have insisted on asking how gender affects or is affected by every branch of human inquiry (even those such as the physical sciences, which seem to have no openings for such questions). And with very good reason we have been annoyed by the absence of reference to gender in inquiries about race or class, racism and classism. Perhaps it seems the best response, to such a state of affairs, first to focus on gender and sexism and then to go on to think about how gender and sexism are related to race and racism, class and classism. Hence the appeal of the work of Nancy Chodorow and the variations on it by others. But however logically, methodologically, and politically sound such inquiry seems, it obscures the ways in which race and class identity may be intertwined with gender identity. Moreover, since in a racist and classist society the racial and class identity of those who are subject to racism and classism are not obscured, all it can really mask is the racial and class identity of white, middle-class women. It is because white, middle-class women have something at stake in not having their racial and class identity made and kept visible that we must question accepted feminist positions on gender identity.

If feminism is essentially about gender, and gender is taken to be neatly separable from race and class, then race and class don't need to be talked about except in some peripheral way. And if race and class are peripheral to women's identities as women, then racism and classism can't be of central concern to feminism. Hence the racism and classism some women face and other women help perpetuate can't find a place in feminist theory unless we keep in mind the race and class of all women (not just the race and class of those who are the victims of racism and classism). I have suggested here that one way to keep them in mind is to ask about the extent to which gender identity exists in concert with these other aspects of identity. This is quite different from saying either (1) we need to talk about race and class instead of gender, or (2) we need to talk about race and class in addition to gender. Some feminists may be concerned that focus on race and class will deflect attention away from gender and from what women have in common and thus from what gives feminist inquiry its distinctive cast. This presupposes not only that we ought not spend too much time on what we don't have in common but that we have gender in common. But do we have gender identity in common? In one sense, of course, yes: all women are women. But in another sense, no: not if gender is a social construction and females become not simply women but particular kinds of women. If I am justified in thinking that what it means for me to be a woman must be exactly the same as what it means for you to be a woman (since we both are women), I needn't bother to find out anything from you or about you in order to find out what it means for you to be a woman: I can simply deduce what it means from my own case. On the other hand, if the meaning of what we apparently have in common (being women) depends in some ways on the meaning of what we don't have in common (for example, our different racial or class identities), then far from distracting us from issues of gender, attention to race and class in fact helps us to understand gender. In this sense it is only if we pay attention to how we differ that we come to an understanding of what we have in common.

Notes

1. Notice how different this is from saying that whether one is *female* is unaffected by what race or class one is.

2. Among the philosophers and political theorists who have incorporated Chodorow's work into their own analyses are Jane Flax, "Political Philosophy and the Patriarchal Unconscious: A Psychoanalytic Perspective on Epistemology and Metaphysics"; Nancy C. M. Hartsock, "The Feminist Standpoint: Developing the Ground for a Specifically Feminist Historical Materialism"; Naomi Scheman, "Individualism and the Objects of Psychology"; and Sandra Harding, "Why Has the Sex/Gender System Become Visible Only Now?"—all in *Discovering Reality: Feminist Perspectives on Epistemology, Metaphysics, Methodology, and the Philosophy of Science*, ed. Sandra Harding and Merrill Hintikka (Dordrecht: Reidel, 1983). See also Isaac D. Balbus, *Marxism and Domination* (Princeton: Princeton University Press, 1982).

Chodorow's work also has been incorporated into the literary criticism of Judith Kegan Gardiner, "On Female Identity and Writing by Women," *Critical Inquiry* 8, no.2 (1981): 347–61, and of Elizabeth Abel, "(E)Merging Identities: The Dynamics of Female Friendship in Contemporary Fiction by Women," *Signs* 6, no.3 (1981): 413–35. Students of psychoanalysis such as Jessica Benjamin and Evelyn Fox Keller have found Chodorow's work helpful in explaining their own positions, Benjamin in "Masters and Slave: The Fantasy of Erotic Domination," in *Powers of Desire: The Politics of Sexuality*, ed. Ann Snitow, Christine Stansell, and Sharon Thompson (New York: Monthly Review Press, 1983), 280–99; Keller in "Gender and Science," *Psychoanalysis and Contemporary Thought* 2, no.3 (1978): 409–33. Chodorow's work has also influenced the far-reaching work of Carol Gilligan, *In a Different Voice* (Cambridge: Harvard University Press, 1982). Chodorow's book and earlier articles were the subject of a critical symposium in *Signs* 6, no.3 (1981), with comments from Judith Lorber, Rose Laub Coser, Alice S. Rossi, and a response from Chodorow. Iris Young recently has expressed doubts about the wisdom of Flax's, Hartsock's, and Harding's use of Chodorow, in "Is Male Gender Identity the Cause of Male Domination?" in *Mothering: Essays in Feminist Theory*, ed. Joyce Trebilcot (Totawa, N.J.: Rowman and Allanheld, 1983). In the *Mothering* volume also appears Pauline Bart's highly critical review of Chodorow's book, a review first found in *off our backs* 11, no.1 (1981). Adrienne Rich has pointed out the heterosexist bias in *The Reproduction of Mothering* in "Compulsory Heterosexuality and Lesbian Existence," *Signs* 5, no.4 (1980): 631–60. As discussed below, Gloria Joseph has addressed the fact of the absence of a discussion of race and racism in accounts like Chodorow's.

3. Nancy Chodorow, *The Reproduction of Mothering: Psychoanalysis and the Sociology of Gender* (Berkeley: University of California Press, 1978). All references are to this edition and are cited parenthetically in the text.

4. Chodorow, Reply to "On *The Reproduction of Mothering*: A Methodological Debate," with Judith Lorber, Rose Laub Coser, and Alice S. Rossi, *Signs* 6, no.3 (1981): 502, 503. Hereafter referred to as "Reply."

5. Chodorow, "Gender, Relation, and Difference," in *The Future of Difference*, ed. Hester Eisenstein and Alice Jardine (New Brunswick, N.J.: Rutgers University Press, 1985), 3–19. Reprinted from *Socialist Review* 9, no. 46 (1979): 51–69.

6. See note 3 above, specifically articles by Bart, Rosaldo, Young, and Rich. See also comments by Mark Poster in *Sociology and Social Research* 63 (1979): 394–96.

7. This chapter can be seen in part as one way to carry out Michelle Rosaldo's suggestion that we look at sexual inequality in light of its connections to other forms of inequality in any society. See "The Use and Abuse of Anthropology: Reflections on Feminism and Cross-cultural Understanding," *Signs* 5, no.3 (1980): 389–417.

8. Chodorow, "Gender, Relation, and Difference," p. 12.

9. For discussion of this, see Young, "Male Gender Identity"; Roger Gottlieb, "Mothering and the Reproduction of Power," in *Socialist Review* 77 (September/ October 1984).

10. Chodorow, "Reply," 514.

11. For a recent account of Emmet Till's murder, see Juan Williams, *Eyes on the Prize* (New York: Viking, 1986), 41 ff.

12. For a recent attempt to explain how Descartes can avoid this criticism, see Norman Malcolm, "Descartes's Proof that His Essence Is Thinking," *Philosophical Review* 74, no.3 (1965):315–38.

13. See Iris Young, "Is Male Gender Identity the Cause of Male Domination?" for a discussion of the distinction between gender differentiation and male domination.

14. Mary Burgher, "Images of Self and Race in the Autobiography of Black Women," in *Sturdy Black Bridges*, ed. Roseann P. Bell, Bettye J. Parker, and Beverly Guy-Sheftall (Garden City, N.Y.: Anchor, 1979), 115.

15. Nikki Giovanni, *Gemini* (New York: Penguin, 1976), 24.

16. Barbara Cameron, "Gee, You Don't Seem Like An Indian From the Reservation," *This Bridge Called My Back*, ed. Cherrie Moraga and Gloria Anzuldua (Watertown, Mass.: Persephone Press, 1981), 46–47.

17. Cherrie Moraga, "La Guera," in *This Bridge Called My Back*, 28.

18. Gloria Joseph, *Common Differences: Conflicts in Black and White Perspectives* (with Jill Lewis) (Garden City, N.Y.: Anchor, 1981), 80.

19. Daryl Dance, "Black Eve or Madonna? A Study in the Antithetical Views of the Mother in Black American Literature," in *Sturdy Black Bridges*, 127. Here Dance is referring to *Black Rage*, by William H. Grier and Price M. Cobbs (New York: Basic Books, 1968), 61.

20. Ibid., 128.

21. Dorcas Bowles, "In Search of an Ethnic Self" (Northampton, Mass.: School for Social Work, Smith College, n.d.).

22. In the *Signs* symposium on Chodorow (note 2 above), Judith Lorber quotes Mary Lyndon Shanley on the apparent universality of emotion: "Hunger is hunger, pride is pride, and love is love—but these feelings, while universal, are evoked, expressed, and experienced differently in different societies" (see Mary Lyndon Shanley, "The History of the Family in Modern England," *Signs* 4, no.4 [1979]: 750).

23. Dance, "Black Eve," 129, quoting John A. Williams, *Sissie* (New York: Farrar, Strauss, 1963), 38–39. See also the conversation between Hannah and Eva in Toni Morrison's *Sula* (New York: Bantam, 1975), 58–60.

24. Lillian Smith, *Killers of the Dream* (New York: Norton, 1949), 82.

25. Ibid., 87.

26. Ibid., 89. Some of the most moving parts of Smith's memoire/essay are her descriptions of the white children's confusion about the resistance to the double mes-

sages of "Christian" parents about the importance of fellow feeling among all mankind. But the children were powerless to act on their perceptions, and on their more truly Christian affections. This is a reminder of how misleading it is for Chodorow to describe the mother/children domestic "sphere" as characterized by the absence of authority relations.

27. From Moraga and Anzaldua's introduction to part 2 of *This Bridge Called My Back*, 23.

28. See Alison Jaggar's *Feminist Politics and Human Nature* (Totawa, N.J.: Rowman and Allanheld, 1983) for an especially useful account of socialist feminism.

29. This has been suggested by Barbara Ehrenreich and Deirdre English in *Complaints and Disorders: The Sexual Politics of Sickness* (Old Westbury, N.Y.: Feminist Press, 1973), 11–12. See also Rosaldo, "The Use and Abuse of Anthropology."

30. See Jaggar, *Feminist Politics*, 99ff. for a review of reasons some feminists take sexual identity also to be in some important sense a cultural creation.

31. In *Labor and Monopoly Capital* (New York: Monthly Review Press, 1974), Harry Braverman described "problems" among workers that industrial engineers were called in to try to deal with:

> The problems addressed are the problems of management: dissatisfaction as expressed in high turnover rates, absenteeism, resistance to the prescribed work pace, indifference, neglect, cooperative group restrictions on output, and overt hostility to management. (141).

> The hostility of workers to the degenerated forms of work which are forced upon them continues as a subterranean stream that makes its way to the surface when employment conditions permit, or when the capitalist drive for a greater intensity of labor oversteps the bounds of physical and mental capacity. It renews itself in new generations, expresses itself in the unbounded cynicism and revulsion which large numbers of workers feel about their work, and comes to the fore repeatedly as a social issue demanding solution. (151)

CHAPTER 13

Asian American Literary Traditions: Real vs. Fake

Frank Chin, Jeffery Chan, Lawson Inada, and Shawn Wong

In 1974, we edited *Aiiieeeee! An Anthology of Asian American Writers* (Howard University Press), and at that time we said,

> . . . American born and raised, who got their China and Japan from the radio, off the silver screen, from television, out of comic books, from the pushers of white American culture that pictured the yellow man as something that when wounded, sad, or angry, or swearing, or wondering, whined, shouted, or screamed aiiieeeee! Asian America, so long ignored and forcibly excluded from creative participation in American culture, is wounded, sad, angry, swearing and wondering, and this is his AIIIEEEEE!!! It is more than a whine, shout, or scream. It is fifty years of our whole voice[1]

With *The Big Aiiieeeee!*[2] we say there is no memory of us that does not include the makers of our heroic tradition. But white and yellow America not only forgot, but warred against the whisper, the very memory of their names. All discussion, speculation, and definition of the Chinese American and Japanese American character, personality, culture, mind, and literature has ignored the heroic tradition. For one-hundred years we've been seen and bred and taught to see ourselves without a heroic tradition. It's as ridiculous as growing up without ever having heard of *Little Red Riding Hood* and *The Three Little Pigs*. Ridiculous because the language of childhood is the language of the heroic tradition.

The first Chinese and Japanese children destined to settle in America with big ideas learned how to use their language from the telling and retelling of tales from the heroic tradition—from *The Romance of the Three Kingdoms* and *The Water Margin*, the universals in Chinese and Japanese childhoods since the Ming, to Chushingura, the tale of the loyal forty-seven Ronin, a story deep and essential in every Japanese childhood since the seventeenth century. These were the tales that taught the first Chinese and Issei to be, how to stand and how to talk. The plots, characters, and moral and social values of these heroic works and others were universally told and known among the Chinese and Japanese immigrants. These tales were the hard core of childhood and were bred into the nerves of the languages the Chinese and Japanese brought with them.

The Christians teaching our American-born grandparents Chinese in missionary schools in San Francisco did not teach the heroic tradition. The Christian missionaries produced converts who produced us—children with no heroic tradition, only Christian science fiction. Our childhood, the heart of our language, is what was taken out of our ear and replaced with nothing but the hisses and whistles of self-contempt and humiliation.

Chinese and Japanese from China and Japan who read this, the immigrants who have settled here after the last lifting of the immigration quota, will think of us doing what we don't have to do, talking the obvious and long-known stuff of a universal childhood with the seriousness of some big idea. We feel a little old talking to people our own age about the stuff of the universal childhood. There is an age beyond which you cannot be taught the alphabet, if you've never had an alphabet. There's an age beyond which it's a waste of time telling you *Little Red Riding Hood*, when you're too far beyond the good these tales have done for people your age. We compromised the joys of ruthlessly criticizing the quality of writing with the teaching of the alphabet and remedial reading. At first it was not a role we relished. The four of us felt silly talking to each other about our childhoods for hours on end.

The pervasive presence of the morals, principles, and sense of form in the works of the heroic tradition we discovered in Louis Chu and the Issei writing behind barbed wire cannot be taught, only talked about, its effects described, in a language voided of the works and made a foreign universe. So, again, as in the first *Aiiieeeee!* we are writing in our language without translation, appreciating the appropriate licks of the stuffed shirts, the ingenious, the rebels of our tradition, with appropriate forms of scepticism and awe. All of us who cry the blues about poor dummies working too hard to make a buck to spend time making art and writing may enrich the melancholy in the dark of a given fantasy of hairless Orientalia, and arouse a positive feeling for these poor dummies who couldn't wash clothes and write at the same time. But they are liars.

The Big Aiiieeeee! tells the tale of how the heroic tradition came, settled, spawned, and was then destroyed by Christian white racism and applied social Darwinism inside concentration camps. And how, every now and then, comes another arrogant and whimsical "Aiiieeeee!" fresh out of the past, to remind us of when we were a people with a vision, honor, integrity, and something to say.

We had looked forward in *The Big Aiiieeeee!* to including solid poetry with a little introductory word play flashing on the glitter and riches in the works we presented. Then we read all the works we had accumulated, old and new, between the first *Aiiieeeee!* and this—the fiction, the poetry, the social science, the histories, the cookbooks. We read them all. If they were by, about, from, or to yellows, we read them a little more seriously than before. We read big newsstand magazines and the arty little magazines. We watched TV. We read first-generation works in translations we had to work to get and we read the latest student writing put between covers and sold as poetry. Patterns we hadn't expected emerged.

The American-born, exclusively English-speaking Asian Americans were dominated by the Christian vision of China as country without a history, and a philosophy without substance or balls. The social Darwinist social philosophers and fictioneers of the turn of the century taught history we accept as both fact and stereotype today, feeling there is no other history to know.

The cultural and literary prejudices of our training in the universe of Western civilization did not prepare us for the discovery of a comprehensible, indeed, an easy to understand and express set of Asian universals codified and explicated in the heroic tradition in Chinese literature. The heroic tradition is to Asian civilization what the Greek epic tragic tradition is to Western civiliza-tion.] More embarrassing was the realization that the works of the heroic tradition are as popularly known today in the Asian-speaking world, including the Chinatowns and Little Tokyos of our youth, as they were two-thousand years ago.

The values and universals of Confucius found their most popular and enduring expression in popular-told forms of storytelling and verse. The basic works of the heroic tradition are Sun Tzu's *The Art of War* and Wu Chi's *The Art of War* from about 350 B.C., Lo Kuan Chung's *The Romance of the Three Kingdoms* and Shih Nai'an's and Lo Kuan Chung's sequel of *The Three Kingdoms, The Water Margin*. The Japanese continued the heroic tradition in *Momotaro* and *Chushingura*. With the exception of Sun Tzu and Wu Chi, all of these works are not high fallutin' esoteric objects of mystery, but univer-sally loved children's books. The moral universals and the dramatic forms, structures and characters of the heroic tradition were the basis of all Asian American writing in Chinese and Japanese languages, and expanded the En-glish of Wong Sam, Sui Sin Far, Louis Chu, Kyo Koike, Toshi Mori, Kazuo Miyamato, James Sakamoto, James Omura, and Chiye Mori.

We could not have made the distinction between the Chinamen and the Christian Chinese American literary histories and sensibilities without help. We could not have substantiated the bitter hard feelings of betrayal spoken out loud and in print and the unwritten silence of Nisei and Sansei writers and public figures without the help and encouragement of a small band of unex-pected, talented, and driven scholars, scientists, translators, folklorists, crimi-nals, impassioned archivists, and Japanese American writers and researchers

who want the silences filled and the horrors of betrayal and behavior modification told, but can't bear to tell it themselves. The sickly one who drinks
too much coffee and writes on napkins, the grandmother out of showbiz going
blind in the archives searching after truth, these noblest of the pained, are the
honest scholars that the college-age camp generation did not produce. They
made us promise not to name them. They fear social ostracism and betrayal to
this day.

Our reading of the Old Nisei, Toshio Mori, Kazuo Miyamoto, and James
Sakamoto pointed us in the direction of the martial classics. Peter Suzuki, the
Nisei anthropologist doing anthropology on the anthropologists working in
the concentration camps, shared the Issei and Kibei poetry the social scientists
collected, translated, and misinterpreted in camp. The Issei poetry drove us
back to the basic works of any Asian's childhood. These were the stories in
which the first Chinese Americans, the first Issei, brought to light their
language and salted their tongues. Louis Chu's *Eat a Bowl of Tea*, a Chinese
American novel of the sixties, is layered with references and allusions to the
phrase, number, word usage, plot, and situation of the works of a Chinese
childhood in Kwangtung or Hong Kong, from the basic books on the art of
war to the sexual intrigues of *The Dream of the Red Chamber*. Life was war
from one end of life to the other.

We reread the disaster fiction of the turn-of-the-century writers gone
mad—Jack London's "The Unparalleled Invasion" and P. W. Dooner's "The
Last Days of the Republic"—end with the yellows destroying the white race
by the force of their overwhelming breeding. These works reflected the typical thinking of white America in the teens, twenties, and thirties of the
American twentieth century. They are not works to be dismissed as vicious
and sentimental racism about yellows written at a time of momentary insanity.
The social Darwinists saw America as a white continent according to the laws
of survival of the fittest. Patriotism was a matter of white supremacy. They
openly said that the survival of American greatness and superiority de-
pended on the survival of the white race. They believed that interbreeding
"mongrelized" the race and produced offspring who were the worst of both
worlds.

In his introduction to Lothrop Stoddard's *The Rising Tide of Color*
(1926), Madison Grant wrote:

> If this great race, with its capacity for leadership and fighting, should ulti-
> mately pass, with it would pass that which we call civilization. It would be
> succeeded by an unstable and bastardized population, where worth and merit
> would have no inherent right to leadership and among which a new and
> darker age would blot out our racial inheritance. The Nordic race has been
> driven from many of its lands, but still grasps firmly the control of the world,

and it is certainly not at a greater numerical disadvantage than often before in contrast to the teeming population of Asia. It has repeatedly been confronted with crises where the accident of battle, or the genius of a leader, saved a well-nigh hopeless day. . . . Fight it we must, but let that fight be not a civil war against its own blood kindred but against the dangerous foreign races, whether they advance sword in hand or in the more insidious guise of beggars at our gates, pleading for admittance to share our prosperity. If we continue to allow them to enter they will in time drive us out of our own land by mere force of breeding.[3]

The yellows threaten—in American pulp and intellectual fiction, in the bombast of the U.S. Congress and Senate, in the graphs and maps of American social scientists like Madison Grant—to destroy white America by a race war, where sex and reproduction are the weapons. What the pulp, intellectual, and social Darwinist writers of the turn of the century wrote was a white racist nightmare—a vision of being assimilated by the yellows. White assimilation by yellows unquestionably meant the extinction of white history and the white race. London, Dooner, and Madison Grant all end their nightmares with an epitaph to Western civilization and the white race.

The whites see being assimilated by yellows as negative and undesirable. No matter how they costume their tongues, the Christianized Chinese Americans, the Nisei social scientists, the Japanese American Citizens League (JACL) New Nisei, the Asian Americans of the sixties and seventies all see the disappearance of the yellow race in America as being good for the yellows.

None of the Asian American sociology, history, ideology, or art tells Asian American history based on contemporary Asian American sources. That's why we're together again, researching, writing, and editing all the books we expected yellow critics, culture vultures, and other scavengers to write in the last ten years.

We are not critics. Our critical anatomy of Chinese American and Japanese American writing is woefully uninhabited by critics, critical theories of Asian American writing, schools, postures, and movements. Instead we are infested with sociologists and holy Joes, picking at the bones of our poetry and tearing the lids off our prose looking for a mastodon frozen stiff in a block of ice.

We have done our scholarly homework haphazardly and reluctantly after the first *AIIIEEEEE!* essay. But no matter how careless, lazy, and serendipitous our method of searching the past for the works, and the works for the past, what we have found to read was stuff that had not been read for years. Stuff our people had written and our people had forgotten. As Asian American writers, we respond as much to the search for and discovery of our literary tradition as to the voices of Wong Sam, Nagai Kafu, Kyo Koike, Sui Sin Far, and James Y. S. Sakamoto, the writers and word magicians we knew wrote in the past because we wrote like them in the distant present and knew we were not the beginning. These are the voices of Chinese American and Japanese American writers bound by visions of Chinamen and Nikkei integrity in the face of inevitable, if not imminent, racial extinction. In our search, we discovered a sweet morbidity, aching epitaphs of the doomed, before they die; flowing celebrations of them, before they die.

Sociologists are the architects of the apocalypse that rids the earth of the infidels and heathens forbidden to enter the promised land. The awful power of the white supremacist God the sociologists serve leaves the heathens blank, naked, with nothing on but awe for white might and moral superiority. And, after the freeing and fleeing of the Israelites away from Pharaoh into forty years of wilderness toward the Promised Land, the generation of converts that knew Pharaoh and grew old beholden to his temples and tombs, graven images, idols and art, were all dead outside the promised land of milk and honey. Moses was of that forbidden generation. That's part of his heroism. The process sociologists call "absorption and assimilation" and posit as a scientific law governing the shenanigans of every non-white American people is the biblical apocalypse, the death in the wilderness of all the converts before reaching the Promised Land and stepping into the atmosphere of the chosen in God's own choice real estate.

The historians, the sociologists, the yellow practitioners of the white "sciences" said they knew nothing about Asian American literature because there was nothing to know. In *AIIIEEEEE!*, with nothing up our sleeves, we produced proof of a Japanese American and Chinese American literature that the sociologists and historians said did not exist. This proof that had eluded the massed expertise, training, and instrumentation of the great white sciences was simply books, the works themselves. Sung, who says we were working too hard to write; Kung, who says we were too low-class to write; Okimoto, who says we were too full of self-contempt to write, and that if we could write we would have nothing to say—all had obviously let their library cards lapse. We found John Okada on the shelf of a grocery store; Louis Chu we found in the card catalogue of the Oakland Public Library; Toshio Mori we found on the shelf of a used book store we had gone into seeking shelter from a rainy day in Berkeley. Our method was not scientific. We tried the scientific sociological method, and, using that method, we could not find them. No longer able to deny the existence of an Asian American cultural sensibility, sociologists spent thousands of dollars of grant money to prove it did not exist, was never there. They grudgingly acknowledged the fact of the works we had found, but would deny that between the works is a link of vision, history, cultural integrity, and literary ambition. Chinese America and Japanese America are not metaphors for white America. We outlined this tradition and its sensibilities in the first *AIIIEEEEE!*

The Christian missionaries, the historians, the sociologists, characterized us as sojourners come to America to get rich quick and retire to Lotus Land. They characterize us as coming with no visions of settling and establishing a new integrity. We are victims of the so-called dual personality identity crisis, they say. The sojourner theories, our lack of vision, the dual personality and the identity crisis, like the nonexistence of Asian American literature, are all the wondrous fabrications of white science and Christianity. Even the language they use smacks of church. As the Christian missionary would convert us to see the light of the true faith, so would the sociologist/historian assimilate us into the "mainstream" where we would serve the "host" society and spend the rest of our lives seeking the acceptance of the "dominant" majority. Call it conversion, assimilation and absorption, it all spells extinction— apocalypse for the heathen Chinee. Chinatown as the Apocalypse.

So-called sociologist D. Y. Yuan, Professor of Sociology, Brooklyn College, did a so-called analysis and called it *Voluntary Segregation: A Study of New York Chinatown*.[4] It reads like the report of surrender made by the losing general or the report of a victory by the winning general.

> Effort was made in the analysis to exclude mutually the voluntary and the involuntary choice (factors).[5]

Translated, this means, "We" if you're the winner, "You" if you're the loser, "set out to make the Chinaman impotent with a confusion of choices."

> The involuntary choice of the Chinese preceded the voluntary development of New York's Chinatown.[6]

Translated, this means, "Before whites drove the Chinese to Chinatown, they were settling down all over town and setting up shop."

> The period of defensive insulation is a period between these two, the last period being gradual assimilation.[7]

This means, "For awhile, whites kept all the Chinamen in Chinatown. Now, whites are letting them out of Chinatown slowly." This is the zoo display, taming and domestication period. The Chinaman whom whites let survive out of Chinatown is not the same Chinaman they drove into Chinatown so fiercely that he made Chinatown an armed fortress.

In short, the stages of the development of Chinatown may be illustrated in the following chart. The hypothetical stages are based on the analysis.[8]

Hypothetical Stages of the Development of Chinatown[9]

involuntary choice (discrimination & prejudice toward the Chinese)	defensive insulation	voluntary segregation	gradual assimilation
(1)	(2)	(3)	(4)

We have a million ways of saying it. Betty Lee Sung puts it nicely.

> Dispersion away from the vortexes of San Francisco and New York should be encouraged. This ought to be the long range goal of the Chinese because distribution reduces the degree of visibility.[10]

Dopey Derald Wing Sue, Ph.D., and dopey Stanley Sue, Ph.D., of the four boys named Sue, stooges for Charlie Chan Shangri La and otherwise, try to attract attention in the psychology profession without waking anybody up or competing with whites. To prove they are not going to say anything to upset whites in their work, they cite nothing but whites and other yellows who cite the white word on yellows as if it were Scripture, in everything they write, even resorting to citing themselves, to remind the chuckling audiences how seriously Sue and Sue take themselves.

The Sue and Sue capsule version of Chinese American history in their "Counseling Chinese-Americans" published in *Personnel and Guidance Journal*[11] is true to the classic form and content of Yuan and Sung. They have more style. Their language flows a little more easily. It has a sinister beauty to anyone hip to Chinese America. These boys are flashier. More swish. Unlike Yuan and Sung, Sue and Sue make a direct appeal to white male fantasies of being the manliest among any and all groups and races of yellow men. Shangri La Charlie Chan, the white man as passive lover. Manliest man among yellow women. Their resemblance to Charlie Chan verges on plagiarism.

> The Chinese individual in America is in a position of conflict between the pulls of both his cultural background and the Western value he is exposed to in school and by the mass media.[12]

Notice that the subject of this sentence, the representative of our history, the all-purpose mythical Chinaman, "The Chinese individual in America," isn't born anywhere. He has a "cultural background" that is not related to "the Western values he is exposed to in school and by the mass media." Sue and Sue are writing as if the "Chinese individual" is commuting between planets. He's Chinese to Western values, and Western to Chinese values. Although born in America, he has been born foreign. In a word, this is nuts. They have done nothing more than restate Charlie Chan's, "Am I then an American? No. Am I then a Chinese? Not in the eyes of Ah Sing." Ah Sing being Chinese in the Chinese sense of Chinese. Now they start giving the white man a massage in their parlor.

> American values emphasizing spontaneity, assertiveness, and independence are often at odds with many Chinese values.[13]

The Sues are comparing the white self-image of American pop culture with the values of high Chinese morality and high culture. They are comparing John Wayne and Mickey Spillane to the ethics of Confucius and Buddhist theology. The high moral self-image of the whites, most would agree, is to be found in their Bible. That tells the history of men seeking to perfect themselves into passive believers in one God, to submit and be of the meek who shall inherit the earth, whose wills are divested of revenge. For the Bible says, "Revenge is mine saith the Lord." Most readers of English, Christian and non-Christian alike, are familiar with that biblical saying. We wonder how they've managed to avoid contact with the Christian monotheistic nature of the way time is told; the history is written and the language is spoken. Perhaps they thought the image of the whites that emerges from the works of pop culture more accurately reflects their abiding self-image. If that were the case, they would have compared the pop white self-image with the image of the yellow that emerges from yellow pop culture. They would have compared John Wayne to Kwan Kung, or to balance their comparison of John Wayne with Confucius they would have compared Kwan Kung with Jesus Christ. The comparison is an embarrassing example of their ignorance.

> As Chinese people progressively adopt more of the values and standards of the larger community as their own, the transition is not always smooth. Indeed, culture conflict seems to be an intimate part of the Asian-American experience.[14]

This is Christian theology, not history. It is the Tower of Babel inflicted upon the Chinese through Charlie Chan. All pre-Chan Chinese American writing—ALL OF PRE-CHAN CHINESE AMERICAN WRITING—resolves any "cultural conflict," recognizes racism and assumes a certain arrogance to be universal among Chinamen. Whites created the "culture conflict," the "identity crisis." The Sues champion it. The sensibility of this pre-Chan, pre-sociologist group of writers is remarkable for displaying roots going back to Kwan Kung, Canton, and the Chinese first-person pronoun, "I." This sensibility we call here "Chinaman." There are those of us who want into white the way some of us want into white neighborhoods and churches. The hidden ultimate good in the sociologies of the Sues, Sung, and Yuan, is white acceptance and extinction of the yellow distinction through assimilation. The most popular form of Chinese American writing has been the autobiography, not the autobiography of accomplished nobility casting a critical eye from the end of a lifetime, but an autobiography modelled formally on the work of white missionaries, typified by Charles F. Shepherd. These autobiographies, first published by religious houses, were in fact testimonies of conversion and salvation. We call these autobiographies Christian Chinese American autobiographies and the sensibilities of these autobiographies "Christian Chinese American," "Chinese American," or "Charlie Chan Shangri La"; at worst, we call them "sociology."

Those of us who know nothing else make their reputations investing in the beliefs that we, unlike any other immigrant group, had pilgrim visionaries come with no commitment to the expression and expansion of specific moral and cultural values they cannot express or expand on in the nation of their birth.

The pioneer white racist of nineteenth-century European pop, son of an admiral and wed to one of Wagner's daughters in his old age, saw in Hitler the Houston Stuart Chamberlain; he who shook hands with Hitler, leader of the great Teutonic people of his heroic Greco-Roman, Teutonic, Christian vision, could be the model for the vision of Chinese lack of history and moral worth written up by the sociologists Yuan, S. W. Kung, the boys named Sue, and Betty Lee Sung, now Betty Lee Sung Chung and who-knows-what-next? Sociology invents a new pseudo-mathematical language of white supremacy, and white supremacy is the only truth these sociologists creating Chinese American history out of thin air can say.

Beyond the names of Christian missionaries in the 1920s, the past is a void. The reason they know nothing about it, they say, is because there is nothing to know (S. W. Kung). A history of divided, primitive bands squabbling, and nothing but nastiness, living in humiliation and victimization, and no more. White history only records the names of the eight Irishmen who helped spell the total of four-hundred Chinamen who rolled the flatcars of rail, unloaded the rail off the flatcars, dropped the rail on the crossties, positioned the rail, spiked the rail down to the ties bedded in a hill of gravel, between six in the morning and six at night—all to lay ten miles, two-hundred feet of track, which broke the record of six miles, eight-hundred feet set by the Irish Union Pacific gangs working from three in the morning by lamplight until the next midnight, for the most track laid in a twenty-four-hour day. The names of the Chinamen are lost. The names of the Irishmen who worked on the Chinaman Central Pacific gang are all that remain of the Chinaman record-setting gang. In the famous photograph known as "The Golden Spike," with two engines sniffing each other out, with men all over, with flags and bottles, there are no Chinamen. These obvious clues, if not examples, of white supremacist values from white racist Christian fantasy destroying specific Chinese American history have not used their special "in's" and equipment to search and research out the history of their people, whom the whites destroyed. Just like the white racist Chamberlain, the yellow sociologists, the New Nisei Bill Hosokawa and Jeanne Wakatsuki Houston and James D. Houston in duo, characterize Asian American history as being composed of conversion, a process with its own apocalyptic extinction and philosophically and historically unintegrated individuals.

The first books Chinese American Christian autobiographers write are all blatantly untypical expressions by untypical Chinese Americans. Yung Wing and Leong Gor Yun are the converts aged in heathen ways and forbidden to the promised Absorption and Assimilation from on high. Pardee Low is named after a California Governor surnamed Pardee, and translates his Chinese name into English, doing to himself what white Christian missionaries had only done to Chinese women, not men. The women were the chosen of assimilation, not the men, but the men of this dream don't care, for theirs is a culture steeped in passivity. All the generalities about Chinese American history and culture the sociologists come up with are straight from the Chinese American autobiographies. The Chinese American autobiographies are straight from the missionary memoirs and ecclesiastical novels of Chinatown Cinderellas, Charles Shepherd, Jack London's *The Chinago* and *The Unparalleled Invasion*—all of which came from the need to avenge the moral failure represented by the failure of the greatest religious mission in the history of mankind mounted against China, and the kick in the nuts to the only great and true civilization, known as Christendom, by merely being unaccounted for in the Gospel, and unaccountable by all the known science and renowned know-it-alls of the time, especially the Popek whose word was law once upon a time. The mere existence of the equally great or even greater Chinese civilization was itself a moral affront to the one civilization built in the image of the one God, who demands His solitude and privacy in the universe. The first commandment, "Thou shalt not hold any other God before Me, for I am a jealous God," was an order to the world that Western civilization was committed to enforce against the Chinese, who represented the opposite of all white moral and cultural values, that the sociologists and Christian Chinese American autobiographers write in pure Christian pearls of Buck Rogers. The morally and culturally opposite is the land of white self-contempt turned out in drag fantastic. What could be more alien to the greedy, hard-bargaining Marco Polo, turgid with dreams of lira to burn, than to be loaded down with several hometown fortunes in free samples by the Chinese and asked to go home and take orders? Polo came back with a diary wacky with misinterpretation, childish what-ifs, and a palpitating amazement and shock at everything he saw. Pirates, loonies, and hucksters take off, imagining China, the land of the morally unimaginable in bogus diaries of Marco Polo that flood literature and religious Italy with strange practices, geographical Christendom. The China that took root in white imagination was a white getaway from the oppression and fear of Christian domination. Writing and reading Chinese in new, revised, and enlarged diaries of Marco Polo, was a way to romp in the realm of the indecent and morally unspeakable in praise of the moral superiority of Christendom. The first science fiction was a white escape from church rule and the rigors of Christian morality. Since Polo's bogus diaries, the quintessential, inconceivable alien, complete with entirely alien thought processes, logical, social, sexual and moral systems, in white science fiction has been Asianlike in the age of ray guns and broadswords, beaming from Flash Gordon's nemesis, Ming of Mongo, a Dr. Fu Manchu, to the sexually inscrutable Darth Vader of *Star Wars*. It is the one vision of the alien, whose mere existence is offense against the morality and manhood of Christendom. The China that Chinese America takes for real is a product of the white closed system.

When historian Roger Daniels says that John Okada's *No-No Boy* should be published without an introduction, especially an introduction like the "ethnic ego-tripping" to *AIIIEEEEE!*, Daniels is no longer the objective, scientific observer of matters Asian American, but speaks as a philosopher-king; not the recorder of Japanese American history, but its master. He speaks as a priest of white supremacy and uses the language of science as an instrument of war against Asia America. In the eyes of white scientists, it is bad enough to have discovered books they said never were; they cannot stand Asian American writers arguing and examining and celebrating the word of Asian American work without their permission and authority. They did not simply teach us English. They taught us English to give us a measure of our acceptance by whites. The better we spoke English, the more accepted we were. Our ambition to speak English was a sign of our ambition to assimilate, out-white the whites, beat the whites at their own game. All the time feeling progress was being made and acknowledging our dependence on whites for all meaning. They did not teach us English for us to make the language our own. They gave us English to force us to define ourselves in their terms.

We are the white philosopher's metaphor people, the race that pathological white supremacists produced through white Christian science fiction, monotheistic rhetoric, and monotheistic and ecclesiastical logic enshrouded in white science, which preaches: (1) all civilizations and cultures are founded on bodies of religious (or superstitious) law; (2) all law is the result of culture's effort to codify the mysteries of the supernatural; (3) society is inherently good; (4) society must survive for the individual to survive; (5) the individual is dependent on society; (6) the majority rules; (7) the minority must yield to the majority for the sake of the survival of society; (8) peace is real and possible; and (9) life is peace.

By the low-down, weed-eating Cantonese-cum-Chinaman, the Christians worked themselves crazy to work out of existence and out of history the sense of form: (1) Life is war. You are born in war. You will die in war. (2) I am the law. The only law is the law of my word. No other laws bind me. (3) Society is natural. There will always be a society. "Nations rise and fall. Empires come and go," the Three Kingdoms open, like "once upon a time," in what had become the epic in the fairytale childhood of the Cantonese for a thousand years. The story of the three individuals from three different parts of the fractured China and three different classes. There is Low Bay, the white-skinned, the fair, the pretender to the throne of the Han, a scholar. Low Bay was great for books, great for learning from specific moments of history, from specific heroes. Ride, Low Bay! Kwan Kung, the fugitive, wanted for murder, winner of a fair fight in a territory run by the dead fool's family; fierce, gigantic, all fight, nothing but killer instinct. Kwan's not even his real name. He took it on himself and made it mean nothing but him. A loudmouth, openly out to be a great hero, Kwan Kung was an outlaw's outlaw, the total anarchist riding only to keep his word and nothing else, refusing to be civilized by the titles heaped on him by fading religions and jittery dynasties. When in doubt, they all went to Kwan Kung. The Buddhists, the Taoists, the Mings, the Chings—everybody from the Tai Pings to the Boxers tapped Kwan Kung for their anger and modelled themselves on him, mining their readings for the genius of war.

The lesson to the Cantonese passing the Three Kingdoms took the form of mook yer, the seven-syllable line after seven-syllable line chanting personal and personally improvisatory folk, among the women working together and watching their babies. Low Bay, Kwan Kung, and Chang Fei were the Mother Goose and Little Red Riding Hood of Cantonese childhood at the same time the first immigrants were sucking their thumbs and wallowing in rhythmic romances of pasty-faced princes, leopard-faced ranchers with big eyes, and a red-faced, wild-eyed runaway murderer, all promising to keep promises to each other above any law. The lesson to the Cantonese was that all are born soldiers into the world at war. The social style and table manners produced by such an individualistic, self-centered view of the moral universe was arrogant, belligerent, and anti-social. To the Chinese outside Kwangtung, the Cantonese were famous for their suspecting everyone and trusting no one, not even, so go the jokes, their families. The Cantonese were famous for their personal identification with Kwan Kung. The Kwan Kung mania of the Cantonese was celebrated in a joke, saying the Cantonese needed Kwan Kung, the god of war and plunder, because they could trust nobody else.

They gave us English to make it impossible for us to tell our lives in our own words. The language of our legitimacy was not our own. We were to make white truth of our lives in white language.

As impossible as it was for China to exist according to the Gospel, so it was impossible for the English language to communicate anything but the white sensibility. Many of the English Christian Chinese American auto-biographies that were called gibberish and that whites found unintelligible communicated a great deal to the Chinaman. The sociologists are the latest refinement of the missionary-created Christian Chinese American religious fantasy come true. History is written in the names of leaders, intellectuals, influentials, and the works of the artists, visionaries, and writers. The sociologists say we have no literature and tell our history from Christian autobiographies and works of missionaries. We propose to follow the history of disintegration. Through the work of leaders, influential on the work of Asian American writing and Asian American writing, from its specific roots in specific Asian cultures to an American Chinese language of print in the first Chinatown papers of 1854 to the bilingual "sets" of Wong Sam and Assistants in 1875 to the present, following the rise and fall of the Chinaman tradition and the rise of the Christian Chinese American.

Roger Daniels is right. We are ethnic ego-trippers. What writer isn't? Literacy, literature, and language in every culture, in every civilization, are monsters that the masters, the philosopher-kings, emperors, warlords, and presidents have tried to keep on leash since the beginning of time. Daniels' objection to our introduction (essay) is not scholarly (for our scholarship is sound) but rather racial and moral. He sees and reacts to the violation of all the moral imperatives built into the grammar, structure, and vocabulary of his English language. He takes offense to protect his history and language, and by judicious manipulation of publishing will protect his language from misuse.

Aristotle, like Daniels, worried about the power of language being put to evil work, language being inherently good; the purpose of language being to persuade and lead the speakers of the language to good. Rhetoric was language put to its moral purpose. The rules of rhetoric were moral, not linguistic or grammatical. Aristotle's rules of discourse were, in his ears, linguistic, but in talking about language and its techniques and powers he discovered, much to his moral horror, that language has a power all its own. That language is as morally plastic and effective as the speaker. That even the language designed by philosopher-kings and engineered by one-track minds creates the need for a power greater than the individual to make individuality right, the need to perpetuate the belief that one all-powerful, all-seeing, all-knowing, whimsical, indifferent, non-communicative, unprovable, nameless god was better than self-confidence and a life of history and the senses, or a pantheon or a collection of gods with limited powers—that even such a language can be spoken naturally ignorant of the language's intent or of the language's inventors and their message, carrying the prejudices and history of a culture Aristotle and Plato would take as horribly alien. Pope Innocent IV did, and was hard-pressed as the foremost, the ultimate, the pontiff, to explain a civilization all the known science and the Gospel itself said couldn't, shouldn't, didn't exist. From the beginning, China, Chinese culture that was to become Chinese America, was for the whites more than a matter of moral fable, imagination, or philosophical contemplation than reality.

The Tower of Babel of Biblical science fiction asserts as God's word that differences in language, like differences in religion, are barriers to understanding. The possibility of speaking more than one language, of being naturally fluent in several occasional and ceremonial and regional languages, is implicitly rejected, much less explored or practiced in America among whites. Good people speak one language only. The one Truth is carried in the one language. A white being fluent in another language, especially a non-white language, is looked on as heroic and extraordinary, fraught with danger like the risk of madness, exotic poisonous snakes, alcoholism, and forms of the clap that eat penicillin. Another language might capture your tongue forever. Only great white hunters—private eyes throwing their lives away into two-hundred-dollar-a-day cases, spies, expensive murderers, and nuclear physicists travelling inside the atom past Germany, Russia, China, America, toward new worlds untouched and unknown by any word yet heard—can afford the risk. The handlers of many languages in their mouths strike white sensibilities and are popularized in paperback in the rack at the supermarket, or television, in movies, as violent men, as men who talk turgid, purple, crooked convolutes instead of straight, kamikaze head-on crashes . . . after all, they're only words . . . and you can talk straight without badmouthing, without put-down . . . traitors talk more than one language like a native. Language should be the gauge of loyalty, but it isn't.

Whites believe we should be humble before the English language, taking it for no more and no less, applying it no more and no less than the white rules of usage allow. The work of Wong Sam, Sui Sin Far, Yung Wing, Leong Gor Yun, Earl der Biggers, Pearl Buck, James Hilton, Kazuo Miyamoto, James Y. Sakamoto, Pardee Low, Jade Snow Wong, Bill Hosokawa, Monica Sone, Louis Chu, Maxine Hong Kingston, Shawn Wong, Lawson Inada, Charles Dickens, Mark Twain, and Rod Serling can all be taken as written in the same language. But they're not the same at all.

Notes

1. *Aiiieeeee! An Anthology of Asian American Writers*, (Washington D.C.,: Howard University Press, 1974) vii.

2. *The Big Aiiieeeee!*, forthcoming publication, New York: New American Library, 1991.

3. Lothrop Stoddard, *The Rising Tide of Color Against White World-Supremacy*, (Westport, Ct: Negro Universities Press, 1971, c1920) xxix-xxx.

4. D. Y. Yuan, "Voluntary Segregation: A Study of New York Chinatown," in *Minority Responses*, ed. Minako Kurokawa, (New York: Random House, 1970).

5. Ibid., 135.

6. Ibid.

7. Ibid.

8. Ibid.

9. Ibid., 136.

10. Betty Lee Sung, *Mountain of Gold* (New York: Macmillan, 1967), p. 261

11. *Personnel and Guidance Journal* 50:(8), April 1971.

12. Ibid., 638.

13. Ibid.

CHAPTER 14

Time and Time-Again: Notes Toward an Understanding of Radical Elements in American Indian Fiction[1]

Kathryn Shanley

For the past several months, a commercial for cellular phones has been running on television depicting a sequence of customers pulling up to what appears to be a drive-through, fast-food menu-mike. A young woman's voice pipes out, "Good Morning! May I take your order, please?" The first customer, a middle-aged businessman, harried and brusque, blurts out his "order" for increments of time; the rhythm of his speech mimics a typical take-out order for, say, a cheeseburger, a large coffee, cream and . . . an order of fries: "an hour or so, a couple of minutes and . . . a few seconds to spare." As he drives on up to the pay window, the second customer, a middle-aged Black man who appears in his place at the menu-mike, merely says, "give me a minute." The third customer, a young woman professional who then takes *his* place gives the particulars of what she desires in the line of take-out, snarf-down time. And so it goes. Depending on whether the commercial is being used in a fifteen- or thirty-second slot, the number of "customers" of course varies, but the tension increases many times over.[2]

The desire to "buy time" is a familiar theme in the folklores of many European cultures; the tales usually end with that culture's personification of the Grim Reaper (Death) arriving altogether too soon to collect his due. Ingmar Bergmann's "The Seventh Seal" is perhaps the most refined statement of the theme in modern times. What is particularly chilling about the 1989 American version is that both aspects of the bargain—the reward and the punishment—are meted out over a lifetime. Not only is such fantastic bargaining a bad idea—a principal moral in such tales—but the "customer" repeatedly suffers the impossibility of satisfying such a desire *throughout his lifetime,* as opposed to being confronted with "time running out" at the moment he nears death. In other words, Death is greeted a thousand times with a thousand whimpers, rather than once with a howling cry.

The Grim Reaper motif does not exist in traditional American Indian tales, for tribal peoples approach death more as a synchronic aspect of continuing life than as the negative pole of a dualism. As Stanley Diamond outlines so well in his introduction to Paul Radin's *The Trickster*, in Judeo-Christian thought,

> Both God and the devil are at an infinite and dissociated remove from human experience, and this reflects the structure of civilization. Conversely, among primitive [sic] peoples, all antinomies are bound into the ritual cycle. The sacred is an immediate aspect of man's experience. Good and evil, creation and destruction—the dual image of the deity, as expressed in the trickster—are fused in a network of actions that define primitive [sic] society . . . .In primitive [sic] perspective, human beings are assumed to be capable of any excess. But every step of the way, the person is held to account for those actions that seriously threaten the balance of society and nature[3]

Moreover, in many American Indian "Origin of Death" myths, we are told we must die so that ecological balance can be maintained in the manifest realm and/or so that as two-leggeds we will have sympathy for one another. In a version of the Blackfeet origin of death myth, for instance, Woman decides "it will be better to die forever, so that we shall be sorry for each other."[4]

Abstracted and commodified time in the American Grim Reaper tale of the 1980s is a symptom of a basic cultural disharmony, a product of what Edward Sapir terms a "spurious culture." Though written in 1924, Sapir's observations, in "Culture, Genuine and Spurious," could serve as a commentary on the "Time Teller" commercial for cellular phones described above. He writes,

> No harmony and depth of life, no culture, is possible when activity is well-nigh circumscribed by the sphere of immediate ends and when functioning within that sphere is so fragmentary as to have no inherent intelligiblity or interest. Here lies the grimmest joke of our present American civilization. . . . Part of the time we are dray horses; the rest of the time we are listless consumers of goods which have received no least impress of our personality. In other words, our spiritual selves go hungry, for the most part, pretty much of the time.[5]

My intent here is not to present another diagnosis of or prognosis for the ailing American ethos; neither do I intend to hold up classical or contemporary American Indian cultural world views and communities as utopian models. Rather, I intend to examine a fundamental difference between Euro-American and American Indian worldviews that persists today—a difference that centers around perceptions and conceptions of time. It is essential to have such an understanding of this difference if contemporary Native American cultural movements are to make sense to dominant culture—but to make sense as revitalization, not nostalgia.

First, in order to elucidate what I mean by "radical" I will talk about where Indians stand legally at the present time. Then I will discuss the relationship of American Indian time/space "models of the universe" to: on the one hand, Euro-American readings of Indian cultural movements as nostalgic, and on the other hand, the persistence of and implicit insistence upon cultural "difference" evident in contemporary Indian politics and the literature that supports those political movements. The writings of Leslie Silko, James Welch, and Gerald Vizenor capture, to one degree or another, a Native American sense of "mythic time"; however, the "radicalism" inherent in their works is often missed because of the confusion between definitions of what's radical.

"Radical" defined as "arising from or going to a root or source; fundamental; basic," more aptly describes what I am highlighting in American Indian fiction than does "radical" defined as "favoring or affecting revolutionary change."[6] Although the authors mentioned do, implicitly at least, advocate changes in government policies, my choice is to emphasize how those works are rooted in Native American concepts of "the center of time." Further, this approach shifts the focus away from traditional historians' preoccupation with documenting and ordering, through a single narrative perspective, the demise or disintegration of Indian cultures.[7] Oddly enough, "radicalism," as I am envisioning it, shifts the focus toward the "conservative" center of continuing Native American traditions; "conservative" in Native contexts, however, should not be confused with its meanings in mainstream politics; rather, it should be seen as a reassertion of the value of the kinship structures implied in "all my relatives," the phrase spoken in Lakota ceremonies to connote the connectedness of the supplicant to all living things and the sacredness within the circle of believers participating.

Second, in order to elucidate what I mean by "Indian time" here and to suggest how it functions both "within" history and "outside of" history, I will review briefly, the significance of Indian literature's emergence, however limited, into a mainstream readership. The literary movement Kenneth Lincoln has termed the "Native American Renaissance" essentially began with the reprinting and popularization of *Black Elk Speaks*.[8] The text functioned, according to the Lakota scholar Vine Deloria, Jr., as a veritable "North American bible of all tribes" to youths—Indian and non-Indian alike.[9] Its apocalyptic vision not only fit with the tumultuous energies of the youth of the time, energies bent on protesting the world as handed down to them, it also reasserted a tribal model of the universe, one which subverts the progress-oriented conceptual foundations of American history—particularly as it relates to Indians' defeat.

For many Indian and non-Indian peoples alike, the text provided the means for a sort of debriefing from Anglo ways; for others, a first textual encounter with Lakota (or, for that matter, any tribal) system of beliefs and rituals. The effects of missionary, government, and public school education, of legal restrictions on religious practice, of policies such as relocation, had placed Anglo values in the foreground, the present and future of history and things-Indian in the background and past. The changes that began with the Red Power Movement of the early sixties were, however, more substantial than mainstream America may be aware.

Books like *Black Elk Speaks* and Dee Brown's *Bury My Heart at Wounded Knee,* which became popular at approximately the same time, revived America's sense of the injustices dealt Indians.[10] But for the most part, few people since have tracked the legal changes wrought for Indians by the social activism of that time, at least not in the sense that those changes have been synthesized for the populace; nonetheless, a new phase in Indian law began at that time. As Charles F. Wilkinson states in *American Indians, Time and the Law,* because of the unique treaty relationship between Indians and the U.S. government, "The modern cases reflect the premise that tribes should be insulated against the passage of time."[11] In other words, tribal perspectives and rights *under the law* rest on treaties made in good faith over a century ago. In fact, Wilkinson concludes, from surveying the court decisions of the last twenty-five years, that

> The decisions . . . stand for the idea that this promise of a measured separatism normally should not be eroded by the press of civilization or the passage of time. At the same time, tribes have the right to grow and to take on the accoutrements of modern society in order to implement legitimate tribal interests.[12]

Because the Court now (more or less) recognizes Indian tribal sovereignty, all decisions subsequent to the 60s have reflected (more or less) the fact that "Indian tribes possess a right to change and to grow: *they are not frozen in time.* Indian tribes are permanent entities in the American political system."[13] (Emphasis mine.)

The "insulated against time" legal precedents Wilkinson speaks of are reflected in Black Elk's story of his vision, and most importantly, in the faith undergirding it: a faith in his story's power to change the course of history with timeless truth. Because Black Elk is simultaneously a living, historical being, through whose vision and human agency his people can benefit, *and* an eternal being—the Sixth Grandfather—he brings Indian "historical" form as well as content to contemporary "time."[14] In the version of *Black Elk Speaks* available to the youth of the 60s and 70s, Black Elk tells of the source of his power:

> Of course it was not I who cured. It was the power from the outer world, and the visions and ceremonies had only made me like a hole through which the power could come to the two-leggeds. If I thought that I was doing it myself, the hole would close up and no power could come through.[15]

In other words, Black Elk "empties" himself in the service of a great power, a force "outside" of, yet central to, historical events—events in "time," since he means to serve his people as well. The controversy surrounding the authenticity of the text notwithstanding, as a popular text *Black Elk Speaks* provided many Indian people with a way of reconciling historical outcomes with the possibility of future prosperity.

Views of time/space like Black Elk's (via Neihardt) are the rule rather than the exception in American Indian thought. In addition to being well-documented in the ethnographic literatures, they are central aspects of Indian religious revitalization movements around the country today, more than, but including, the familiar practice of doing things on "Indian Time"—when everyone's ready. Perhaps the most notable examples in ethnographic literature are derived from Hopi and Navajo sources.

Although amply documented, Indian world view continues to appear suspect, a "cult" phenomenon, when verification is attempted through scientific method. The startling vision of the Hopi time/space model as presented by Benjamin Whorf in his classic 1936 article, "An American Indian Model of the Universe," for example, continues to be controversial.[16] According to Whorf's claim, in Hopi metaphysics the individual inhabits the "subjective realm" (unlike the place the individual has in "the flowing time and static space" of European metaphysics). It is

> the realm of expectancy, of desire and purpose, of vitalizing life, of efficient causes, of thought thinking itself out of the inner realm (the Hopian heart) into manifestation.[17]

Efficient causes, for the Hopi, are more than the getting-the-job-done that immediate ends require, to borrow Sapir's terminology; efficient causes are the "inherently harmonious, balanced, self-satisfactory" blend of immediate and remote ends in a "genuine culture."[18] Among poverty-stricken Indian peoples who have been forbidden to practice their tribal religions for the better part of this century, kinship structures have often been kept intact, enough so to allow at least for sharing what limited resources have been available.

Documentaries of reservation life often do not capture this, because
America's Pavlovian response to visual representations of Indians evokes
images of "the Indian" as welfare spectacle, as Kitsch Indian, or as Indian
Anachronism Erectus—"the dance or bleed" presentations of culture. The
argillite sculptures of Haida artists in the early nineteenth century capture the
Indian perspective well: as mythological figures' bodies flow into one another, often sharing the same tongue. In sculpture, Eagle's wing becomes
Killer Whale's fin, or vice versa. When the artists began carving pieces using
the non-Indian sailors and their dogs as subjects, the figures never touch.[19]
The interrelatedness, in other words, of all living things is apparent in many
aspects of Indian material cultures—past and present.

We must nonethless be careful about making generalizations from a
Hopian world view to something like an "Indian" world view; just as we must
clearly depart from the cliched version of Indian world view presented in box-
office movie favorites like "Poltergist Two"—that is, Indian as haunting spiritual mascot of the continent. For cultural studies critics, the question then
becomes: How do we make the leap from ethnographic literatures to contemporary legal realities to contemporary writers such as Vizenor, Silko and
Welch. Can Indian authors be fluent in the thought-world of languages they do
not speak and have never spoken fluently? (Certainly that question demands
more space than this chapter allows. For my purposes, I would say yes, to a
significant extent they can be and are.)

Reluctant to generalize the varied cultures of Native American peoples
into a single "Indian" identity, Jarold Ramsey warns against concocting "an
unlocalized Indian mystique . . . out of a wide, loose, and sometimes contradictory assortment of native materials."[20] Although his cautionary remarks
on the subject are, for the most part, appropriate and need to be made,
Ramsey also reveals something of his own biased conception of time when he
concludes,

> Perhaps a centralized American Indian racial identity and aesthetic *will*
> someday emerge in this country, encouraged by archaelogical and philologi-
> cal investigations into what the native cultures have in common as to origins,
> folkways, and languages and mythologies, and urged along by political and
> indeed literary assessments of what they share now, surrounded by and
> implicated in Anglo cultures.[21]

The way that Ramsey nominalizes his sentences' subjects is quite revealing. Who is going to do the archaelogical and philological investigations, the
political and literary assessments? The "authentication" process he imagines
to be necessary before "racial identity and aesthetic" generalizations can be
made precludes an Indian discourse which, I maintain, already exists. No

doubt the last several centuries of intensely oppressive circumstances have taken a toll on Indian belief systems, a phenomenon that is difficult to summarize, but we should not deny that there is a contemporary Indian identity and aesthetic. One has grown from resistance to domination. Movements such as the Ghost Dance, the National Congress of the American Indian, the National Association of Tribal Chairpersons, American Indian Movement (AIM), the International Treaty Council, and so on, have each in their unique way contributed to a kind of unity that is nonetheless mindful of tribal differences. Indian country today is a far cry from what Ramsey fears such unified visions of it can produce, "a grotesque native reinvention of that discredited Anglo utensil, the Melting Pot."[22] One might argue, in fact, with Ramsey's idea that the melting pot has been discredited, especially given the current mainstream ethnicity school in academia.[23]

Fearing that Indian cultures will become as "spurious" as American culture has become (if indeed American culture can be seen as one monolithic culture) is legitimate, given the encroachment of media culture and tourism on Indians, the effects of poverty, and the limited access those populations have to the means of achieving economic autonomy and prosperity. However, such a fear also betrays a nostalgic view of Indians which refuses to recognize significant and often good (in those peoples' own terms) cultural transformation and change. In fact, I would argue that no one is more aware of the difficulties and absurdities involved in reconstructing, recreating, revitalizing, and maintaining Indian traditional practices than are Indians themselves. But I would also argue that an important self-critical humor is alive and well in Indian communities today, and that it arises in part from age-old clown traditions. As a continuation of a highly developed art of self-mocking evident in sacred clown traditional practices, Indians mock Europeans, and no doubt have, ever since first contact and as a reaction to being denied other discursive grounds. The nineteenth-century White Man mask in the Provincial Museum in Victoria, B.C., with its pale face, vacuous stare, and ermine mustache, is but one example.

The "absurd hero" lately returned to "serious" Western fiction, bleeding through, no doubt, from past epochs, has never been entirely lost to American Indian thought. Even the extreme shame and lost honor resulting from the colonialization process is buoyed up from total despair by an absurd, frequently self-mocking, sort of humor; this is particularly evident in James Welch's work. For example, in *Winter in the Blood,* when the wife of the professor from Michigan calls across the front seat to her daughter, who has just returned to the car from vomiting by the side of the road, "Are you ok, honey?" the protagonist, hitching a ride and seated beside the pale, carsick child, himself answers. He feels so sorry for himself that he perceives any sympathy aired as belonging to him.[24] More to the point, the protagonist

refuses to be "white" in order to "succeed" in his environment; instead, he
skirts existing mythical and historical script formulae available for him and
opts for the chance at a brand of personal sovereignty more Indian than
otherwise.

The Airplane Man in *Winter in the Blood* comically takes on the dimensions of an American absurd hero; he either does not know or cannot say who
he is or where he comes from, because he is so fundamentally dishonest. Nor
can he say where he is going, other than "to Canada," or why. Like the drive-
through "customers" in the ad, he's trying to cheat on time; in his case, it's
time he's overdue in spending in the penitentiary. The novel's protagonist,
though seemingly as lost in Anglo time and space as all the other characters, is
allowed a peek through to the "outer" time/space Black Elk spoke of. But
Welch will not allow him either to be "saved" by recognizing the glorious
"past" of his ancestors or to be chewed up and spit out by the dismal "future"
that is sure to be his lot if he continues living his neither old-time-Indian nor
dark-skinned-assimilated-to-white "difference." Jim Loney, the protagonist of
Welch's second novel, *The Death of Jim Loney,* opens the hole to the "outer"
realm a bit wider, though he can finally only "enter" it by dying.[25]

One reviewer laments, "Loney's life is empty and perhaps best left
untold, but Welch's power as a writer makes one wish he had given the book
more of a chance."[26] What it is that Welch won't do is satisfy his reading
audience's need for a nostalgia fix. Even though his latest novel, *Fools Crow,*
comes the closest of the three to evoking Indian-lover sympathies, careful
readers of Welch's work know immediately what he's up to.[27] For one thing,
he's opened the door to dream/vision so wide that the characters who fail to
realize themselves are those people who stubbornly back away from the social
responsibilities which come with Pikuni ways of knowing/being. The most
significant achievement of the book, in my opinion, is its recovery of the full
dialectic of honor/shame as a Pikuni social contract. Humility replaces humiliation, and "crying for pity" becomes, once again, a fundamental aspect of
ritual renewal—recognition of the pitifulness of the human condition and
recognition by the tribal group for the suffering and sacrifice it entails.[28]

During times of personal and cultural transformation, coping with our
perceptions of ourselves as foolish requires the sort of humor and satire
Gerald Vizenor also employs. In his essay, "Socioacupuncture: Mythic
Reversals and the Striptease," he pokes fun at Indian and non-Indian alike
by suggesting a program of "socioacupuncture" to rid the American cultural mind of its need for the "neosavage" and the "metasavage." Although
Vizenor's work ranges widely in genre from rather straight-forward cultural
recovery texts, such as *anishinabe adisokan: Tales of the People* and *anishinabe nagamon: Songs of the People,* to his surrealistic and satirical novel,
Darkness in Saint Louis Bearheart, to more recent narratives of mythic rever-

sals and philosophical inquiry, all his works seem aimed at "mythic strategies for survival."[29] He says as much in "Socioacupunture," when he writes,

> The obsession with the tribal past is not an innocent collection of arrowheads, not a crude map of public camp sites in sacred places, but rather a statement of academic power and control over tribal images, an excess of facts, data, narrative interviews, template discoveries. Academic evidence is a euphemism for linguistic colonization of oral traditions and popular memories.[30]

As the movement among the Lakota and the Navajo to take control of the production of their own literary and historical publications catches on among other tribal groups, perhaps we will see a reversal, if not an abatement, of the "linguistic colonization of oral traditions and popular memories" Vizenor rightly identifies. Wolverine, Fools Crow's animal helper, in Welch's *Fools Crow*, is an animal who is reputed for getting out of the most sophisticated traps. Welch has apparently borrowed Wolverine's power as well, to escape the historical script of the Baker Massacre, by visioning survival beyond that horrific event.[31] Similarly, Vizenor has taken on Wolverine's most objectionable trait—he pisses on his spoils so that no one else will dare touch them. Such acts of resistance to colonization through literature are radical.

Without a doubt, Indian writers whose audiences cross cultures have an extremely problematic task before them: appealing to Euro-American literary tastes in essentially Western literary forms while, at the same time, somehow representing Indian thought and values. In *Ceremony*, Silko performs the sort of mythic reversal Vizenor calls for when she enters "mythic" time to relate the "history" of the creation of the White Man as witchcraft gone wrong. Borrowing aspects of several southwestern Native American traditions, the novel begins with Thought Woman, and her thought "thinking itself out of the inner realm into manifestation." The narrative revolves around its mythic hero, Tayo/Arrowboy, and his need to be cured of a time/space disorder. When Tayo's cure finally comes, it's as tenuous as the "cures" Welch's protagonists make for themselves, for the lived experience matters most.[32] America already has enough Indian ghosts to mourn. Indian time/space values, in Silko's short stories "Storyteller" and "Yellow Woman," guide both female protagonists, as each becomes comfortable with herself situated in the center of mythic/real time and as each determines her own version of her history accordingly.[33]

Indian self-determination, as it is worked out, individually and tribally, takes many forms in life and literature. A poster announcing an important Omaha event reads: "The Original 155th Annual Omaha Pow-wow, August 28 through September 1, 1985." Three years later, a poster announcing the annual pow-wow proudly designates it as the "Original 184th." What kind of math is that? Or is it math at all? In the summer of 1988, the Omaha began a process of reclaiming their sacred Pole from the Peabody Museum, an artifact of their culture that had been physically alienated from them for one hundred years. The Pole, however, referred to by Omaha people as "Venerable man" and as "the tree that stands burning," is anything but artifact—it lives.[34] In fact, as the museum staff were bringing the Pole up from the basement, the elevator refused to respond to commands—something that apparently had not ever happened before. A curator at the museum who reported the event to anthropologist Robin Ridington said, "I don't know what this means, but you can add this to the story."[35] What does it mean for this Pole to be alive?

Just as the Peabody Museum's function as "safekeeper" of the Sacred Pole has come to an end, so has western history's claim that the pow-wow is a secular Indian celebration engendered in modern times. It's not, as it might at first seem, that the Omaha poster-maker is writing history from the top down; neither is he (I surmise) naive or lacking in a sense of humor. Rather, both events signify Omaha belief in the continuous nature of time/space. The details of record—to whom has the Pole belonged for the past one hundred years? and who falsifies or verifies when "in time" an aspect of Omaha culture "began"?—depend for interpretation on who has the power or authority to determine the discursive terms. There can be no doubt that popular memory is shaped, in part, by ethnographic writings, and it was the discovery of new information from ethnographic sources that led to the updated declaration of the "origins" of the Omaha pow-wow. But even "origin" has its own meaning for Omaha people, a meaning that transcends linear time: "fundamental," the same word used to define "radical."

What is "radical" in contemporary Indian life and literature may not be accessible to people who disallow a connection between the power of Black Elk's story (his mythical power to make an impact on history) and the endurance of the regenerative religious powers of the Lakota people themselves. What is radical in contemporary Indian literature may be missed by readers of Vizenor, Welch, and Silko, if they do not recognize the self-conscious (perhaps self-aware is a better term) devices they employ to thwart, through mythic reversals, the "scripts" given them. What's radical in contemporary Indian movements to restore their religious artifacts to their rightful "centers in time" will be regarded as naive and nostalgic as opposed to vital and vitalizing, if observers of such events remain spectators, detached from the humility implied in desiring to constitute a community. As the Zuni men who visited Frank Hamilton Cushing in 1886 on the East Coast remarked, Americans are a strange people:

> Waihusiwa: "[T]hey have enough to eat and enough to wear and what they eat and what they wear are also of the best. . . . "

Heluta: ". . . but the sentiment of home affects them not; the little bits of land they may own, or the house they may have been bred in, are as nothing to them; and more than all, their thoughts do not seem to dwell contentedly even on their their own wives and children, for they wander incessantly, wander through all difficulties and dangers, to seek new places and better things. Why is it they are so unceasingly unsatisfied?"

"I think why," said Palowahtiwa; "above every people they are a people of emulation; above every kind of man or being a people of fierce jealousies. Is that not an explanation?"[36]

Whether those words are actually the words of Zuni men or of Cushing himself, a man known both for his own storytelling powers and for his knowledge of Zuni ways, they ring true a century later.[37] Living on "islands" called reservations, Indians seek to preserve (by their "measured separation" from mainstream American society) the hope of "a fulfillment of the ultimate promise, that [reservations] be homelands."[38] Time does not stand still for Indians, any more than it does for any other people; rather, time comes around again, returns home.

Notes

1. This chapter originated as a paper given at the American Studies Conference, "Creativity in Difference," Miami, FL, October 27–30, 1988. Panel: "The Radical Novel and Cultural Difference;" chair: James Henretta. Other participants: Robert Shulman (University of Washington), Alan Wald (University of Michigan), and Paul Lauter (Trinity College).

2. "Time-teller," KING Broadcasting Company, Seattle, WA.

3. Stanley Diamond, "Introductory Essay: Job and the Trickster," in Paul Radin, *The Trickster: A Study in American Indian Mythology* (New York: Schocken Books, 1972), xxi.

4. Clark Wissler and D.C. Duvall, "Mythology of the Blackfoot Indians," *Anthropological Papers of the American Museum of Natural History,* II:1:21.

5. Edward Sapir, "Culture, Genuine and Spurious," *The Selected Writings of Edward Sapir* (Berkeley: University of California Press, 1967), 321.

6. William Morris, ed., *The American Heritage Dictionary of the English Language* (New York: Houghton Mifflin Company, 1975), 1076.

7. For an overview of recent thinking about the problematic in points of view in writing American Indian history, see: Calvin Martin, ed., *The American Indian and the Problem of History* (New York: Oxford University Press, 1987).

8. Kenneth Lincoln, *Native American Renaissance* (Berkeley and Los Angeles: University of California Press, 1983; John G. Neihardt, *Black Elk Speaks* (Lincoln: University of Nebraska Press, 1932; 1983).

9. Vine Deloria, Jr.'s "Introduction" appears in the 1979 Bison Book Edition. Neihardt chose to create the tone of defeatedness in Black Elk's story which, in my opinion, affected Indian and non-Indian readers differently. While empowering to Indians, perhaps as a vindicating last word, the tone of the story recalled America's guilt over its treatment of Indians, no doubt enhanced by the assessment of American involvement in the Viet-nam War as immoral.

10. Dee Brown, *Bury My Heart at Wounded Knee: An Indian History of the American West* (New York: Bantam, 1972). The book went through thirteen printings (by Holt, Rinehart) in 1971 alone; special printings included Book-of-the-Month Club, Playboy Book Club, and Popular Science Book Club, all in 1971.

11. Charles F. Wilkinson, *American Indians, Time and the Law* (New Haven: Yale University Press, 1987), 32.

12. Wilkinson, *American Indians*, 120.

13. Ibid., 53.

14. In Raymond DeMallie's *The Sixth Grandfather* [(Lincoln, Nebraska: University of Nebraska Press, 1985)], DeMallie gives a brief biography of Black Elk's life and makes available the original transcripts on which the book is based. He also provides a topical outline of events related in the original transcripts, but left out of the printed text. The term, the Sixth Grandfather, refers to Black Elk's role in his vision as one of the six powers of the universe.

15. Neihardt, *Black Elk Speaks*, 208–9.

16. See: Robin Ridington, "On the Language of Benjamin Lee Whorf," (forthcoming from Rowman and Littlefield, 1990, in *Anthropological Poetics*, edited by Ivan Brady).

17. Benjamin Whorf, *Language, Thought, and Reality*, ed., John B. Carroll (New York: John Wiley & Sons, 1956; 1962), 59, 60.

18. Sapir, "Culture," 314.

19. Victoria Wyatt, "Ethnic Identity in Times of Change: A Case Study in Investigating Attitudes Towards Culture," presentation for panel, "Native American Identity: Stereotypical Portrayals and Responses to Social Change," chaired by Rita Napier, University of Kansas, American Studies Association, October 29, 1988.

20. Jarold Ramsey, *Reading the Fire: Essays in the Traditional Indian Literatures of the Farwest* (Lincoln, Nebraska: University of Nebraska Press, 1983), 184.

21. Ramsey, *Reading the Fire*, 185.

22. Ibid.

23. For example, Alan Wald argues [in his article, "Theorizing Cultural Difference: A Marxist Critique of the 'Ethnicity School,'" *MELUS* 14 No. 2 (Summer 1987): 21–33 that by subsuming "race" within the general rubric of "ethnicity," the unique perspectives of people of color, *based on race and racism,* get lost in American immigration history. Besides the Indian experience in America, many other peoples came here, not as immigrants but as indentured servants or slaves, and were denied an opportunity to become full citizens, let alone the possibility of "melting" into the mainstream.

24. James Welch, *Winter in the Blood* (New York: Harper & Row, 1973), 127–29.

25. James Welch, *Death of Jim Loney* (New York: Harper & Row, 1979.)

26. Irene Wanner, *"The Death of Jim Loney,"* *Iowa Review* 10 (1979), 111.

27. James Welch, *Fools Crow* (New York: Viking Penguin, 1986).

28. "Crying for pity" refers to the lament of a vision seeker, most particularly in Gros Ventre and Blackfeet religious traditions.

29. Gerald Vizenor, "Socioacupuncture: Mythic Reversals and the Striptease," in *The American Indian and the Problem of History,* ed., Calvin Martin (cited above), 181; *anishinabe adisonkan: Tales of the People* (Minneapolis: Nodin Press, 1970); *anishinabe nagamon: Songs of the People* (Minneapolis: Nodin Press, 1970); *Darkness in Saint Louis Bearheart* (Minneapolis: Truck Press, 1978). Two recent novels by Vizenor are: *Griever: An American Monkey King in China* (New York: Illinois State University/Normal Fiction Collective, 1987), and *The Trickster of Liberty: Tribal Heirs to a Wild Baronage* (Minneapolis: University of Minnesota Press, 1988). For a selected bibliography of Gerald Vizenor's work, see A. LaVonne Ruoff, *American Indian Quarterly* IX:1 (Winter 1985), 75–78.

30. Vizenor, "Socioacupuncture," 29.

31. The Baker Massacre occurred in the winter of 1870 on the St. Marias River in Montana; a troup of cavalry mistook a band of peaceful Pikuni (Blackfeet) for a band of "renegades" who had been raiding Napikwan (white) cattle. One hundred and seventy-three Pikuni were killed, only thirty-three of whom were men. See George W. Manypenny, *Our Indian Wards* (Cincinnati: Robert Clark & Co., 1880), 281.

32. Leslie Silko, *Ceremony* (New York: Viking, 1977; Penguin, 1987).

33. Leslie Silko, *Storyteller* (New York: Viking, 1981).

34. Robin Ridington, "A Tree That Stands Burning: Reclaiming a Point of View As From the Center," forthcoming (1990) in *Anthropology and Literature,* Special Steward Journal, 17:1–2, ed., Paul J. Benson.

35. Personal communication between Robin Ridington and the author, October 1988.

36. *Zuni: Selected Writings of Frank Hamilton Cushing,* ed., Jesse Green (Lincoln, Nebraska: University of Nebraska Press, 1979), 414–15.

37. See: Jesse Green, "Translation," *Zuni* (cited above), 331–345.

38. Wilkinson, *American Indians*, 121.

CHAPTER 15

The Sign in Sidney Brustein's Window: Toward a Transformative Aesthetic

Johnnella E. Butler

> *The question is not whether one will make a social state-*
> *ment in one's work—but only what the statement will say,*
> *for if it says anything at all, it will be social*
> Lorraine Hansberry

In reviewing the critical commentary and analyses of Lorraine Hansberry's *The Sign in Sidney Brustein's Window*, although the volume is not great, the most representative works make one think that there is little else to say. A look at the play, however, within the context of a twenty-five-year hindsight, reveals that the play, its political and historical contexts, and Hansberry's stated intention in writing the play, all place her as a precise explicator of contemporary American political and intellectual life and reminds us that she was an artistic visionary who dared to write an Afro-American play with only one Black character.

Contemporary critical commentary about the play and about Hansberry ran the gamut from Cruse's diatribe against Hansberry as an Afro-American writer with a middle-class background,[1] to condemnation of the play as a failure in its form or as an attack on liberalism and homosexuals,[2] to insightful and empathetic analyses such as those rendered by Jordan Miller and C. W. E. Bigsby.[3] Recent criticism, most notably by Margaret Wilkerson and Steven Carter, hone the diamonds from the work begun in the 1979 *Freedomways* issue in Lorraine Hansberry's honor and promise more in-depth discussions of her posthumous works and her essays and other commentary.[4] None, however, investigate the question of the aesthetic categorization of *The Sign in Sidney Brustein's Window*. Such a consideration goes to the heart of the social function of theater because it involves the intersection of the cultural (What is the aesthetic?) and social (What does the aesthetic say or do?), and the still-debated segregation of Black theater (despite the current success of some of the more obviously "universal" works such as *Fences*).

Criticism that approaches this problem generally mentions the fact that the play had only one Black character and implies what that might mean, or suggests a difference in the aesthetic of the play because all but one character is white. Margaret Wilkerson and Jordan Miller, respectively, serve as a good example of the former and C.W.E. Bigsby of the latter.

Wilkerson:

> A play of ideas, *Sign* angered and confused critics for two basic reasons. First, it was not about the black experience; in fact, it had only one black character in it. Lorraine Hansberry, hailed by the establishment as a new black voice, had written about white artists and intellectuals who lived in Greenwich Village. Second, the play firmly opposed the vogue of urbane, sophisticated ennui and the glorification of intellectual impotence so typical of the period. It dared to challenge the apathy of the American intellectual and his indifference to the serious problems overtaking the world.[5]

Miller:

> At this point then, we take the following stand. We refuse to discuss the merits of Miss Hansberry's two plays on the basis of any form of racial consciousness. We are going to avoid any temptation to place them in any niche of "social significance." In short we take no sides, and we maintain the right, indeed the critical obligation, to judge them as exceptional pieces of dramatic literature quite apart from any other factors.[6]

Bigsby:

> In an interview with Harold Cruse, Bigsby, referring to *Brustein* says: "Now Hansberry, among other black playwrights, has moved outside the sphere of the ethnic theater, and you say elsewhere in your book that the black playwright can only come to fruition within the context of an ethnic theater."[7]

Wilkerson, in 1983, states the facts. She discusses the plays as to their intrinsic worth and their political and historical contexts; she does not broach the aesthetic argument, yet she clearly sees Hansberry as an Afro-American writer in both the Afro-American and American literary traditions. Miller, writing in the late 1960s, is very much aware of the burgeoning assertion of the Black Aesthetic, and he implies a disavowal of any race consciousness on the part of the whites determining what are "exceptional pieces of dramatic literature." Bigsby accepts quite openly a difference between ethnic literature and mainstream literature and, as such, implies limitations in *Raisin* that stem from his seeing it only as a Black play. *Brustein* holds no such limitations for him.

The Sign in Sidney Brustein's Window is a play by an Afro-American playwright who writes out of a simultaneously Afro-American and American aesthetic sensibility. As Steven Carter, in an overview of Hansberry's articulation of this aesthetic, summarizes:

> As her prospectus for the John Brown Theater implies, she felt no compunction about drawing upon the dramatic traditions of all cultures and all times to further the presentation of her own heroic and social vision. Unlike some contemporary black nationalist playwrights, who make a blanket condemnation of Western European civilization and strive to avoid using its dramatic techniques, Hansberry wished to combine the best of the West with the best of African culture. . . . All of her plays utilize classic European dramatic forms, while often incorporating elements of both Afro-American and African culture.[8]

The "Original Prospectus for the John Brown Memorial Theater" states quite precisely her social vision and aesthetic stance:

• A theater dedicated to, and propagated by, the aspirations and culture of the Afro-American people of the United States.

• A theater wherein the cultural heritage of that people, which owes to their African ancestry, will find expression and growth.

• A theater which, at the same time, will readily, freely and with the spirit of the creativity of all mankind, also utilize all and any forces of the Western heritage of that same people in the arts.

• The drama, the music of oppression here: the new and old forms invented by the sophisticated and unsophisticated sons and daughters of 20,000,000 black and presently unfree Americans and—their allies, by which we shall mean all and any who identify with the heroic intentions of these Afro-Afro-Americans. In that spirit and in unmistakable recognition of the oneness of the cause of humanity has this theater been named after a white man who dismissed all qualifying considerations and apologies for the slave system and answered the slavery of black men with the consecration of rifles.

• Thus, will the contributions of all who wrote, sang, composed, painted, acted in behalf of the implacable will of man for freedom be represented.

• *In particular this theater will strive to perfect the idiom, the invention, creativity of the American Negro in the drama, dance and song. It shall simultaneously draw upon world culture to enrich this bounty.* It shall be bound by *no* orthodoxy in this regard—and no beholden posture to the commercial theater of its time, nor to the idle, impotent and obscurantist efforts of a mistaken avant garde [i.e., the playwrights of the Theater of the Absurd]. It shall draw its main sources from the life of the Negro people and their allies and, at all times, this theater shall consider itself above those blind allegiances and hypocrisies which so often come to dominate and sterilize revolutionary apparatuses. It shall imagine, always, the Truth to be the stars—and the energy required in conquering their distance from this planet equal to the task.

• Toward these ends, then, let all artists of grand imaginations and skills be welcomed here! Let the myriad artists of all peoples be represented here; *let all who find a poetic work in behalf of the human race and that of its portion which is, in particular—black, be welcome here.*

• *Let the arts renounce all tyranny in this place—to the sound of the black cheers and laughter.*

And in that laughter be some measure of the everlasting veneration of a patriot: John Brown. (Emphasis added)[9]

As Carter comments, Hansberry's "consciously paradoxical act of naming a black community theater after a white man emphasizes the consciously paradoxical nature of Hansberry's world men and art. . . . ." She "insisted on 'the oneness of the cause of humanity'" and was concerned about a black theater that would " 'draw on its main sources' from the allies of black people as well as from Blacks themselves"; "a Pan Africanist who wished to place the Western heritage of Afro-Americans alongside the African heritage; a revolutionary dramatist who strove to be an artist as well as a propagandist."[10]

A look at *Brustein* through they eyes of two most representative critics, and another look within the understood context of the many discussions over the past twenty years of an expanded or even redefined aesthetic, will demonstrate that *Brustein* is such a play. In so doing, I will describe the aesthetic operative in *Brustein*, which is consistent with the intellectual and cultural heritage of Afro-Americans and the personal stance of the playwright Lorraine Hansberry.

Jordan Miller, in his 1969 piece, *Lorraine Hansberry* discusses the play as a good, old-fashioned realistic drama, admittedly anachronistic in the mid-sixties, but perhaps welcome in such a time of turmoil. He places the play into a category "[he] likes to call the Comedy of Sensibility, an invention, [he] believes more or less his own but which [he] find[s] more suitable to plays of this sort than 'social drama,' 'thesis play' or even that self-contradictory if highly pedigreed 'tragi-comedy.'" He reminds us that the basis of comedy is the continual reminder that humans are ridiculously fallible. *Brustein's* characters are certainly comic, and he further explains his category in that "their comic nature keeps us from becoming sentimentally involved with them, while at the same time our emotional response to them is directed toward a refined sensitiveness, with especial attention to their pathetic nature—in short, they arouse our sensibilities."[11] He concludes his discussion of Hansberry's two plays, *A Raisin in the Sun* and *The Sign in Sidney Brustein's Window*, with the following assessment:

> Two plays only, the total product of Lorraine Hansberry, playwright. We owe her a great deal, for she demonstrated that a good old fashioned play is worth having around. She showed us that good people are worth knowing on the stage, and that the struggles to live with pride and dignity are worth it. If the world of art—the world itself—is to survive as a going concern, it is going to have to take people for what they are and the polarization of cliches and slogans, color and economic status will have to give way. Lorraine Hansberry has shown a good direction to follow.[12]

C. W. E. Bigsby's discussion of Hansberry's *Brustein* seems to touch all bases—bases that can of course be expanded upon and debated. He discusses the play's commitment and the playwright's commitment to life, hope, and human potential. He dissects the play's depiction of Sidney's "[fluctuation] between the two poles of liberalism; Thoreauesque dissociation and enthusiastic political involvement." He answers the play's contemporary critics who see *Brustein* as simply an attack on liberals and demonstrates how her "portrait of bewildered liberalism . . . lies at the very center of a drama . . . essentially concerned with the plight of the individual in a society in which commitment is considered passe." Further, he argues that to accuse her of attacking homosexuals is to "misunderstand her point . . . that personal vision is of interest but that it cannot be taken as being of universal significance."[13] Most penetrating is Bigsby's discussion and analysis of *Brustein* as

> One of the most complete disavowals of absurdist drama which has yet been made. In its concern with the nature and purpose of art it goes beyond the introspection of *The Connection* and even the self-conscious dramas of Pirandello. Clearly Sidney's attack on the callow prophesies of Golding and Beckett represents the credo of a dramatist who believes passionately in the validity of insurgence and the redeemable nature of man. The play is the voice of social protest, no longer touched with the embarrassing simplicity of the thirties but rather redolent with the cutting sophistication which Albee had introduced into the American theater.[14]

A comedy of sensibility, a portrait of bewildered liberalism, a disavowal of absurdist drama, a play of ideas; *Brustein* is all this and more. The "more", however, is difficult to demonstrate. It involves an expansion of the concept of a play about ideas, and the *context* of the "comedy of sensibility," of the portrait of bewildered liberalism, and of the disavowal of absurdist drama. It is this context that makes the discussion of, for example, the good that is always apparent in even the most depraved of Hansberry's characters, more than just an author's viewpoint but a real potential, stating that the other side of evil is good, the other side of joy is sorrow, the other side of up is down, and vice versa. The sensibility of this paradoxical context is apparent in Margaret Wilkerson's discussions of Hansberry, and at the end of the article entitled "The Sighted Eyes and Feeling Heart of Lorraine Hansberry," she points out that "The theater was a working laboratory for this brilliant woman whose sighted eyes and feeling heart caused her to reach out to a world at once cruel and beautiful."[15]

The context of the play involves the vision of the playwright; her vision that something is drastically wrong with an intellectual posture that negates joy, beauty, and love, and the human responsibility and commitment that makes them possible. She tells us that she wrote *Brustein* because

> Mine is, after all, the generation that came to maturity drinking in the forebodings of the Silones, Koestlers and Richard Wrights. It had left us ill-prepared for decisions that had to be made in our time about Algeria, Birmingham or the Bay of Pigs. By the 1960's, few enough American intellectuals had it within them to be ashamed that their discovery of the "betrayal" of the Cuban revolution by Castro just happened to coincide with the change of heart of official American government policy. They left it to the TV humorists to defend the agrarian reform in the end. It is climate and mood of such intellectuals, if not those particular events which constitute the core of a play called *The Sign in Sidney Brustein's Window.*[16]

In Sidney's development from a negation of good and beauty in the real world to an acceptance of the responsibility and commitment to believe in it (and thereby bring about its fruition), Hansberry does not suggest a reformist posture or even the creation of new alternatives *within the same context.*[17] She advocates a transformation to a different context of harmonious balance with human beings and their community being the measure. The transformed Sidney, whom Gloria forced to confront the horror of negating despair, has hope. He now sees more concretely the conundrum of life that evil is just the other side of good, that

> . . . death is waste and love is sweet and that the earth turns and men change everyday and that rivers run and people wanna be better than they are and that flames smell good and that I hurt terribly today, and that hurt is desperation is—*energy and energy* can *move things.* . . . (emphasis added) (p.142)

Lastly he tells Iris that strength comes of sorrow:

> Yes . . . weep now, darling weep. Let us both weep. That is the first thing, to let ourselves feel again . . . then tomorrow, we shall make something strong of this sorrow. (p.143)

Sidney (his Beat contemporaries and the absurdist dramatists) sees only the good *or* the evil, the joy *or* the sorrow. We see Sidney at the beginning of the play conflicting philosophically with Alton, asserting that the only form of compassion left is "avoid[ing] the impulse to correct all movements, causes, clubs and anti-clubs" (p. 9). The mode is cynicism, denial of good, and it is an absolute negating mode with little room for alternatives other than escape. Even when Sidney does hang the sign and actively support Wally, he is still in an absolute, dichotomous mode; one is either good or bad; can be helped or not; is anti-political or seeking totally political rectification. His credo is expressed throughout, and we see no change until Gloria's suicide.

> Sidney: . . . Don't venerate, don't celebrate, don't hallow what you take to be—(*Facing out to the audience with a bit of a smile*) the human spirit. Keep your conscience to yourself. Readers don't want it—they feel pretty damn sure that they can't afford it. (p. 7)

Stage directions are important in this play, for throughout they underscore Hansberry's meaning. Sidney's smile in the above quote conveys his cynicism, and his facing out to the audience makes clear his direct address to both Alton and the audience. The choice of music in the play is equally meaningful. For example, in the same scene, shortly after Iris enters, about to discover Sidney's next ill-conceived money-making scheme:

> (*. . . The music comes up. It is a white blues out of the Southland; a lyrical lament whose melody probably started somewhere in the British Isles more than a century ago and has crossed the ocean to be touched by the throb of black folk blues and then, finally, by the soul of back country crackers. It is, in a word, old, haunting, American, and infinitely beautiful; and, mingled with the voice of Joan Baez, it is a statement which does not allow embarrassment for its soaring and curiously ascendant melancholy. SIDNEY busies himself at the drawing board, with an occasional side glance toward IRIS. The song, "Babe, I'm Gonna Leave You," dominates utterly. IRIS changes the subject). . . .(p.11)*

Obviously, the song accentuates the melancholy and suggests the despair that Sidney's cynicism evokes, and it anticipates much of the mood of the rest of the play. However, Hansberry's choice of song, and moreover, her explanation of the song—the need for which is not immediately apparent—suggests a syncretism that occurs in music and that she urges to occur in American intellectuality. The surface unlikelihood of Afro-American blues and the "soul of back country crackers" merging with a lyrical British Isles melody is just as unlikely as the twentieth-century Western intellectual mind thinking non-dichotomously and communally. *Brustein* shows us how dichotomous thinking destroys a sense of humanity and ultimately, in some instances, ourselves. The cultural syncretism that brought the songs together stands as a model for the cultural, aesthetic, and specifically intellectual syncretism that has to take place for Hansberry's generation—and indeed our generation—to see and rescue the beautiful in the ugly, the good in the evil.

The characters in *Brustein* each seek contentment through negation and escape, not through working through to a balance. Sidney negates the problems of urban life, of his community, of his wife by his escape into his fantasy mountain world. Iris escapes her failure to be a successful actress—or simply a fulfilled person—by negating her supportive familial past, by accepting Sidney's image of her as the long-haired, primal mountain girl, taking that to be her role as wife and thereby negating who she really is. Alton negates the suffering of others and has little compassion for it, seeking answers for his own pain among those he thinks share in absolute terms the same pain. Mavis negates the painful reality of her marriage with her upper-class facade, and while she accepts responsibility, she sees its working out as "giving," "saving," with a passive recipient. She thinks she can save Gloria. David, the post-modern, absurdist playwright, negates the active humanity of his audience and sees no good, just death or chaos, as the ultimate definer. He negates the oppression of others by generalizing his own oppression as a homosexual, and is therefore blind to Alton's conflicts and Gloria's pain. Max and Wally seek alternatives within the context of the superficial negation of the "bad." They are dedicated to reform, change, not transformation. And Gloria, who needs love and someone to care enough to say "Stop!" rather than to just let her be or to try to save her, suffers the logical end of the bohemian approach to life: self-destruction.

As Wally and Alton try to convince Sidney to support Wally and the Reformers, he struggles with the potential drug death of a neighborhood kid, Sal Peretti. It is such drug problems the Reformers promise to rid the community of as they rid it of "Bossism." Sid capitulates, we see in the next scene, but not before, in scene 1, he tells Wally and Alton:

> . . . But the truth of the matter is, dear friends, I am afraid that I have experienced the *death* of the exclamation point. It has died in me. I no longer

want to exhort anybody about anything. It's the final end of boyhood: the death of the exclamation point in my life. (p. 23)

He has accepted that life is essentially hopeless, that to interfere is useless:

. . . As a matter of fact, to get *real big* about it, I no longer even believe that spring must necessarily come at all. Or that if it does, that it will bring forth anything more poetic or insurgent than—(*with a flourish*) the winters dormant ulcers. (p. 22)

Wally's snide, yet unknowing comment about Gloria foreshadows the tragedy that takes place, which *does* restore his vision, Gloria's suicide. Alton, mugging, speaks of how great Gloria is, and Wally, never losing sight of his need for Sidney and his newspaper says:

So where is this perfection? Why doesn't she drop by and help restore Sidney's vision? (p. 25)

Her suicide catalyzes Sidney to finally accept responsibility in this world, and to realize that responsibility involves accepting with and working with both the good and bad rather than negating the reality by just letting Gloria be.

The play is about ideas, but it is, moreover, about the context within which ideas and their subsequent actions form, and within which individuals live. It is about conflict and the assertion of self within the domain of the conflict of everyday life, simultaneously an ordinary and an extraordinary problem of human nature. Hansberry is certainly in tune with the "present" of her play, for these ordinary characters and their lives are a microcosm of the extraordinary, if you will, macrocosm of the Truman and Eisenhower era. (And of course, we see frightening similarities today.) The bohemian or Beat Generation or post-modern climate aided and abetted the dichotomous Cold War mentality, giving rise to McCarthyism. The intellectual and political confluence allowed for no balancing of extremes, and instead, went to extremes.

Brustein's characters are caught up in the exaggerated Western posture of the rational, the objective, the individual. Yet Hansberry throughout implies an opposite posture, not unlike that George Kent suggests in his study, *Blackness and the Adventure of Western Culture.*[18] An opposite sensibility is there for Hansberry in Afro-American cultural, political, and intellectual life. It is particular to the vernacular of Afro-American literature and life, and it is the source of the Afro-American's survival as a people. Thus, I argue that although the play has only one Black character, it is aesthetically a Black play because its author's perspective is a uniquely black one. The point is not that she disavows the theater and politics of the absurd, it is *how* she does so—by exposing the Western dichotomous approach to life, revealing another approach *and* boldly suggesting the Afro-Americans' unwitting participation in it.

Here it is necessary to look closely at Alton Scales, the one Black character. Hansberry gives us ordinary characters, but they are fully drawn for the time they spend on the stage with us. For example, Wally and Max are short-lived in the play, yet we have a real sense of them as they affect the action of the play. Alton Scales, the Negro who could pass for white, leaves the play abruptly after learning of Gloria's life of high-class prostitution. His angry protestation of not accepting "white man's leavings" is more than an angry betrayal of his own prejudices, as contemporary reviewers of the play have stated.

Here we have a somewhat typical Negro bohemian, a Communist until the Hungarian Revolution, who although light enough to "pass," insists on being recognized for who he is. Iris and Sidney view him in the typical liberal way of his being Black not making a difference:

Iris protests Sidney using the phrase "bites the dust" and Alton thinks she makes too much of it as her cause, yet takes it lightly.

Alton: I got your point, so knock it off.

Iris (*turning on him*): You knock it off, sometimes, Alton! It's a bore. You and the causes all the time. It's phoney as hell!

Alton (*Sharply, back at her*): I was born with this cause.

Iris: That's what I mean! Fun with illusion and reality: white boy playing black boy all the time.

Alton: I *am* a black boy. I didn't make up the game, and as long as a lot of people think there is something wrong with the fact that I am a Negro—I am going to make a point out of being one. Follow!

Iris (Pragmatic bohemia): But that's what makes it so phoney. The country is full of people who dropped it when they could—what makes you so ever loving different?

Alton: It's something you either understand or don't understand. (He shrugs.)

Iris: Well, I guess everybody has to do something with their guilts.

Alton (*Flaring*): Guilt's got nothing to do with it. . . .

Sidney: Come on, this is a stupid conversation. Be a Martian if you wanna. (p. 41–42)

Iris makes a niggling comment about heroes everywhere and no battles won and Alton indirectly apologizes. But Hansberry has made clear the pervasiveness of imposed sameness that pervades one intellectual context of the play, bohemia, absurdity, what have you, and implies its uselessness to Alton, in this instance, for whom the other context is necessary (as it is for all the characters). It is, ironically, that imposed sameness and the blindness to difference that forces Alton to leave. That blindness is part and parcel of the either/or, negating posture of the bohemian intellectual and it prompts not an engagement with feelings and reality, its beauty and ugliness; rather, it prompts an escape and the illusion of an alternative to the liberal, white world. Sidney, a Jew, sadly taunts him: "A star has risen over Africa— . . . over Harlem . . . over South Side. . . ." Alton responds, "Yes." Sidney continues: "The new Zionism is raging . . ." (p. 102–103). Alton turns to leave.

This is a brilliant, prescient stroke of genius on Hansberry's part that we can only recognize now in hindsight. Here she warns of the separatist stance of many Black Americans, suggesting with her other intellectual posture that negation and positing self on negation is not the answer. That she has a Jew compare Alton's leaving to a new Zionism may show some growth in Sidney, but more so, poignantly explicates the comparable historical experience of Blacks and Jews that has resulted in their "bittersweet encounter."

Hansberry's sense of the interactive unity among ideas, actions, and human beings allowed her an early perception of the connection among the "-isms," long before many of her contemporaries; her early understanding that, to paraphrase Malcolm X, a Black person with a Ph.D. in the white world is still " a nigger"; her refusal to submit to the post-modern view of the world and the subsequent artistic expression; and her dissection and depiction of ordinary characters and ordinary events that reveal an ultimate humanity and magnanimity in the hearts of Negroes in the midst of their "plight," of whites in the smugness of their liberalism, and the Negroes and whites in their efforts to be, to exist, meaningfully; all this, among her other gifts apparent in her plays and commentary, rank her among the most useful and insightful Afro-American and American intellectuals. She convincingly stated her concept of the universal:

> . . . in order to create the universal, you must pay great attention to the specific. Universality, I think, emerges from truthful identity of what is. . . . In other words, I think people, to the extent we accept them and believe them as to who they're supposed to be, to that extent they can become everybody.[19]

She says "ego, like everything else, exist(s)(ing) in time and context. . . . For the supreme test of technical skill and creative imagination is the depth of art

it requires to render the infinite varieties of the human spirit—which invariably hangs *between* joy and despair."[20] Contributing to this view, she saw
realism as "not only what is, but what is possible," as Wilkerson reminds us,
quoting from *To Be Young, Gifted, and Black.*[21]

For the 1950s this was a truly controversial view of the much-distorted
and appropriated concept, "the universal," and yet it anticipated the articulation of the Black Aesthetic in the 1970s and the present-day evolution of the
understanding and acceptance of a pluralistic aesthetic. Reading Hansberry, it
becomes clear that her conception of the universal, so logical and so in tune
with Shakespeare and Achebe, is exactly what allows Wilkerson to establish
Hansberry as a visionary who "sensed the mood of the times and anticipated
the future." That sense of the universal allowed Hansberry the context to write
plays that are simultaneously, by traditional norms, both Black and American.[22] For example, *A Raisin in the Sun, Les Blancs*, and *To Be Young, Gifted,
and Black*, all fit easily into the category "Black American"; yet they just as
obviously sing an American song of the American Dream, freedom from
oppression, individual and group freedom.

In depicting the truthful identity of what is in her plays, Hansberry, "in
her singularity, in her particularity [she] was a voice of the whole United
states, of its dynamic culture and its tortured politics," as Jean Carey Bond
stated in the 1979 *Freedomways* issue devoted to her. Lorraine Hansberry had
a personal singularity and particularity as a Black middle-class woman whose
generational experiences (like those of generations before her) did not seduce
her to see herself apart from less fortunate Black lower-class people or from
the Afro-American and African past. Furthermore, her generational experience caused her to struggle with the intellectual atmosphere of her time, an
atmosphere that promoted the Western absurdity of life and ultimate despair.
To paraphrase Hansberry, she gave us acceptable and believable writing as to
what it is supposed to mean, and to that extent it is comprehensible to
everybody.

Hansberry has presented in the play *The Sign in Sidney Brustein's Window* a particularly Afro-American cultural and intellectual mode that is implicitly in conflict with and that explicitly should replace a particularly Western, American cultural and intellectual mode, if indeed the end of all is the
blossoming of humanity. She does this through characterization that always
suggests the potential for good; through stage directions by their integral
connection to the *meaning* of the play; and through the numerous encounters
characters have with themselves and others in their negation mode of the
unpleasant, the taxing, the ugly. She depicts their negation and escape, for
example, to pastoral fantasies (Sidney), chaos (David), and an all-Black reality in the same mode (Alton). Thus, *Brustein* is indeed a "comedy of sensibility," but sensibility, with the understanding of Hansberry as "beyond the

'universal,'" has a meaning far beyond the arousal of the audiences' sensibilities that Miller suggests.

The mode of that sensibility, sung in the spirituals and lived through the past three-hundred years by Afro-Americans, demands engagement with and a harmonizing of the opposites, of the good and bad.[23] It is the same mode that gave Nat Turner and Linda Brent the faith in their rebellions, that gave civil rights lawyers the eager patience of thirty years to pave the way for *Brown v. the Board*. Thus, the aesthetic sensibility of *Brustein* is essentially Afro-American. The sign in Sidney's window then marks the beginning of Sidney's transformation to an insurgent and stands as a reminder at the end of the play of the corruption and static negation his former intellectual posture rendered. *The Sign in Sidney Brustein's Window* is ethnic theater; specifically, Afro-American ethnic theater is American theater; and the play, its characters, and themes can only be understood and fully useful in this context.

Notes

1. Harold Cruse, *The Crisis of the Negro Intellectual* (New York: William Morrow, 1967), 267–84. Cruse's discussion of Hansberry needs serious consideration, for it implies key questions about the polarities the Afro-American artist finds himself or herself working within as they assert themselves and are judged within the context of the Western sensibility.

2. See Ernest Kaiser and Robert Nemiroff, "A Lorraine Hansberry Bibliography," *Freedomways* 19, no. 4 (1979): 285–304. This bibliography gives a complete listing of Hansberry's works and their critical commentary. The entire issue, subtitled "Lorraine Hansberry: Act of Thunder, Vision of Light" is a Hansberry retrospective. While it contains some pieces that are mostly sentimental, it also provides content basic to further study of Hansberry.

3. Jordan Miller, "Lorraine Hansberry," in *The Black American Writer, Volume II: Poetry and Drama*, ed. C. W. E. Bigsby (Florida: Everett/Edwards, 1969), 157–70; and C. W. E. Bigsby, *Confrontation and Commitment: A Study of Contemporary American Drama, 1959–66* (Mo.: University of Missouri Press, 1967, 1968), 156–73.

4. 1980s issues of *MELUS* and of *Black American Literature Forum* contain excellent work by Wilkerson and Carter, both of whom are featured in the 1979 *Freedomways* issue cited in note 2.

5. Margaret Wilkerson, "The Sighted Eyes and Feeling Heart of Lorraine Hansberry" *Black American Literature Forum* 17, no. 1 (1983): 12.

6. Miller, "Lorraine Hansberry," 160–61.

7. C. W. E. Bigsby, "Harold Cruse: An Interview," in *The Black American Writer, Volume II: Poetry and Drama*, ed. C. W. E. Bigsby (Florida: Everett/Edwards, 1969), 231.

8. Steven Carter, "The John Brown Theater: Lorraine Hansberry's Cultural Views and Dramatic Goals," *Freedomways* 19, no. 4 (1979): 186–187.

9. *The Black Scholar* (July/August 1979): 14–15, cited in Carter, "John Brown Theater," 186–87.

10. Carter, "John Brown Theater," 187.

11. Miller, "Lorraine Hansberry," 168–69.

12. Ibid. 170.

13. Bigsby, *Black American Writer*, 156–73.

14. Ibid., 167–68.

15. Wilkerson, "Sighted Eyes," 13.

16. Cited in "Introduction: The One Hundred and One 'Final' Performances of *Sidney Brustein*," by Robert Nemiroff, in Lorraine Hansberry, *The Sign in Sidney Brustein's Window* (New York: Random House, 1965), xvi.

17. All reference to *Brustein* in the text refer to the edition cited in footnote 16.

18. George Kent, *Blackness and the Adventure of Western Culture* (Chicago: Third World Press, 1972). Kent's work offers the first literary analysis of the Afro-American literary tradition from the standpoint of cultural sensibility—the awareness of the Afro-American self as it explores, confronts, accepts, and challenges Western culture through literary expression. See also Johnnella Butler, *Black Studies: Pedagogy and Revolution: A Study of Afro-American Studies and the Liberal Arts Tradition Through the Discipline of Afro-American Literature* (Washington, D.C.: University Press of America, 1981). Chapter 4, "Afro-American Sensibility and Afro-American Literature: The Ambivalent Aesthetic," speaks to an ambivalence that Hansberrymakes a workable, generative paradox.

19. Lorraine Hansberry, *To Be Young, Gifted and Black: Lorraine Hansberry in Her Own Words*, adapted by Robert Nemiroff (New York: New American Library, 1970), 128.

20. "Introduction," by Nemiroff, in Hansberry's *Young, Gifted and Black*, 1x.

21. Wilkerson, "Sighted Eyes," 13.

22. We have yet to coin a term that describes and indicates the American aesthetic that simultaneously incorporates both the Western and the ethnic American.

23. I am indebted to Paul Carter Harrison, *The Drama of Nommo* (New York: Grove Press, 1972) for catalyzing my teaching of Afro-American literature and my writing over the years, and to my colleague John C. Walter for helping me think this seemingly contradictory approach through precisely.

CHAPTER 16

Armenian American Women: The First Word . . .

Arlene Avakian

The material for this work on Armenian American women was collected through a series of six group interviews with a total of thirty Armenian American women in Massachusetts. Part of the "Women in Transition" project of Rites and Reason, the research theater of the Afro-American Studies Program at Brown University, the aim was to do a preliminary study of a group of white ethnic women in conjunction with a similar work on African American women. The Armenian American part of the project was severely limited due to the almost complete lack of scholarly work on Armenian women.[1] Indeed, there is a dearth of research on Armenian Americans as a group.[2] These interviews represent the first documentation of contemporary Armenian American women's lives.

As a first generation Armenian American woman whose work focused on American women's lives, there was much that I wanted to know. I was curious about the degree to which Armenian women were finding their voices. What had they heard about women's role from their mothers? Did they obey those rules about women? What were they telling their daughters? Did they work outside the home, and if they did, was the reason economic necessity or personal satisfaction or both? How did employment affect their lives at home? In short, I was interested in knowing what their lives were like as women, and what consciousness they had of those lives.

It was clear from everything in my own experience that Armenian culture was and still is highly patriarchal. Among the very few resources on Armenian women is *Armenian Village Life Before 1914*, by Villa and Matossian. Their description of Armenian village weddings indicates graphically the degree of women's oppression among rural folk. A married woman, according to Villa and Matossian, "became mute, lost her individuality, and fell under the absolute control of her elders."[3] The silence of the married woman began at the celebration immediately following the wedding. The bride was veiled, seated in a corner, and required to remain silent, keep her eyes

271

lowered, and kiss the hands of all the guests who approached her. Patrilocal residence was the mode and the bride was dominated by her mother-in-law, who determined the length of the period of silence. During this time the new wife would be allowed to talk only to children while in the presence of the family and to her husband only in private, a rare occurrence within the cramped quarters of village homes. Depending on the mother-in-law's judgement, the period of silence could last from a few months to more than ten years. The daughter-in-law was often released after the birth of the first grandson. While this description of the suppression of women outstripped anything in my experience, it was also not totally inconceivable. There were many occasions when the women in my family remained "mute."

Also central to my concern was the effect of the 1915 Turkish genocide of the Armenian population.[4] Starting in 1914, shortly after Turkey had entered World War I on the side of Germany, the Armenian intellectuals in Constantinople were arrested and killed. Shortly after this incident, the mass killing of Armenians began in earnest. Under the orders of Talaat Bey, the Minister of the Interior, and Enver Pasha, the Minister of War, Armenians were "deported" into the desert. According to the oral histories of the survivors and other eyewitnesses to these events, the "deportations" were in reality death marches. The "deportees" were rarely allowed to take anything with them to sustain themselves along the journey, neither food, clothing nor money. Since the government provided nothing for them, the majority of people died of starvation and exposure.

Often, before the "deportations" began, able bodied men were inducted into the Turkish army where they were used as laborers and had the status of slaves, since they received no pay for their work, nor did they have an appointed tour of duty. They were simply used until they died. Additionally, perhaps to stave off the possibility of rebellions on the marches, the able bodied men of a village were killed before the "deportations" began. The result of these policies was that within a period of a few years, one-and-one-half million Armenian men, women, and children in Turkey were killed, 82 percent of the population.

Of the small percentage of survivors, many were women who through luck, courage, and determination managed to save their lives and sometimes the lives of their children. Some of these survivors emigrated to the United States where they picked up the pieces of their shattered lives and started anew. What is the effect of that survival on attitudes towards men and women among contemporary Armenian American women?

My aim was to determine what Armenian American women see as salient issues in their lives. Armed with the lists of questions I had so carefully prepared, I anxiously awaited the arrival of the women to our first group meeting. Arranged by a member of the "Women in Transition" project, it consisted of a group of her mother's friends who she could convince to come out on a snowy night. After describing the project and telling the women we were there to hear from them about their concerns as women, a lively discussion began. I realized that my lists of questions had not only been unnecessary but also might have been inappropriate. If we really were there to hear about these women's concerns, perhaps we should be as non-directive as possible in order to be able to get a sense of what issues Armenian American women considered important. I had no delusions that we were observing women interacting as they naturally would. We had obviously created a situation by bringing them together with the explicit purpose of discussing women's roles, but I felt we could learn more from listening than from trying to direct the conversations into areas we thought were the most important.[5] The pattern that emerged at that first meeting was to be repeated in all of our subsequent interview sessions with other groups of women. With only the most minimal facilitation from me, the groups focused on women's issues.

We formed two more groups in the Boston area with the help of Ruth Thomasian, founder and director of Project SAVE, an archive of photographs of the Armenian people, who had joined the project as a consultant. We chose the groups in an attempt to be as inclusive of various segments of the Armenian American community as possible within this limited project. The first group represented a wide range of ages and classes and consisted of women who belonged to the Ramgavar faction of the Armenian political spectrum. For many generations, the Armenian community has been politically divided between Ramgavars and the Tashnags. Ramgavars, or assimilationists, believe that wherever they are, Armenians must make do as best they can. This does not mean, however, that they assimilate into the culture or the country they are in, for Ramgavars all over the Middle East and in the United States and Canada have built strong Armenian communities. The Tashnags are nationalists in the sense that they work towards the repatriation of the traditional Armenian homeland, which presently lies within the boundaries of Turkey and the Soviet Union. Each group has its own community, usually centered around a church, which has traditionally taken an important role in the debate.[6]

We were advised by the Armenian teacher (Armenian is taught as a foreign language in three Boston area high schools) to interview her students, recent immigrants as well as second-generation Armenian Americans. The principal of Watertown High School arranged two meetings for us by selecting those students who he knew to be immigrants, and for the group of second-generation students he chose female seniors with Armenian names, starting at the top of the class rank. All but one of these students also turned out to be immigrants.

After meeting with the group of Tashnag women, we realized that while many of the women in the two groups we had already interviewed worked, none were professionals. Ruth Thomasian, using her contacts within the community, organized a group of professional women.

After all the sessions in Boston were held, I felt somewhat disturbed that my own experience as an Armenian American woman was not adequately represented. Not willing to believe that I am completely out of tune with my countrywomen, I wondered if there might be something in particular about the women we had interviewed that made me feel very different from them. I then realized that all of the women we talked with were very much connected to the Armenian community, through the church and/or Armenian community groups. Most of the women with children were very much concerned that their children learn Armenian and, indeed, many of the children are fluent and literate in Armenian. For many of these women, social life is exclusively with kin and/or other Armenians. As one women in one of our groups put it,

> We are not fully Americanized, especially the Armenians in Boston. Do you realize that there are not more than one hundred Armenian churches in the country and that seven of them are right here in the Boston area.

Although Armenian was my first language and both of my parents are immigrants who socialize only with kin, my focus as a young adolescent was becoming as American as possible. My parents offered only minimal resistance to my desire to assimilate. I do not presently live in an Armenian community, but I do identify as an Armenian and wanted my experience included in the study.[7] I therefore considered it vital to the project to have at least one session with women who are not now part of an Armenian community. I chose Amherst, Massachusetts because there is no Armenian community in the immediate area and I knew of a few Armenian women.

The difference between this group and the other four was striking. The Amherst group was the only one that agreed in their general criticisms of the roles of Armenian women within Armenian culture. It was also the only group in which a majority of the women were single, either never married or divorced. Of the sixteen adult women in the Boston area that we interviewed only one was never married and three were divorced. The Amherst group was also the only one, outside of the high school immigrants, who talked about the difficulties of being Armenian in American society.

While there were women in most of the groups who wondered why we would focus on women's experiences and opinions, and there was some initial resistance to the idea of discussing women's issues, each group lasted longer than we had anticipated, and at the end of the sessions many women expressed an appreciation for having had the opportunity to get together to talk about their concerns as women. The most striking instance of an initial reluctance followed by an intense involvement was in our first meeting. The group had been assembled by the mother of one of the project's team and consisted of nine of her friends and acquaintances. When I asked why they had come, most answered that they only came as a personal favor to the team member. We began at 7:30 in the evening and after four hours of highly animated and sometimes heated discussion, I tried, unsuccessfully, to end the session. Finally, an hour-and-a-half later, the women were ready to leave. The most initially resistant and even hostile group we interviewed was one of the high school groups, and yet even they stayed well beyond the allotted time for our discussion, and that was on a Friday afternoon after school. (The discussion began in the last school period.) Although very few of the women we interviewed would call themselves feminists, our experience with these group of Armenian American women made it very clear that they are concerned with issues in their lives as women.

All of the groups focused heavily on marriage and family issues: there was general discussion of marriage; power issues between husbands and wives; women's proper role as wives; women and marriage and childrearing. Other issues that emerged in all the sessions were: education; general discussion of women's role in society; the church; Armenian culture; relationship to American culture; the genocide; and women's work and careers. One of the issues that did not come up was the political divisions within the Armenian community around reclaiming traditional Armenian land and the role of terrorism in achieving recognition of the Armenian cause; one group responded to a question asked by one of the project team about terrorism, but the discussion lasted only a few minutes. Another issue not discussed was women's sexuality. There was only some response to questions about the double standard for female and male sexuality.

While most of the discussions encompassed a wide range of issues, I have grouped them into six categories: general discussion of women's roles in society; marriage and family; relationship to American culture; mother/daughter relationships; work and career; and the genocide. I have chosen to quote extensively from the women we interviewed and have made only brief comments at the beginning of each section.

General Discussion of Women's Roles in Society

If my mother wasn't strong she wouldn't have survived.

My mother told me when I came here [to Boston after her marriage] to just be quiet and everyone would know that I'm a good girl.

In most of the groups, the discussion of women's roles took place within the context of marriage and, therefore, will be discussed in that section; however, the professional women brought up some of the difficulties they encountered in their fields as well as some of the ways they had found to cope with them. In discussing the problems relating to male colleagues, two of them had the following exchange:

> A man who demands respect for himself as an individual and as a person isn't even considered a demand. It's considered a right simply because he is standing there. Just the very fact of his manhood demands a certain respect in our culture. A woman just by being there doesn't receive it and if she makes any motion physically or verbally to call your attention to the fact that a person expecting and demanding respect is standing there can be perceived as arrogance. So you have to get to be very accomplished in the manner in which you handle that. It's difficult.

> I was in California to be the featured speaker on an afternoon program. . . . The other speaker, who was a male and a graduate student, had an appointment with an older Armenian to get some information . . . and he asked me to sit in. . . . And as we sat around the table, the graduate student asked his questions. I participated—made some comments—so that any person with any intelligence (that's a sentence born of irritation) would have known that I knew something about this. . . . When we finally got finished . . . the older man said, "And what are you doing in San Francisco? Are you here for a visit?"

> . . . there's nothing in the environment that says, "Yes, you are a worthy person. You are a knowledgeable, competent person." You have to carry that around in your own head all the time while people around you are saying that you are not there.

One of the women in the group who had gone to one of the top women's colleges in the country felt that there was much in her education that worked against her sense of self as a woman.

> There was some factors at Radcliffe that worked against being independent and against being self-realized. . . . I didn't recognize it at the time. At Radcliffe and Harvard you were told you were the best. . . . Looking back you were a second class citizen. The freshman classes were separate. . . . They built Lamont Library and they didn't let women in there. I used to make a joke by saying that it was the most glorified men's room on campus. . . . And when you had large lecture courses . . . you would be the only girl . . . and you didn't like to open your mouth and the men could talk circle over and around you. And there was the common perception, that I must have bought at the time, that the women might get good grades because

they're conscientious, but the men were really bright. All of this verbal
ability . . . it really has a perceptive effect on you. . . .

Speaking of her classes, a college professor noted that her female students are still quiet, but she attributes that reluctance as much to conscious choices as she does to intimidation.

They are really concerned with how they are going to be perceived by the young men in their classes and whether or not they are going to be considered desirable mates or not. . . . Young men in the class want attractive women who they think they can control. Young women will not speak up in a class even when they know the answer until a young man speaks.

Another academic raised the issue of women's need to be loved and the following discussion ensued:

It is a very unusual young girl . . . who has enough intellectual drive to put that in its place—that drive to love and be loved. . . .

That's the whole point though. Here we're getting back to this business of love and loving in its proper place. Sure, why should a woman have to put being loved and loving in its proper place? At any point in life you want to be loved and to love. And you want to be valued for who you are, but. . . .

While these discussions could be about women from any segment of the society, a woman from one of the other groups, an unmarried high school teacher, expressed her feelings about the effects of being raised in a culture in which women defer to males on her ability to maintain her sense of self in intimate relationships with men.

As I look back I realize that I had the special feeling as I was growing up. I was treated intelligently . . . but there's an erosion . . . living—raising children in a suburb, you very rarely had discussions with anyone, and so, in a sense . . . you were not testing your intelligence against other people's intelligence. You were not getting feedback . . . a positive demonstration of your competence, either by a salary or a promotion or even verbally. . . . I mean there were always certain levels at which I knew I was very competent in my profession which was wife, mother, housemaker, cook, whatever—to the point of French food—Julia Child and all that. . . .

I will end this section by complying with a request by one of the professional women that I use the following statement somewhere in my report of the session; "Men in our society apologize for their weakness, women for their strength."

Marriage and Family

I've observed one thing about Armenian women. Armenian women are very
affected by their parents. I've seen Armenian women go both ways. Either
they are hard working, conscientious about their heritage—I don't want to
say aggressive—strong women, or they become wives, take the back seat,
they become the worst of what femininity is. Too bad there is not a happy
medium. I think I'm really driven to do, I don't know what, to be something.

In all the groups, marriage and family were central to the discussions.
The overwhelming majority of the adult women are presently married. For the
women in their forties and fifties, dating was either not allowed or strongly
discouraged. The most extreme was a woman in her seventies, an immigrant,
whose marriage was arranged by her brother.

I never see him alone. I never say hello to him. He never say you like me or I
like you—no. We just marry. He [her brother] say you have to marry to this
man. He look like good man. . . . He going to support you. Any trouble you
come back to me. If you marry the person you like I don't look after
you. . . . I don't like in the beginning. I don't want to marry. . . . He says
you don't know nothing. . . . You marry and you make a home. That's all.
We marry. We have a good life. We have children.

A woman in her fifties responded that when she was young she said, "I'll
never marry an Armenian because I want to be dated for six months before I'll
ever take an engagement ring." Her uncles who had authority over her mother
because her father was dead, forbid her mother to allow her to date Americans. She recollected that they said, "Don't let R____ go out with any non-
Armenians and spoil our name." She met her husband at her sister's wedding
in Boston. He came to visit her in Iowa where she lived with her mother. A
few months later he came again, this time bringing his father along. Attesting
to the importance of family ties in the selection of a mate, she stated that
among the reasons for marrying her husband was "his first cousin was married
to my first cousin and he liked my mother and she liked him."
     Another woman in her forties remembers that her mother recognized the
difficulty of finding mates in the American setting. Her mother told her father,

You give her an education, you give her a car, you let her have clothes, you
give her money. What is she supposed to do? Put on her clothes, sit in the
car, put the money in her pocket and sit in the car in the garage? You can't do
that. You have to let her go out. She has to meet people. This isn't the old
country. They're not going to come to the house and ask for her hand.

Whether they actually did go out on dates, met their husbands through family or an Armenian group, all but one of the married women in our groups were married to Armenian men. They expressed the desire that their children marry Armenians, although most were willing to accept the mate regardless of nationality. All of the high school women, most of whom were immigrants, except one whose mother was not Armenian, said their parents expected them to marry Armenians. Many of the women, except for the Amherst group, also preferred Armenian friends.

> We have very good friends. . . . They are like family and they are Armenians. I have to stop and think that they are Armenian. Yet when I think about it, we don't have American friends that we are as close with.

> Without realizing it you are much more friendly and relaxed with Armenian friends than with American friends. You find that they are more interesting.

> My longest lasting friends are Armenian. Somehow the closeness that you have with an Armenian group—you're much more relaxed.

Among the issues raised, the most controversy was with regard to the relationship between wives and husbands. Some of the discussion centered on whether Armenian women are submissive or strong. The most extreme view was held by the seventy-two-year-old woman whose arranged marriage was described above.

> Life was under the commander—under the husband commander. But today—no husband and no commander and that's why life is so easy. . . . When you under the husband you have to obey and he bring the living. Today's living is my pocket is mine and your pocket is yours. . . . The man have to be the man the woman have to be woman in the house. Because no rule for the children, no rule in the house—nothing. If we have no government we have no country either. Husband same thing as government in the house. Whether he is a good husband or a bad husband, he still has to be the boss.

While not completely agreeing with this point of view, another woman did say, "very few Armenian women dare contradict or override their husbands." In her own marriage she says it is her husband who makes all of the decisions.

> We can't do anything without his approval. If we went for a ride we have to ask him to stop for ice cream. He says "no." I say, "the kids want to stop for ice cream." "No. We are going home." Everything had to be what he wanted. Whether it is selfishness or manliness, I don't know.

She did, however, make the decision to go to a real estate school despite his disapproval.

> My husband was furious. He wouldn't help me. I had to catch the 6:30 bus. He came home at 5:45. He wouldn't help me. I had the kids all ready for bed. If I was home, he would help me.

She did, in fact, pursue a career in real estate regardless of his opinion. Although she perceived her husband as having all the power to make decisions in the family, he was clearly not the "commander" across the board.

Despite a general agreement that men have power within the family, in all of the sessions some women talked about the strength of their mothers. This was most evident, however, in the nationalist group.

> My mother was always a very independent, strong person. She was strong mentally, physically and emotionally—in every way. And she had my sister and me and she brought both of us up to be independent and complete people. My father worked long hours . . . so we did all the yard work, took care of the porches, the car. . . . Mama taught us how to do everything. Mama was a fantastic example. She was such a strong woman. . . . So, I also raised my children very independently.

Another woman described her parents' relationship as being one of two equally strong people.

> My mother took off and went to Boston, found a job and came home and said, "I've got a job." They had only been in this country two years. My father was upset in the beginning but then realized that they needed the money. . . . They had their arguments on different things. I remember when my father would have to write something. He would say, "let me read to you what I have written." After the first couple of sentences she would butt in and he would say, "wait until I am finished." But this is what they did all the time. He wrote. She would have to listen until he finished and then start talking them all down again. . . . He would always listen, but if he felt strongly he would argue the point and she would bring him down. They were both strong, opinionated. They matched wits.

Her mother, she thought, was exceptional because she had had an education.

> Women are strong but they are not able to express it as much. My mother could only go so far in school because she was a girl, but she insisted on going through anyway. She read everything she could get her hands on. So in

her case, she can talk about it. Most Armenian women are strong, but don't show it in so many ways.

The restrictions put on strong women by Armenian culture were explored by another woman.

My mother was also strong but she was part of the Armenian tradition where the woman couldn't be as strong. My father was very strong. They never had fights that I knew about, but I could definitely sense that there were conflicts. My mother would do things. . . . She could turn the outdoors upside down. And my father didn't approve. I don't think it was because he minded her improvements, but what he minded was, I don't thinks she cleared it with him or what. . . . Not only did she garden. . . . We had to wallpaper. We had to paint. We had to do our home improvements. My father was not of the temperament to do those things. . . . My mother just could do anything. . . . She was frowned on for it. My father was never able to enjoy her accomplishments.

While women from all of the groups talked about the strength of women, it was never clear what strength meant. One group explored the concept of women's strength within the context of the Armenian patriarchy and made the distinction between strength and power.

What a contradiction the women continue to live. I see it in the Armenian families I know. This great strength in the women and the great power in the men and those don't come together. The men don't have the same strength and the women don't have the same power. My grandmother is an incredibly strong woman. She's one of the most powerful, articulate, charismatic women I will ever know, but she's very deferential to men—just pampering of men and they are what's right and women are not visible unless they are attached to a male. It's a very painful thing to experience and she could not be a more strong, more clear, more independent woman.

The concept of power was also explored by another woman in the same group.

. . . when we talk about power we have to understand something. It is power only where their families are concerned. Those women understood something. Those men have no power outside of the family. They have none—none. A man is born into this world and everything around him says, you can become something; however, if you can't get it in the world you can get it at home. My father was not a powerful man outside the home. . . . He was scared everyday of his life to go out and work in a world that didn't accept him, in which he really did not belong and which he didn't totally understand.

Whatever was meant by the strength of women in the Armenian community, only a few women considered their relationships with their husbands as equal partnerships. And these were generally described as being in opposition to their parents' relationships. A woman in her late thirties says

> My mother and I are very different. My mother waited on her family hand and foot. I see Armenian women that way, but it didn't rub off on me. . . . Somewhere along the line the tradition broke. . . . I worked when my children were in school. My husband and I share.

Much more common among the women in all the groups was the feeling that Armenian women suffered a loss of identity in marriage as a result of deferring to their husbands. One woman did not marry until her early thirties, she said, because

> . . . I was very much aware of what I would have to give up when I got married. My mother had a strong identity and she gave that to me and probably the male images I saw did not appeal to me. . . . I insured myself by marrying late. I had twenty years in a career. . . . Our generation, in the fifties, you either became a teacher, nurse or it was assumed that you would get married. It was the typical thing. They became Mrs. Somebody. They stay home, raise their children. They don't know who they are when they marry that young. And then later, they realize what's happened. I used to think my girlfriends were crazy.

Almost all of the adult women in our groups worked, although most did not think of themselves as career women. Their work was peripheral to their lives. The exception to this case were the professional women, all but one of whom thought husbands' careers should always take precedence over that of wives.

> I have always felt that his career came first. There was always that tacit understanding and if I was invited to a conference and he was busy, I would just stay home. His was more important. . . . I still do.

> The whole subject is so loaded. . . . First of all, practically speaking, my husband's career, for many reasons, came first, traditionally and practically.

> . . . I am just asking us also to look at the fact that there are times . . . when it's appropriate that the woman's career should take precedence over the man's, and for our minds to be open enough to accept that. . . .

I was making a conscious decision. . . . I just felt instinctively—first of all,
I am not an assertive person, but second, I thought that it would be too much
of a strain on the marriage. Just instinctively, not that my husband ever said
anything or did anything. . . . I probably would do the same thing
again. . . .

While the decision to try to combine career and marriage and family
might bring up some difficulties, deciding not to pursue a career at all was not
easy for the professional women. One of the women in the discussion above
recalled her life as a housewife and mother.

I remember, at that time, I used to say, the sudden change from being in the
world without children and with children, I used to say—not in a heavy
way—was like having a ball and chain.

Another woman agreed.

There was no support for women with children. It was a fantastic loss of
freedom. I was totally unprepared for it. And there is nothing in society to
support you or help you.

Yet, when her children were in high school and she began to take
courses, she responded negatively to the suggestion of one of her professors
that she go to graduate school.

No. Some people can do that, but I feel that I wouldn't be doing my husband
and the children the justice. I wouldn't be able to give them the attention I
feel they deserve.

All of the high school women want to get married, but they all also have
career goals. Some were disturbed that their mothers who worked outside the
home were also responsible for the housework.

All I know is, Armenian women they go to work, be good housewives and
have children. They have the same tradition. They don't change. But when
you come here at a small age your views . . . become more Americanized. . . . I don't think they should cook all the time. I think they should
share housework equally. They should help each other. Share the burden. . . . My mother goes to work, does the housework, cleaning, cooking.
It's very hard on her. My brothers and father don't help. They still have that
overseas way—taking it easy.

Seeing traditional gender role definitions in another light, a young woman responded,

The major thing is Armenian women . . . they never change. . . . American women work, but are not housewives. They are used to eating outside. They work outside. Armenians not like that. I like to work. I like to be home too.

Another young woman, also a recent immigrant, disagreed.

They are good wives, but sometimes they're too much. Always home. They always tell you what to do. They have old ideas. I want—go out—find out what life is—travel.

Agreeing with this point of view, a young woman who has been in this country for six years said, "Nothing should happen to your career. Life doesn't stop after marriage—right?" Most of these young women do not expect it to. Although they might disagree on whether or not traditional values should change, these women want it all—families and careers.

Mother/Daughter Relationships

I said to her, "marriage is not the end of life. . . . What you do is go to school. You can have it all."

You people seem to be knocking down marriage.

No we're not.

A home is very important.

We agree.

There is more to life than that.

Most of the women we interviewed who have daughters want it all for them too. In discussing her feelings about her daughter, who left college and is about to be married, one woman expressed the view that a woman needs more than marriage in life.

She has great potential and is not living up to it. . . . I said, "What if you don't marry M____, or what if it doesn't work out? What is going to make you happy? What are you going to do for the rest of your life? You can't say that marriage is it." She should not think of marriage as a career. Not in this day and age.

Speaking from her own experience, another woman told us the advice she gave her daughter.

I taught music. Then I got married and quit my job to raise a family. There was no question that I would do that. Now that I need to support myself I am behind the eightball. I have an entry-level position in a jewelry store. I resent very much being in a position where if I remained in my profession I would have a comfortable life style and now I can't support myself. . . . I told my daughter, "You go into a profession where you can comfortably support yourself. Don't let it dry up like I did. You never know what happens. I never dreamt in my life that after twenty-five years I would get up and get a divorce.

Another woman, who had a career for twenty years but is now home with her two young daughters, expressed a concern that she is not providing a proper role model for them by being a housewife. Another hoped her two daughters would have careers and she encouraged them to set up their own businesses.

Education is highly valued by all the women we spoke with. Again and again we heard how important it had been to the older women's parents that their children were able to get an education, perhaps reflecting the difficulty Armenians had doing so in Turkey.

The fact that we could go to school and have independence. We live in the best country in the world . . . my mother—everyday she said she was glad she was in America. . . . I follow along with my mother. I thank God that I'm here and my children can go to school . . . my mother couldn't go to school. . . . My mother was illiterate and even though my father died she made sure we all went to high school. My Godfather said, "send the children to work." But she was adamant that her children would go to high school.

I remember my father saying—emphasizing the education, "You're so lucky you have a library, you have books. You would have been shot in Turkey if you had been found with a book."

In some families, however, daughters were not encouraged to pursue higher education. One of the professional women, who holds a Ph.D. from a prestigious university, recalls

My family did not particularly think the education of women was important. They never put any obstacles in my way, but on the other hand, they never pushed me. . . . I think they always felt I didn't know what I was doing, and they were probably correct in that. I think they've always given me a lot of freedom, but on the other hand, I've always felt that since they weren't really in favor of this, that I shouldn't expect any money to support me. So, I always earned my way through all the way.

In other cases, the education of sons was given precedence over that of daughters.

I'm sure this is typical of many Armenian families. They will send the boys
to college and not the girls because they couldn't afford it. . . . So I knew all
along, I had one brother and two sisters, that my brother would go to college
no matter what it took and the girls were older and we would help to put him
through. Fortunately, he went on scholarship, because I decided I'd go to
college two years after I was in high school.

My mother, though she was a very good student . . . had to leave school
because her father died and they didn't have enough money to send the girls
and so, that was that.

Sometimes, mothers encouraged the education of daughters.

My father couldn't care less, never encouraged his daughters to go to college, but ever since we were in elementary school my mother brainwashed
us that there was no question that we would go to college. So, of course my
sister and I did.

Most of the high school women's parents expect them to go to college,
but not one of them plans to go away to school.

My parents won't let me go away either. I don't know why, but. . . .

That's really weird. Because, like, I've mentioned that to my mother. . . .
How about if I want to go away to college? She goes, "No. There's too many
schools right here."

There is general head-nodding in agreement to this comment. She goes
on to describe how she imagines a conversation between an "American"
college-bound youngster and her parents.

An American kid well . . . someone who was probably, you know, whose
parents had been brought up here, they wouldn't talk the same way. They
would say to their parents, "you don't have anything to say about it."

Picking up on this scenario, another of the young women added

The parents wouldn't say anything about it. They'd say, "where do you want
to go to college?" The kid would say, "I want to go to California." "I'll give
you the money."

Coming to the defense of Armenian parents, a young woman said,
"They're scared of American influence—drugs and stuff." Most of the wom-
en we interviewed who went to college lived at home. The few who did go
away generally came home every weekend. One woman recalled what hap-

pened in her extended family when she decided to go away to college and her parents allowed it.

> I was the first one to attend a four-year college—days . . . and the big thing was his sisters and brothers. They said, "You're not going to let her go away and she's sixteen years old? . . . She's going to get pregnant."

This sense of the dangers presented to daughters by the world was part of the reason the high school women thought their parents would not let them attend colleges away from home, but they also felt that the strong sense of family also contributed to their parents' desire to have them home.

> My mother trusts me a lot now. I don't think it's the fact of drugs or anything like that. I think she just is too scared to let go. You know it will be the first time that the kids will have left home like that for her. My brother left and she didn't like it. He moved away from the state. . . . He has been living away for about three or four years and she has never gotten this idea. . . . It used to make her sick at nights. And he's twenty-six, twenty-seven. It's not the fact that I'm a girl and I'm seventeen. . . . It makes her sick because of the way they were brought up in the old country. Families lived together and they see each other constantly. I have a huge family . . . every weekend they're always together. They have the best time together.

Older women recalled the control their fathers exercised over them and the role their mothers played.

> She was responsible for me and my sister having a life. . . . My father had one answer for everything, "no." That was it. We didn't discuss it. "No." I was quite old before I would realize the process. . . . I would go to my mother and ask her, "can I go to the dance?'" and she would say, "ask your father." She would defer to him always. I would say, "you know he is going to say no," and she would say "ask him." So, I would ask him and he'd say "no." . . . I would come back and I'd cry and carry on and she'd say, "well, maybe he'll change his mind." Always, the next day, he'd have a change of mind. It took me years before I realized that my mother would sit up with him all night, quietly. It was my mother. It was always that way. She never, never took credit for it.

For another woman the process was quite different.

> My mother could influence him, but she could never stand up to him. . . . Occasionally she would say, "why don't you let them go?" She deferred to him.

She questioned whether her mother was simply unable to stand up to her father or if she agreed with his restrictions on their daughters. She also felt that being out at all was illicit. Upon returning home from a date one night, her father asked, *"Oor manatzer?"*, which she translated as "where did you get left?" "I didn't go and get left anywhere."

This sense of the world as a fearful place coupled with the feeling that children should not live apart from their parents until they married could make leaving home difficult for those who did not marry.

> I was in my late twenties when I finally left home. After high school I . . . started to work for M____. I was with them about nine years when they . . . offered the opportunity to move. I didn't go with the first batch, but several men and their families moved out there. One October I took a vacation with a friend and went . . . to visit. . . . When I arrived two of the men I had worked for had secretaries that were pregnant and would be leaving in a year. . . . They were sort of teasing me and asking if I'd like my old job back. And I said "yes." What amazed me was that I realized that I could make decisions for myself being twelve-hundred miles away from home. And all the way home I just had to psych myself up that I was going to inform my parents. I was all they had. I was my mother's fourth child and the only one to survive. . . . So, I was their whole life. So for me to come home and announce . . . I was now twenty eight and I was going to move to S____.

Some parents are ambivalent about their daughters' ability to take care of themselves. A woman in her early forties related a conversation with her father.

> My father, in his old age, is standing there and his eyes are filled . . . and he say "What are you going to do when we die? Who is going to take care of you?" And he was so sincere, so overwhelmed by the possibility that I reached out to touch him. I almost had tears in my eyes myself. It's going to be alright Pa, I've taken care of myself all these years. Before I can get the words out of my mouth he says to me, "But you're the strong one. You have to take care of the others."

As indicated in some of the comments about going away to college, some of the fears that parents have about their daughters have to do with sexuality. One of the groups had a heated discussion in response to a question I asked about whether they had different ground rules for boys and girls. The opinions expressed ran the gamut from those who thought that both females and males "have to know and respect their bodies," to those who felt that daughters had to have different rules, "For one simple reason. Girls get pregnant and boys don't." There was disagreement about this issue in another group as well. One woman had no problem with her son moving in with his lover, but another said, "I would be very upset if my daughter lived with a man. I would be upset for my son too." This sentiment was echoed by another woman who said, "I think my daughters are very precious and it's a very precious gift to give a man—to give yourself."

There was general agreement in all the groups, on the other hand, that male children were preferred over female children.

> My mother always loved boys. She never had any, and she has four grand-sons and two granddaughters. She never gave two hoots for the poor girls, but boys, oh she doted on the boys.

> Uncle Joe always talked about his sons. He ridiculed his brothers for having daughters. When he was an old man he told me it was not lucky to have sons, because he was alone. . . . But he crowed like a rooster every time he had a son.

There was very little discussion about whether they wanted their children to marry. It was hoped that they would and that they would have children. Most women in the Boston area groups were positive towards the institution of marriage, even though they might have expressed some problems in their own relationships. Only the women in the Amherst group were critical of the institution.

Another topic about which there was little discussion was the importance of religion. It was assumed that good parents should take their children to the Armenian church, and the overwhelming majority of the women were active church members. A few of the women, however, were disturbed that the church is so male dominated. One woman would not take her children be-cause she felt "very strongly that the Armenian church is anti-feminist."

Work and Career

> When I graduated from college I wanted to be a lawyer . . . and then I thought it was a very unfeminine thing to do. I didn't want to be a woman lawyer and so—going for a master's degree was less of a commitment.

> I'm a senior in high school and don't know what I want to do. I'm going to college next year. . . . Once I make up my mind nothing's going to stop me . . . no man is going to stop me.

Despite the fact that most of the women work, and some have worked for many years, there was very little discussion of work in most of the groups, with the exception of the professional and the high school women. For these two groups, work was a major topic. All but one of the high school women expected to have professional careers.

> I want to be a legal secretary. I don't want to be just a housewife. I can work part time and be a housewife. I want to be a lawyer, but . . . we can't afford it. . . . I want to be a legal secretary so we can go to school.

> Our parents became just housewives. I want to be more than high-school educated. I want to make money to help my husband. My mother works in the hospital. . . . I want to be professional. My mother tells me she doesn't want me to be like her. She thinks she's unlucky. She got married when she was seventeen.

> My father wants me to have a career.

> Our parents are like that. Armenians encourage us. They did not have much education because there were private schools and they did not have the money.

When I asked if they thought they might encounter any problems as women, two of the women responded as follows:

> By the time we graduate from college . . . there should be no difference between you and a guy. You can do anything you want. It's going to be easier by the time we get to the point when we're going to look for a job.

> People make too much of a big deal out of it. . . . If you're good enough they're going to take you. It's not that bad. Everybody makes the biggest deal out of it and then, women, they turn around and they want it easy just because they're women. They use it as an excuse. And there is no excuse. The excuse is themselves. If you want a job, go out and earn it.

> I know it's not exactly the same, but if you want something bad enough, you're going to get it.

The older women complained that they did not have the kind of advice that would have helped them to make intelligent career choices when they were young women. They also focused, as noted earlier, on the difficulties of being women professionals and being taken seriously.

Relationship to American Culture

> My mother prayed everyday—every time she sat down—"Thank God. Thank God we are in America."

I was dark. I was exotic looking. I had all of the features that the Anglos said were trampy . . . and when they looked at me they assumed what they had absolutely no right to assume.

The most striking difference between the group in Amherst and the groups in the Boston area was their perceptions of American culture and how they related to it. The women interviewed in the Boston area are, for the most part, deeply entrenched in the Armenian community. With the exception of the high school students whose peers teased them for being foreigners, they seem neither to have problems being treated unjustly by non-Armenians, nor do they experience significant conflict arising from being raised in Armenian homes and living in American culture. The women who no longer live in an Armenian community, on the other hand, focused on such problems with no prodding from me, while those who remain within the community did not respond at all or only minimally when I asked questions about their relationship to the larger culture. The assimilationist women did not respond to my initial question, and when I asked the question again, one woman answered that American girls are promiscuous and she felt that was a problem, because she was concerned that her daughters would be influenced by them. There was no other response from the group.

The nationalist women responded by saying that they had been given such a strong and positive sense of being Armenian that they never had any problems. One woman talked about her family's relationship to children of immigrants from other countries.

We grew up in a multiethnic neighborhood. None of the children spoke English. When my brother went out he sang Armenian songs and all the kids in the neighborhood learned these songs in Armenian.

Indicating that some people might have problems in school, she related a conversation she had with a friend who decided against giving her child an Armenian name.

She said, "I didn't want my child to be exposed to the treatment I had growing up." She related the story that no one could pronounce her name and she was held back. She was ashamed of her name. I never knew anything about that. My name is A_____, my brother was A_____. Not one of us had any problems. The teachers would stutter when they came to my name and I would stand up and say "my name is A_____," and I would spell my name and sit down so they wouldn't say is this a boy or a girl. I did this in every grade. It never dawned on me that I was proud. I knew that it was my name. It came from my parents. They were both very strong. Even now, my daughter is the same way.

In response to a question of whether they felt a disjuncture between home and the larger society, the professional women had the following discussion:

> I don't remember feeling other. I can remember feeling other, but never less than. My daddy always told us how wonderful we were.

> I wonder if young women can be strong enough to stand up for themselves. They are living in two distinct worlds and it is too hard to integrate them.

> I always felt a special source of strength. I felt lucky to be Armenian. I thought we were special. We had a more colorful life. I was embarrassed because people could not pronounce my name.

> I was proud of our history.

The dissenter in the group was a woman who teaches English as a second language to the Armenian immigrant students and who also teaches Armenian in the high school.

The students were fairly clear that they live in two worlds—the Armenian and the American. Some are trying to bridge them and others remain within Armenian culture as much as possible. Those who had been here for six years or more related the problems they encountered in school when they first arrived.

> It was definitely hard. It used to be hard, being made fun of. It wasn't hard when we were just a few, but the fifth, sixth, and seventh grades were very hard.

> We were the only ones, remember?

> They used to call us Armors. The way they dressed. With the clothes they had. They didn't speak the language.

> When you come at a younger age it's real hard. . . . Up to the sixth grade I had a lot of problems. The group had a lot of problems. Over the years they accepted us. They got beat up. I was the only student who didn't get beat up. . . . I always tried to be friendly, ignore the remarks.

Those who had been here for more than six years generally said they wanted to assimilate and contrasted themselves to the recent immigrants. Assimilating to American culture, however, did not mean giving up Armenian friends.

> I've adjusted. I came at an early age. I don't think as they do [referring to the recent immigrants in the room.] I'm more friendlier with my Armenian friends because most places I go are Armenian oriented. When I came here there were not a lot of Armenians. Everywhere I went there were ten families of Armenians and we became a group. . . . Now I have American friends.

Among some of the more recent immigrants, the two worlds are so incompatible that they prefer to remain totally within their own community.

> I can never get along with American kids. They think a whole different thing. Can talk for a while, but come time when there is nothing to talk.

> Thinking mentality is much totally different. We feel much comfortable with Armenians.

But their choice is not without some feeling that they are not being seen by the dominant culture.

> You become shyer when you are in a different country. . . . But when you come to this country they don't know you and what good things you can do for them. They don't know you.

All of the immigrant women identify the main issue that separates the two worlds as the differences in relating to males, with most of the recent immigrants wanting to hold on to their traditions and those who came to this country when they were in elementary school closer to their American peers in attitudes, if not always in ability to live out what they think. Speaking of American women their age, the following discussion ensued, with the recent immigrants proclaiming their difference from Americans and those who had been in the United States for more than a few years attesting to their preference for the American attitude towards dates:

> Dating boys is common to them. We don't think that way. We are more conservative.

> That's all they think about. There is more to think about than that.

> I go out with my friends. I have much more fun in groups.

> Count me out.

> Armenian kids think differently than the way Americans think. I like the way Americans think.

> You don't go out on dates. That's the difference in our thinking. Over there you don't go out with guys and stuff. Here I can go out with a guy and have a good time and no one thinks its forever. The way they think, you know, if you go out with a guy, you're married to him.

The issue of dating had also been a problem for some of the women in the other groups when they had been adolescents and young adults.

> I was sixteen years old and I made a date with a guy and my father didn't talk to me for two weeks.

> When I was about twenty-five I went to a psychiatrist for about a year. I really had problems with the two worlds. There were so many double messages. I mean there was no dating or none of this stuff. I would be on committees in high school for the dance and I couldn't go to the dance. . . .
>
> My father would not let me join the Armenian Youth Federation. Because that's dating. You meet boys there.

As indicated by the second comment, the conflicts with American culture were broader than whether or not American practices were adopted. Some women suffered from assumptions made about Armenians.

> N_____ is primarily an Anglo town. . . . I learn very quickly . . . so I learned to read and all that very quickly. So what they did with me was to jump me two grades because I was bored. . . . I went into the ninth grade when I was twelve years old and I had been at the top of my class all the way into the eighth grade. There had never been any doubt that I would go to college. That's what I heard all my life. Well, the first day of high school, I'm in all these artsy craftsy classes. I really didn't understand it, but what I did understand was I knew you had to have a language to go to college and I wasn't in any language classes. So, I go marching down to the counselor and I explained to her that I am going to college and don't I need so many years of language. She looked at me and said, "My dear, your parents can't afford to send you to school. You are not going to college. You don't need that. You need to learn how to make a living." You have to understand how mortified I was by this and I went home to tell my mother.

Her mother, who she described as having "an incredible sense of self," informed the school that her daughter was going to college and that they should put her into the proper classes. The school complied but she felt that "they made my life miserable."

The Genocide

> My mother, who had no one, she spent all of my youth with me and she couldn't read so she wasn't reading me fairy tales—instead she was talking about the massacres.
>
> Because of what the Turks did to the Armenians, my mother told me what they did and I thought it was awful to be stamped out. I thought I had a special responsibility. Everything I do seems to try to prove my identity—that I am Armenian—that I want to show other people.

A major factor in the life of most Armenians is the 1915 genocide in which one-and-one-half million people were killed and thousands more were dispersed throughout the Middle East and the United States. The group of women who were the most reluctant to discuss the genocide and its results were the assimilationist women. While it necessarily came up in conversation, since many of them were children of survivors, when asked directly about it they responded that they "didn't want to go into all that." The nationalist women, on the other hand, brought up the issues quite frequently. Stories about the genocide generally emerged when women over thirty-five discussed their childhood years, as it was part of their environment whether or not their parents were survivors. The extent of the perceived effect of the genocide on people's lives can be captured in the following discussion:

> I heard about it a lot when I was a child, but it's only in the last few years that I've listened. It hasn't affected me. I can understand it. Yet, it's like something that never happened.

> Don't you resent it? Don't you think about the outcome of it . . . the fact that your whole cultural history was destroyed—annihilated. . . . You don't have the right to go into the library and look up your ethnic history. I didn't have the right to find any Armenian costume design history until these plates came from Armenia in the late sixties. . . . You have to have these things because you have children. You have a responsibility to educate them as to their cultural heritage. . . . They have the right to know about their heritage. A lot of things that were brought to this country before the genocide were found and the people themselves were delighted to show the things. They automatically became real to themselves. Their ancestors became real. The heritage became real. They had seen the objects they possessed, but it was almost as if they looked through them like they were invisible because they didn't have the consciousness to even have the luxury to think of their background because the shock of coming here was such a trauma that the luxury of looking at their history was new to them. . . .

> My mother was the sole survivor of her family and I heard stories when I was young. I am very close to my mother emotionally and physically. I went to see "Annie" and everyone else is laughing and I am crying and it is shortly after my mother died and I just related to the orphans and my mother and the other Armenian orphans. I always felt cheated growing up that I had no family.

And some of the survivors felt a special responsibility to their parents.

> When you are the offspring of a survivor you try to become strong. You sort of become like the parent of the survivor. You feel so sorry for them you want to do everything for them. I gave English lessons to my mother's

girlfriends. Armenians of M_____ were like one family. They visited each other and I went with my mother and heard all the survivor stories. It is a burden for a child. I felt I had to be strong in order to survive.

Other women wondered about the effect of the genocide on their parents' lives. One woman thought that her mother's inability to trust anyone was directly related to what she had experienced in Turkey as a young woman.

They're going from one city to another as they had to do and there were highwaymen—robbers—on the road. They stopped the carriage and wanted the money. My mother was very pretty. This robber grabbed her and wanted all of the money. And he also referred to her as being attractive. She was crying and saying she had no money. He grabbed her by the hair, spun her around. As long as I have known my mother, she's had headaches. If the Turkish driver did not come to her aid—the family couldn't of course—who knows what would have happened. He said that if the robbers had not taken her, he would have. My mother does not trust anybody.

The telling and the retelling of the stories of the genocide was explored by another woman.

My mother always told me about her life and it's very important that she did, and I know other Armenians did that. For years, and I know this is another legacy of the genocide, the only people they had to talk to—the only audience they had was us. The world did not care—it never cared. They know that. They would not have died if the world had cared. . . . So that it would not die. it is the idea of the telling and the retelling and expiating the pain by telling it and telling it and telling it. And in the telling it becomes easier to live with. It's a recognition that we were people and they did this to us. I was somebody. . . . My mother believes that she and her people survived the genocide because God put out his hand to and chose them. . . . That's the only justification they have. It's the guilt of survival.[8]

Conclusions

For the Boston area women, the Armenian church and community was a backdrop to our discussions. Women did not raise issues in these areas, it seems to me, because they are so much a part of the fabric of their lives. While there were a few complaints about male dominance in the church, there was no controversy over the value of the Armenian church to one's life and the lives of one's children. Only one woman did not take her children to church because she felt it was anti-feminist and therefore a bad influence on her daughters. Similarly, the importance of living within the Armenian community was not raised by the adult women, most of whose close friends were Armenian. For the high school women, on the other hand, the issue of whether or not one should associate exclusively with Armenians and participate only in Armenian activities was a point of heated debate. The importance of maintaining the language and encouraging children to learn it were also givens. The values of visiting and taking one's children to Armenia was also accepted without question. Many of the women in our sessions and their children had been to Armenia and some were planning second trips.

There were, however, other issues over which there was substantive disagreement. While the institution of marriage was not seriously questioned by the Boston area women, there was a wide range of opinion about the proper role of wives. Although only one woman in her seventies expressed the opinion that women should be totally subservient to their husbands, other women indicated in other ways that they subscribed to gender roles in which women had primary responsibility for childrearing and housework and men were expected to support the family financially. Most of the married women stopped working when they married or had children, although some did return to work after their children were in school. Some of these women were content to be at home with their children and were very critical of women with children who worked; others complained about their loss of freedom and the lack of support for women with children in our society. This discussion, among women in their forties, was very much like that of non-Armenian women who became mothers in the 1950s. One of the working mothers shared child care, cooking, and cleaning with her husband, but most women either gave up their jobs and careers while their children were young or managed both work and their responsibilities as wives and mothers.

Among the professional women, there was disagreement over husbands' careers taking precedence over that of wives. Two of the women felt that there should be no question that their careers take a back seat to their husbands', and one woman argued strongly for the possibility that there ought to be some discussion about whose career should have primary importance at various points. All agreed that this issue was a difficult one.

The women in the Amherst group were the only ones who had substantial criticisms of marriage as an institution. Two of the women had made the choice not to marry and another, in her late forties, had married only recently and was not sure she had made the right choice.

There was agreement on the value of education for both daughters and sons. Most of the adult women's parents, however, had given preference to the education of sons. Even those women whose parents did expect them to go to college agreed that traditionally Armenian families are not concerned with education of daughters. Stories of parents expecting daughters to work to help put their brothers through school were not uncommon.

While there was little disagreement over the hope that daughters would have careers, there was controversy over premarital sex for females, and, in some cases, male children, with the majority of women holding the opinion that women should remain chaste until marriage, and the minority accepting sexuality as a healthy part of their children's lives whether or not they were married. The issue of parents' attitudes about relating to the opposite sex was clear cut for the high school women. Most of their parents did not allow them to go out on dates, and while they did want them to go to college, not one of them was permitted to consider going away for school. Some of them accepted their parents' decisions, but others were frustrated by what they saw as overly restrictive rules.

In recalling their adolescent and young adult years, many of the older women recalled that their parents also controlled their behavior. Only two of the adult women who had been to college lived away from home, and one of those was expected to come home every weekend. Most of the older women left their parents' homes only when they were married. For the few women who did not marry, the decision to live on their own came late and with difficulty. There are, however, those women who defied expectations. One of the women left home at nineteen to pursue a career as a designer and chose not to marry until she was forty. Another woman emigrated alone to this country from Lebanon when she was in her mid-twenties, against the wishes of her older brother.

In each of the discussions with the adult women, there were some women who talked about their mothers as strong women. The few women who thought of themselves primarily as professionals attributed their sense of themselves as competent, even exceptional in their fields, to the influence of their parents, particularly the models of strong women provided by their mothers, although none of them had been professional women. Yet the majority of women felt that even if the women in their families were strong, they deferred to males. Focusing on this phenomenon, the Amherst group made a distinction between strength and power, attributing strength to the women and the power to the men. All agreed that Armenian culture is patriarchal and that women's lives are circumscribed by those parameters.

The majority of the adult women in the Boston area groups did not perceive any problems being Armenian within American culture. Some women did not respond at all to this issue, but those who did said they never felt inferior because their parents had instilled in them pride in their heritage as Armenians. The high school students experienced verbal and even physical abuse from American students. The high school teacher worried about the ability of her immigrant students to negotiate what she described as the two worlds of home and family and the American environment of school and work. In their descriptions of their school years, the adult women in the

Amherst group discussed similar problems. One woman felt that she was discriminated against by teachers and harassed by her peers. Another felt she suffered psychologically from living within the dichotomy.

One of the things that could make Armenians feel "different" is the experience of the genocide, but not all women were willing to discuss its effects. While the genocide came up in every discussion with the adult women, one group flatly refused to focus on what it meant to them. In other groups, some women attributed their mothers' strength to having survived the genocide and its aftermath. Those women who were willing to discuss the effect of the genocide on their lives felt it was either a burden to hear stories of massacres and/or that it gave them a sense of purpose in life, a feeling that they had a mission to let the world know who they were—that they were Armenians.

There were many differences among the women and some points of heated controversy, but one thing was the same for all groups. They all continued long past the allotted time and most of the women felt that we had only begun a conversation that was long overdue. Although most of the women indicated that they had not thought about being Armenian women before coming to the session, all of the discussions remained focused on women's issues without direction from me. There was a sense in all of the groups that the women deeply appreciated the opportunity to discuss their lives as women with other Armenian women. Women in the adult groups expressed the desire to meet again to continue the discussion, despite the fact that most of the women in the Boston area groups know each other very well and see each other frequently.

In many ways, this project is the first word on Armenian American women. It is a conversation that needs to be continued.

Notes

1. Published scholarly resources on Armenian American women are virtually nonexistent. There are a few dissertations on the Armenian family and community life: Richard Tracy LePiere, "The Armenian Colony in Fresno County, California: A Study of Social Psychology," Ph.D. dissertation, Stanford University, 1930; Harold Nelson, "The Armenian Family: Changing Patterns of Family Life in a California Community," Ph.D. dissertation, University of California, Berkeley, 1954. An article on "Ethnicity and Feminism Among American Women: Opposing Social Trends?" by Harold A. Takooshian and Catherine R. Stuart, *International Journal of Group Tensions* 13, forthcoming, compared Armenian American women's attitudes towards feminism with women in the general population. The Fall 1988 *Ararat* (An Armenian American Quarterly available through Armenian General Benevolent Union, 585 Saddle River

Road, Saddle Brook, N.J. 07662–9975) is a special issue on Armenian Feminism, ed. Arlene Avakian.

2. Robert Mirak's recent *Torn Between Two Lands: Armenians in America 1890 to World War I* (Cambridge: Harvard University Press, 1983) is the only comprehensive study of Armenians in the United States. This volume also has an extensive and useful bibliography.

3. Mary Kilbourne Matossian and Susie Hoogosian-Villa, *Armenian Village Life Before 1914* (Detroit: Wayne State University Press, 1982), 72. This work is excellent on women's roles.

4. Leo Kuper in his 1981 book, *Genocide: Its Political Use in the 20th Century* (New Haven: Yale University Press) includes an excellent chapter on the Armenian genocide.

5. This decision was made spontaneously because the discussion focused immediately on women's issues and was very lively. Although we clearly had created a situation by bringing the women together and telling them that we wanted to talk with them about women's issues, I was unwilling to interject myself and my issues into the discussion. Doing so would have been intrusive. While I continued to carry my questions with me to subsequent meetings, I never used them, because each group began to discuss women's issues on their own.

6. More detailed information on these two political factions can be found in Mirak's volume.

7. Using the insights from self-reflexive anthropology, (e.g., James Clifford and George Marcus, eds., *Writing Culture: The Poetics and Politics of Ethnography* (Berkeley: University of California Press, 1986); Deborah Gordon, "Writing Culture, Writing Feminism: The Poetics and Politics of Experimental Ethnography," *Inscription*, nos. 3 & 4 [1988]) I was aware that my study was not objective. On one level I was observing the reality of Armenian American women's lives as they understood it, but it was also true that I had created a particular reality through the arrangement of the meetings, my self-description, and the very existence of the project. I undertook this study partially because I am interested in ethnic women. What compelled me to do it while holding a full-time position doing full-time graduate work was that I am an Armenian American woman who had recently connected to my ethnic identity. My agenda, then, had as much to do with myself as it did with my "subjects." When I did not "see myself" in the study, I needed to know why. I asked questions about the composition of the group. We were able to contact the women we interviewed because of their connection to the Armenian community, and in most studies of ethnic groups it is precisely people like our subjects who are studied. Because I self-identify as an Armenian woman and there was some disjuncture between myself and the women I interviewed, the question of determination of who is a member of an ethnic group arose. The decision to interview a group of women who were not connected to the community was made as a result of using my own experience as a valid part of the data. All of the women we interviewed who were not connected to an Armenian

community did, in fact, self-identify as Armenian American. I was also influenced by native anthropologists such as John Gwaltney, whose *Drylongso* (New York: Vintage, 1981) is enhanced by both his personal experience as an African American and his acknowledgment throughout the text of subjects' response to his blindness.

8. See Helen Epstein, *Children of the Holocaust* (New York: Putnam, 1979) for responses of survivors and their children.

PART IV

Ethnic Studies, Women's Studies, and the Liberal Arts Curriculum: Retrospect and Prospect

We have a legacy of history to present as completely and as fairly as possible to our students. And, we have a legacy of concerted efforts over the past twenty years that has allowed us to limp along towards that goal. The gender and race biases that have plagued Ethnic Studies and Women's Studies respectively, the insistence upon the maintenance of approaches, perspectives and paradigms inherent to our "traditional" scholarship, with its reinforcement of white male privilege and Euro-American superiority are viewed in this section with an eye towards reaching a fair, equitable curriculum, productive to all.

Beverly Guy-Sheftall notes the gender bias in Black Studies as well as the race bias in Women' Studies. She deals with the views of Black Women scholars in both camps and gives eleven suggestions for bringing about a more comprehensive race/gender program. While her presentation, as part of the National Women's Studies Association 1989 Plenary, "Feminist Transformations of the Curriculum: Engendering Knowledge," cites Black Studies and race bias against Black women in Women's Studies, it can serve as an analogy for other Ethnic Studies and other women of color. There is much work to be done.

Placing Bloom in the current conservative political milieu, Jonathan Majek refutes Bloom's claims in *The Closing of the American Mind*, that Black students are now engaged in racial separation and that Black Studies have failed. Furthermore, Majek accuses Bloom of elitism, sexism, and indeed, of a closed mind. "American political principles are embodied in the constitution and in the people and *not* in the universities" he reminds us and Bloom. He pictures Bloom "like the Platonist he is, whose soul seems to yearn for a different century if not a millenium." As for Bloom's sexism, he quotes him: "The Muses never sang to the poets about liberated women.

In the final chapter, "Praxis and the Prospect of Curriculum Transformation," Butler and Walter identify the approaches and changes put forth in the volume and offer recommendations for the continuation of the transformation

303

effort. The value of this book in providing a theoretical foundation, in demonstrating scholarship, and in establishing a firm direction for the liberal arts to respond to the demands for inclusiveness and truth are reiterated and discussed practically.

CHAPTER 17

A Black Feminist Perspective on the Academy

Beverly Guy-Sheftall

Two of the most important challenges to the American academy over the past two-and-a-half decades have been the emergence of Black Studies and Women's Studies. Advocates of both movements have argued convincingly that the typical college curriculum is based upon a world view that is largely Eurocentric and that does not reflect the fact that more than half the world's population are female and people of color.

Thinking about and celebrating twenty years of feminist scholarship caused me to reflect upon the work of women of color and my own twenty-year involvement with race and gender issues, which began formally in 1968 with long and lonely stays in the Atlanta University library trying to figure out how to write a master's thesis on Faulkner's treatment of women, Black and white, in his major novels. Though the Black Studies movement and African American scholarship had called our attention to ways of analyzing images of Blacks, especially racist stereotypes in literary texts, the idea of feminist literary criticism, which was to borrow heavily from this earlier work by Black literary scholars, was only in its embryonic phase.

For this reason, my own need of a conceptual framework for the work that was to engage me intensely for the next two decades was difficult to construct. When my teaching career began a year later, there was no Women's Studies movement to speak of; few, if any, critical works on women writers; no histories of African American women; profound silence about the existence of Black lesbians; no biographies of Black women writers (there are still only a few); no acknowledgement of a rich feminist tradition in African American intellectual and literary history. The absence of all this must have motivated a group of Black women academics and writers to involve ourselves in the development of what was to much later be called Black Women's Studies.

Black Women's Studies, which emerged in part because of the failure of Black and Women's Studies to deal with the experiences of Black women

nationally and globally, is the scholarly investigation of the history, crea-
tive/intellectual expression and experiences of this unique segment of the
population. This relatively new field confronts the problem of gender bias in
Black Studies and race bias in Women's Studies and analyzes the myriad ways
in which gender/race form an "otherness," both in relationship to Black men
and in relationship to non-Black women. All three of these oppositional
movements within the academy call into question the philosophical frameworks and values of the American college curriculum.

The most noteworthy developments in Black Women's Studies have
come primarily from a group of women scholars who have been teaching and
doing research on Black women for at least the past twenty-five years; a group
of writers, artists, and intellectuals whose foremothers are Phyllis Wheatley,
Anna J. Cooper, and Zora Neale Hurston; a group of activists and community
organizers whose first-hand experience with the lives of Black women shaped
their vision; and a younger group of women, and to a lesser extent men, who
as graduate students or junior faculty have been inspired by the new scholarship on women of color and who have access to resources that only two
decades ago were nonexistent. This activity, without which it would have
been very difficult to do the kind of feminist transformation of the curriculum
in which the Women's Studies movement is now engaged, included a number
of critical publications. Books included Toni Cade's *The Black Woman*
(1970); Gerda Lerner's documentary history, *Black Women in White America*
(1972); *All the Women Are White, All the Blacks Are Men, But Some of Us Are
Brave* (Hull, Smith, and Bell-Scott, 1982); *Sturdy Black Bridges: Visions of
Black Women in Literature* (Bell, Parker, and Guy-Shoftall, 1979); *The Afro-
American Woman: Struggles and Images* (Harley and Terborg-Penn, 1978);
Black Women Novelists: The Development of a Tradition, 1892–1976
(Christian, 1980); Bell Hooks's *Ain't I A Woman: Black Women and Feminism*
(1981) and *From Margin to Center, Feminist Theory*; Mary Helen Wash-
ington's *Black-Eyed Susans* and *Midnight Birds*; *When and Where I Enter:
The Impact of Black Women on Race and Sex in America* (Giddings, 1984);
Filomina Steady's *The Black Woman Cross-Culturally*; and more recently
Johnnetta B. Cole's *All American Women*, a widely-used textbook in Women's
Studies courses. I also want to mention the work of other Black women—
Audre Lorde, Alice Walker (who taught the first course on Black women
writers), Johnnella Butler, Bonnie Dill, Michele Wallace, Toni Morrison, and
numerous others, who also contributed to what can only be called a renaissance of Black women writing. The founding of *SAGE: A Scholarly Journal
on Black Women* in 1983 was a milestone in promoting research on Black
women throughout the world and an obvious manifestation of the "coming of
age" of Black Women's Studies.

Despite all of the important activity that has taken place in Women's

Studies, there came to be in the eighties many among us (advocates of Black Studies, Ethnic Studies, and later Black Women's Studies) who became discontented and frustrated. Many, mainly women of color, began to critique both Women's Studies and curriculum integration or transformation projects for their relative lack of attention to questions of racial, class, or ethnic/cultural differences. They (we) argued passionately that femaleness or womanhood is not a monolithic category. Professor Johnnella Butler, who co-directed one of the first projects that attempted collaborative efforts between Women's Studies and Ethnic Studies asserted:

> Women are separated from each other by race, class, ethnic group, religion, nationality and culture so that they appear to share more of a common identity with men of their own immediate group than with women outside that group.[1]

One of the most brilliant and hard-hitting analyses of the insensitivity of Women's Studies to race, class, and ethnicity can be found in the pioneering work of feminist theorist Bell Hooks. In a passionate defense of Black Women's Studies, which appear in a special issue of *SAGE* on Black Women's Studies, she reminds us:

> Our collective work (the work of Black feminist scholars) made it possible for individuals active in feminist movement to demand that Women's Studies courses acknowledge that they claimed to be talking and teaching about women when the actual subjects of study were white women. . . . However, the insistence on recognizing differences among women, of ways the intersection of race, sex, and class determine the nature of female oppression has not sufficiently altered hierarchical structures within Women's Studies scholarship. Most programs continue to focus central attention on white women, subordinating discussions of Black women and other people of color. Since most Women's Studies programs fail to be inclusive in ways that radically subvert and challenge racism and racial hierarchies, the development of Black Women's Studies is a necessary corrective.[2]

Butler has also argued eloquently for "paradigm shifts" within Women's Studies that would make more visible the situation of women of color. Like Hooks, she rejects the woman-as-oppressed-group model so prevalent in early feminist scholarship:

> White women function both as women who share certain similar experiences with women of color and as oppressors of women of color. This is one of the most difficult realities to cope with. . . . White women who justifiably see themselves as oppressed by white men find it difficult to separate themselves from the effects and shared power of white men. The fact is that white

women share with white men an ethnicity, an ancestral heritage, a racial dominance and certain powers and privileges by virtue of class, race and ethnicity, by race and ethnicity if not class, and always by virtue of white skin privilege.[3]

In her assessment of Women's Studies at twenty, entitled "Difficult Dialogues," Butler continues to argue that Women's Studies itself needs radical transformation in order to reflect all women's experiences. She goes on to say that her eight years of experience in the vineyards, so to speak, consulting and conducting workshops for Women's Studies, Ethnic Studies, and English departments have led her to the sad conclusion that Women's Studies, ironically, will be more difficult to transform than Ethnic Studies, despite its previous lack of attention to gender and its persistent homophobia.[4] Having spent a considerable portion of my professional career also involved with Women's Studies, English departments, and to a lesser extent Black Studies, I am more reluctant at this point to say which is the most difficult to transform.

During the late seventies, as the Women's Movement grew in momentum and as the Black Liberation Movement receded, it seemed, into the background, some of us left Black Studies or tried to infuse gender there (sometimes a difficult enterprise). A few associated themselves with Women's Studies, and advocated loudly for paradigm shifts that would more adequately address race/class/ethnicity issues and eradicate frameworks that were constructed from the notion that "woman" is a monolithic category. Others tried to maintain a foot in both camps so that Black womanist or feminist perspectives would permeate both disciplines, one of which had been historically insensitive to gender and homophobia, and the other one of which had been insensitive to race and class, and too bound up in Western epistemologies and cultural contexts. It was especially difficult to be a Black woman committed to the eradication of racism and sexism and heterosexism during this early period. You were sometimes perceived to be a traitor to the race, anti-male white-oriented, and lesbian. White feminists sometimes perceived you to be angry, militant, too emotional, even racist, because you were constantly mentioning the "R" word (race), when the appropriate and more urgent preoccupation should have been gender and sexism. Obviously, you did not really understand the pervasive and more all-embracing manifestations of patriarchy. Racism was, after all, a *consequence* of patriarchy, not an evil in and of itself. If you really understood feminist theory, which obviously only white women had produced, you would not keep bringing up race/ethnicity. It was hard to convince anyone that Black women had been thinking and writing "feminist" since the early 1800s and that their perspectives came from their analyses of their own realities rather than from an embrace of white female notions. You were even sometimes problematic among many members of the group that perhaps you cared most about—other Black women.

I want to describe briefly one case of an attempt at curriculum integration in a context that still has, relatively speaking, little Women's Studies activity, despite its role in the development of Black Studies, and that is the historically Black college. In 1983, under the auspices of the Women's Research and Resource Center, Spelman College, the oldest Black women's college, engaged (with the assistance of a Ford Foundation grant) in the first curriculum integration in Women's Studies project on a historically Black college campus. Specifically, the objective was to invigorate the liberal arts curriculum by redesigning courses so that they would reflect the new scholarship on women generally, but especially the new scholarship on women of color, both in the United States and abroad. In order to bring this about, a carefully articulated program of faculty development, course refinement and modification, and course development was initiated. An interdisciplinary faculty team of twenty were involved from the Spelman campus. Eight courses in the core curriculum were redesigned, including Freshman English, World Civilization, World Literature, Introduction to Sociology, Introduction to Psychology, Survey of Fine Art, World Religions, Afro-American History, Introduction to Philosophy, and Science and Society, the last being the least successful of the efforts. Much of the "pioneering" work involved the English Department, which compiled a new race and gender balanced reader that was international in focus and included short stories, poems, essays, and excerpts from the personal narratives and autobiographies of major thinkers and writers as well as lesser-known ones.

The extent to which Black Women's Studies was incorporated into this core requirement was also apparent in the English Department's decision to use Maya Angelou's *I Know Why the Caged Bird Sings* as the one complete text that all first year students would read in English 101. The English Department also designed a new world literature course that represented a radical and refreshing departure from conventional world literature courses in most colleges and universities in the United States, which focus unduly on the West. The new course is truly a *world* literature course and is cross-cultural in its approach. It does not begin in Greece and reflects the fact that human civilization began on the continent of Africa.

As a result of the Ford-funded Curriculum Development Project in Black Women's Studies (whose second phase was funded in 1987), Spelman now has the distinction of being the only historically Black undergraduate college with a viable Women's Studies program (which includes a minor) and a mainstreaming project in Women's Studies. Spelman's project is also unique because of its special attention to minority women and its cross-cultural dimension. We have truly tried to acknowledge the diversity of women's experiences throughout the world and feel that we have helped to reconceptualize Women's Studies in such a way that it is respectable and in keeping with its own goals of ridding the academy of androcentric as well as racial and class biases.

Considerable experience with curriculum development projects over the years has convinced me that a number of strategies are likely to result in serious efforts during the nineties to bring about a race- and gender-balanced program:

1. acknowledgement that paradigm shifts are necessary in both Black and Women's Studies

2. resources for faculty development seminars that explicitly address race/class/ethnicity issues and the need to be inclusive

3. acceptance of the complexity of the process

4. recruitment of more women and minority faculty, and support during the tenure process

5. alliances/coalitions between faculty and programs involved with Black Studies, Ethnic Studies, and Women's Studies

6. development of a healthy *respect*, not tolerance, for differences that does not embrace color-blindness, which usually continues to see whiteness as the norm

7. maintenance of a good sense of humor

8. willingness to move beyond narrow, disciplinary boundaries; the work is interdisciplinary

9. willingness to take risks

10. willingness to teach material with which one is unfamiliar or which might make one uncomfortable

11. willingness to include material that does not focus only on gender or race

During the final decade of the century we face a number of challenges as Black and Women's Studies advocates. At one extreme is the question of our continued survival given the existence of scarce resources and fierce competition among diverse programs on college and university campuses. Some would argue that the institutionalization of Women's Studies is proceeding more smoothly than Black Studies, despite its longer history in the academy. It seems counter-productive for Black Studies and Women's Studies to engage in unnecessary battles given their own marginality in the academy where financial resources are concerned. Both programs, critical to the success of real transformation of the liberal arts curriculum, have much to learn from each other. As we approach the turn of the century, it would be appropriate and even revolutionary for both programs to join forces, when necessary, to achieve the common goal of creating an inclusive curriculum that would benefit us all.

Notes

1. Johnnella Butler, "Difficult Dialogues," *Women's Review of Books* 6 (February 1989): 16.

2. Bell Hooks, "Feminism and Black Women's Studies," *SAGE: A Scholarly Journal on Black Women,* VI (Summer 1989), 54–56.

3. Butler, "Difficult Dialogues," 16.

4. Ibid.

CHAPTER 18

A Critical Assessment of Bloom: The Closing of an American Mind?

Jonathan A. Majek

Educational reform became a very popular cause in the 1980s. This demand for reform may be indicative of a general uneasiness about the future and a lack of confidence in the prosperity of the Reagan years.

The federal government has run up a huge budget deficit and the United States has become a debtor nation instead of a creditor nation. Indeed, there is great concern that the United States is losing its competitive edge to foreign nations, particularly Japan. So once again, the United States is turning to its educational enterprise for some solutions. That enterprise, however, is in trouble, as attested to by numerous critical reports and books.

Of all the books on higher education, none received so much publicity as Allan Bloom's controversial book, *The Closing of the American Mind*.[1] It was on the *New York Times* best-seller list for twenty weeks.[2] It also enjoyed widespread popularity in France, where it is sold under the title *L'Ame Disarmèe* (The Disarmed Soul).[3]

The popularity of the book indicates that Bloom obviously has something important to say that many people are not only willing to consider but also that many others may be tempted to believe. There is, moreover, no doubt that the current conservative mood in the country has enhanced the popularity of the book. But Bloom, himself, seems to be a neo-conservative, judging by the content and style of his book. "The Neo-conservative style," Peter Steinfels points out "is formal, literary, learned and serious. . . . It is scholarly and yet unlike scholarly publications, it is combative, and yet, unlike the denunciatory literature of the Left and Right."[4]

This analysis focuses on two related aspects of Bloom's critique of higher education in the United States. I will examine his analysis of race relations in academe, particularly his assertion that Black students are now the ones engaged in racial separatism. Second, I will consider his claim that Black Studies have essentially failed. But first, I will provide a brief overview of Bloom's general critique of higher education. Before analyzing Bloom's critique of higher education, I shall first describe his idea of a university, because it is, in my opinion, the real basis of his critique.

Bloom reveals that in his youthful days before he entered college, he had rather fanciful ideas about the university. He imagined it as a temple "dedicated to the purest use of reason." It was a place that provided an atmosphere for free inquiry; a place that fostered camaraderie based on shared experiences. The university protected the tradition. It was a place where what he considered "authentically great thinkers" engaged in theoretical life. These great thinkers owed their authority not to power, money, or family, but natural intellectual gifts that commanded respect.

When one examines Bloom's adult view of the university, it becomes quite clear that he has not outgrown his youthful ideas. Here is his adult view:

> The university is the place where inquiry and philosophic openness came into their own. It is intended to encourage the noninstrumental use of reason for its own sake, to provide the atmosphere where the moral and physical superiority of the dominant will not intimidate philosophic doubt. (p. 248–49)

The problem for Bloom is not only that the reality of the university today is at variance with his ideal, but also that the semblance of the institution he had known, especially in the fifties, is no more—hence his rather bitter critique. The decline of the academy, according to Bloom, has been brought about by, among other things, relativism, the legacy of the sixties, and feminism.

Bloom asserts that one thing a professor in an American university can be "absolutely certain" of is the fact that most of the students believe that truth is relative. "They are unified only," he says "in their relativism and in their allegiance to equality" (p. 25). According to Bloom, this student relativism has not been corrected but reinforced by an educational system that emphasizes an aberrant form of openness—an openness that is, in the last analysis, really a form of closedness. Bloom cites a number of practices in academe that foster this kind of openness.

The study of history and culture, for instance, is conducted in such a way as to show "the world was mad in the past; men always thought they were right, and that led to wars, persecutions, slavery, xenophobia, racism, and chauvinism" (p. 26). The objective of such a study, as Bloom sees it, is "not to correct the mistakes and really be right; rather it is not to think you are right at all" (p. 26). Moreover, there has been an evolutionary shift, in the last fifty years, from the education of the democratic man to the education of the democratic personality. The former emphasized man's natural rights as the basis for unity and brotherhood regardless of class, race, religion, national origin, or culture. The latter education only emphasizes openness. According to Bloom this kind of education "has no shared goals or vision of the public good" (p. 27).

Another practice fostering this wrong kind of openness is the one that requires students to take a course in non-Western culture. Bloom concedes that such courses are indeed taught by "real scholars" who love the areas of their studies; however, the intent of such courses, he claims, is demagogic. The students are forced "to recognize that there are other ways of thinking and Western ways are no better" (p. 36). Bloom counters this alleged attempt to reduce ethnocentrism in the West by asserting that all those non-Western cultures are just as ethnocentric. He declares that "only in the Western nations, i.e., those influenced by Greek philosophy, is there some willingness to doubt the identification of the good with one's own way" (p. 36). Martha Nussbaum points out that such a statement shows Bloom's "startling ignorance" of classical Indian and Chinese critical and rationalist traditions.[5] Besides, one does not have to be a philosopher in order to engage in self-criticism. Ironically, Nussbaum sees Bloom's confident assertion as "a cogent, though inadvertent, argument for making the study of non-Western civilizations as an important part of the university curriculum."[6]

Bloom's description and analysis of the sixties suggests the picture of an angry man, perhaps a man traumatized by the experiences of that turbulent decade, particularly his own experiences at Cornell. As he denied being so traumatized in a *Time* interview with William McWhirter, one can concede that point.[7] However, the undeniable fact is that he *is* very angry.

Bloom cautions the reader that the fact the universities are no longer in convulsion does not mean they have regained their health. For Bloom, what happened at the universities in the sixties was "an unmitigated disaster"—the relaxation or abandonment of certain academic requirements; the grade inflation and so forth. Indeed, he personally knows nothing positive that ever came from the campus upheavals of that period. He rejects what he considers a mythology that has grown around the student activism of the sixties. According to this mythology, Bloom points out, (1) the "Fifties were a period of intellectual conformism and superficiality, whereas there was real excitement and questioning in the Sixties" (p. 322); (2) McCarthyism had an extremely negative impact on the universities; and (3) the students had superior moral concern.

The imperative of the sixties, he says, was to promote equality, and stamp out racism, sexism, and elitism. Accordingly, the faculty in the natural sciences, the social sciences, and the humanities were asked to change content and standards. The student activists made these demands after brandishing firearms—hence Bloom's frequent reference to "the guns of Cornell." Unfortunately for Bloom, there was no solidarity among the so-called community of scholars. He relates with bitterness that he saw those whose duty it was to take a stand respond instead with cowardice and casuistry.

At Cornell—the institution that epitomizes for him all that went wrong with academe—Bloom served on various committees. On these committees he says he "continuously and futilely voted against dropping one requirement after the next" (p. 321). In the end, the old core curriculum was abandoned. Now, in the eighties, although the universities are returning to requirements, Bloom is not consoled. He writes:

> The university now offers no distinctive visage to the young person. He finds a democracy of the disciplines—which are there because they are autochthonous or because they wandered in recently to perform some job that was demanded of the university. This democracy is really anarchy, because there are no recognized rules of citizenship and no legitimate titles to rule. (p. 337)

Bloom laments the disintegration of liberal education and wonders as to why these universities that can perform monumental tasks such as splitting the atom and finding cures for terrible diseases cannot develop a modest program of general education for undergraduate students. What he sees now in place is a narrow preprofessional specialization that Bloom thinks separates students from one another.

Of all the professional degrees, Bloom singles out the MBA for special criticism—and a very harsh one at that. He considers the emergence of the MBA as the equivalent of MD or the law degree, "a great disaster." He talks disparagingly of the MBA as "a diploma that is not a mark of scholarly achievement" (p. 370). Moreover, Bloom points out that economics has become very popular as *the* prebusiness major. The economics majors, he contends, are not motivated by the science of economics, but by money. Although he says there is nothing wrong with that, it is their smugness that infuriates him. Bloom observes that a premed who takes biology appreciates physics whereas the prebusiness economics major has no interest whatsoever in either sociology, anthropology, or political science, all because he is "persuaded that what he is learning can handle all that belongs to those studies" (p. 371). Even though it is true that the economist enjoys an undeservedly high status in the society, Bloom's criticism of the prebusiness economics major is not evenhanded in light of the fact that he regards premed and prebusiness students as "distinctively tourists in the liberal arts" (p. 370). The reason for such lighter criticism of the premed student seems to be that Bloom has a grudging respect for the intellectual capacities of the natural scientist.

Bloom's appraisal of feminism's impact on academe is essentially negative. He regards feminism as an enemy of the classic texts—more so than the struggles of the past two decades against elitism and racism. Those struggles, he points out, had no effect on students' relations to books. Bloom then asserts without any evidence that for feminists, *all* literature is sexist. He then declares sarcastically that "The Muses never sang to the poets about liberated women" (p. 65). Bloom believes that failure to read good books not only enfeebles the vision, but also leads to "a fatal" tendency to believe that the only things of importance are to be found in the present.

Bloom does not see much evidence of influence of feminism, particularly the militant feminism, on women students in the university. However, he concedes the fact that once in a while strident voices do get heard, especially in the student government and in the campus newspapers. By and large women students, he says, do not feel discriminated against or ridiculed for their career choices. Sex, he quips, does not have political agenda any more in universities, except among homosexuals.

With respect to the relations between the sexes, Bloom says that the challenge came from two sources, the sexual revolution and feminism, in that order. While both movements sought to suppress modesty—which Bloom considers *the* female virtue—their aims were, however, different. The obvious goal of the sexual revolution was freedom, whereas feminism is after equality. Sexual revolution proved to be short-lived, according to Bloom, while the "grimmer, unerotic" feminism has endured. Sexual revolution sought to bring men and women together, but feminism not only wants them to be separate but has reduced sex to a thing-in-itself. As Bloom sees it, feminism is an abstract project that requires political activism. "It ends," he says, "as do many modern movements that seek abstract justice, in forgetting nature and using force to refashion human beings to secure that justice" (p. 100). This insinuation of authoritarianism is both unwarranted and indefensible. In the first place, the feminists have never advocated the use of force or any other extra-constitutional means. Second, the women's suffrage, for example, was won with relative ease. As J. R. Pole has observed, "The women's movement represented a remarkable example of political persuasion."[8] There is no doubt that this success was enhanced by the factors of race and class. The leadership of the women's movement was mostly white from the middle and upper classes.

Bloom's analysis of race relations can broadly be divided into three parts: student life, curricular concerns, and administrative policies.

With regard to student life, Bloom points out that the "brotherhood" of the sixties did not culminate in integration. Instead it veered off, he says, toward Black separatism. As a result, he declares, Black and white students do not become real friends and that this is not the fault of the white students. According to Bloom, white students are almost always too eager to prove their liberal credentials, only to be rebuffed by the Black students. As is the case throughout the book, Bloom does not delve into the reasons, and in this instance the reasons for the lack of communication between those students.

This lack of communication, for which Bloom blames Black students and absolves white students, is rooted in the history of race relations in the United States. One thing that Bloom does not seem to understand is the fact that Blacks are very sceptical of those whites who want to prove their liberal credentials because those credentials are often full of stereotypes. Indeed, Black people did not survive thus far in America misjudging white people's attitudes and behaviors.

White students, just like white people in general, want to be in control even in interpersonal communications with minorities. A Black person is likely to be put on guard when a white person says "some of my best friends are Black." It is even worse with some white students who want to "talk jive" with their Black schoolmates. Interestingly enough, these ostensibly liberal white students are generally not quite willing to talk to their Black school-mates off campus unless it is at their initiative and in a place of their choice. There are, however, times when genuine human contact, "soul to soul," as Bloom calls it, does occur between white and ordinary Black students and not just the few "perfectly integrated" ones that Bloom would have us believe.

One of the most visible cases of Black separatism, according to Bloom, is to be found in the student cafeterias and dining halls. He goes on to point out that "they stick together" was a phrase used in the past by prejudiced people, but now it is merely a factual observation. I think that phrase has not lost any of its prejudicial content. Indeed one can ask Bloom why the white students stick together? The fact that this is not said about them proves my point. The fact is that white America has not resolved the question of race, particularly as it concerns Blacks. Many white Americans cannot stand to see a group of Blacks together, particularly if they appear to be enjoying them-selves.

Bloom seems to blame Blacks for not becoming assimilated like the white ethnics. "The heat is under the pot," he say, "but they do not melt as have *all* other groups" (p. 93). Once again Bloom demonstrates his lack of appreciation for history. He seems to forget the fact that it was his own ethnic group, the Jewish Americans, who came out early and very strongly against the idea of a melting pot for fear of losing their cultural and religious identity. One of the leading proponents of that Jewish American view was Horace M. Kallen, who advocated cultural pluralism.[9] Contrary to what Bloom says, it was not Blacks but white ethnics who picked up "ethnicity," particularly in the seventies. Michael Novak's *The Rise of Unmeltable Ethnics* is just one among many important books of the period. Novak, who assumed the role of an apologist for white ethnics, defended the utility of ethnicity. He wrote:

A Pole who knows he is a Pole, who is proud to be a Pole who knows the social costs and possibilities of being a Polish worker in America, who knows where he stands in power, status and integrity—such a Pole can face a black militant eye-to-eye. A Pole uncertain whether he is American or Polish, WASP or racist, worthy or despicable, feels emotions too confused for compromise, emotions most easily discharged as hate.[10]

With regard to curricular matters, Bloom claims that since World War II, there was intensive effort in major universities to educate more Blacks. Decent men in these institutions, he says, began to argue and took sides on the issue of whether or not to lower standards in order to admit large numbers of Black students. Once again Bloom makes blanket and unsubstantiated statements. The reality of that period was exclusion of qualified Black students and their unequal treatment on campuses, as shown by the two leading cases involving higher education decided by the U.S. Supreme Court in 1950: *Sweat v. Painter* and *McLaurin v. Oklahoma State Regents*.

It was in the late sixties that real efforts were made to enroll more Black students, largely as a response to the civil rights movement. The attacks on admission criteria, as well as certain curriculum content, were effective not because of the intimidation by Black student militants but rather because the facade of class privileges was no longer defensible. Black Studies were established in order to bring into the mainstream an important facet of the American experience. Contrary to Bloom's rather wishful assertion, Black Studies have not failed. They are alive as Afro-American Studies or under some organizational rubric. Scholars in Afro-American Studies have generated credible research. A number of these scholars, moreover, are not even Black—a good enough reason to show that Black Studies are not only alive but on their way toward institutionalization.

Finally, there is Bloom's analysis of administrative policies. Bloom claims that "a little black empire" has gained legitimacy in academe. Its main mission is the defense of its Black subjects from racism. This little empire, says Bloom, does secure from the administration, among other things, the following privileges: (1) permanent quotas, (2) preference in financial aid, and (3) racially motivated hiring of faculty. In what follows, I will analyze each of these alleged Black "privileges" to show first, that they are not unique to Blacks in academe, and second, that there is no such empire at all.

Allan Bloom's book was published in 1987, nine years after the U.S. Supreme Court disallowed admission quotas in the Bakke case. It is astonishing for a scholar like Bloom to omit such an important decision. Perhaps he is waging his own private war against the establishment in higher education. Preferential treatment in admission is not an exclusive Black privilege. Veterans, for example, enjoy certain preference in higher education and so do white women, particularly in the professional schools. Moreover, in those "leading universities" that Bloom talks about, children of alumni have always received special treatment in admissions. The question, therefore, is this: Why is racial preference any more objectionable to Bloom than the others in view of the fact that racism is pervasive in academe? Furthermore, the U.S. Supreme Court allowed the institutions of higher education to take race into account in their admission policies as a meliorative measure.

Regarding the issue of financial aid, I really do not see why Bloom ever bothered to talk about it since the kind of students who receive financial aid are beyond the purview of his book. In the preface of his book, Bloom describes his student "sample" as follows:

> It consists of thousands of students of comparatively high intelligence, materially and spiritually free to do pretty much what they want with the few years of college they are privileged to have—in short, the kind of young persons who populate the twenty or thirty best universities. (p. 22)

Obviously Bloom has no interest in those students who are not "materially free" to undertake liberal education on a full-time basis. The fact that escapes Bloom is that these kinds of students are becoming common in the colleges and universities as a result of the great expansion in higher education. Moreover, as Nussbaum points out, 40 percent of students nationwide are over twenty-five years of age.[11] They are now referred to as the nontraditional students on most campuses. Many of these students as well as those of college age go to school part time.

Financial aid is provided as a rule on the basis of need, even that designated for minority students. Also, as a rule, Minority Affairs offices do not handle financial aid. They simply identify minority/disadvantaged students who need financial assistance.

Racially motivated hiring of faculty is the third privilege Bloom claims the "little black empire" exacts from the university. If indeed it could do that the little empire would not be so little any more. In fact, there is no such empire at all. The "little black empire" does not hold up under scrutiny based on three criteria of power. It does not have autonomy with respect to budget, personnel, and programming; in other words, it is not any different from other units that provide specialized services in academe. Thus, this "little black empire" is nothing but Bloom's contribution to a vocabulary of provocative and emotionally charged words that the opponents of affirmative action use quite frequently. In any case, there is nothing immoral or illegal about a racially motivated hiring if the aim is justice and fairness. The U.S. Supreme Court has upheld such hiring. Many Fortune 500 corporations have not only complied with the decision, but have also vigorously pursued affirmative action goals. A recent survey conducted by the *Black Enterprise* magazine shows that at IBM, through its affirmative action efforts, 12.3 percent of its 3,850 managers are Black.[12] Most Americans, and that includes Bloom, know very well that IBM and comparable corporations are not in the charity business.

There is no better way to round off this analysis than to quote from Justice Harry Blackmun's opinion in the *Bakke* case:

> In order to get beyond racism we must first take account of race. There is no other way. And in order to treat some persons equally, we must treat them differently. We cannot—and dare not—let Equal Protection Clause perpetuate racial supremacy.[13]

A Critical Assessment of Bloom

Bloom's provocative title draws one's attention to the book, but it is the subtitle that establishes Bloom's purpose for the book. To that end one is led to expect an exposé on *How Higher Education Has Failed Democracy and Impoverished the Souls of Today's Students*. The book begins auspiciously enough with a brilliant foreword by the Nobel laureate, Saul Bellow. But right away, in the preface, Bloom not only lets the reader down, but also he himself loses credibility as a defender of democracy by focusing on a relatively small number of students—those unencumbered by any material concerns. As a result the book ceases to be compelling; it merely becomes interesting.

That Bloom is a meritocrat is undeniable, but he is one with rather undemocratic tendencies. In fact he does seem ambivalent if not distrustful of democracy. Although he applauds democracy in America for making the university the home of its political principles—a rather odd claim—he does not like other aspects of democracy. Bloom misses a vital point here. American political principles are embodied in the constitution and in the people *not* in the universities. These institutions merely carry out peoples' mandates.

Bloom does not like the egalitarianism in a democracy. It makes it hard, he says, "to make any claims of superiority, particularly in the domains in which such claims have always been made—art, religion and philosophy" (p. 337). It seems Bloom confuses superiority with excellence. He also dislikes democracy's concentration on utility because that makes theoretical distance seem immoral, especially when there are pressing problems. "The deepest intellectual weakness of democracy," he declares, "is its lack of taste or gift for the theoretical life" (p. 252). With these kinds of views, I don't see how Bloom can successfully fend off any charges of elitism. He comes across like the Platonist he is, whose soul seems to yearn for a different century if not a different millennium.

The problem of relativism among today's students is not a recent development, as Bloom would have us believe. Mortimer Adler, who is a long-time proponent of the Great Books approach, accuses Bloom of "historical myopia." He points out that he wrote an article in 1942 complaining about student relativism.[14] That was when the standards were supposedly higher and, obviously, there were no Black Studies or Women's Studies to "dilute" the liberal education curriculum. Bloom does not consider the fact that the relativism that he attributes to a faulty education may indeed be a part of a normal maturation process.

With respect to Bloom's criticism of feminism, it is as one-sided as it is shallow. He devotes too much time and space to sexual relations. As a result he has very little to say about historical, academic, or constitutional aspects of the feminist agenda.

Bloom's critique of race relations is also unbalanced. He blames Blacks in general and Black students in particular for the deterioration of race relations in academe mainly because of their support for affirmative action. Moreover, he psychologizes them invidiously, claiming that Black students keep away from white students for fear of being looked down upon by the better-qualified white students. My response to Bloom would be in kind. Isn't all this attack on affirmative action by white males an attempt to hide their own incompetence? Why then are they now trying to limit Asian American student enrollments? By sheer fact of numbers there should be, and indeed there are, more incompetent white men holding good jobs than there are minority men and women and white women.

Finally, one of the highlights in Bloom's critique of higher education has to be his eloquent appeal for liberal or general education. He deplores the fact that "there is no vision, nor is there a set of competing visions of what an educated human being is" (p. 337). As a result of this lack of vision, coupled with what he describes as "a bewildering variety" of departments and courses, a student nowadays finds it easy to make a career choice and pursue appropriate training. Bloom is not happy either with what he calls "composite courses" that are designed for general education these days. He claims that such courses lead to trendiness and that they lack "substantive rigor."

What does Bloom prescribe? The old Great Books approach, but with a new methodology if not a new attitude. He writes:

> Of course, the only serious solution is the one that is almost universally rejected: the good old Great Books approach, in which a liberal education means reading certain generally recognized classic texts, just reading them, letting them dictate what the questions are and the method of approaching

them—not forcing them into categories we make up, not treating them as historical products, but trying to read them as their authors wished them to be read. (p. 344)

Bloom is, of course, aware of and agrees with the objections to the cult-like status of the Great Books. Nevertheless, his main reason for recommending them is that students become excited and satisfied after going through a Great Books program. The big question for Bloom, then, is this: What makes this kind of excitement qualitatively different from, say, that of a graduate with a bachelor of science degree in computer science who is paid more than someone with a Ph.D. in humanities? Surely there must be more to liberal education than mere excitement.

In conclusion, I will have to give Bloom the benefit of the doubt on the charge of racism by intent. He is however guilty, on evidence, of elitism, sexism, and closed-mindedness about diversity in the United States. The paradox though for Bloom and people of his ilk who disparage areas of study such as Black Studies or Women's Studies is that they are calling for the restoration of the old Eurocentric core curriculum at a time when institutions of higher education are trying to cope with diversity. The challenge for these institutions is how to devise liberal or general education programs that would prepare students for living in a multiracial, multicultural society.

Notes

1. Allan Bloom, *The Closing of the American Mind: How Higher Education Has Failed Democracy and Impoverished the Souls of Today's Students* (New York: Simon and Schuster, 1987).

2. Michael W. Hirschorn, "Best-Selling Book Makes the Collegiate Curriculum a Burning Issue," *The Chronicle of Higher Education* (16 September 1987), p. A–1.

3. Maxine Greene, "Further Notes on Bloom and the New Bloomusalem," *Phi Delta Kappan* (June 1988), p. 757.

4. Peter Steinfels, *The Neoconservatives*, (New York: Simon and Schuster, 1979), p. 70.

5. Martha Nussbaum, "Undemocratic Vistas," *The New York Review of Books* (5 November 1987), p. 22.

6. Ibid.

7. *Time* (17 October 1988), p. 76.

8. J. R. Pole, *The Pursuit of Equality in American History* (Berkeley: University of California Press, 1978), 315.

9. Ibid., 247.

10. Michael Novak, *The Rise of Unmeltable Ethnics* (New York: The Macmillan Company, 1972), 250.

11. Nussbaum, "Undemocratic Vistas," 22.

12. *La Crosse Tribune* (4 January 1989), p. B–5.

13. *Regents of the University of California v. Bakke*, 438 U.S. 407 (1978).

14. Hirschorn, "Best-selling Book," A–22.

CHAPTER 19

Praxis and the Prospect of Curriculum Transformation

Johnnella E. Butler and John C. Walter

Transformation begins with the incorporation of the subject content of men and women of color and white women into our curricula, our scholarly methodologies, and our pedagogy. This is a huge task, for ultimately this material must permeate the entire curricula as well as continue to be developed as specific academic departments to generate the scholarship in Ethnic Studies and Women's Studies that will be, among other purposes, incorporated into all other disciplines. The issue of transformation looms large, for transformation goes beyond the classroom with fundamental implications for the subject, structure, assumptions, and boundaries of our scholarship, and raises fundamental implications for our everyday lives. In this book, we have begun to articulate clearly a theory and provide examples of scholarly and curriculum transformation. In this final chapter, we address these issues head-on, with the intention of anticipating some of the reactions, questions, hesitancies, and resistances most frequently raised around this volatile and radical issue.

Our goal is to encourage praxis in its fundamental sense of reflection and action. The academic and social change envisioned through transformation will not come easily. We are only beginning to undo the effects of the distortion and inequities set in motion 500 years ago when Columbus brought massacre and the most brutal form of slavery known to these shores, all in the interest of spreading "Western Civilization" with all its long lasting assumptions of racial, cultural and male superiority. This praxis must be pursued with a constant, eager patience that has as its reward, in our lifetime, the concrete beginnings of change for the better for all.

To us, theory is the essential understanding of just what we are doing, given a specific task, and the identification of what our efforts entail. In order to correct the insidious distortions of the liberal arts curriculum, with its severely flawed understandings of U.S. people of color and white women as well as its distorted self-worth of white cultures, ethnicities, and males, we must begin by recognizing that race, ethnicity, gender, and class form the basis of our societal human identities and that they are basic categories of analysis as well as of existence in the world we have concocted. We must then be able to envision a pluralistic existence based on the connectedness among human beings, and among the earth, its creatures, its fruits. The way in which we organize our knowledge, furthermore, must reflect that connectedness, placing great value upon interdisciplinary and comparative ways of organizing our scholarship and pedagogy, recognizing and utilizing power and authority not in an hierarchical, monolithic way, but in ways that recognize and utilize the diverse manifestations of power and authority within the context of the connections among humans and between humans and the world.

Once our reflections bring us to an understanding of the kinds of changes and correctives necessary to give us the foundation in our educational system of a equitable and just society, plans of action begin to emerge. Questions around those actions are few in number, yet monumental to answer and solve. We may ask, for example:

1. Are these ignored, distorted, subordinated people and their history, legacies, and experiences important to understanding and expressing our American selves?

2. If so, how then do we go about transformation? How do we begin moving beyond our restrictive racist, ethnocentric, sexist, heterosexist, and classist cultural, political, social and economic definitions of the past and present reality of the United States?

3. And how, in our eagerness to correct, do we avoid the simplistic and often vengeful alternative of replacing the old norms with new ones, based on the extremely individualistic, hierarchical, merchandizing, power-obsessed values that have come to define the American past and most of our identities? How do we distinguish between cultural sharing and cultural appropriation which carries with it a power imbalance potent enough to redefine the cultural source in ways hostile to its very being?

These questions emerge from the scholarship of Ethnic Studies and Women's Studies. They seem to be the questions that plague those most committed to designing a college and university curriculum reflective of the closest approximation of the truth and the closest approximation of inclusiveness. These and similar questions bother and even outrage others who are either less committed or skeptical or who oppose and challenge the content of Ethnic Studies and Women's Studies and its central role in transformation with questions of "standards," fear of or refusal to learn more and different things. These questions address areas of concern and areas of our lives in the United States that are sacred to the maintenance of the status quo. The Bloom, Hirsch, and Bennett notions of cultural literacy, the calls for "law and order" within college and university curricula and scholarship from the various bigoted enclaves of academia, seek to perpetuate the essentially elite English and northern European heritage that has characterized American education from its beginnings. Such values attached to this Euro-American hegemonic focus are frequently espoused by many assimilated U.S. citizens of European as well as non-European and even Jewish heritages, who simultaneously declare an ethnic and even racial distinction from a perceived majority of Americans. These longstanding and transitive values have become aesthetic, social and paradigmatic norms to which all else compares inadequately and is of minimal value, if any at all.

In our colleges and universities, as we begin these efforts, we must recognize and contemplate the analogy between transformation's essential insistence upon the interaction between the communal and the individual and the interaction between diversity and sameness as well as the implicit change it brings to the organization of our scholarship and academic institutions. Communal and individual, diversity and sameness are analogous to inter-disciplinary and disciplinary. What is clear is that connections are essential and inescapable in this world. We must begin to think and organize our studies around the *reality* of these connections. For example, sociology may appropri-ately appear to stand alone, be foregrounded as a discipline, but it also has implied connections with other disciplines. Simultaneously, those implied connections operate as part of a matrix of which sociology is a part, and we then have interdisciplinary sociology. We have interdisciplinary approaches to literary study with literature as our focus. *Diversity and the goals we have set through recognition of our human diversity will only amount to emphasizing difference and therefore reinforcing stereotypes and hierarchies and imposing norms if we do not simultaneously identify connections, samenesses.*

Many well-intentioned frequently ask, "In the next ten or twelve years, will the need for Ethnic Studies and Women's Studies disappear?" This is a variation of question one. There is so very much that is unknown, unidenti-fied, unstudied about our pasts and presents in both this nation and abroad. Ethnic Studies and Women's Studies, separately, together, and in interaction with the so-called traditional disciplines, are where we will find the structural, scholarly, and pedagogic contexts for understanding our human selves, with all our multiple identities. They provide the contexts for the overwhelming amount of knowledge and information that flow from recognizing all that has been lost because of racism, ethnocentrism, sexism, heterosexism, classism, colonialism, and apartheid. They reveal human creativity, possibility, and alternative philosophies while providing space for the reconciliation of the pain and anger of those who suffered and the guilt and anger of those who plundered. Most significantly, Ethnic Studies and Women's Studies hold the potential for identifying new ways of being with one another in this world. This is not a unidimensional or short-term proposition.

Questions two and three—"How then do we go about transformation?" and "How, in our eagerness to correct, do we avoid . . . replacing the old norms with new ones, based on the (same) . . . values. . . ?"—demand much reflection, and gradual, clearly focussed action. We may agree with the fundamental change in Western thought that transformation requires; however, we must go *beyond agreeing* to *reshaping* our institutions, our departments, our rewards system, our senses of who we are to reflect that change from "cogito, ergo sum" to "I am we."

Furthermore, these questions of transformation mean we must teach ourselves as we teach; they mean that we must take risks through informed explorations of areas with which we are not familiar; they mean that so-called "minority studies" must have priority in our traditionally white academic enclaves. Just as Women's Studies must give up the primacy of gender for an understanding of gender and sexism and heterosexism interacting with race, class, ethnicity and their "-isms," so too must our literary canons, our sociological and anthropological paradigms, our conceptualizations of history, politics, economics, our math and science, give up white male and female racial and class hegemony, white male and female cultural and ethnic hegemony, white patriarchal hegemony. In similar fashion, "minority" and white women academics must identify ways in which their scholarship reflects and assumes the very hegemonies we seek to dispel. Constant self-critique, a voracious academic appetite to read, discover, generate ideas and approaches, affirming connections as we identify difference—these are only a few of the hallmarks of transformation. So beginning, we can realize the budding theory and scholarship in volumes such as this.

The contributors to this book obviously argue and demonstrate that we must begin first with the understanding that race, ethnicity, gender, and class form the basis of identity and culture. Second, the content of Ethnic Studies and Women's Studies deals directly with these fundamental aspects of identity and culture. Third, from the evident initial stages of much of the thinking and research in this book, it is apparent that Women's Studies has the urgent task of developing scholarship and methodology that is not racist, classist, ethnocentric and heterosexist, and Ethnic Studies has the equally daunting task of developing scholarship and methodology that is not sexist, heterosexist, classist, ethnocentric, or racist. *If these fields do not meet this task, we may as well give up on any fundamental change.* Fourth, Women's Studies and Ethnic Studies (and we reiterate that Ethnic Studies means African American Studies, American Indian Studies, Asian American Studies, and Latino American Studies both separately and comparatively) must be recognized as fields of study with academic departments to generate scholarship in these areas that will be, among other practical purposes, incorporated in all other so-called disciplines. Fifth, this task of curriculum transformation has as its organizing principles race, class, gender and ethnicity, with their respective "-isms," and attendant social phenomena such as assimilation and acculturation. These organizing principles and categories for analysis lead to others such as age and physical handicap, categories which are refined and somewhat defined by race, ethnicity, gender, and class. Sixth, to develop the scholarship of Women's Studies and Ethnic Studies demands that we understand and analyze power relationships in society, and that we seek to empower our students to interact rather than reinforce the established function of power to dominate hierarchically, thereby encouraging them to foster false senses of each other.

In short, to consider praxis and the prospect of transformation means that we take seriously, analyze and seek to understand the complexities, horrors, and beauties of our collective pasts. No longer can we, as a nation or as scholars and teachers, ignore or deny the holocausts associated with Columbus sailing the ocean blue in fourteen hundred ninety-two. No longer can we discount the connection between the present and past realities and peoples of the United States and colonialization, to which physical, social and cultural genocide were and are central experiences. Furthermore, we cannot ignore that a significant number of those subjected to our colonial, racial holocausts studied us well and imitate us well. The changing demographics in the United States as well as those of the entire world underscore the connections between incorporating the study of our U.S. racial/ethnic groups and of *all* women into our curricula so that they can be properly understood both in and of themselves and as they interact with and have had to relate with the dominant white society. In a similar fashion we can proceed to understand the shifts in identity, power and perception of our global society.

If this final chapter sounds like an exhortation to action, that is what it is intended to be. If you find it to be "a revolutionary puree", then you have missed the point of this book entirely. If you seriously want to begin or continue transformative work, here are some concrete suggestions:

1. Faculty development is key to this effort. Release time, sabbatical time, and summer workshops must be funded as regular on-going parts of budgets, as well as supplemented by outside funding.

2. College and university presidents and provosts must not simply echo educational forecasters that diversity is the issue of the 90s. They must strive to understand the depth and complexities of this reality beyond perceiving of it as just another issue. College and university presidents must signal that curricular, scholarly, and pedagogical transformation is the *top priority*. Ultimately, this is the key to providing a productive education for our citizens so that they are informed, active participants in our governance.

3. We must rethink just what is essential for our students to know. We all can agree that they must be critical readers, adequate writers, and critical thinkers; that they must have math and science skills. We need, however, to

agree that they must understand the history, literature, and social organization of United States society complete with the truth about the horrors upon which this land was built that gave rise to brutal assimilation for many whites, anti-semitism, anti-Catholicism, racism, sexism, and classism, continued today in so many brutal forms of oppression. They need to know why, in order to effect any change for the better of all.

4. Lastly, as we endeavor we must continue in the tradition of the well-known admonition from Audre Lorde that we cannot dismantle the master's house with the master's tools. As scholars and teachers, as men and women, we must constantly analyze the assumptions, predispositions and prejudices we bring with us to the classroom and to our scholarship. We must struggle to critique one another with a love and generosity aimed at the betterment of all. We must go beyond our egos to admit when we are wrong, when we are confused, what our limitations are. In short, we must live "I am we."

This text could not begin to address all the areas of curriculum transformation. We intended to give concrete direction to the effort, knowing that you the reader, the professor, the student, the administrator will appropriately transfer and further develop our messages. If in the last decade of this century we can sincerely commit to curriculum transformation and all its implications, we will have realized the most noble dreams of the massacred American Indian and the African American slave—a freedom that embraces love, opportunity, and respect.

Contributors

Howard E. Adelman is Director of the Program in Jewish Studies at Smith College. He holds degrees in Jewish Studies from Cornell, the Jewish Theological Seminary, and Brandeis. His main area of research is early-modern Jewish history, and he was involved in publication of *The Autobiography of a 17th Century Venetian Rabbi: Leon Modena's "Life of Judah"* (Princeton, 1988). He is currently working on a book on Jewish Women in Italy. He serves on the Board of Directors of the Association for Jewish Studies.

Arlene Avakian teaches in the Women's Studies Program at the University of Massachusetts at Amherst. Her major research focuses on the interaction of race, class, gender, and ethnicity. Her autobiography, tentatively titled *Lion Woman's Legacy*, an exploration of these issues, will be published by The Feminist Press in 1990. Avakian edited a special issue of the Armenian American Quarterly, *Ararat*, on Armenian feminism and continues to facilitate workshops on the role and status of Armenian women.

Evelyn Torton Beck, Professor of Women's Studies and Jewish Studies, has directed the Women's Studies Program at the University of Maryland-College Park since 1984. Her books include: *Kafka and the Yiddish Theater: Its Impact on his Work* (1971); *The Prism of Sex: Essays in the Sociology of Knowledge* (1979); and *Nice Jewish Girls: A Lesbian Anthology* (rev. exp. ed. 1989).

Katharine Bolland, a 1988 graduate of Smith College, is currently a Research Coordinator with the Department of African-American Studies at the University of Washington in Seattle.

Johnnella E. Butler is author of *Black Studies: Pedagogy and Revolution, A Study of the Liberal Arts Tradition Through the Discipline of Afro-American Literature* (1981) and numerous articles on curriculum transformation from the perspective of the intersection of Black Studies, Ethnic Studies, and Women's Studies. Her chapter, "Transforming the Curriculum: Teaching About Women of Color," first appeared in the undergraduate text *Multicultural Education: Issues and Perspectives*, edited by James and Cherry Banks (Allyn Bacon, 1989). She is one of the contributors to the American Council on Education's *Minorities on Campus: A Handbook for Diversity* (1989), and served on the National Task Force for the Women's Studies Major, as part of the American Association of Colleges project, "Liberal Learning, Study in Depth" from 1989-91. A member of the Executive Council for the National Association for Ethnic Studies (1987-1990), she has either codirected or been a major participant in curriculum transformation projects nationwide since 1981. She is Associate Professor of American Ethnic Studies and Chair of the American Ethnic Studies Department at the University of Washington.

Jeffery Chan, Frank Chin, Lawson Inada, and Shawn Wong coedited *Aiiieeeee! Anthology of Asian American Writers* (Howard University Press, 1974) and *The Big Aiiieeeee!* (New American Library, 1990). Jeffery Chan is professor of Asian American Studies at San Francisco State University. Frank Chin is an award-winning playwright and author of *The Chinaman Pacific and Frisco R.R. Co.* (Coffee House Press, 1989), a collection of short stories. Lawson Inada is Professor of English at Southern Oregon College. Shawn Wong is an Associate Professor of American Ethnic Studies at the University of Washington in Seattle.

Johnnetta B. Cole is the President of Spelman College, the leading historically Black college for women in Atlanta, Georgia. Dr. Cole brings to the presidency years of active teaching and research at Washington State University, the University of Massachusetts, and Hunter College, with visiting teaching positions at Oberlin College, U.C.L.A., and Williams College. She is widely published in Cultural Anthropology, Women's Studies, and African American Studies. Dr. Cole graduated from Oberlin College and holds a master's and a doctorate in Anthropology from Northwestern University.

Ruth Frankenberg is an Acting Assistant Professor of Women's Studies at the University of Washington, Seattle. Her research focus is on the social processes through which white women take their places in racially hierarchical societies such as the U.S.A. Her book, *White Women, Race Matters: The Social Construction of Whiteness*, is in progress.

Beverly Guy-Sheftall is Associate Professor of English and Director of the Women's Research and Resource Center at Spelman College, Atlanta, Georgia. She is also coeditor of *Sturdy Black Bridges: Visions of Black Women in Literature* (Doubleday, 1979), and founding coeditor of *SAGE: A Scholarly Journal on Black Women*. Her book, *Daughters of Sorrow: Attitudes Toward Black Women, 1880–1920*, will be published by Carlson Publishers in 1990.

Jonathan A. Majek is the Director of the Institute for Minority Studies at the University of Wisconsin at La Crosse. He also teaches the principle courses for the certificate program in Minority Studies. His research focuses primarily on comparative analyses of minority experiences.

Caryn McTighe Musil has been the National Director of the National Women's Studies Association since 1984. She has been teaching, writing, and speaking about Women's Studies for two decades. Having given up her faculty position to move into administration, she is discovering how effective a Ph.D. in English can be in fundraising.

R. A. Olguin is an Assistant Professor of American Ethnic Studies at the University of Washington. He received his Ph.D. from Stanford in 1986 and has been at the University of Washington since then. Olguin has authored articles on the philosophical implications of Ethnic Studies as a discipline and is working on a manuscript, *Ethnic Studies and the Liberal Arts: The Politics of Criticism*. He is a board member of the National Association for Chicano Studies and is in the Board of Directors of the Society for Values in Higher Education.

Ruby Sales is a Ph.D. candidate in American History from Princeton University. She is writing her dissertation, a biography of Lucy Diggs Slowe, educator, activist, and theoretician who played a prominent role in higher education and African American political life. Sales came to the academy after working for the Student Non-Violent Coordinating Committee (SNCC).

Betty Schmitz is currently Special Assistant to the President of the University of Maryland at College Park, implementing a campus-wide program to improve the status of women. She has directed and codirected five major curriculum transformation projects and is the author of *Integrating Women's Studies Into the Curriculum* (Feminist Press, 1985) and of numerous articles on the same topic. She is one of the evaluators of the Ford Foundation Project on Integrating Women of Color into the Curriculum, co-directed by Johnnella Butler and Angela Ginorio of the University of Washington.

Elizabeth V. Spelman is Associate Professor of Philosophy at Smith College and also teaches in the Women's Studies Program. Her contribution to this volume is an abridged version of a chapter from her recent book, *Inessential Woman: Problems of Exclusion in Feminist Thought* (Beacon Press, 1988). The book is an exploration of the ways in which white middle-class privilege thrives in the concepts and methodologies of some strands of feminist thought, and an examination of the ways in which gender, race, and class identity are inextricably intertwined. Vicky Spelman also is the author and coauthor of a number of articles in feminist theory, ethics, theories of the emotions, and social and political theory.

Kathryn Shanley (Assiniboine) teaches American Indian literature at the University of Washington. Currently she is writing a critical work on James Welch's fiction and poetry.

John C. Walter is Professor of American Ethnic Studies at the University of Washington. A specialist in American and African American History, he has written widely on F.D.R. and the Navy, the history of the Caribbean immigrant, and is the author of *The Harlem Fox, J. Raymond Jones and Tammany, 1920–1970* 1990 American Book Award winner. He was president of the New England region of the National Council for Black Studies from 1976 to 1980 and is currently the President of the National Association for Ethnic Studies. He is one of a few Black male scholars actively involved in seeking to bring together the perspectives of Black Studies and Women's Studies through curriculum transformation work.

Laurel L. Wilkening, Ph.D., is Provost and Vice-President for Academic Affairs, Professor of Geological Sciences, and Adjunct Professor of Astronomy at the University of Washington in Seattle.

Index

335